The Girl on the 6th Floor

Wide Awake Through the Nightmare

Brian Nichols

Rockford
Publications

To Jenny

I hope that you never ask, "Why me"

But believe that there is always a reason why

PREFACE

My name is Brian Nichols, and the story I am about to tell you is true.

This is the story about an illness my daughter, Jenny, had – or rather, has; now, more than a year later, I still don't understand that aspect of it. The name of the illness is not important right now. Before Jenny came to them, even the doctors that treated her had never heard of the illness with which she was eventually diagnosed. Very few doctors had. The information that I have is that the world famous Mayo Clinic had only seen 10 patients with the illness prior to Jenny's diagnosis.

Even if you have heard of the illness, in my opinion the name means little, as I believe the name itself is misleading. The technical names and descriptions of the illness mean nothing until you have actually *witnessed* someone with this illness. Only then can you truly understand not only its complexity, but more importantly, the profound effect it has on everyone involved – not only the patient, or even the family, but also the health care professionals.

This is the story of what Jenny's closest family members witnessed – me, Jenny's mother, Barb, Jenny's younger sister by two years, Michelle, as well as my sister Debbie. I will attempt to find the right words to tell this story as accurately as possible.

On occasion I would stand outside Jenny's hospital room and try to prepare first-time visitors for what they were about to see, which always proved to be difficult, at best. As it would turn out, I always failed to accurately prepare the visitor for what they ultimately encountered. Even while it was occurring, there were many times no words could describe what was happening to Jenny. And, trying to describe it now – well, is anyone able to accurately describe a nightmare once it is over?

Jenny Nichols, April 9, 2013

Jennifer Camille Nichols grew up in Rockford, Minnesota, a town of about 4,400 people, located 25 miles northwest of Minneapolis. It is what many people refer to as a "bedroom community." While there is very little retail or entertainment within our town, it is perfectly located in the sense that almost everything we need is no more than 10 to 20 minutes away.

Rockford is an ideal community in which to grow up. It is large enough that you don't know everyone, but small enough so a person can contribute to the community and have an influence on the people that live there. The school district was tremendous while both of my daughters attended and helped shape Jenny into the person she has become. The school was large enough to offer a wide variety of extracurricular activities, yet small enough that everyone who signed up could truly participate and play a significant role.

In particular, sports have always been an important part of our family's life. My wife and I sincerely believe that participation in athletics is one of the best ways to teach children "life lessons," but I couldn't have known that Jenny's involvement in sports was preparing her for what was the fight of her life as she battled the illness she would endure.

Jenny was never the most athletic or talented kid on any team she participated, but she had a good work ethic, a consistently positive attitude, and a deep determination to do her best in whatever she was involved. These attributes were honed by participating in various school and traveling sports teams on a year-round basis from the time she was 10 years old. Jenny focused on volleyball and basketball and went on to play both sports through four years of college.

Over the month that would account for the worst part of the nightmare you are about to read, there was a good chunk of time that the doctors could do nothing for Jenny. Even when they could finally help her attack the cause of the illness, it was still up to Jenny – seemingly, on her own – to fight the demons that literally had a grip on her brain. During the course of her illness, I witnessed how the very attributes that Jenny had engrained through years of athletic endeavors would be the tools she would require to be able to travel through the living hell into which she was forced.

At the start of this event in March 2013, Jenny was 16 days short of her 26th birthday. She was working full-time at Barnes and Noble Bookstores in Minnetonka, MN, where she was the Lead of the Children's Department. Jenny genuinely enjoyed this job – not only because of the tasks involved in her work, but more so due to the people with whom she worked. She was truly happy there. As the events of the following months would play out, the individuals she worked with, as well as the company itself, would play a key role in Jenny's battle through what was about to transpire.

Part 1

"Odd Behavior"

March 27 to April 5, 2013

CHAPTER 1

"Hi. Is this Jenny's Dad?"

"Yeah."

"This is Stephanie, one of the managers at the Barnes and Noble where Jenny works. I'm calling to let you know that Jenny was just found unconscious in a snow bank outside of the store."

Almost everyone has experienced a life-defining moment, but how often do those experiences also forever redefine the meaning of and our reaction to specific words and phrases?

The word "deterioration" can have many meanings. Many times it refers to the effect weather has on an old building. Unfortunately, it can also refer to someone's health. People can deteriorate as well – usually via old age, but also at the hands of drug abuse, and even cancer or some other devastating disease.

"A parent's worst nightmare" can also encompass a multitude of things, based specifically on what a child is experiencing at that very moment. I imagine most people fear the death of their child and believe that would be their worst nightmare. While I do not argue that idea, I have to think that any situation in which a parent does not know whether their child will fully recover also deserves the phrase.

With that phone call from Stephanie, my family began a five-month odyssey that went beyond anything we could have predicted or even dared to imagine. The word deterioration has forever taken on new meaning. We now understand firsthand that we dare not put boundaries on what a parent's worst nightmare really is, because we may have to be wide-awake for most of the thousands of hours that we are forced to experience it.

Stephanie informed me that an ambulance had been called, and put me in touch with an EMT who stated that Jenny was already in the ambulance and being transported to a nearby hospital. I questioned the EMT as to whether Jenny had been assaulted, and she assured me she had not, but rather believed that Jenny had suffered a seizure.

Who could have imagined how the confirmation of a seizure over assault would qualify as the last bit of reliable, and relatively good, information I would receive for weeks. Yet, it would be another two days before there would be any indication that something was seriously wrong with Jenny, and even then, I think I denied what I was seeing. Rather than coming on suddenly and with any clarity, this nightmare unfolded slowly.

Initially there were only hints of what was to come. The demons controlling this roller coaster ride only showed their faces for brief moments, and were oftentimes dismissed with feeble explanations. With almost every event that took place, I would think, "This can't get any worse," only to realize just hours later that it had. Eventually there came a time when I realized that I could not awaken myself from the nightmare.

The moment that I took Stephanie's phone call will be etched in my mind forever. I was standing behind my car, with the trunk open, in the parking lot of one of my business customers in Prinsburg, Minnesota. A feeling of helplessness immediately washed over me. I needed to get to a hospital that was an hour and a half away in St. Louis Park – Jenny needed me, and there was nothing I could do for her from where I was right now.

I immediately began driving toward the hospital while simultaneously trying to contact Barb, my wife and Jenny's mother, at work. The nature of her job made her difficult to reach at times, and today was no exception.

As I continued to drive toward the hospital that afternoon, I decided not to call John, Jenny's boyfriend of three years. He had started a new job the week before and I did not want to call him while he was at work. Instead, I called my business partner, Bonnie, to inform her of what was happening, and I asked her to be prepared to go to the hospital in the event that Jenny's condition worsened before Barb or I could get there, since she was much closer to the hospital than we were.

As I look back on this entire event, I think of all the times that my ignorance to the reality of the situation caused a naïve belief that "it's not so bad." This belief led to many bad decisions, or what now appears to have been irrational behavior, and to regrets that I will carry with me for the rest of my life.

Once I had finally made contact with Barb, and after some discussion, I made the first of my bad decisions. We decided to meet at home and go to the hospital together. It made sense at the time. Had I known then what I know now, I would have asked my business partner to drop everything and get to the hospital as fast as she could, and I never would have taken the time to go home and wait for Barb to get there. I am not sure when I will be able to forgive myself for making some of the decisions I made that day, but having received a phone call from a person I had never met telling me something so unusual had happened to my otherwise healthy daughter – well, it didn't sink in for a while.

Barb and I arrived at the Emergency Room of Methodist Hospital somewhere around 5 p.m. I will never forget my first glimpse of Jenny through the narrow window in the door to her room. For reasons that still are not clear to me today, Jenny appeared to be much smaller than she actually was, sitting in that bed. In that moment, she became my little girl once again, and I had let her down by taking so long to get to her side.

She had on a hospital gown and was under a blanket pulled up to her waist. The usual collection of monitors and equipment found in any

Emergency Room were around her, yet she was not hooked up to any of them. She was conscious, and in fact, had her phone in her hands and was tapping away, presumably sending a text.

While the look on her face was intent, it had a bit of fear in it as well. Sitting there in that room alone must have felt like an eternity to her. Why had I gone home to wait for Barb? Why had I not asked Bonnie to go to her right away? For as helpless as I felt being so far away when I first received the call, I still have not forgiven myself for not realizing that Jenny was even more helpless waiting for someone, anyone that loved her, to arrive and comfort her. I followed Barb into the room, and as Jenny looked up and saw us, she began to cry very hard.

What we did not know at the time was that for some reason, even though our phones would show that we had coverage, text messages were not being delivered while we were in the Emergency Room. The phones would show that the messages were sent, but not a single message Jenny sent while she was sitting in the Emergency Room waiting for someone who loved her to arrive had gone through.

Two months later, I went through Jenny's phone to see who and what she had texted during that time. She had sent texts to Barb, John and me. It was clear she had been expecting either Barb or I because most of the texts were sent to us: "Where are you guys? I'm so scared and confused." I can easily imagine the loneliness and helplessness she felt while sitting in that hospital room alone with no clear understanding of how she got there, along with the confusion and disappointment of sending out texts only to have no one respond for almost two hours.

Once Jenny had settled down, the questions turned to what had happened – for all three of us. Jenny had no recollection of events from the time she parked her car in the parking lot of the small shopping mall called Ridgehaven in Minnetonka, Minnesota on her way to her job at Barnes and Noble in that mall. We could not answer her questions, and she could not answer ours. Each question Barb and I had searching for details of what happened leading up to Jenny getting to the hospital were responded to with, "I don't know," "I'm confused," or just frustrated tears. Jenny was asking us what had happened to her, and in return, we had no response.

Jenny seemed perfectly fine once she calmed down and began engaging in normal conversation with us. There was no sign at all of what we would ultimately learn was inside of her and what would take over her mind and body.

Little did I know that the nightmare had already begun. At that moment, what was simply mild concern over the details of what had happened would transform into a series of events that would spiral so far out of control that, shocking as it seems, at one point I would offer a prayer that doctors would find cancer within my daughter. What would turn into my own version of a parent's worst nightmare would become so haunting that I would be forced to stand by helplessly and watch my otherwise previously healthy 25-year-old daughter's physical and mental stability deteriorate. Moreover, the changes were relentless and unforgiving. Before we had the chance to adjust to what was happening, Jenny's condition would get worse. Not day by day, but hour by hour. This all happened while she was under the care of medical professionals who were unable to identify the cause, stop it from happening, provide her any relief, or save her from the demons that would haunt her as we all stood by and watched.

CHAPTER 2

Once Barb and I were able to talk with Jenny's doctors, we learned that they had already conducted a CT scan, EEG, and a few other tests before we had arrived. All the test results came back "normal," and it was determined that Jenny had no physical condition, such as a tumor, that had caused the seizure. The diagnosis, in a nutshell, was that Jenny had a seizure of an unknown origin.

While we still had many questions, we were relieved when the doctors told us there was nothing seriously wrong. Although very rare, it is not unheard of for a seizure of unknown origin to occur. Jenny was released from the Emergency Room without being admitted to the hospital, and we left there around 7 p.m. the same evening. We were told to be watchful and aware, but left fairly certain it was just a one-time event and nothing to be overly concerned about. There were not even any follow-up appointments scheduled.

As I look back on it now, I very easily convinced myself that the seizure was a result of Jenny being tired and under a significant amount of stress as a result of working two jobs. The doctor recommended she take it easy and not drive a car for a few days. We left the hospital believing it was all behind us and just a small scare. Little did we know that the journey had really only just begun.

Barb and I went to Jenny and John's apartment, and decided to stay for a while to observe Jenny and give ourselves some assurance that she was indeed okay. Other than a weird craving for some ice cream, Jenny seemed perfectly fine on all fronts. Around 9 p.m., Barb and I left to make the 30-minute drive home.

During the trip home, as well as while preparing for bed, we received some texts from Jenny. Looking back, they were a bit odd, but I can't say I thought much of them at the time. If the events of the following three months hadn't happened, I never would have given them a second thought. One of the texts said, "I get the giggles over the stupidest things tonight." These types of texts were out of character for Jenny, but more so it was the frequency of them that seemed a bit odd. Over a 45-minute span she had sent about 10 texts that were rather pointless. I wrote them off as giddiness, a result of coming down after a stressful event.

Barb and I had been lying in bed for only a minute or two when Barb's cell phone rang. Caller ID said it was Jenny calling, but it turned out to be John on the other end. He informed us that he was calling from his truck as he followed the ambulance that was hauling Jenny back to Methodist Hospital.

John recounted the hour since we had left the apartment. Although it was late in the evening and both of them were tired from the events of the past few hours, Jenny would not let the ice cream craving go and had convinced John to take her to Dairy Queen. After they had returned to the apartment, Jenny looked into a mirror and became mesmerized by her own image and stared for a few moments, oblivious to all else. Then her neck twisted in an unnatural direction, and she made a sound that resembled a growl before falling to the floor as a Grand Mal seizure ensued. Little did we all understand that John was the first to see, first hand, the demons that had taken over Jenny's brain. John did everything needed to keep her safe and helped her ride out the seizure. He then called 911 and an ambulance was dispatched.

At this point, Barb and I made another decision that now sounds irrational; John told us he would be with Jenny at the hospital, so Barb and I stayed in bed and attempted to sleep. As terrible as it sounds now, the reasons for this decision seemed very logical to us at the time.

We assumed that Jenny would be admitted to the hospital that night since it was the second time in less than eight hours she had been taken there by ambulance. Due to the obvious mistake made earlier in the day when Jenny was left at the hospital alone for so long, we took precautions to be sure she would not be left alone at all moving forward. The three of us put a very simple plan in place for how we could best manage our employment obligations as well as make sure that Jenny had a family member with her at all times between that moment and the weekend. John had essentially taken the first shift since he was following Jenny to the hospital; therefore, it made sense for Barb and me to get some rest. The plan was for me to replace John at some point during the night, and for Barb to go to work in the morning in order for her to be available Thursday night and into Friday. At this point we had no idea what to expect in terms of how long Jenny would be in the hospital, but it seemed wise to be prepared.

It also seemed logical to believe that our plan only had to get us to the weekend. Surely, Jenny would not be in the hospital more than a day or two. No one stays in the hospital more than overnight these days. Modern technology allows doctors to identify and treat illnesses in a matter of hours. Common sense and every level of conventional wisdom had me believing this was a short-term situation because, while seizures are a serious issue, up to this point she had had only two, and everything I had learned over the past few hours told me that seizures could be controlled with medication if necessary.

Ironically, the decision not to leave Jenny alone would never change, but the reasons for it, and the reality of actually trying to accomplish it, would change dramatically. The demands on our lives outside of the hospital, as well as our own health, would be greatly affected as time passed.

CHAPTER 3

Friday, March 29 to Sunday, March 31, 2013

By Thursday morning, the doctors had begun giving Jenny the anti-seizure medication Keppra, as well as repeating the entire battery of tests that were done during her first visit to the Emergency Room. Once all of this was completed, the plan was to observe Jenny for a couple of days to be sure the seizures were under control. Blood tests were conducted every three hours or so to check the level of the Keppra in her system. The good news was that she experienced no more seizures, so it appeared that the medication was doing its job. However, Jenny was now classified as an epileptic.

It was on Friday morning that Barb and I first began to notice a change in Jenny's behavior. We discussed it and agreed something was "off," but even talking it out between us, we couldn't put our finger on it – it was just something a parent would notice, even if we couldn't define it. Although odd, it wasn't dramatic enough to make us terribly uncomfortable, but we did mention it to the doctor and were told that it was likely caused by Jenny's body adjusting to the Keppra. We had read a lot about the drug by this time and knew the side effects as well as the pros and cons, most specifically "unusual mood or behavior changes," so we easily accepted the doctor's explanation.

Even today, I have no doubt that the doctors were doing the best they could, given the facts presented to them. Jenny's change in behavior was definitely subtle enough to be missed by anyone that didn't know her well. It was even difficult for Barb and I to quantify in our minds.

The "odd behavior" that Jenny began to exhibit can best be summed up as hyperactivity, but it initially only came in short spurts, a few seconds at a time. Jenny would get so full of energy that she had a hard time sitting still, and she would talk loudly. Although her words were clear and each sentence made sense, there was no overall logic to what she was saying. She seemingly spoke every thought that crossed her mind. There were short bursts of this behavior and then she would return to "normal" for long periods. This made it very easy to dismiss the behavior as a reaction to the medication. Another logical explanation was that Jenny was just going a bit stir crazy after being penned up in the hospital for 36 hours.

The blood tests to confirm the Keppra levels met what the doctors felt was appropriate continued throughout the day, and adjustments were made as deemed necessary. As far as the doctors were concerned, the day was progressing nicely, but Barb and I saw Jenny getting "weirder" with each passing hour. The doctors and nurses listened to our concerns and talked to Jenny to get a feel for it themselves, but the behavior was difficult to define in a way for the doctors to identify it. In addition, because it came and went so rapidly, more often than not, we were the only ones in the room with her when it was exhibited. (I didn't know it then, but there was also a subtle attribute of Jenny being able to act completely normal when any non-family member was present. This would be a phenomenon that would continue throughout her illness.)

At about 3 p.m. on Friday, the doctors decided Jenny's seizures were under control, as she hadn't had one for more than 40 hours after experiencing the first two within eight hours. The medication was at a level that their experience dictated was appropriate, and thus the paperwork process was started to discharge her from the hospital. Barb and I had concerns, but we didn't think those concerns merited keeping Jenny in the hospital. We didn't push it any further with the doctors, especially since we knew Jenny would be seeing a neurologist at an appointment scheduled for the following Friday, a week away.

However, Barb was concerned enough that our car was barely moving out of the hospital parking lot before she had her phone in hand to make an appointment for Jenny with her primary care doctor. The appointment was set for the upcoming Monday.

Jenny went home to the apartment that evening. John had also noticed the changes in Jenny's behavior and remained attuned to them as the weekend progressed. When John dropped Jenny off at our house on Sunday, the 31st – Easter Sunday – he told us that it was getting worse.

While the change was subtle on an hour-by-hour basis, not having seen Jenny for nearly 48 hours we immediately noticed a significant change compared to how she was behaving on Friday evening. Jenny's younger sister, Michelle, had come home for the holiday and immediately noticed the change in Jenny as well.

Barb always prepares amazing meals on the holidays, and this one was no exception. I was a bit surprised when we sat down as a family on Sunday evening for dinner and Jenny didn't eat much of anything, although in hindsight, I guess I might have seen it as another sign that something was wrong with her. Instead, I attributed it to the fact that Jenny's tongue was sore and severely swollen due to having bitten it a number of times during the seizures. It was ultimately a prelude to what was to come, as Jenny's appetite ultimately dwindled to nothing over the coming weeks.

By Sunday evening, Jenny's behavior was becoming more of an issue. It could still be described as hyperactivity, but it was escalating. Jenny was talking almost constantly, going on and on nonsensically. It was as if her thoughts were racing at an impossible pace, faster than she could express them, yet she seemed to need to verbally express everything that crossed her mind.

Perhaps I was being liberal with what I was willing to accept, but I told myself that everything she was exhibiting so far matched the list of possible side effects of the Keppra. The doctors had warned us that it might take a while for her to adjust to the medication, and at this point, it wasn't as much concerning as it was just weird.

All of us went for a walk with Jenny on Sunday evening, figuring that the exercise would help calm her down. During the entire walk, Jenny was speaking very fast but making little sense. Jenny recognized that she was hyperactive, but she also had no control over it, so her overactive mind went to work on the problem. During the walk, Jenny began using a phrase that proved to be something we would hear from her countless times over the next two or three weeks: "I figured it out."

Her mind was working so fast that each time she came up with a possible solution as to why she was acting so hyper she would say, "I figured it out," before really thinking the entire problem all the way through. Every time, Jenny believed she had reached a monumental and irrefutable conclusion. She would give Barb a fast, albeit partial, explanation of what was going on in her head, exclaiming, "I figured it out," and then ask, "Don't you get it?" When Barb answered, "No," Jenny would simply start over and repeat the same incomprehensible explanation.

Even though Jenny didn't seem to realize that she wasn't making any sense, she did understand that her audience was unable to comprehend what she was attempting to explain. She became frustrated and sometimes even angry at whomever she was speaking to, which consequently made the thoughts spinning in her mind race even faster.

While Jenny vaguely remembers almost everything before the first seizure, and even a few events leading up to the second seizure, she has no recollection of anything after that, including any of the Easter Sunday events. The demons in her head already had a grip, but they were just starting to show themselves, and while I knew something wasn't quite right, it still wasn't entirely clear that anything was seriously wrong. I continued to accept that it was just a reaction to the medication.

Yet, as uncomfortable as we were with the changes in Jenny that we had witnessed between Wednesday, when she experienced the first seizure, to how she was behaving by this Sunday evening, it proved to be nothing compared to what we would see occur over the next four days…and the weeks to come.

CHAPTER 4

Monday, April 1 and Tuesday, April 2, 2013

Monday morning I left home at 2:30 a.m. for a business appointment out of state. Jenny was sleeping when I left, and as odd as her behavior had been, it was still a minor issue when I considered the big picture. Throughout my drive that morning, my only concern was the seizures. What caused them? Why now? Will they be permanently brought under control? But ultimately, and most importantly, how will this change Jenny's life in the long run? Not once on that drive did I give a thought to how she was behaving.

Barb took Jenny to the doctor appointment that morning, and in what proved to be a pattern at this early stage of her illness, Jenny was able to maintain relatively normal behavior during the visit. While the doctor listened to Barb's concerns, Jenny was clearly uncomfortable trying to contain her hyperactivity. Yet once again, the diagnosis was that Jenny was having a reaction to her medication and it would just take some time to adjust. As before, we accepted the diagnosis and believed Jenny's behavior was just a bizarre short-term condition that would soon be forgotten.

However, by that evening, the rate of change in Jenny's condition was escalating at a noticeable rate. As I describe all of this now, it is almost embarrassing that I was willing to accept what the doctors said, and that I was willing to ride it out.

After spending the weekend with us, Jenny's sister, Michelle, had departed to return to her own home that morning. John, Barb, and I began a vigil of working together to ensure Jenny was supervised by a family member at all times. What kept us dedicated to this task was the anticipation of the April 5th appointment with a neurologist. Surely, that doctor would have some clearer answers, or make some more adjustments to the medication to get Jenny back to being herself, and life would have some semblance of normalcy again.

By Tuesday morning, Barb and I were convinced that Jenny's behavioral changes had to be caused by something more than simply her body adjusting to the new medication. Jenny was talking almost constantly and her words began to become garbled, but it was more concerning that there was no thought process as her comments were incomplete and random in their order. If we would try to respond to what she had said or even question what she meant, it was almost as if she hadn't heard us speak and she would just continue on with the next random comment. She was also extremely hyperactive and having a hard time sitting still for any length of time. Yet, the descriptions I use now are based mostly on hindsight knowledge as this trend would continue and become more defined as time passed. As it was occurring we still had a hard time describing it, just as when she was at the hospital four days earlier, and certainly had no way to put any medical definition to it.

As Jenny continued to "babble" with increased verbosity, verbal exchanges became more difficult as we could not make sense of her choice of words. In addition, her hyperactivity had reached a point that she'd had little quality sleep since Saturday. Her body was clearly tired, even if her mind had little interest in resting. Jenny could rationally understand that she wanted and needed to sleep, so she would lie down and attempt to nap, but only moments later she would get up. There was never a specific reason to get up, she seemed to simply want to talk some more – whatever was on her mind just had to be spoken.

Later that day, John took Jenny to a chiropractor that his family trusted and had visited many times over the years. Everyone hoped that he might have some answers and be able to shed some light on the situation for us. Our lack of understanding about what was happening was harder for us to accept than was the task of dealing with the problem itself, so we began looking to anyone who might have some kind of answer.

Sure enough, John called immediately following the appointment. "Problem solved!" he proclaimed. Jenny could be heard in the background chanting, "We figured it out, we figured it out!" I remember her sounding very robotic and even rehearsed. As I recall, the explanation provided by the chiropractor was that Jenny had something pinched in her neck that was limiting the blood flow to her head. We all desperately wanted to believe that this was the answer. Jenny even called Michelle to explain that the chiropractor had fixed her and it was all solved. While Michelle listened to Jenny, she was more levelheaded than the rest of us and did not accept the diagnosis. Because Michelle had not experienced the strain of the previous four days of dealing directly with Jenny, she was not as inclined as we were to accept any diagnosis that sounded plausible.

As relieved as I was by the call from John, and really wanted it to be true, I remained only cautiously optimistic. In just five days I had already grown accustomed to the fact that Jenny's condition changed constantly. While I was hopeful, I did not allow myself to relax too much at this bit of news; too much had transpired and the trend was too consistent to be confident that this wasn't just a momentary reprieve from what we had been witnessing.

What I now know is that Jenny was simply processing the explanations offered by other people in her own way. Despite the illness that had already begun to take control of her mind, Jenny was able to adjust her behavior for short periods based on new information she received, and somehow this also provided her with the ability to act "normal" when non-family members were present. A doctor had treated her, there was a plausible explanation for the problem, and at least for a short time, her body reacted positively.

Unfortunately, and perhaps, as expected, it wasn't very long before Jenny returned to the behavior she was exhibiting before the visit to the chiropractor. By Tuesday evening, her hyperactivity and the nature of her random thoughts concerned us enough that the three of us agreed Jenny should not be left alone at any time, not even at night when she slept – or when she would try to sleep – when we hoped she would sleep, so we could sleep ourselves.

CHAPTER 5

The previous two days had been fairly difficult, and we did not feel it was safe to leave Jenny alone. It was not that she exhibited any behavior that indicated she was a danger to herself or anyone around her. It was simply that she was so unpredictable we just didn't know what could happen and wanted to be as careful as possible, so we kept our 24-hour vigil.

Although I was not aware that is what it was at the time, as best as I can determine, this was the day that Jenny experienced her first hallucination, and it proved to be one of the first "What the..." moments for me in this journey.

Jenny had received a large water cup with a watertight cover and large, heavy-duty straw from Methodist Hospital during her short stay there. She had instantly become attached to the container, had filled it dozens of times and carried it with her constantly.

Out of the blue on Thursday she said, "My straw is broken," and insisted that I fix it, clearly assuming that fathers can fix anything. The problem was that when Barb, John, and I each examined the straw closely, we found nothing wrong. It worked just fine.

"What's wrong with it, Jenny?"

"It has a hole in it!"

(I resisted the temptation to resort to my usual sarcastic mannerism to ask, "Shouldn't it have two holes in it?")

For nearly an hour, Jenny insisted that she could not get any water out of her cup because there was a hole in the straw, despite the fact that when one of us would try to suck water up the straw it worked just fine. However, Jenny couldn't seem to get anything out of it. She insisted that she needed the straw fixed and would not move on to anything else until it was. I finally switched the straw with a very similar one Barb had in one of her cups and handed it back to her, saying I had fixed it. She was happy and went back to what she was doing.

Somehow, Jenny's belief that the straw was broken was so strong that her attempts to suck water up it had failed. Whether or not this meets the definition of a hallucination, I have no idea. What I do know is that hallucinations would prove to be a major symptom of her illness and would play a key role in causing many of the horrific scenes that would occur over the coming weeks. This first experience was actually funny because I still had no idea what I was dealing with, and it was absolutely no comparison to what I would see later on. All I was thinking at that point was, "What the

15

heck is happening?" When combined with the events of the previous few days, this somehow just blended into the process and it didn't stick out as significant until weeks later when we recalled all that had happened.

Late in the afternoon, John raised the possibility that something traumatic may have occurred at Jenny's other job at the YMCA the day of the first seizure. Working there part-time, Jenny had come from a shift at that job when she arrived at Barnes and Noble the afternoon of the 27th. Was Jenny simply evoking some sort of self-defense mechanism? While there was no evidence of this being the case, we were willing to accept any possibility. I called Jenny's supervisor at the YMCA and discussed the issue, and was, of course, assured that she was not aware of any such situation. I can't say I gave it any serious consideration after that, but it does speak to our desperation for any clue as to what was causing Jenny's behavior.

While we frantically sought to make sense of what was happening and were focused on taking care of Jenny, we actually had lost perspective of how extreme her behavior had become. Other than an additional trip to the chiropractor, we had been keeping Jenny away from everyone except family. She called in sick to both of her jobs that week. She stayed either at our house, the apartment, or went to John's parents' house depending on our schedules and who could manage to be with her. Inadvertently, we had so isolated Jenny during the week that we had developed an unconscious naiveté to Jenny's condition. The combination of having two doctors tell us that what was happening was not that far out of the ordinary given the medication she was taking, as well as our singular focus on the goal of simply managing Jenny until the appointment with the neurologist on Friday, we became blind to how ridiculous the situation had become. We were clinging to our belief that Jenny was still adjusting to the Keppra, because none of us had ever seen or heard of anything like what was happening.

That changed drastically that evening when the isolation we had created around Jenny was broken and a relative stranger encountered her.

Barb, Jenny, John, and I spent the evening together. We had decided that John would head back to the apartment that night and Jenny would stay with us as this would allow John to attempt to get a good night's sleep and go to work the next day. As John was headed out the door to his truck, our Schwan's salesperson arrived. Jason had been on our route for quite a while, so was somewhat familiar with our family. As I greeted Jason at the front door upon his arrival, he must have either sensed the tension, or recognized the fatigue on my face immediately, because almost no conversation ensued beyond the usual greetings, which was unusual.

Within seconds of Jason's arrival, both Jenny and John came down the stairs from the upper level of the house to pass through the entryway on their way outside for John to leave. Jenny walked out the front door with

16

John to say goodnight, passing by Jason as he and I spoke. I said goodnight to John, and as I turned to continue our conversation, I noticed the dumbfounded look on Jason's face. Although he had only encountered Jenny for about five seconds as she passed by him in the entryway, it was obvious that he sensed something was wrong. Jenny is a very friendly person, and would always at least greet someone as she passed by. Jason knew her well enough to know that, so he must have been surprised when Jenny simply walked past him without so much as eye contact as she repeatedly mumbled, "Jenny going home with John." The look on his face said it all. I'm not even sure he actually asked me what was wrong, but I began to tell him the story of the previous Wednesday when Jenny was found unconscious in the snow bank.

I was not even 15 seconds into the story when both John and Jenny were back at the front door. John was escorting Jenny back into the house because she was trying to get into his truck rather than simply saying goodnight and sending him on his way. I had to guide Jenny back through the door and turn her up the stairs while she continued to robotically repeat, "Jenny going home with John." She still had not even acknowledged that Jason was there. Once she was going up the stairs, I turned my attention back to Jason, but he continued to watch Jenny. After a moment, I could tell by the movement of his eyes that Jenny was coming back down the stairs. I turned to look behind me just as Jenny passed by attempting to go back toward the front door. I took her arm and had to use some force to turn her around to head back up the stairs. Barb was there now, took Jenny from me, and escorted her the rest of the way to up into the living room.

I had become a bit shell-shocked by what was happening and turned back to Jason, having no idea what to say. Jason just stared at me for a moment; I imagine he was waiting for me to finish the story I had started a few moments earlier but wasn't sure he should or could ask me to continue. I took a moment to sit down on the steps that Jenny had just used and rested my elbows on my knees. I became a bit exasperated as the realization of how bad Jenny's condition had gotten suddenly hit me. After a moment of staring at each other, I put my head down into my hands.

Jason hesitantly asked what was wrong. Since I really had no clue, I stated the first thing that came to mind, simply as a way to give him some kind of a response; although I had already put the possibility out of my mind, I used the question John had raised earlier. "We really don't know, but we are concerned there might be a possibility that she may have been assaulted at work. We are taking her to a doctor tomorrow."

For some reason, it took Jason's reaction to open my eyes and see that we had been kidding ourselves as to the severity of the situation. At that moment, the appointment with the neurologist couldn't come soon enough because the only hope I had was that this specialist could identify what was wrong.

CHAPTER 6

Jenny's Journals

On that Thursday afternoon, Barb had suggested to Jenny that she begin keeping a journal of what she was thinking and experiencing. Jenny dove into the project enthusiastically, grabbing a spiral bound notebook and began writing. This notebook would stay with Jenny throughout her illness, although she would use it only sporadically after the first week. (Today the notebook also contains notes written by Barb, Michelle, John, and I and creates a somewhat odd historical record of some events during the course of Jenny's illness, including such things as food orders for all of us at the hospital on any given day.)

The following are actual clips of Jenny's notes from the first day she started journaling – the afternoon of Thursday, April 4th:

> So I woke up from my nap today right around 2 o clock and don't remember much of anything

(Barb wrote the note, 'right around 2 o clock')

We are not sure what time she made the next note, but from then on, almost everything she wrote had a time attached to it:

> Then I woke up and started freaking out because I hurt so bad. My arm was in pain and I was confused for what was going on.
>
> 2:55 Dad fell asleep
> Maya is on the couch
> My left arm itches really bad by my elbow
> my right toes are all tingly
> My tongue feels swollen
> My bottom lip feels open like it is sore.
> Water bottle spilt

(Maya is one of our dogs.)

Jenny appears to be recording everything that she sees or feels is wrong, because Maya should not be on the couch, and everything else she writes is negative.

The next two entries are in my writing. I do not recall what Jenny was doing at the time, but the two entries are exactly an hour apart. I obviously hadn't slept long, since at 2:55 she said I was sleeping:

> 3:07 *Can't stop crying*
> *Was doing better*
>
> 4:07 *Feels a panic attack coming on*
> - *She understands that. Good sign*

Jenny took over writing again:

These side effects suck

400 Side effects
the images are all jumpy

Example

At 5 o clock I was feeling fine again.
I watched Ch 11 news.

She crossed out the four lines above just after she wrote them.

5:44
my tongue is feeling slightly swollen
have not been confused since the
Twins game this afternoon My arms are
itchy I have eaten cheetos
Have been texting my sister and John
I feel like I have more energy
Been drinking Sprite
I want to go to B+N to look at books
and research

19

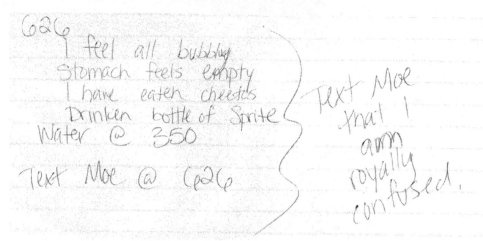

("Moe" is our nickname for Michelle, Jenny's younger sister.)

At some point during the next 30 minutes, I took the journal and wrote what Jenny was telling me she had been experiencing while watching the Twins game on TV earlier in the afternoon:

"Recent memories are playing in head randomly but can't control or rewind them"

There were two journal entries indicating that Jenny went for a walk around the park at 7 p.m. that night, and she noted that John was due to arrive at 8 p.m. that evening; she then made the following entry:

> 733 Took antihistamine   Face felt swollen
> Sent Moe text –   and itchy
>   So you know I am wearing your
> wolves sweatshirt. It is very comfy.

The next two entries (not included) indicated that Jenny watched *Big Bang Theory* (her favorite TV show) and then started to watch *American Idol*.

> 744 Weighed myself 148.2
>
> 744 Things are starting to click and
>   I understand things
>
> 750 John text me he was on his way

(The weight that Jenny recorded was off by more than 15 pounds.

752 Read my past journal entries and everything made sense.

754 Figured out how to write in my journal so things make sense when I go back to it

756 Text John Yay

758 Watching Am Idol, judges did not use their save

758 John text me here

801 I explained to John I figured out how to write into my journal to help with my confusion because my mom was slightly confused.

  I have omitted seven entries Jenny made from 8:03 to 9:20 p.m. Most referred to what TV shows she was watching (she was jumping back and forth between sitcoms as well as the Chicago/Brooklyn NBA basketball game), as well as recounting brief conversations with Barb and John.

848 End of basketball game, Time to go home

9:00 John went home to sleep
Jenny is staying at Mom+Dad's tonight

Going to work with My Mom tomorrow 8:45
Buying mom lunch
Jenny is keeping card to buy lunch

  Jenny made the entry at 8:48 p.m., at which time the incident with John leaving and encountering the Schwan's delivery person took place. In an effort to help Jenny comprehend that she was staying at our house with us, since Jenny had very quickly developed an attachment to the journal,

21

Barb made the five lines of entries at 9 p.m. The notation by Barb appeared to work, because Jenny stopped making a fuss about staying at the house that night.

From 9:04 to 9:20 p.m. there are six entries omitted. One noted that I took her phone away from her for the night (an attempt to get her to focus on sleep instead of texting John and others). She noted what she had for dinner earlier in the evening, commented that her handwriting looks like her Mom's, and mentioned what basketball game had started on TV.

All of that was followed by this entry:

922 When things make perfect sense, page is blank

I am not clear on what she meant by this. I assume in her mind she only made entries when she was confused, but there were no blank pages.

After one final entry at 9:24 p.m. stating that she had gotten caught up on the TV show *Scandal*, Jenny stopped making entries for the night. Although I do not recall exactly why she stopped journaling, I assume it was that I had taken it away from her, just as I had her cell phone, in an effort to get her to sleep. She had become somewhat obsessed with journaling, and the absence of the phone made it so the journal was all she was focused on.

The goal was to settle down for a good night's sleep. That didn't go so well.

CHAPTER 7

Friday, April 5, 2013

The tactics we employed that week to accomplish our stated goal of managing Jenny until the time of the neurologist appointment sounds so odd now. It feels as if we were the worst and most naïve parents of all time believing if we rode out the storm until we got to that appointment, a simple explanation or a miracle cure would be unveiled. In what seems like a silly defense now, I know my error was a blind faith placed in the earlier diagnosis combined with the belief that a specialist such as a neurologist would have the answers.

Jenny's behavior was not improving in any way – in fact, it grew steadily worse. Although I remained convinced the symptoms were becoming more inconsistent with those attributable to "adjusting to medication," the fact that there were no signs of additional seizures was good. The plan laid out on Thursday evening was for me to stay up with Jenny through the night and then go to work the next morning and Barb would take over supervising Jenny. This type of rotation would become our "normal" for the time being.

Jenny's periods of odd behavior had ebbs and flows. They would arise slowly, peak, and then go away for a while. On Thursday night and moving into the early hours of Friday morning, Jenny had been wound up for a particularly long time. The topics of conversation were more random than they had been previously, and were switching from topic to topic even more rapidly. By 2:30 a.m., my estimation is that Jenny had slept for a total of five or six hours since Tuesday morning, and the sleep took place in short, restless spurts. She was clearly tired, as were John, Barb, and I.

My shift of monitoring Jenny this night actually consisted of me almost constantly begging her to lie still for just five minutes. It was a grownup version of being in the car with her as a five-year-old, and playing the game of seeing if she could go one minute, two minutes or three minutes without saying a word. My theory was that because she was so tired, I hoped I could get her to agree to sit still long enough so she might automatically fall asleep.

I also had a completely selfish motivation – God, how I wanted to sleep. She was lying on the couch in our family room, and I was sitting in the recliner next to her. When I would ask her to lay still for five minutes, hoping she would fall asleep, the challenge for me was to sit still for five minutes and not distract her while still managing to stay *awake* myself.

The strategy was failing miserably. While I was struggling to stay awake, Jenny was not able to be still long enough to fall asleep; and her thoughts were coming faster and becoming more random than ever. I resorted to having the TV on while the rest of the house was dark and quiet, hoping this would at least keep her from wandering around, and promote her remaining, at the very least, lying on the couch.

This plan didn't work either. Instead, Jenny was on a rant as she tried to explain what the Keppra was doing to her brain. It was one of those moments she believed she had "figured it out." In reality, she was making a long leap from a conversation she had overheard Barb and I having earlier in the evening. She would not make eye contact during these rants, but looked off somewhere, usually at the ceiling, just letting the thoughts in her mind flow out of her mouth.

As Jenny continued to discuss the Keppra, she suddenly turned, looked at me, and said, "Mark Rosen sucks." Then, just as suddenly, she went back to lying on the couch, looking straight up at the ceiling, and continued her analysis of Keppra and how the chemical breakdowns work on the inner structure of the brain – of which she had no such knowledge.

For the record, no one in our family, including Jenny, has any issues with Mark Rosen. None of us, to my knowledge, have ever even met him. Our only connection to him is watching his reports as the lead sports anchor on a local television station. Regardless, during the course of the night Jenny would randomly, yet very sincerely, turn to me four or five times and say, with complete conviction, "Mark Rosen sucks."

I can't say Jenny never criticizes people, but for her to say something potentially hurtful about anyone, and so blatantly, is rare. On occasion she will openly express a negative thought about someone, but she never does so as definitively and repeatedly as she did this night, and especially about someone she does not even know. Clearly, not only were her thoughts rapid and random, but an odd change in her personality was showing itself as well.

Another new dimension to Jenny's situation revealed itself late during that long night with her. Jenny and I are both huge Minnesota Twins baseball fans. I had missed the game played earlier that afternoon, and had turned on the late night rebroadcast of the game on TV. As Jenny watched the game during her rants, she began repeating the comment, "time is getting stuck." While this was similar to some of her other meaningless babble, she was looking intently at the TV as she said it, and seemed to repeat it more than any other statement – enough so that it got my attention. This marked the first time I saw a definable problem with how her brain was functioning.

I asked Jenny what she meant by the statement, "time is getting stuck." I wanted to know what she was seeing on the TV to cause her to make this statement. Although trying to comprehend most of what she had said over the past few days had been a very frustrating proposition, I prepared myself for the difficult task of trying to figure out exactly what she meant.

As she repeatedly tried to explain it to me, what I came to believe was that the video she was seeing of the game did not match the audio of what the broadcasters were saying. It took about 30 minutes for me to understand that, in her mind, the broadcasters were saying what was happening in the game but the video would get stuck. This wasn't any kind of technical malfunction, as I could see that everything was fine on the TV. However, for Jenny, time was getting stuck because she could hear the broadcasters talking about the action, but the video was not keeping up. As we watched the game together, she pointed out that the announcers said the batter hit a single, but she insisted he had never left the batter's box. I could see that the video was not actually freezing. Play had continued, but somehow in Jenny's mind it was not at the same pace as the announcers were speaking.

After giving Jenny's statements quite a bit of thought, my assessment was that due to her hyperactivity and the rapid progression of thoughts going on in her head, she was simply losing focus on the game. She would process other thoughts in her mind and would then return her attention to the game, expecting it be exactly where she left off, and would not see what she expected the action to be. Her mind processed the discrepancy as time getting stuck in order to make sense of it. For example, she would hear that a batter got a hit by a pitch, but by the time her rapid series of thoughts got around to processing that specific piece of information and she looked at the screen, the next batter would already be up to bat. As a result, she would not see what she expected to see, which was a batter trotting to first base. She believed it was still the same batter standing in the box. I have no clue if my assessment is accurate or not…and as of yet, I had no idea that this is what our world would be like for the next month, and beyond.

Although I was perplexed about everything going on and my lack of clarity as to the reason for it, the "time is getting stuck" exchange gave me the idea to grab my digital voice recorder. My intention was to create a record of Jenny's speech and thought patterns for the doctor we would see later that day. Part of the difficulty we were having explaining the behavior to others was due to Jenny's ability to return to somewhat "normal" when people other than John, Barb, or I were around. The challenge became to provide evidence of the behavior "strangers" were not seeing when they were present. I needed a way to give the doctors definitive proof of the changes in Jenny's behavior. Although this would not allow them to *see* anything, at least they could hear it. I ended up recording Jenny's rambling rants for the next 45 minutes.

At 5 a.m. that morning, Jenny picked up her journal and started again.

5:00 I discovered the loop I am stuck in
      My body reset, Magic School Bus
   Does John know?
        What all does he know?
      I know I am a Kids Lead @ B+N
      Do I hold a manager position as well
      I didn't really sleep

Dad + I had a great convo last night,
Where is the remote to change the channel
5:38
   I keep creating new loops
   wake up confused
   Read my journal and it all makes sense.

5:41 Morning movie review
        Evil Dead

At 5:43 and 5:46 a.m., Jenny made entries very similar to that of 5:41 a.m. when she began to write exactly what she was hearing on TV. Then she made the following entry with no time notation:

My loop is repeating over + over

Jenny continued to record nearly everything she heard and saw on TV for six more pages, with 33 entries between 5:49 and 6:17 a.m. Sometimes there were multiple entries within a single minute, and she recorded the same time with each entry. Her entries were so detailed as to what she heard spoken on the television, she had even listed the admission charge for a Minnesota United FC Soccer game. The exception to this was an entry that, again, had no time notation, but is shown between the 5:55 and 5:56 a.m. entries:

555 Shakira on the Voice
Love Blake

The clock seems to not be moving
at all but so much is
happening

556
WCCO Radio Tune in to
listen

At 6:17 a.m., things began to get even more confusing for Jenny.

617   7 Day Forecast
       Construction
       94 by clearwater/ St Cloud
619 Last remember
NFl require teams for cameras

Sleep express commercial

~~received~~ ~~became confused~~

~~Need to go to bed~~

~~time remember~~ ~~lack of sleep~~
609 is the time gap

653 Commercial break

27

It is difficult to see all that she crossed out, and various and inconsistent times had been written, but all of the journal entries dealt with lack of sleep. Then she jumps from 6:19 back to 6:09 and makes a notation of a time gap. I am not aware of, or do not recall, exactly what she was doing or experiencing from 6:19 to 6:53 a.m.

This continued, almost nonstop until 7:18 a.m. when she stopped to get ready to go to work with Barb so they could leave for the neurologist appointment directly from there, rather than needing to come back home to pick up Jenny for the appointment. This plan allowed Barb to get to work for at least a while.

Barb and Jenny left for work about 7:30 a.m. as planned.

The initial review of the journal entries, from Thursday night through that Friday morning, seem to reveal a rather chaotic thought process, or at least confusion, and the entries appear to be random. However, upon closer examination, the entries could be interpreted as simply a deliberate attempt to grasp what was going on around her; rather, to decipher the difference between what she was thinking in her mind as opposed to what she was hearing on the television. It was almost as if Jenny understood that she was not able to tell the difference. In fact, an entry that Jenny made later that morning while in Barb's office shows her continued confusion:

8:30 At ~~mom~~ mom's work

    I am confused & it doesn't make sense

    I feel I'm on info overload.

845 Started crying cuz mom was
    trying to get off work,

Another view is that it may not have been so much about *what* she wrote, as it was the frequency of the entries. As Jenny's illness progressed, she would demonstrate a tendency to get fixated on random things, but it would be another two weeks before this would be clear. In this case, it was a fixation of recording nearly every single thought that crossed her mind.

The experience with the Schwan's deliveryman the night before had given me serious doubts about waiting for the neurology appointment, but the nightlong rants had convinced me that, at the very least, I had to call and

28

consult with a doctor. The only question I had was which doctor. I knew contacting the neurologist would be difficult, at best, and I did not want to call a general "nurse's line" as I was too tired to even think about trying to explain all this over the phone to someone who was new to the situation.

I decided to wait until 8 a.m. when the office of Jenny's primary care doctor opened which would allow me to talk directly to the nurse that saw Jenny on Monday. I knew that speaking to someone who had seen her earlier in the week would not make it any easier to explain the current situation, but at least I knew the person on the other end of the phone would know some of the history of what was going on, and perhaps understand that my concerns were real.

I began preparing for work myself, intending to get to the office for a few hours before the neurologist appointment. I had one eye on the clock the entire time I was getting ready to leave, intending to be the very first call the doctor's office would take that day.

The operator answered the phone at exactly 8 a.m. and connected me to the nurse. The nurse listened intently to what I had to say, asked a few questions, and clarified the symptoms I had described.

Her response was, "Get Jenny to the Emergency Room right away!"

I hung up and called Barb, who had been at work for only a few minutes. I told her to get herself, and Jenny, back in the car.

CHAPTER 8

Although there is at least one hospital closer to our home than Methodist Hospital in St. Louis Park, I do not recall us discussing where we were going to take Jenny. It felt like common sense to take her back to where the treatment had begun.

Barb stopped to pick me up on the way to the hospital. We arrived at the Emergency Room, Jenny was admitted immediately, and doctors began to make their assessments.

After some time, a doctor came in to relay his conclusions based on the tests and examinations, go over the plan of action they were proposing, and answer any questions. The doctor sat down and very patiently and clearly explained all aspects of the situation. He made sure all of our questions were answered, but also encouraged conversation to be sure that we had a chance to process what he told us as new questions were bound to come up, and indeed they did. The conclusion was that Jenny was having an allergic reaction to the Keppra, not simply having a hard time adjusting to it, as had been previously thought.

For a week we had been witnessing behavior that we knew was very odd for Jenny, changes that were so severe it was as if she had developed an entirely new personality. Yet even if a stranger actually saw the behavior, it would be difficult to explain it as being out of character for Jenny. This trend continued in the Emergency Room.

During the doctor's visit, Jenny sat in her bed and appeared to be listening very intently to everything he had to say. She even asked a few intelligent questions. The doctor did a great job of including all three of us in the discussion, making sure all of us were clear on what was happening, and understood what the plan was. He concluded with the statement, "So are there any other questions?"

Jenny immediately responded, rather harshly, "I don't mean to be rude, but can you please get a doctor in here that can explain to me what is going on?"

There was an awkward silence, and the doctor looked between Barb and me in surprise. He may have easily excused Jenny's response as part of her being confused by the allergic reaction to the medication, but I believe he interpreted our silence as confirmation that we agreed with Jenny. After a moment, he very professionally excused himself saying that he would have another doctor come in to explain everything again.

What he did not realize was that Barb and I were stunned into silence. While to the doctor, Jenny's behavior may have appeared to be a normal, albeit very rude reaction to not understanding what was happening, we knew it was completely out of character for Jenny. The true and healthy

Jenny would have asked as many questions as it took to understand, or at least that she was comfortable asking. When the doctor had asked if we had more questions, she would have either asked more questions, or allowed the doctor to leave and then turned to us for clarification of what she didn't understand. The Jenny we know would never have said what she did. None of the explanations or literature about the adjustments to the Keppra, nor the newly diagnosed allergic reaction, spoke to the personality changes we were witnessing.

Sure enough, the previous doctor sent in the Emergency Room Chief of Staff. He dutifully went through the same conclusions and plans. This time Jenny produced no inappropriate outbursts.

I asked the doctor if I could join him in the hallway, which he agreed to and we both stepped out of the room. I had intended to ask him some questions, but suddenly my fatigue, combined with the stress of everything I had seen over the past week, compounded by the unnatural outburst Jenny had just exhibited, took over. Surprising even myself, I began to cry nearly uncontrollably. I tried to speak through my sobbing and, honestly, my embarrassment. "That is not my daughter in there," I said. "There is something else wrong. I don't know what, but this has to be something more than an allergic reaction to a medication!" I pulled out the digital voice recorder and asked him to listen to a portion of what Jenny had sounded like the night before.

The very busy doctor was patient and tried to be consoling, however, deep down I knew, even as we were standing there in the hallway that he believed me to be an overly concerned and out of control father. He very professionally told me what he believed I needed to hear, and I acted as if I believed he had taken me seriously and was doing more than giving me lip service. Then I let him go on his way.

He was not interested in listening to the recording I had made.

Once again, I had failed to convince someone of what I knew with my entire being to be true. This was the point that I gave up trying to explain it to doctors. Part of the plan of action included that Jenny would stay in the hospital to begin the process of switching her from the Keppra to a different anti-seizure medication. I hoped that during this hospital stay someone would eventually see what I was seeing. When and how this would happen I had no idea, but I was convinced that they would see it for themselves very soon and "figure it out." Then this would all be over…in just a few days.

Later that afternoon, Jenny was admitted as a patient into Methodist Hospital. She was taken to the 6th floor where neurological patients are treated and affectionately referred to as "6Neuro" by the staff. It would be 74 days before Jenny would sleep anywhere other than a hospital bed.

Part 2

"Deterioration"

April 5 to April 30, 2013

CHAPTER 9

Friday, April 5, 2013: Day 1

The next three and a half days were the calm before the storm.

While Jenny was being transferred to the 6th floor and being settled into her room, I went to call Michelle, who was a part-time teacher in Wabasso, Minnesota, a town about two hours southwest of Rockford. We had kept her up to speed on Jenny's progress during the week in very general terms, but she had not received an update since early Thursday evening, so she was obviously surprised to hear that her sister had been admitted to the hospital. Michelle was going to be heading home for the weekend anyway, but upon hearing what was happening with Jenny, she immediately headed for the hospital and arrived later that evening.

Upon admission, a diagnosis for Jenny's condition needed to be listed. Due to the lack of any definitive evidence of any other cause, the doctors labeled it as an allergic reaction to the Keppra being used to control the seizures. The immediate plan was to begin the tenuous process of weaning Jenny off the Keppra and switching her to another anti-seizure medication, Dilantin, to see if anything changed, but the process takes days.

I remember feeling very at ease once Jenny was settled into her room on the 6th floor. I suppose it was due in part to the exhaustion I was experiencing from all that had happened in the 10 days since Jenny's first seizure. In a strange way, I was actually pleased that Jenny was admitted to the hospital as it made it much easier for Barb, John, and me to keep an eye on her. More importantly, I was very anxious for the nurses and doctors to see Jenny's behavior first-hand for a longer period of time than just brief examinations. I was unconvinced that she was having an allergic reaction. In my mind, the only real question that remained was whether the doctors were going to wait for the medication switch to be completed, or if additional tests would be done in the meantime to look for other possibilities.

I have no recollection of the doctors acknowledging that they were directly concerned about Jenny's behavior at the time of her admission. Months later, I reviewed the notes of the doctors who observed Jenny that day and saw they did, indeed, acknowledge that Jenny's behavior was suspect and very possibly a symptom of something more serious than an allergic reaction, but they needed solid evidence to support this. Our inability to definitively identify the changes we witnessed in a way that the doctors could quantify made it impossible to reach any valid conclusions. My concern that day was that based on Jenny's rapid deterioration thus far, if her behavior was not caused by the Keppra, how much worse would she get before other causes were seriously considered.

Enter Dr. Daniel Freking.

Dr. Freking was the neurologist on call at the time of Jenny's admission and began to put us at ease immediately. He first conducted his preliminary examination of Jenny and administered a series of motor skill and memory tests we would see repeated dozens of times in the coming months. He then began to ask us a multitude of questions covering a whole spectrum of possible causes for Jenny's condition. This immediately increased my confidence that we would get to the bottom of this very quickly. Whether he didn't believe it was an allergic reaction, was a very thorough doctor, or was simply following a hunch, I may never know for sure. While Barb, John, and I explained everything we had witnessed for the past week to Dr. Freking, he asked questions to clarify what we were saying – he was actually listening to us!

Not long after the doctor left, a nurse and an orderly came into the room in somewhat of a rush. We were told that Jenny was "going downstairs for a test." The sudden sense of urgency led me to believe that something was seriously wrong, and I became quite nervous. Earlier in the day, blood had been drawn, and a series of other tests run but the results had not come back yet. Now there was an urgency to get Jenny downstairs for a test that had not been explained to us any further. After recovering from my initial shock and concern, I started pressing for answers. Dr. Freking was paged, and he came to Jenny's room almost immediately to inform us that he had decided that on the off chance that the Keppra was not the cause of Jenny's changes in behavior, he had better start looking for other causes.

The urgency stemmed from Dr. Freking's desire to get a lumbar puncture (spinal tap) done before that procedural room closed for the weekend. With that news, it felt as though my heart started beating again. I'd love to say that was the only time I overreacted during the rest of Jenny's illness, but unfortunately, it wasn't.

Things were underway, and I already felt much better just knowing that at least one doctor was willing to look beyond the Keppra issue.

Dr. Freking went over what each test was and why he had ordered them. Some of the tests such as the MRI and EEG, were a repeat of tests done earlier and were going to be used for comparison more than anything else, but there were quite a few tests for a variety of illnesses such as West Nile virus and Lyme disease.

The lumbar puncture was of the most concern to me. It seemed a bit extreme, even with what I had been seeing, but when I voiced my concern Dr. Freking responded, "I'm ordering that on the 2% chance we find something." I quickly came to view Dr. Freking as a tenacious man, who was very forward thinking. Ultimately, his decision saved Jenny at least a couple days of additional deterioration.

The results of the various tests started to come in late that evening. The most puzzling result was that the EEG showed a problem on the right side of Jenny's brain, but the MRI was "unremarkable," meaning that nothing abnormal was found. This contradictory information seemed to become an afterthought that afternoon, but it actually would be of monumental interest in weeks to come.

The most immediate issue was the result of the lumbar puncture testing. A preliminary test result of the fluid that afternoon showed that the white blood cell count in Jenny's spinal fluid was extremely high, at 62, when it should have been zero. This was an indication that an infection of some kind was in Jenny's brain. Unfortunately, the test to determine the actual cause of this could not be done at Methodist and the fluid was sent to a lab elsewhere in the Twin Cities, but there was no way to get the results until Monday or Tuesday.

This was the test result that confirmed what Barb, John, and I had felt since the beginning: something serious was wrong with Jenny. The actual cause of the seizures and of the "odd behavior" was still not known, but at least now, there was some solid evidence that something other than an allergic reaction was going on.

Confirmation of what the infection was would take a few days, so some assumptions needed to be made that ultimately resulted in two decisions: the switch from Keppra to Dilantin would continue as a precaution, since the process had already begun; and Jenny was started on an antiviral medication designed to attack a few specific infections of the brain. Based on the educated guesses of the doctors, the assumption was that the infection was more than likely Herpes Simplex.

All of these medical details were trivial to me. As far as I was concerned, at least something positive was being done, which was reason enough for us to begin feeling some optimism. All there was to do was sit and wait as each of these two processes took place. The weekend was relatively quiet compared to the previous 10 days, and this calm before the storm proved to be the first of many experiences that created a false sense of security. We were at the hospital. I was confident in the doctor that was on the case and the staff he had around him. I had every reason to believe this would all be over soon.

What proved to be one of the great ironies of this portion of Jenny's illness was that the seizures always remained the primary indicator of her health. Seizures are always a manifestation of something else that is wrong. Either a patient is epileptic, or there is an underlying illness of which the seizures are a symptom. Throughout the weekend, the doctors said that Jenny could go home when the seizures were "totally under control." How this control was accomplished was irrelevant to me; my only goal was to get her home.

By Sunday night, Jenny was actually showing significant and consistent signs of improvement in terms of her awareness and behavior. However, over the course of the weekend, another EEG was performed, and during that 20-minute test, Jenny had another significant seizure, although it was not outwardly visible in that there were no tremors. Clearly, there were hurdles to overcome, but overall the weekend seemed to be going well.

By Sunday night, I had hope and was confident that progress was being made, as evidenced by an email I sent:

> *Had a GREAT day. Still more confusion and frustration than not, but first positive day since this all started back on the 27th. We won't know anything for sure until tomorrow or Tuesday when the test results are back on the spinal fluid, but it appears that the doctors guessed right and are administering the right medication to begin her road to recovery.*

On Monday morning I sent an email to my business partner updating her on everything going on in which I said, "I will be back to work in a day or two." My optimism was tempered however; there were still some unanswered questions that I discussed in another email that read:

> *In reality, we know nothing until the "culture" comes back – thank God he rushed the spinal tap, otherwise whatever it is that is causing this would have had two to three more days to grow and cause more problems. On Saturday morning Jenny was acting in such a way that I believed we needed a priest, not a doctor.*

We felt better and believed positive progress was being made. What we remained completely unaware of was how many surprises the demons in Jenny's head had in store for us. It really was the calm before the unknown, oncoming storm.

CHAPTER 10

Days 4 & 5

That first Monday in the hospital felt like a better than average day when compared to all that had happened since Jenny's first seizure on the 27th of March. There had been many reasons for optimism over the previous 48 hours. Jenny's behavior appeared to be improving, although it was by no means "normal," far from it, but Sunday and Monday were an improvement compared to Friday and Saturday. Of course, I took that as a very good sign and gave credit to the antiviral treatment that was being administered. All of us seemed to relax and our belief was we were simply waiting for it to finish its job, and then we could all head home.

The notebook Jenny used to make journal entries the previous Thursday and Friday had made the trip to the hospital with her. However, with rare exception, entries made at the hospital were by either John or Barb; Jenny made only a couple of simple entries, for the most part. The vast majority of entries simply traced Jenny's sleeping, eating, and bathroom habits. There were also a few notes about the various doctor's visits to her room.

It was not until a few weeks later that we noticed/recalled some entries Barb had made into Jenny's journal on the evening of Monday, April 8th, which ultimately foreshadowed what was to come:

> 7:00 Got confused, couldn't remember how to count picking at IV
> 7:15 wont pee — still confused
> 7:40 went pee — still playing w/ IV
> 7:45 much calmer — John went home
> 8:00 Want pee
> 8:15 – 8:40 Major hallucinating — the room getting bigger & bigger & going to explode or pop, then her body was swelling (in her mind) & arms & hands were getting bigger & bigger and were going to pop —

As odd as the entries of "8:15 – 8:40" were, it may sound even more odd that the events these entries refer to are, indeed, barely even footnotes today when held in comparison to what was to come. Jenny had been showing improvement since Saturday night, or so we thought. It was our belief at the time that any "odd behavior" Jenny was demonstrating was

39

waning. The odd hallucination wasn't given any thought that day mostly due to the fact that she was receiving medical care and we had allowed ourselves to believe she was, indeed, improving. The event and journal notation ultimately was completely forgotten due to what came afterward.

It was on Tuesday, the 9th, that things really began to turn for the worse. If the weekend was the calm before the storm, we should have seen a few clouds rolling in on Monday, because by Tuesday we knew a very strong front was on its way. That was the day the demons inside Jenny's head first showed how cruel they were going to be – not only to Jenny, but also to those of us around her who loved her.

Knowing what I know now, I have no idea how or why Jenny was able to act as she did the previous two days. I believe that part of it was that she truly wanted to get better, and was simply reacting to the positive news of the treatment, similar to her reaction after the initial visit to the chiropractor the week before. In any case, we now understand that nothing had really changed for her. In fact, she was getting worse.

The list of disappointments on this day is long and began when the extreme behavior seen the previous week started to return. Given the positive signs since the treatment had begun, I had allowed myself to become too optimistic – my roller coaster ride of emotions that would be part of the coming months had truly begun. What I came to call "the deterioration" began to reappear and increased rather rapidly.

That morning, the first indication we had that things were taking a turn for the worse was noted in a journal entry by Barb:

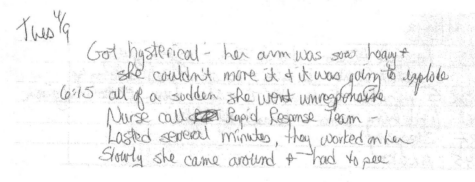

Tues 4/9

Got hysterical - her arm was sore baggy + she couldn't move it & it was going to explode
6:15 all of a sudden she went unresponsive
Nurse call Rapid Response Team -
Lasted several minutes, they worked on her
Slowly she came around + had to pee

In hindsight, it appears almost comical to me that Barb would note that Jenny "had to pee" on the same line that "she came around" after being unresponsive to the point that the Rapid Response Team had to be called in. This is an indication of how bizarre the situation had already become for all of us.

The next disappointment we endured that day, after having wanting so badly to believe Jenny was improving, was when the lab results from the spinal fluid came back: every single infection that was tested for – all of them – came back "negative." The fact remained that the white blood cell count was high, and we still did not know why.

I've learned a lot of things over the past year. Some of it would actually be very interesting if I wasn't learning it while waiting for doctors to find the answer to what was wrong with my child. Medical tests look for specifics, and the results are either positive or negative. Tests only tell us whether a particular disease is present; they don't tell us what is wrong.

The tests coming came back negative may not have been as important if Jenny's behavior had continued to improve. I could have simply pointed to the changeover from the Keppra to the Dilantin. However, reviewing everything that had happened during the 13 days since Jenny's first seizure, I came to understand that we knew nothing more than we did on March 27th. I had no idea where we would go from here, and even more disturbing, I was not aware if the doctors did either.

On top of all this bad news, Jenny began to experience additional seizures late in the day. I had been told over the weekend that Jenny was going to be hospitalized until the seizures were under control, and now even that seemed further away.

All of this made it feel as if we were back to square one. With good reason. We were.

Throughout all of this, Jenny never lost sight of her main goal. Every time a doctor came into the room, Jenny asked the same question, "When can I go home?"

For a very simple yet significant reason, this question was becoming even more urgent with each passing day. When Jenny was admitted to the hospital on the afternoon of April 5th, it never crossed my mind that Jenny would be there seven days later. April 12th was significant for two very big reasons: The first was that it was Jenny's 26th birthday, and the second was that Jenny and I had started something of a father/daughter tradition that whenever the Minnesota Twins played a home game on her birthday, we would go to the game. This tradition was important to both of us. The Twins are a passion that Jenny and I share. It is our thing.

On Monday, Jenny started expressing concern about being out of the hospital in time to make the game. I thought we were okay that morning, but by Tuesday afternoon, I had my doubts, although I didn't want to be the one to break the news to her. So on Dr. Freking's last visit for the day, I deliberately asked him, "Will Jenny be out of here by Friday?" Dr. Freking very definitively said "No" without a moment of hesitation, and Jenny immediately burst into tears. It took everything in me to hold back from doing the same thing.

The final and biggest hit of the day came late that evening when all of us came face to face with the true drama of what we were going to be dealing with in the coming weeks.

From the time that Jenny's "odd behavior" began, there were variations in how she would act at any given time. During the first week or so, Jenny was "normal" the majority of the time. Her strange behavior was so subtle at first that it was almost imperceptible. Yet, beginning the second week, with each passing day the amount of time that Jenny was "with us" became less and less as the odd behavior became more prevalent. Additionally, the odd behavior itself was getting worse, both in terms of the amount of time it was happening, and it's intensity.

Regardless of what stage of her illness Jenny was in, the one constant was that there were "peaks and valleys" in how she behaved. The peaks were intense periods that would last anywhere from a few minutes up to as long as an hour and half. During these periods, there was absolutely no reaching Jenny. She would just "leave" us.

Even when she was able to communicate, or at least appeared to be attempting to communicate with us, she would not react directly to any one person even when we were responding to something she asked of us. Depending on what was happening in her head at the time – depending on how cruel the demons that had control of her wanted to be – she would think things, see things, feel things, and hear things that were not real in any way. These were the times that we constantly worked to be prepared for – mentally as well as physically. Her behavior became increasingly unpredictable and she became incredibly difficult to manage. These times were the very reason that we made the decision that we could not leave Jenny alone, even when she was in the care of the doctors. Barb and I could not imagine Jenny experiencing any of this without someone who knew and loved her next to her while it occurred.

We came to refer to these intense peaks in her behavior as "episodes." I don't remember when we started to use the word, but it really was an appropriate description of them. Just as every single episode of any TV show has something unique that sets one apart from all the others, so did Jenny's episodes. What she experienced during these episodes, and how she behaved as a result was rarely the same. There were an infinite number of variations in behavior, which made it difficult to describe them to others. It just became easier to sum them up in one word, even though the word really only meant something to those of us closest to her every day. Even the nursing staff began to use the word.

Barb, John, Michelle, my sister Debbie and I, who were with her more than any other family members or medical care providers the entire time, rarely attempted to explain what was happening, or had happened, during these episodes. There were almost no similarities in them, and more often than not, there was no reason to try to explain it – and oftentimes, they were inexplicable anyway. We simply would say, "I couldn't answer the phone when you called because Jenny was having an episode." We rarely even asked each other what had happened. We knew what we meant when we used the word and what we had to deal with, but the details and facts eventually became irrelevant because each one was different…and usually horrible, in their own way. Sometimes the episodes would actually be interesting in one way or another, but more often than not, they were at least a bit sad. Occasionally they could be funny, but humor became less and less common as the illness progressed – and the episodes became scarier – for both Jenny and those present to witness them at the time.

Up to this point Michelle had only heard our attempts at describing these episodes to her on the phone, but she didn't truly understand what Barb, John, and I already knew – the episodes were actually indescribable, no matter how simple they were. Michelle had yet to witness one of the most intense episodes with her own eyes. That was about to change.

Due to some weather issues in southwest Minnesota, Wabasso schools had let out early on that Tuesday, and since the results (or lack thereof) of the spinal tap confirmed something serious was going on, Michelle decided to get a substitute teacher for the remainder of the week. She had arrived at the hospital earlier in the day so she, Barb, John, and I were all gathered in Jenny's room, standing around her bed, assessing the day and bringing Michelle up to speed. The natural light of the sun was still illuminating the room enough to see without any other lights on, but it was late enough in the day that it was beginning to darken the corners of the room.

Jenny was lying in bed during our conversation, not doing anything in particular, and not really involved in our conversation directly. Then, out of nowhere, she asked Michelle to "take the truck out of the room."

Based on the direction of her stare, it was clear that she believed there was a truck, I assumed the size of small toy, at the head of her bed. Michelle was a bit surprised but amused at the same time as this was the first time that she had heard one of the sometimes silly requests Jenny would come up with. She looked to each one of us for guidance, assuming that we would have complete understanding of how to handle the situation. However, the truth was that all of us were still learning how to deal with Jenny during her episodes, and there was still a constant learning curve that we would, ultimately, never master.

For lack of a better idea, we quietly and subtly suggested that Michelle go through the motions and pretend to pick up the truck and take it into the hallway, which she did. After going through the motions of picking up an imaginary truck from Jenny's bed, she walked out into the hallway for a few seconds and then came back into the room. For a moment, it appeared as if that would be the end of it. We all returned to what we were doing before the strange request.

Then, just as suddenly as before, Jenny turned to Michelle and asked her what she did with the truck. Michelle informed Jenny that she had put it in the hallway, but Jenny did not believe her and said she wanted to go out into the hallway to check.

One thing we had learned very early on was that it was best not to let Jenny into the hallway during her episodes, so I denied her request. Beyond the need to keep Jenny in the room in case her behavior escalated, I knew, of course, there was no truck in the hallway. I did not know if Jenny would see a truck if she went into the hallway, nor did I know what would happen if she didn't see one.

Through all of the many weeks of Jenny episodes, I never did manage to figure out how much our actions incited worse experiences for Jenny or if they would have happened anyway. So ultimately, I will never know if not allowing Jenny into the hallway that day triggered what happened next, or where it would have gone on its own.

Initially, it seemed that Jenny was going to let it go, but very soon she began to act quite agitated. None of us could figure out what was happening yet, but among the many emotions Jenny seemed to be feeling, it was clear that fear was at the forefront. At first, she appeared to be trying to look under her bed while she was still in it. The design of hospital beds made this a difficult task and she appeared in danger of falling on her head, so we stopped her. She didn't want to get off the bed, but she clearly still felt the need to see under it. Perhaps it was something she said, I don't recall, but I began to understand that she wanted to be able to see the truck under her bed without being in a position where it could hurt her. Jenny's emotions began to escalate rapidly, and fear remained prevalent.

By this time, another 10 to 15 minutes had passed and the room was getting a bit darker as the sun neared the horizon. I am not sure why it did not dawn on me, or anyone else, to turn on a light since the long shadows and dark corners increased my uneasiness while witnessing one of Jenny's most extreme episodes up to that time.

Jenny was petrified of whatever it was that was under her bed, wanting to see it but also afraid to get out of her bed to do so. This went on for a few minutes. By this time, I knew Jenny was in a full-fledged episode, and I was prepared to let it run its course. The four of us stood around Jenny's bed and did our best to support her. Michelle and I stood on opposite sides of the bed and each held one of her hands, mostly to comfort her, but in some ways using them as leverage to keep her in her bed. Her hands were sweaty and she had a very tight grip.

In a matter of a few seconds, Jenny went from fear on her face and concern in her voice to absolute terror displayed in every aspect of her body and behavior. At first none of us could figure out what the issue was, but then Jenny exclaimed that now the truck was about to drive over her bed! What I initially believed was a small toy truck now seemed to be a life size truck of some kind to Jenny. Not only had the truck become larger, it was moving toward the bed with the intent to cause Jenny great harm. Judging by where Jenny was looking, she believed it was coming from the direction of the window.

Jenny appeared as scared as I ever recall seeing her. She began to repeat over and over that the truck was coming at her in the bed. Everything was happening so fast, the emotions were so strong, and this type and intensity of episode was new to me. I was confused about what she was experiencing. However, the fear that I saw on her face and heard in her voice was very real. She was crying, and it was clear that she was in a panic.

Her requests to get out of bed turned into demands, and lasted so long, we finally allowed it. Once she was standing on the floor, Jenny went to the foot of the bed and began to pull on the footboard. She was asking for someone to help, but not speaking directly to any of us. It was very clear that she believed the danger was so obvious that all of us would quickly join her in the struggle to move the bed before the truck ran over her.

Hospital beds are not light, of course, and the brake was set. Jenny was in her bare feet and it took her a while to find the proper leverage to pull on the bed. With her first few pulls, she was unable to move the bed at all. Jenny looked around and realized that all of us were just standing and watching, allowing her to do the work on her own.

Realizing that none of us was helping her move the bed, Jenny's fear and desperation escalated. She turned to each of us one at a time and made a personal and direct appeal for us to help her. "Help Dad. Dad will you help me? Help me move the bed out of the way!" The terror and panic was so real to Jenny, but I did not help her move the bed because I had no idea where it would lead if I reinforced what she was imagining.

When she had pleaded with each of us individually, to no avail, she got the desperate tone in her voice of someone who is looking for anyone to help her, but knows she is on her own. She continued to tell us that the truck was about to run her over, and cried so hard that snot ran from her nose. She was sweating so profusely that she left puddles of perspiration on the floor, and slipped on them from time to time. I am not sure how much of the sweat was because she was working so hard at moving the bed, and how much was caused by the panic itself. At one point, her determination was so fierce that she actually managed to move the bed five or six inches, shocking us all.

This whole episode was most disturbing to Michelle, since she hadn't seen anything remotely like it yet. She left the room, not wanting anyone to see her cry, especially Jenny. John and I stayed with Jenny and Barb went out into the hallway with Michelle to comfort her.

Michelle told me later on that she and her mother hugged and cried together in the hallway. Barb assured Michelle that it would be okay after a little while, but that this is what Jenny's episodes sometimes looked like. Michelle had no idea that it had gotten to that point, and tried to understand how we could just watch all that happen.

As cruel as it may sound, more often than not we stood by and watched as Jenny engaged in various behaviors during her episodes. We made sure she was safe, but beyond that, all we really could do was just let the episodes run their course. Sometimes there were episodes when Jenny desperately pleaded with us to be active participants because of the hallucination she was experiencing. While we desperately wanted to help in any way we could, and oftentimes made futile attempts at asking her what it was we could do, more often than not we could only offer the sound of our voice telling her that we would stay by her side no matter what. Perhaps we were only making ourselves feel better by hoping that she didn't feel she had to experience it alone.

I am not sure anything could have prepared me for the helpless feeling of standing in Jenny's room that night as she begged me to help her move the bed. As much as I wanted to save Jenny from what she was experiencing, and despite the great price I would have been willing to pay to do so, I knew there was nothing I could do. I was deep into my worst nightmare while watching Jenny experience one of her own.

Jenny continued to struggle until her body could take no more. Her muscles were shaking in both her arms and legs from pulling on the bed. She finally reached the point that she had no physical fight left in her and allowed John and I to guide her to the bed and get her settled in. I assumed the episode had run its course, but Jenny was still mumbling something over and over. She spoke so softly that I couldn't make out the words. I put my ear down close to her mouth but still couldn't figure it out. I said, "Jenny, I can't hear you, you need to speak up," meaning of course, just speak loud enough for me to hear. Suddenly she began screaming, "HURRY UP, HURRY UP, HURRY UP" repeatedly. It was loud enough for Barb and Michelle to hear clearly out in the hallway with the door to the room closed. The desperate tone in her voice was even more unnerving than what I had just witnessed, and was enough to give Barb and Michelle a new set of emotional chills as they comforted each other. Jenny was still horrified of the truck, and continued to try to get me to move the bed. In her mind, she was running out of time. I realized that the demons in her head had not yet released her from this particular episode. Her body may not have had enough strength to go on, but her brain was not worn out yet.

After a few minutes of lying in bed, Jenny went as straight and stiff as a board. She had her eyes closed as tight as any child watching a scary movie and not wanting to see what came next. Jenny was waiting for the impact of the truck that she was now convinced was unavoidable. All I could do was stand by her side and offer her my hand. She grabbed my fingers and squeezed so hard that her knuckles were white. Michelle and Barb came back into the room and Michelle offered her hand to Jenny, who squeezed our hands tightly.

Finally – after what seemed like hours – the episode ran its course. I actually have no clue how long it was. We rarely did once any of her episodes were over. They usually came with no clear beginning, so we never thought of looking at the clock, and when they got intense, it really didn't matter how much time passed, it never passed quickly enough.

After she calmed down enough to relax, Jenny opened her eyes and, as always, looked to her best friend, her biggest fan and her strongest supporter, her sister. Michelle commented that Jenny looked tired. Jenny asked Michelle why she was crying. Nobody in the room expressed it, but I am sure everyone was as shocked as I was that Jenny did not appear to remember what had just happened. Michelle said she was fine, but Jenny started saying that it was her fault that Michelle was crying, and kept apologizing. Soon the two were crying again, together this time.

Although Jenny did not seem to remember details, she had enough presence of mind to realize that she was lying in a hospital bed and the fact that everyone around her was more than a bit disheveled must have been the result of something that she had done. It was just another bit of pain from which I could not save my daughter. Of course, none of this was her fault, but how could that possibly be explained right now.

Jenny cried herself to sleep while her sister held her. The cumulative events of the day made it clear that this was far from over, and it was far from the last tears that would be shed during this nightmare.

CHAPTER 11

A Closer Look at Jenny's Journals

The spiral bound notebook that was initially used by Jenny to record what she was thinking and feeling on April 4th, gradually became a catchall scratch pad throughout the course of Jenny's hospitalization. During the first week after Jenny was admitted to the hospital, Barb and John continued to make consistent entries.

By the time the notebook ceased to be used, it contained 40 pages of assorted "notes" that varied from the detailed play-by-play of Jenny's evening on April 4th, to the recording of food orders for everyone in the room on any particular day. As Jenny grew more ill, the use of the notebook waned considerably. The first 28 pages of the journal covered a period of eight days, from April 4th to the 11th, and then at that point all consistent use of the notebook stopped. The final 12 pages were sporadic notations covering a variety of inconsistent topics.

The irony of how detailed the notations were was that the notebook largely went unexamined until *months* after Jenny's discharge. The truth is, on April 11th, I turned the page to write down the phone number for the Corporate Offices of Barnes and Noble to return their call and I don't believe any of us ever looked back from then on. This was not intentional, and certainly not because of a lack of interest. Due to the manner and rapid pace Jenny began to deteriorate at that point, there simply was no time to go back and look…and, in a way, there really was no point. Truly, each day, and even each hour, brought new revelations and a new set of challenges that seemed to deem the previous day insignificant. Ultimately, there was no time to make use of the notebook. It was originally intended to find patterns and significant peaks and valleys of Jenny's behavior and status. However, the reality of the situation became that everything was new and unique each day, so there was no pattern..

Now, in hindsight, it is well worth taking a closer look at some of the notations that took place from four days prior up to this point in the story.

Although Jenny had been acting and talking "odd" since March 29th, it was very easy to define it as a possible side effect of the Keppra she was taking. It was at 1:30 a.m. on April 6th that an otherwise insignificant notation written in the journal by John may have been the first sign of serious trouble with Jenny's thought process: *"Woke up confused & thought was on the show Walking Dead."*

Just two hours later, he made another note: *"Woke up very confused. Talking about time continuum. Keeps pulling off tape (to her IV needle).*

BOGO was on her mind. In a twisted house – feels like in a Dr. Seuss Book." (It may be worth noting that Barnes and Noble was doing a Dr. Seuss theme in their store right before Jenny got sick.)

Then at 10:20 that morning, John's notation in the notebook was, *"Thought our words were like a Dr. Seuss book."*

And at 11:20 a.m., *"Jenny realizes 'hasn't been alone for a week, made my Mom cry. That's really bad'."*

John left a bit before noon that day and Barb took over making entries into the notebook. At 1 p.m. Jenny got back to her room following an MRI and she made the statement, *"Felt like Horton."* (Barb also noted here that Jenny had been working on the Dr. Seuss theme at Barnes and Noble.)

There are then a full four pages of notations that cover the next 36 hours until 10 p.m. on April 7th. The entries are made primarily by Barb, and are nothing more than details of the comings and goings of nurses, doctors, and visitors as well as Jenny's activities, including going for additional tests.

But at 10 p.m., I made a few notations that show Jenny and I were having another discussion about "time getting stuck." We clearly were watching the clock together, but Jenny did not have the ability to tell time. At one point during our "argument," Jenny even pressed the nurse call button in an attempt to get someone else on her side, to no avail.

The notations once again return to relatively normal entries until the evening of April 8th when the two significant entries detailed in the previous chapter occur.

Then everything took an incredible turn for the worse.

At some point between 10:15 on the morning of April 9th, and 1:20 p.m. on April 10th there is a single page with a single entry that covered the entire top half of the page. None of us is aware of exactly when it was written:

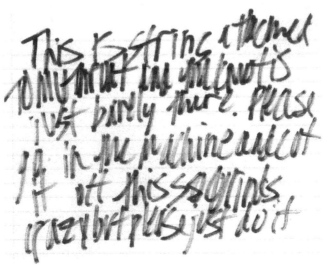

As best as we can tell, the writing says, *"This is string attached to my throat and you knot is just barely there. Please go in the machine and cut it off this sounds crazy but please just do it"*

Barb, John, and I did not keep track of who stayed with Jenny that night; but given that there was a 27-hour gap with no entries in the journal, and I was not one to keep too many notes in this notebook as I had my own journal, it is presumed that it was me. The assumption is that I fell asleep at some point during the night and Jenny made the entry during that time. The very first notation on the afternoon of April 10th was written by me, on the page following the one Jenny made this entry on. Since the page had somehow been turned before anyone noticed it and none of us had a reason to turn back the pages, this entry would not be seen until months later.

I am left to wonder what any of us would have thought had we seen that page in the notebook the day in was written and taken the significant amount of time it took to figure out what it said. The hallucinations were getting extreme, and the demons were torturing Jenny. To a degree, I believe we were able to survive the coming weeks because we had a naïve belief that, no matter what was happening at any given moment, "it can't get any worse than this." Since I've looked at this notation hundreds of times since I first discovered it, and I still get the chills when I look at that entry today, I suppose that it is a good thing that I didn't see it back then.

CHAPTER 12

Day 6

If you are looking for this book to document everything the doctors said and did throughout Jenny's illness, you will be disappointed. The truth is I don't recall many of those details, in particular for a three-week stretch that started on or about this date.

I have a large collection of medical records from Jenny's hospitalization in binders and envelopes stored in a plastic bin in a closet. Although I did use the information to clarify many things during the writing of this book, I suppose I also could dig through it to glean some of the information documented there; but I'll be the first to admit I'm not smart enough to understand much of what the doctors worked so hard at making perfectly clear to us. I knew the doctors and nurses were doing their job, and I knew that Barb was monitoring all of it, so I chose to concentrate on other things. Honestly, I never tried to comprehend much of what the doctors told me. My goal was to have a general idea of what was happening and how I could help my daughter. Beyond that, the medical details didn't really matter to me.

That statement would sound very surprising to anyone who knows me well. I have always been a very detail-oriented person. I can be, I suppose, what many people refer to as a "control freak." However, once it became painfully clear that the doctors would need some time to figure out what was wrong with Jenny, I surprised myself with how easily I gave up control of the situation and became a very bottom-line type of person. The only fact I really wanted to know was when I could take my daughter home.

I'd love to say that it was a spiritual peace or religious faith that allowed me to do this, but this was not the case at all. I believe in God, but I don't go to church as often as I should and I can't say I pray a lot. I'm embarrassed to admit that I did not pray much even during this chapter of my life. The truth is, after participating in many of the episodes Jenny experienced and watching her sister and mother having to witness and endure those same horrors, well, frankly, I was pretty pissed at God.

One possible explanation for my surrender of control is that I was listening to some of my own preaching. I have been a youth, high school, and traveling soccer coach for over 20 years, and my teams have heard me say countless times, "Worry about what you can control." Maybe I was beginning to practice what I preach.

Maybe.

More than likely, I simply understood I was not mentally equipped to comprehend the medical aspect of what was happening anyway, so I didn't even try.

Meanwhile, Jenny continued to get worse. Her deterioration accelerated, and the frequency and intensity of the episodes increased. Additionally, there were times that Jenny would simply "go away." She would become perfectly still and unresponsive for a few minutes at a time. She would not speak nor respond to any stimuli. Waving hands in front of her eyes would not sway her stare, nor would she respond to any verbal communication. In many ways, it was preferable to have Jenny go away as opposed to the episodes. At least she appeared to be content with what was happening, if not oblivious to it. This would have been more bearable for everyone while the doctors continued their work to find what was wrong.

Although it was not a thought that was at the forefront of my mind, I had come to believe that the times Jenny would "go away" were the current manifestations of the seizures. My thought was that the medication was controlling them but had not yet eliminated them. My belief had never been confirmed or denied by a doctor up to that point, and I never directly asked. In hindsight, this was just my own unfounded logic trying to fill in the vacuum of the lack of information I had. It sounded good to me.

Late that afternoon Dr. Freking asked me to step into a separate room to have a conversation, a request that was rather unnerving to me. Up to this point, all conversations regarding Jenny's condition had taken place in front of her. However, on this day Dr. Freking took me into a family lounge one door down from Jenny's room, where he placed two chairs a few feet apart and facing each other – he was clearly planning on sitting down for a long conversation. I admit that inside I was turning upside down a bit.

I sat quietly as Dr. Freking went through the details of what he knew and what they were going to do to learn more. I'm not sure how closely I was listening; I know I was trying to pick up enough of the key points to relay the information back to Barb, Michelle, and John, but I was really only interested in the bottom-line: finding out what was wrong with my daughter and taking her home.

Apparently, I must have looked quite passive as I sat and listened to him because after he had been talking for a while, Dr. Freking said, "You're kind of like a duck."

What? Back up. What did you just say? I had no idea what he was talking about and strongly suspected that I must have heard wrong, but then he explained that a duck sitting on the water looks very calm but under the surface, the feet are paddling like crazy. He went on to say that on the outside, I was one of the calmest people he could remember, given the circumstances, but he imagined that inside I was going a bit crazy.

Although it gave me a good giggle, the analogy also made a lot of sense. Yet, I was more than a bit surprised to hear that my outward demeanor appeared calm to others as I knew certain members of my family had been on the receiving end of me losing my inner-duck a few times.

Other than the professional medical observation that I had some Zen-like qualities similar to that of waterfowl, there really were no hard facts to come out of this initial sit-down consultation. Dr. Freking discussed a few possibilities regarding Jenny's illness, but he was very careful not to mislead me in any way or offer any false hope. He was very honest, saying that there were more questions than answers right now, but there was also a plan in place to pursue the answers to those questions.

The only significant development of the day was the beginning of "video EEG monitoring." A more common name for the testing, and what we came to call it was "continuous EEG."

An EEG (Electroencephalography) is the recording of electrical activity just below the scalp. The equipment used for basic EEGs is relatively small, utilizes a head cover with probes built into it, and is transported on a cart with wheels that is easily moved from room to room.

For some of the more involved EEG tests done on Jenny, the probes were actually pushed into her skin and then glued in place. There are variations to the process, but in Jenny's case, it involved the placement of 25 probes at various locations all around her head. Each of these probes had an individual wire, and all the wires were joined together in a bag with a shoulder strap that they called a "tether."

Most EEG testing takes an average of 25 to 35 minutes, sometimes running up to about an hour. The continuous EEG was a monitoring procedure that ran for days at a time and was vastly different from the more common procedures in that it included audio and video monitoring as well. All of this data was recorded for review by doctors at any time and included a live feed for viewing in real time by technicians and physicians located elsewhere within the hospital. This made it possible for them to view what Jenny was doing and saying at any time.

There was a button attached to the tether, much like a nurse's call button. Family members were instructed to push that button whenever Jenny displayed any relevant and significant behavior of any kind. In other words, we were to push the button any time she had an episode or "went away."

There was no audible or visual signal in the room that the button had been pushed. Nurses would not respond to the button being pressed, it simply "marked" a spot on the EEG, audio, and video recording for the doctors to refer to for specific brain signals and behavior. I imagine there were a number of things the doctors were looking for, but my understanding of the primary goal of the continuous EEG was to measure the frequency and intensity of Jenny's seizures, and to see what relationship there was between those seizures and Jenny's various forms of behavior.

We had witnessed Jenny having the probes for the EEG "installed" a few times. Each probe was pushed into her skin individually, and a needle was pushed into the center of the probe to dispense glue that secured it to her scalp. The process took 45 minutes during which Jenny held her head in the position the technician asked her to and squeezed her eyes shut in an effort to tolerate the discomfort of the probes being inserted.

While Jenny was extremely patient and cooperative during the installation process, she quickly lost patience with the probes once the installation was complete. They periodically caused irritation, itched, and pulled her hair, depending on what she was doing. It did not take long for the family and nursing staff to discover that we had a new battle on our hands. From this point on, whenever Jenny had an episode and the probes for an EEG were installed, at least some of her time was spent trying to pull them out. Her attempts at removing unwanted "attachments" included pulling at her IV and PICC lines, and at times, the struggle to prevent her from removing them became somewhat of a wrestling match.

In an attempt to protect the probes from Jenny's prying hands, initially the EEG techs wrapped Jenny's head with gauze to cover and contain the numerous wires and hold them away from her face, as well as protect them from accidental bumps. However, this proved to be ineffective for Jenny. The gauze wrap was off her head less than an hour after the tech left the room. The next attempt added a layer of tape along with the gauze but was no more successful. How about an Ace bandage? Nope. Ace bandage and a layer of tape? Again, nope.

Barb and Michelle went hat shopping to see if they could find something for Jenny's head that would provide the type of protection needed from her prying fingers, however nothing adequate for the job was discovered. The challenge of keeping Jenny's hands off the probes was an ongoing and difficult task for most of her time in the hospital.

This point in Jenny's illness was also the beginning of a completely new set of issues, marking the beginning of her slide into depression. Whether this was a result of the infection in her brain or just the reality of her situation setting in, I will never know for sure. While she came out of it for short periods in the coming days, this was the day she was in an almost constant state of sadness whenever she was actually "with us."

CHAPTER 13

Sally & Emu

It was about this time that everyone was introduced to "Sally." Barb was the one who introduced her to me.

By the second week of Jenny's hospital stay, she almost constantly had saline and/or some type of medication being administered through an IV. This necessary medical procedure posed somewhat of a challenge to those of us working with Jenny because once the IV rack became a part of everyday life, any reason for Jenny to get out of bed triggered a process of maneuvers to make it happen.

Whenever we got ready to leave the room for any reason (or even go across the room to the bathroom), the IV rack had to be wheeled along. Inevitably, we had to untangle the sheets and blankets from the hose, unplug the electrical cord for the controller/dispenser and turn off the "unit unplugged" alarm, get it all wrapped up and in hand with enough slack laid out to move, but not so much as to drag or tangle while moving. This process was even more difficult because of the location of the rack – it made sense to keep it on the side of the bed by the window, with the bed separating the rack from the door so that it did not become an obstacle for people moving about the room.

This process really would not have been particularly difficult under normal circumstances, but even suggesting the prospect of going for a walk got Jenny's immediate attention and instant response. For Jenny, movement by anyone in the direction of the door meant, "Let's go," and she would get up and walk to the door without hesitation. Simply touching the IV rack caused the Pavlovian effect of her popping up and heading for the door. The combination of Jenny's determination to head for the door so quickly along with the process of getting the IV rack ready to move created an interesting juggling act at times. First, Jenny would need to be detained in a way that did not get her too upset or in any way make her fight back. Then, after gathering up all the hoses and cords, the rack had to be rolled around the bed and often navigated around chairs, bags and other things that had been spread around the room. Thus, any movement by Jenny away from her bed became an event.

In spite of the effort required, whenever possible we allowed Jenny to wander the hallways of the 6th floor. It was a great way to occupy our time as well as hers, and it was better than fighting with her to stay within the confines of her hospital room or sit still in her bed. Initially our motivation for walking the halls was to burn off Jenny's excess energy, but it never had that effect. Quite the opposite occurred; the more she walked, the more she wanted to continue doing it. But, at least she was happy for a while.

One day, just as I arrived, Jenny wanted to go for a walk, as was often the case. Whenever possible, I was the designated muscle needed in case Jenny got out of control. I walked into the room where I knew Barb and Jenny were waiting for me, and as soon as Barb saw me she said, "Dad's here! Let's go for our walk!" As had become usual, Jenny popped out of bed and headed for the door. I moved to block her way, knowing it wasn't that easy, and Barb said, "Wait, we need to get Sally!"

I had no idea who Sally was or why we needed her. My first thought was that she must be a new nurse, and as Barb went around the bed to get the IV rack I said, "Who's Sally?"

"This is Sally," Barb explained as she pushed the IV rack toward me.

Sally was the first piece of hospital equipment that we named during Jenny's stay at Methodist. Perhaps we named the IV rack simply because it was faster and easier to say, but truth be told, it personalized something that had become a very intrusive figure in our lives. Eventually, even the nurses started to refer to it as Sally. Even now, more than a year later, when Jenny goes in for some of the various treatments she receives, we refer to the IV rack as Sally.

Naming the equipment used in Jenny's treatment didn't stop there.

The other major piece of equipment that was in Jenny's room for long periods of time was the machine used for the continuous EEG, which was also on a portable cart, but significantly larger than the IV rack. In fact, although it was on wheels, this cart of equipment could not be moved because of how it was used, and Jenny was tethered to it by a batch of wires, sometimes for up to 10 days at a time.

The cart contained a small work surface with a full computer, monitor, keyboard, the EEG equipment, and audio and video recording equipment. The cart was set in a way that allowed the machine to view Jenny's entire bed. Once positioned in the room, it was not to be moved in any way by anyone other than the EEG technicians. This equipment took up the space of a rather large chair, and therefore occupied a significant portion of room. Additionally, we had to respect its space more than our own because of the need to be sure the video camera could see Jenny at all times.

This piece of equipment was in Jenny's room for various stretches throughout her stay. We needed to get used to it, not just because of its size, but, more importantly, because we knew it was recording everything said and done in the room. It became more intrusive than Sally and thus needed to be personalized more than any other item.

The equipment had a technical name, of course, but I have no idea what it was. However, on the front of the unit – the side facing Jenny's bed that we could see all the time – there was a model number of the equipment that read "EMU" and then a few numbers. Much the same as it was easier to call the IV rack Sally, we began to call this contraption "Emu." Michelle even printed a picture of an Emu and taped it to the machine. Then, much as the nurses started calling the IV rack Sally, the EEG techs left the picture attached to their contraption and started calling the machine Emu as well.

CHAPTER 14

Day 8

Over the previous three days Barb, Michelle, John, and I had come to understand that something had taken control of Jenny's mind and body. This had become very clear to us based on witnessing Jenny's body moving in unnatural ways, and things she would say that were out of character for her. It was at some point during those past few days that, in my mind, I came to define whatever it was that was doing this to Jenny as "demons." It was the only explanation that made sense to me at the time. Jenny simply looked like she had been possessed.

This day would turn out to be our last day with Jenny – the real Jenny that we could truly interact with and, more importantly, with whom we could reason. The doctors still didn't know what was wrong, and Jenny continued to slip further away with each passing hour. It was the last day we would see Jenny smile without pain and fear in her eyes. Even when the demons in her head would take her away from us, her eyes never stopped communicating for her, and after today, they seemed to be constantly pleading for help. By the end of this day, I had lost all hope that this would be over any time soon. I think all of us saw it coming even though none of us specifically talked about it.

That day was also Jenny's 26th birthday, and given the unspoken reality we all knew was in front of us, there was a sense of urgency to make the most of it. We felt a collective determination to do all we could to make it a day to remember for Jenny. Michelle had been working on a plan for a small party later that evening. Guests were invited, presents wrapped, and a cake and decorations had been purchased.

Oh, were decorations purchased! We may have spent more on decorations for that day than we had for all other birthday parties in Jenny's life combined. Everything had a Twins theme, since Jenny is a huge fan and she and I were supposed to have gone to the game that day. There were blue and red streamers and signs, balloons, and other Twins and baseball related items.

On this day, we ignored almost all hospital protocol, or at least any perceived notions I had of what is allowed in a patient's room. I still look back on this day and marvel at our absolute and complete "throwing caution to the wind" with the planning we did, without ever asking for permission to do anything.

A 48-hour continuous EEG was concluded late that afternoon. When the probes were removed, Jenny's head was a rat's nest of hair with crusty glue left behind that would have appeared to be terrible dandruff to the casual observer. Barb took Jenny down to the shower to get her cleaned up and her hair washed in preparation for the upcoming party, and Michelle and I took that opportunity to get to work on decorating Jenny's hospital room.

I feel it is important to explain something here. Although Jenny could not be left alone to even shower on her own, she still continued to demonstrate certain personality characteristics that let us know that she understood what was going on around her most of the time. Because of her apparent awareness of what was being done for and to her, we preferred to have a family member assist Jenny with her personal needs. Because we were assisting Jenny with her personal hygiene and performing other tasks for her, my fear is that this would reflect badly on the tremendous nursing staff at Methodist Hospital. I want to stress that it was the overall situation, as well as our love for Jenny, that had us doing all we could to keep her comfortable. This need to help our loved one should not be taken as a lack of trust on our part or any lack of effort or compassion on the part of the nursing staff – quite the opposite was true.

Although Jenny was in a room set up for two patients and two beds, by this time in Jenny's stay, the nurses had removed the second bed and given us the run of the entire space. In large part, this was due to the space required for the continuous EEG, but even after its removal, a second bed was never returned to Jenny's room.

While Jenny was in the shower, Michelle and I quickly decorated every corner and bit of wall space. We hung Twins banners on the walls, a huge baseball diamond with "Happy Birthday Jenny" across the window, and various streamers from every conceivable spot in the room, including on Sally. We worked feverishly to be sure to have all the decorations in place before Jenny returned from her shower. We moved chairs around to use as ladders and yelled instructions to each other – actually, Michelle yelled instructions at me, which I quickly followed – and generally made far too much noise for any respectable hospital room. The nurses heard us and came in to see what we were up to; then they just gave us a cheer, smiled, and closed the door to the room so we would not disturb other patients.

Just as we were wrapping up the decorating, two of Jenny and John's friends arrived. Because Michelle and I had not previously met them and were still busy decorating, they decided to wait in the hall for Jenny.

I was curious what condition Jenny would be in when she encountered her visitors. She was fairly cognizant when she left for her shower, so I was confident it would go well. After a few minutes, Barb, Jenny and her two guests came into the room. Jenny was already engaged in a conversation with her visitors, which indicated to me that she was in control and aware of her surroundings. However, I did notice that during the entire visit, Jenny never acknowledged the dramatic change in the room created by the birthday decorations. The conversation she was having included some discussion about the party that would occur later that evening, but she never specifically said anything about the decorations.

After a while, I began to notice that Jenny seemed to be getting more and more uncomfortable even though she continued to visit with her friends. True to form, she maintained a good face for her visitors. Once again, for at least one more day, Jenny was able to resist the demons in her head long enough for a non-family member to see her as normal as possible.

Almost immediately after her friends left, everything changed. Jenny let go of the good face she had been maintaining for nearly an hour and started to cry. Michelle sat on Jenny's bed with her and worked at determining what was wrong. Jenny explained that she felt overwhelmed and that she was seeing things that she did not believe were there. Michelle patiently talked Jenny through each of them.

The first issue was some bruises on her arm. There were, in fact, a few small bruises caused by the multiple IV lines that had been inserted in her arm during her hospitalization. Michelle pointed out each bruise and explained its origin. Interestingly, Jenny did not recall the events that led to them, but she willingly trusted and accepted Michelle's explanation. She was extremely relieved that what she was seeing was, in fact, real.

The biggest issue for Jenny, as she explained to Michelle almost apologetically, was that she was seeing lines and colors on the ceiling that weren't supposed to be there. Even though she was a bit shocked, Michelle began to point out and explain each decoration and reminded Jenny about the party later in the evening. Jenny had been looking forward to the party since we told her of the plans a couple days earlier, even though she had to be reminded of it from time to time. Once again, Jenny was relieved to hear that she wasn't seeing things that were not real, and she relaxed tremendously.

Michelle encouraged her to take a nap so she would be ready for the party and Jenny willingly accepted the suggestion and rolled over for some very rare sleep. Michelle was always the one that Jenny trusted and listened to most. She was a great influence on Jenny and had the uncanny knack of being able to put Jenny at ease. This ability makes sense, as she is also the best at getting under Jenny's skin whenever she tries to.

It had been two weeks since all of this had begun, and we still had no solid answers as to what was going on. The only thing that was perfectly clear was that all of us were experiencing a life-altering event. Jenny suffered the illness, but it was clear that this would have a profound and prolonged effect on Barb, Michelle, John, and me as well.

The nature of what was going on never allowed for preparation for what was about to happen, nor for evaluation of what had happened once it was over. In fact, while it was happening, time passed in a very surreal fashion: it never passed quickly and during the intense episodes actually seemed to stand still. Yet, as much as it would seem that waiting for answers from the doctors would make time drag, Jenny had a way of presenting new challenges so often that there was seldom time to sit and ponder what was coming next.

I don't recall ever feeling that I was capable of any more than dealing with what was right in front of me at the moment. I dared not think about the future once it became clear that there was no end in sight because I had no idea what to prepare for anyway. Since each time that I allowed myself to believe that it couldn't get worse, it did, and I just stopped trying to anticipate anything. Ultimately, all energy and thought was spent helping Jenny through whatever was happening at any given moment, and getting myself through it as well.

The series of events and conversation between Jenny and Michelle that I had just observed on this particular afternoon suddenly had me asking a new set of questions. I looked at the situation from a new angle, considering exactly how Jenny was experiencing these episodes. It sounds so ignorant and selfish now to think that it hadn't crossed my mind before that day.

Very early on, even when Jenny was mostly coherent and was only experiencing what we now consider very mild episodes, she never really understood that what she was doing and/or saying was odd or made no sense. Everything she did was very matter of fact and she never openly looked back on it and questioned what she had done. Even as the episodes and subsequent hallucinations became increasingly torturous, Jenny always claimed that she did not remember anything, and she never appeared to suffer any residual effects of the trauma that had unfolded. I took comfort in that fact and I guess I just allowed myself to believe that she somehow lost all consciousness during her episodes. I had never put it into those words, but on this afternoon, I realized this was only an assumption on my part.

The conversation between Jenny and Michelle questioning the bruises on her arm and not understanding that there were streamers hanging from the ceiling was a new phase for me in the process of trying to deal with what was happening. It was the first time that Jenny expressed concern that she was seeing things that were not real and it upset her that it was happening. It was the first indication I had that told me she knew something was not quite right, and it made me wonder: if she had no recollection of what was happening during the episodes, what part of her brain was questioning what she was seeing now? How did she know? Was there a possibility that Jenny knew what was happening and was a prisoner of the demons in her head? At that moment, I came to realize that there was a real possibility that a completely cognizant woman was trapped inside her brain and forced to experience everything that we only witnessed.

These questions were the genesis of what became my greatest fear for the remainder of Jenny's illness. It had been clear for a few days that Jenny was slipping further and further away and there was nothing I could do about it. That thought alone was an enormous burden, but now my biggest fear became that she was possibly staring at me during these episodes and screaming for me to help her and believing that I was just sitting and watching it happen. Did she think I was unwilling to help her? The demons had now started to haunt me as well.

This question would burn hotter and hotter in my mind in the coming weeks. Even while she was in the deepest recesses of the illness, at least once a day we would see the real Jenny come through in some small way. At times, it was just a flash of competitive determination, something that I equated to her fighting the demons in her head, letting them know that ultimately she was going to win. However, sometimes it was that I saw the Jenny that was, and always will be, my little girl. I saw it in her eyes. Always in her eyes.

Extended periods of sleep were still rare for Jenny, so all of us were very pleasantly surprised when Jenny actually took a long nap that evening. The party was just a loose gathering of only a very few family and friends with no real starting time, so there was no reason to wake her. Even if there had been a set time, we would have let her sleep. Her lack of sleep was becoming so serious that the nursing staff would even delay taking vitals at the scheduled intervals if she appeared to be asleep.

I experienced a weird sense of nervousness for this get together. It is indescribable how desperately I wanted Jenny to be "with us" and actually enjoy the evening, and hopefully remember it as well. The extended nap was a very good sign. Although this would change in the coming days, up to this point, the longer Jenny slept the closer to normal she would be and the longer she would stay with us. I was very excited about the nap, and I still believe that Michelle putting Jenny at ease before she slept allowed for the long rest.

Once Jenny awoke, she ate a small amount of food (something that was also becoming rarer with each passing day) as visitors slowly trickled in with birthday presents in hand. Besides Barb, Michelle, John, and myself, Jenny's godmother Aunt Bonnie showed up as did her cousin Drew and a coworker from Barnes and Noble.

The whole evening was a very low-key affair. Everyone was there to cheer Jenny up and try to put a smile on her face. As all birthday parties do, it started with a horrible rendition of "Happy Birthday" sung with all of us standing around Jenny's bed. Then we enjoyed a Minnesota Twins birthday cake and Jenny opened presents.

Jenny had a huge smile on her face the entire time and was about as clear and cognizant as she had been in a week. The sense of relief Barb, John, and I felt was palpable. We had been with Jenny since the beginning of this horrible journey and were therefore most aware of and grateful for this reprieve. I am not sure anyone other than the three of us, and perhaps Michelle, who had witnessed how bad it could be, had a true sense of what a great evening it really was, but everyone in the room had the joy of seeing someone they love who is in the hospital smile and be happy for a while.

Jenny had a terrific evening and she burned up a lot of energy, but she was truly happy. The party wound down with all of us just sitting around the room while Jenny sat quietly watching the Twins game on TV.

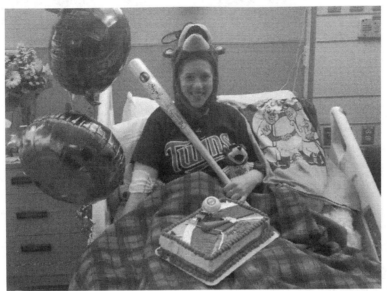

Jenny, on her birthday, with her presents and cake

A residual effect of much of what happened that day also served to clarify our relationship with the nursing staff on the 6th floor. I didn't understand it at the time, but in many ways this day set the stage for how we were able to deal with what was happening to Jenny for the weeks to come.

That day made it clear that the nursing staff on the 6th floor had become part of our family during this week in the hospital. While I know that Jenny and her family were no more special to the nursing staff than any other patient they cared for, we had well exceeded the average stay of a patient on that floor, and the prognosis by now was that we were all going to be together for some time to come.

The nurses never hesitated to do all they could to make Jenny as comfortable as possible, but they also went to some length for the family members. At one point during Jenny's stay, the nurses assisted me in going room-to-room to find the most comfortable recliner on the 6th floor and moved it into Jenny's room. Other than the fact that one of us was present 24 hours a day, I believe we did all we could to blend in as much as possible with other patients and visitors. We tried to stay out of the way when they had work to do, and we tried not to use any more of their time than necessary. Most importantly, we tried to be quiet in the hallways, though we weren't always successful, and did our best to respect the normal protocol one would expect in a hospital.

That all changed on this day.

I don't know how much the nurses allowed us to bend the rules or if we really weren't doing anything that normally wouldn't have been allowed, but the nursing staff showed no concern for the way in which we celebrated Jenny's birthday. At one point in the evening, a nurse's aide came into the room to perform some task and even put on bright yellow birthday hat while he did it. I imagined that he would remove it immediately after leaving the room, but when I left the hospital hours later, as I walked down the hall, I saw him in another patient's room with the bright yellow hat still perched on top of his head as he leaned over the patient he was assisting.

From that point on, I felt as if the nurses were part of our family, and that we were part of theirs. Thank goodness, because it made what was still to come just a bit easier to handle.

CHAPTER 15

Fixation

Many of Jenny's "episodes" had a singular element of some kind on which she would fixate, and was generally very narrow in focus, even when it caused a wide variety of behaviors. It could be an emotion, a thought, something that happened around her, or even something she saw in the room. Just as with all of her episodes, none of the fixations were the same, so it is difficult to explain exactly what they were and how they happened. There are two stories in particular that stick out in my mind as the best explanation of her fixation on the smallest of things that were taken to huge extremes.

On the evening of Jenny's birthday, after the party was essentially over, many of us had settled down in chairs around Jenny's bed and were talking and watching the Twins game on TV. A commercial came on for an upcoming broadcast of a Minnesota Wild hockey game. The graphic on the screen at the end of the commercial showed, "Wild vs. Blue Jackets," along with the time of the game and other relevant information. The commercial had been over and gone for a good three or four minutes when Jenny began telling us, "There are 4 letters in the word Wild and 11 in Blue Jackets." As was the case so many times, it was odd for her to point out something like that, but as we had grown accustomed to her random and somewhat irrelevant statements over the past two weeks, no one in the room commented or gave it a second thought.

A few minutes later, Jenny got one person's attention in particular and repeated the comment, "There are 4 letters in the word Wild and 11 in Blue Jackets." That person agreed with her, and moved back to what else was being said in the room. However, Jenny was not ready to let it go. She turned to Barb and said, "Mom, are there 4 letters in the word Wild and 11 in Blue Jackets." Barb agreed there was. Jenny turned back to the first person and said, "See," very matter-of-factly, then turned back to Barb and said, "He doesn't think there are."

While this behavior was a new kind of "odd," we were still learning that these things could turn into something significant, so we simply continued with our conversation.

Then, Jenny took over the room. It was not long before we realized that what we were witnessing meant that we had to, once again, expand our definition of an "episode" as Jenny began to go from person to person asking them if they knew that the word Wild had 4 letters in it and Blue Jackets had 11. Regardless of the answer given, Jenny's reaction indicated that she believed either the person had argued with her or they "didn't get it." She was never satisfied with the answer, and she became frustrated. Regardless of how we adjusted the words we used to explain that we agreed with her and that she was right, her response showed that she had heard us disagree with her. At one point, she even pressed the nurse's call button, and when the nurse responded Jenny proceeded to tell him that we were confused and that the nurse should help Jenny explain it to us.

After this went on for a while, Jenny pulled out her journal, wrote out the words, and counted the letters for us. I am not sure what she was hearing in her mind, but there was no way to convince her that we agreed and understood. Then, Jenny ripped a page out of her journal. We didn't understand what she was doing as she began to rip the page into narrow strips. All of us watched intently, believing she had moved on to something else. She even got someone in the room to help her rip the strips, as it seemed the process was taking too long for her. Once she had 15 strips of paper, they became props to show us the difference between 4 letters and 11 letters.

This episode went on for about 45 minutes until she finally appeared so exasperated that she gave up.

A week or so later, during one of my all-night watches, an episode occurred that demonstrated how wide the scope of Jenny's fixations could be and how even the simplest thing could have a dramatic effect on her.

That evening Jenny's fixation was to continually leave her room to walk the hallways and talk to people that weren't there. While it was happening on a regular basis and we were doing our best not to let her leave the room without a family member present, this was still a new behavior for the nursing staff. We still had not received a diagnosis, and the hospital – well, all of us – had not yet adjusted to the wide scope of issues Jenny presented.

I had made it through most of the night with Jenny and we had managed not to have any major incidents. Around 6 a.m., Jenny was relatively calm. She was still not sleeping much despite our continual efforts. She would settle in her bed and appear to be trying to sleep, and everyone involved would do everything possible not to disturb her.

Jenny had finally settled down after a long night. She was lying perfectly still in her bed and the room was dark. I was in the recliner in the room with the TV off, and I did everything I could not to make any noise, not even moving in the chair in case it creaked. Sure enough, it worked! I fell asleep!

I awoke to one of the nurses bringing Jenny back into the room while Jenny chanted something about "changeover." Even though I had only been asleep for a few minutes, I was so exhausted that the sleep was deep and it took me a few seconds to come around and grasp the situation. The nurse passed Jenny back to me and left the room. As I tried to move

Jenny back toward the bed, it took me a while to realize that she was fighting me much harder than usual.

Finally, I woke up enough to realize something new and unusual was happening. The room was only beginning to receive some light from the rising sun coming in the window, but it was enough to be able to navigate the room and see where Jenny was, how she was standing, and even the look on her face. I had been asking Jenny to get back into bed, but then I took a step back to get a good look at her and see what she was doing.

She was standing with her feet a bit more than shoulder-width apart, knees slightly bent, and leaning slightly forward at her waist. She had her arms held away from her body, but bent at the elbows. Her position was similar to someone standing in a boat on a wavy lake trying to keep their balance. I heard her say, very urgently and almost in a panic, "Dad, it's changeover, we need to be careful where we walk!"

I had no idea what she was talking about. We had all heard about a hundred other weird statements from her since she became ill, and because of my exhaustion, I can't say that I was interested or even tried to figure it out at first. However, what was different this time, as my fuzzy, sleep-deprived brain slowly began to realize, was that Jenny was genuinely scared. It was not the first time Jenny had an episode in which she was scared, not even close, but we handled this type of episode with much more care and concern.

No matter the type of episode, we recognized that it was best that Jenny stay in her room, but during the episodes that involved severe hallucinations and caused such deep emotions, it was vital to keep her there. I tried to talk her back toward the bed without physically directing her, but she repeated her earlier sentiment with just as much urgency, "Dad, you don't understand! It's changeover and we have to get out of here!"

While I can say that I was always as patient as I could be with Jenny during these emotional episodes, I have to admit that I rarely tried to comprehend what she was trying to say as it had proven to be a fruitless task countless times before. As the "Wild has 4 letters ..." episode showed, even when we knew what she was saying and agreed with her, it more often than not provided no help in actually dealing with her.

I took a step toward her to put my hands on her shoulders and to comfort her. "Dad! Don't move! It's changeover, we need to get out of here!" She was almost yelling now.

As was often the case, there was a contradiction to her statements. We couldn't move, but we needed to get out of there. I had no idea what to do or how to handle this new situation.

What took place over the next 30 minutes was not unusual. I did the best I could to keep her calm and tried to make her feel safe, but I pretty much failed at both. What became apparent was Jenny felt the urgent need to leave the room. I never learned details of the specific motivation for this particular episode, but I have often wondered if it was just another way her brain processed her never-ending desire to leave the hospital, even during the times when she was "Jenny." In this episode, although it was manifesting as something completely different, it was clear her escape instinct was completely engaged.

Any movement I made in any direction other than the door triggered Jenny to go into her "wobbly boat" stance. Over time, she managed to communicate to me that her very real and intense fear was that if we did not get out of the room we would "mess it up," but I was not clear how. It was as if she was afraid to put any footprints on the floor other than toward the door. In addition, if I touched something in the room Jenny went into an uncontrollable rage.

After giving it some very serious thought during and immediately after this specific episode, the most reasonable conclusion I could come up with was that Jenny was fixated on something she had heard in the hallway after she wandered out of the room when I fell asleep. Her trip to the hallway occurred at the exact time that the hospital made the "changeover" from night shift nurses to the daytime nursing staff. Jenny had to have heard one of the nurses say that specific word when she was in the hallway. How that fixation translated to the idea that we couldn't "mess up the room" and had to leave, I have no idea.

This was the world we had entered as a result of Jenny's illness and the demons it allowed to take over her mind and control her thoughts and body. With each passing hour, it was something new. Sometimes it was funny, but more often than not it was puzzling and perplexing. Quite often, it was sad, and at times it was horrifying, for both Jenny and whoever was with her at the time.

CHAPTER 16

Day 9

From this point on, every aspect of life took on an almost constant surreal feel. I suppose it was mostly because my mind and body were so tired from lack of quality sleep as well as being so worried all the time, but in many ways there was an odd pace to everything that happened. Jenny's deterioration accelerated at a much faster rate but quality information came in more slowly. Dealing with Jenny got trickier and any information that did come to us had multiple layers to it. Overall, everything got much more complicated and nothing was simple anymore.

This day marked a significant turning point in Jenny's cognitive condition. It was Saturday, April 13th, the 18th day since her first seizure. This was the day that Jenny really "went away."

Previously the only time we totally lost the ability to communicate with Jenny was during her episodes and the brief moments when she would "go away." Those times had not been as "deep" as they became this day; and while her time "away" was still not constant, the times we still had with her were far too short and very random. We were still able to reason with her and to direct her in certain ways, for now. However, any decent conversation was essentially gone. We could no longer sit and talk about the Twins or what was going on in the world. Remarkably, she still managed to get out the question, "When can I go home?" from time to time, but her ability to absorb what we still tried explaining about what we knew and what was going on had ended. More importantly, and more painful, her ability to tell us what she felt and believed was happening also stopped.

Was it the illness causing this, the depression taking over, or something else? Perhaps Jenny was shutting down out of sheer fatigue, as she had yet to sleep for anything resembling an extended time since April 2nd. Jenny slept no more than two or three hours at a time which would have been fine if she had slept four or five times a day, but Jenny could go as long as 20 to 24 hours between "naps."

Barb, John, and I were more tired than we might have been if we were not so determined that one of us be with Jenny at all times. So far, Jenny had not been alone in the hospital. Barb did the majority of the shifts, which included two out of every three nights. John was only able to do one overnight on the weekend and most evenings. I covered the rest. Early on in Jenny's illness, why we were so determined to always be there with Jenny was probably the hardest part for family and close friends to understand.

With each passing day, Jenny went further "away" and the episodes happened more often and were more intense. Much like the doctors had a hard time understanding what we meant by her "odd behavior" early on, anyone who did not actually see what Jenny went through during her episodes could not understand what they were like. This created a two dimensional problem: while it was difficult to imagine forcing a nurse or a nurse's aide to deal with Jenny during her episodes, it was impossible to imagine leaving Jenny alone with a stranger to help her ride them out as well. Even if we had allowed ourselves to go home to the comfort of our own beds, we could not sleep peacefully wondering what was going on back at the hospital. At least with Barb, John, or I there, we would know someone who loved Jenny was with her to help her through the tough times.

In addition, as Jenny's episodes became more intense, some aggressiveness started to surface with them. Not that Jenny was ever dangerous, but she would get a certain level of determination in terms of what the illness and the demons in her head would make her do. Although Jenny wasn't the biggest or strongest woman around, she was stronger than the average woman her size. When the adrenaline and ferocity of her episodes was added to her physique, she was stronger than she otherwise would have been and was therefore difficult to handle.

In many of Jenny's episodes we needed to physically restrain her for short periods. Physical restraint was a two-sided coin: it was well above and beyond what could be asked of the staff at Methodist Hospital and we wanted to be the ones to make the decisions as to how physical and what type of force was used. Barb could somehow reach Jenny more often and reason with her better than anyone else, and John and I were just plain stronger than Jenny and more comfortable being forceful with her when necessary. Where we had no problem and suffered no repercussions in physically holding Jenny down on her bed where it was easier to manage her, the hospital staff would be more likely to use mechanical restraints. These were very necessary and appropriate protocols in place for the hospital staff, not only for their own safety, but are also generally accepted practices within a hospital. None of the nursing staff actually wanted to use such methods unless it became absolutely necessary. Although it was considered many times, there was only one time that it got to the point that two security guards were outside Jenny's door with the equipment used to mechanically restrain a patient. Thankfully, she settled down just in time.

One of my biggest fears in compiling this story is that anyone would see our experience as reflecting badly on the doctors and staff of Methodist Hospital. The fact that we chose to stay at Jenny's side 24 hours a day at this point in her illness appeared to some outside the hospital as indicative that we were doing more for Jenny than the nursing staff, but nothing could be further from the truth. Without a clear understanding of Jenny's situation, it is not possible to understand the overwhelming responsibility Jenny created for the hospital. Regardless of whether or not I have successfully described Jenny's condition and the challenges she presented to the entire staff at Methodist, it cannot be argued that this situation was extremely unique by anyone's standards, as evidenced by the fact that once the diagnosis finally came, even the Mayo Clinic had seen fewer than a dozen cases. In other words, none of us had any protocols to follow with what we were experiencing, and all of us – patient, doctors, staff, family, and friends – just had to do the best we could moment by moment.

While it was happening, I was extremely frustrated with the progress, due mostly to the stress and sorrow of watching my daughter deteriorate. While I could see the lengths that the nursing staff went to for Jenny, we were not entirely aware of how hard the doctors were working behind the scenes.

There is no way for me to confirm the number of doctors who worked on Jenny's case throughout her illness. I know during the search for the cause of her condition we were visited by doctors from no fewer than three specialties: Neurology, Psychiatry, and Infectious Diseases. These specialists were in addition to other doctors who came and went each day. I know that doctors in other hospitals, other states, and even other countries were consulted at one time or another during the process, and a specialist from the Mayo Clinic came to examine Jenny at one point. There was more than one late night phone call from a doctor doing research, asking us questions about Jenny such as travel and eating habits, as well as possible behavioral patterns we may have witnessed. At one point, there was a lot of focus put on some sushi Jenny had left in the refrigerator for a week and chose to eat anyway. Clearly, they were focused on the case and determined to leave no stone unturned in the search for a diagnosis and treatment.

However, the long delay in finding the diagnosis led to unforeseen and unintended consequences that Barb, Michelle, John, and I were forced to deal with outside of the hospital. One of the most trying and most frequent was explaining the situation to others.

Although none of us went out of our way to inform people of Jenny's condition, word was starting to get out simply because we were not participating in our normal everyday activities. Of course, all of us were missing work, but other regular routines and involvements were ignored as well. I was the head coach of a U14 girls soccer team with players from a variety of towns and schools in our area. Games hadn't started yet, and while I had not actually missed any practices, my coaching was increasingly ineffective, so people were beginning to notice that something was going on.

We avoided telling anyone what was happening because it was extremely difficult to try to explain to people, over and over, that there was still no diagnosis. On the one hand, things were happening and changing so fast that any information we relayed was outdated almost as soon as it was shared; but on the other hand, to continually repeat that we did not know what was actually wrong with her was more than frustrating. It was also impossible to explain what Jenny was experiencing and what we were enduring. It was just easier to tell as few people as possible.

There were two legitimate questions that all caring and interested people asked. The first was, "How's Jenny?" which was certainly a fair and even obvious question. I asked it myself every time I returned to the hospital after being away for any length of time, even after just running down to the cafeteria. However, Jenny's condition was changing so fast even the doctors couldn't keep up, making the question impossible to answer. The second reasonable question people asked was, "What do the doctors say is wrong?" This question was also impossible for us to answer as no one had any idea what was wrong, but saying this led people to believe we were criticizing the hospital and staff. Almost everyone has a multitude of questions when they hear that someone has been in the hospital for two weeks and there is still no diagnosis. I understood that, but I got tired of trying to be polite and attempting to provide information that I barely understood. No one, it seemed, would accept "I don't know" as the answer.

The event that convinced me to stop trying to explain the situation was when I ran into a neighbor who knew Jenny was in the hospital and asked how she was. It was, for some reason, a relatively good day and I simply said, "Doing really well," and we both went about our day. Two days later I saw the man's wife and she said, "It is such good news that Jenny is out of the hospital." This, of course, was not at all what I had told her husband and the frustration of not understanding what was happening to my daughter was exacerbated by being misunderstood when I attempted to explain. On top of the real issues I needed to deal with, this aspect of it simply got to be too much.

Finally, I expressed this frustration to our minister during one of his visits to the hospital. The following Sunday he, thankfully, made a statement to the entire congregation before his sermon to please not ask Michelle and I, who were in attendance, anything about Jenny's condition.

It was the end of April before we would officially make any "public" statements about Jenny's illness. However, the further Jenny deteriorated and the more time that passed without receiving a diagnosis, the more questions began to be raised as to why we didn't move Jenny to another hospital, even among our family and very closest friends. "She needs to get to Mayo," seemed to be the mantra we heard most often (referring to the Mayo Clinic in Rochester, Minnesota). There is a misconception that it is just that easy: jump in the car, drive there, and the doors swing open wide and welcoming with a diagnosis and cure immediately available. While we did consider all of our options and many long discussions took place about the possibility of moving Jenny to Mayo, which had also been suggested by more than a few doctors at Methodist, multiple factors ultimately ruled it out.

The decision was complex, but the truth is that Barb and I were always comfortable with Jenny staying at Methodist. The biggest reason for this was we knew all of the facts that were available.

Everyone was frustrated that the doctors were not finding the cause of my daughter's illness, including the very doctors whose job it was to accomplish the task, but no one was more frustrated than Barb, Michelle, John, and me. We were possibly even more frustrated, however, by the many people who questioned us about whether the doctors knew what they were doing.

In the same way that a relative stranger would have little comprehension of Jenny's true condition with only a passing conversation at a convenience store, no one could have a full grasp of everything that was being done without having been in on the dozens of discussions taking place over many, many hours that we had with the doctors.

Outside of the medical staff, probably no one understood the situation better than Barb and me. However, by the time we were done digesting all that the doctors had told us, gone back with a multitude of questions and digested it all some more, it was a monumental chore to explain it to anyone. We did the best we could to give John and Michelle as much factual information as we could, but the truth is, we were so tired and suffering from so much information overload that it was actually painful to try to explain anything to anyone. The result was that almost everyone in our lives got only very simple summaries.

The best example of what came from all this was a text message exchange with my business partner, one of the smartest people I know and someone who has experienced her own medical crisis. She was pushing me fairly hard to move Jenny to Mayo or another hospital, which I knew she was doing out of caring and compassion. However, she knew better than anyone that I had a hard time thinking straight when I was tired and I finally sent her a text that said something to the effect of, "Bonnie, you are only getting my 30-word summaries of what was said in a 45-minute meeting with the doctor – please stop second-guessing me."

There were many reasons that we did not move Jenny to Mayo, but the very bottom line was that we knew Mayo doctors were already actively involved in the case. In addition, the thought of taking Jenny away from the doctors and, more importantly, the nurses who had proven how much they cared for and loved her actually made it no decision at all. Barb and I never regretted not moving Jenny out of Methodist Hospital.

CHAPTER 17

Day 10

There was no longer any doubt that it was time to face the reality of the situation. Despite an email I had sent the night before that said, "I hope Jenny is out of the hospital this week," it was time to end the denial phase of this process and begin to make plans for how we were going to manage for the long haul.

The funny thing about family crises is that the mortgage company still wants their monthly payments.

As far as Barb, John, and I were concerned, preparing for the long haul meant that we needed to figure out how we were going to keep a family member with Jenny while trying to return to at least a portion of our normal daily lives. There was no way we were going to change our plan to have a family member be with Jenny 24 hours a day, but life did have to go on, so it was time to make changes in how we were doing things. Still, in a strange way, this came up on us suddenly and we had no idea how we were going to do it. Part of the issue was that obviously we didn't know how long Jenny would be in the condition she was in, so we didn't know what we were planning for.

Oh yeah! Family!

How do we dare ask someone to take this on? The phrase "stay with Jenny" sounds so simple. Grab a book and a chair and keep Jenny company for eight hours or so. That's what it's like at a hospital, right?

The problem of course was that it was impossible to prepare anyone for Jenny's behavior. She would display literally hundreds of various behaviors and very few were comparable to any others that occurred before or after. Therefore, what to expect could not be explained. For example, Jenny's hallucination of a truck about to run over her bed and its ensuing panic happened only once, but there were countless other terrifying events. The behavior was never predictable, and there was never a sustained pattern of any kind. While we could tell stories, they did not really give a reasonable expectation of what might happen in the future.

As we considered bringing in more people to stay with Jenny, we were forced to take the difficulties of dealing with her and her situation into consideration as well. Jenny's illness and dealing with it were drastically different from the experience of any other illness. When a person feels a cold coming on, they can reasonably expect to sneeze, cough, and have a runny nose at various times during the course of a week or two. The degree to which this happens varies, depending on a number of factors. However, rarely is anyone surprised by any of the symptoms. In Jenny's case, when I described a behavior she had been demonstrating, it had already passed and would probably never be demonstrated exactly like that again. It was already time to prepare for something new, but there was no way to know what that "new" would be that you were preparing for.

In terms of finding the internal strength to leave Jenny with anyone else reminded Barb and me of the struggle to leave our children on their first day of daycare. What started as a need to stay at the hospital because "this is odd, so we need to hear what the doctor says," turned into "no one else can do this as well as Mom and Dad" (well, okay, as good as Mom). For a variety of reasons, it was tough to turn our daughter over to someone else, anyone else. It was not at all a lack of trust. We certainly trusted our family members, and we had full confidence in the nurses on the 6th floor. Although we were concerned about how someone would care for Jenny and deal with the demands she would put on them, we more so worried about whether it was fair to ask anyone to do so. How a person reacted to dealing with Jenny was a vital part of surviving the hours of challenges that lie ahead. All of the nurses worked hard and did the best they could; but, as an example, one nurse who simply had enough was so frustrated that she stepped back and threatened Barb to "get her under control or I will call security." These were the trained professionals so it was this type of event that made us skittish about who was selected to care for Jenny. We needed to know that person wouldn't abandon their post while we were away.

To be fair to all involved, even after a person was familiar with everything the job would require, caring for Jenny was not easy. It wasn't easy for us, so it was probably even more difficult for everyone else. There was a learning curve involved. Barb, John, and I weren't better at caring for Jenny; we simply had more experience doing it. Barb and I had concern for everyone involved, not just Jenny.

Once Barb and I came to grips with the necessity of allowing other family members to step in to help, our greatest task was figuring out how to prepare them for what they would face. My sister, Debbie, was the first family member to step in to assist in taking care of Jenny during the day.

Ever since Jenny's first seizure, I had been most diligent at keeping Debbie up to date with what was happening, although admittedly, it was primarily via text message. A clear demonstration of how much Jenny's condition, and hence her behavior, would change in just a couple of days can be seen in a journal that Debbie wrote for Jenny during her illness. Although Debbie had seen Jenny just two days before she arrived at the hospital on the morning of the 15th, her surprise at Jenny's rapid deterioration can be heard in the following portion of her journal entry from that day:

> *No one had explained to me prior to my arrival that first day that "Jenny" wasn't always in the room. I could tell simply from the repeated questions you asked and the sometimes-distant silences that*

75

we experienced. You would always come back from the sudden distances to ask me a question you had just asked before you "left."

The fact of the matter is that I believed I had done all I could to prepare Debbie before she arrived that day, yet, that is what she experienced, and her day had only just begun!

So what was it that was so shocking? What was it that a person, whether family member or the nursing staff, had to deal with while working with Jenny?

The shocking and difficult part of dealing with Jenny wasn't anything specific, it was simply that what had to be dealt with changed so often and came in so many different and non-repeating forms. It was confusing for everyone, including the doctors, even when it was happening right in front of them. Barb, Michelle, John, and I had the advantage of seeing this all develop from the very beginning, as well as being with Jenny for hours on end as many of the changes took place in front of us. The doctors were slower to grasp the fact that things were changing so rapidly simply because of the limited contact they had with her. Early on, they only saw Jenny for minutes at a time, and they trusted the input of the nurses more than her family. While the doctors would ask us what we were seeing, in effect, Barb, John, and I were inadvertently supporting the perception that emotional family members struggle to give objective and accurate reports because what we said we saw was never visible to the doctors just hours, or even minutes, later.

One day a doctor came into Jenny's room about 9 a.m. and witnessed her displaying some specific behavior. The doctor decided that she needed another doctor from another specialty to see it and sent a message for him to come and examine Jenny. By 11 a.m. when he arrived, Jenny had completely moved on and was no longer exhibiting even a vague semblance of what he came to see. It was actually quite comical watching his reaction as I am convinced that at first he thought he had the wrong room. He walked out and looked at the room number on the doorjamb in the hallway, apparently not trusting what the chart said. Then he questioned me about the validity of the notes on the chart. I assured him that two hours ago they were very accurate and that he just took too long to get there. I probably sounded like a smart-aleck, and I am pretty sure he doubted every word I said when I told him that if he wanted to come back at 1 p.m. he could witness something completely different again.

From a factual and professional perspective, the doctors and nurses were seeing a wide variety of behaviors from Jenny, and as is standard operating procedure for medical professionals, technical terms needed to be applied to a behavior Jenny displayed, if for no other reason than to put something on the chart that everyone could understand. (I guess "she is acting odd" wasn't part of medical school terminology.)

Reading through even a few of the examination reports from the variety of doctors presents a complex list of sometimes completely contradictory descriptions of Jenny's behavior, personality and/or condition when a doctor was with her. One doctor would refer to Jenny as "catatonic," meaning she was sitting quietly and was completely unresponsive while later in the day another doctor referred to her as "in a state of catatonia," defined as being in a stupor, staring, and not thinking. Catatonia is considered an emergency psychiatric state. The patient is in a stupor in the sense that they are not thinking, processing, or purposefully doing anything, but the body is intensely active. A nonprofessional, like me, could confuse this with being catatonic. The catch was that Jenny wasn't stuck in it constantly; it would pass after a few minutes to an hour.

In addition, at one time a doctor stated that Jenny was in a state of "agitated catatonia," which is similar to catatonia, of course, but with a somewhat angry aggressiveness. The addition of the "agitated" is simply to point out that the patient was a bit angry or aggressive as opposed to simply making random sounds and/or movements as Jenny did quite often.

A list of "behavior problems" can also be seen throughout the doctors' reports: agitation, delusions, and rumination (obsessing over one thing, like "I have to go outside") were just a few.

As if this was not enough to deal with, Jenny had a whole list of "movement problems": tremors, ticks, dyskinesia (Latin for "bad movement"), ataxia (lack of coordination), ataxic gait (clumsy, uncoordinated walking) and finally, decerebrate posturing (fixed hyperextension of extremities), when Jenny was at her worst.

At times Jenny would also get what the nurses called "waxy flexibility." It is a commonly accepted term among the nurses (although I am sure it has a more technical name) and occurs when a patient can literally be "posed" and then stays that way. It happened once or twice a day when Jenny was in her worst condition. We could lift her arms up off the bed and she would just keep them there.

Of course, much like Jenny's episodes, the behaviors Jenny would actually demonstrate at any one time varied day-by-day, and oftentimes, even hour-by-hour. There was little to no pattern of any kind so it could never be predicted what would happen next. Considering these rapid succession of changes, the monumental task the doctors and nurses had in caring for Jenny can be more easily understood. With the idea of accepting a family member's help, throwing someone new into the mix who hadn't witnessed any of this yet would clearly be overwhelming.

These rapid changes also help explain why it was so difficult to come up with a diagnosis. The information that the various test results presented to the doctors was puzzling enough, but so too were the outward physical symptoms. There was no consistency, no pattern, and no relationship between the symptoms and test results.

In addition to all of this, Jenny had six to ten "episodes" each day in which she saw anything from a giant spider on the wall to a person walk into the room and hold a pillow over her face to suffocate her. We thanked God each day for the nurses and nurse's aides that dealt with this; but how could we ask an untrained family member to take on this task.

There were many family and medical professionals that had only seen bits and pieces of this, and in very small doses. Many of them, especially family and friends, would walk away more than a bit stunned. Many were speechless, and some never came back. I believe those who never came back imagined that whatever they saw was something we experienced occasionally, and probably believed they just happened to be present during the worst of it. In reality, visitors never saw the worst.

CHAPTER 18

Day 11

On Monday, April 15th, my sister Debbie stepped in as the first family member to take on the task of caring for Jenny. I thought I had prepared her, but clearly, I had not.

Debbie's journal contains an excellent play-by-play of her first two days caring for Jenny, showing the rapid changes Jenny went through and how difficult the task could be as seen in this edited, partial version of her journal entries covering portions of April 15th and 16th:

My first day with you was extremely enlightening as to what was going on with you, and what your parents and John had been experiencing for the past two weeks...It was a very intense time, those first two days. I was very "green" as to what I was getting myself into. When I would first arrive, you would know who I was, greet me enthusiastically, and we would have a short time together where things were relatively "normal" in terms of what we did and things we talked about. As time would pass, you would have "episodes" where you were gone for a while. It was a toss-up as to who you would be when you came back. Sometimes you would greet me like I had just gotten there, and the day seemed to start over. Other times you were sad and confused, and had something disconcerting or terrible that you thought you had just been through that we had to work our way through to convince you that it hadn't really happened. Still other times, you were someone whom I didn't recognize, and who didn't recognize me, and we had something even larger and more time-consuming to work through to bring you back to me and the real things that were going on, not what you were imagining were going on. Usually, these differences in the "person" that came and went were punctuated by a very short, brief "nap" sometimes as short as a minute or two, and one time – and only once – as long as 45 minutes. The longer the nap, the less assured I was of Jenny coming to visit when she woke up. However, we always worked our way through it and back to it being you and me, as temporary as those times became.

Although Debbie's words are very revealing as to what she dealt with in this specific two-day span, no two days were alike so proper preparation was virtually impossible.

Each new nurse that was assigned to Jenny had to go through the learning curve as well. I have no idea if or how any of them were prepped before they stepped into the room for the first time, but I am sure they had heard the stories at the nurse's station and in the lounges.

Perhaps I am insensitive, but I have to admit that I never gave a thought to what the nurses were experiencing. They entered the room countless times and every time I would allow myself to relax because I knew the experts had arrived to relieve me of what I was dealing with at that moment. As far as I was concerned, these were the trained professionals, and I could see by how they were acting and responding that they were comfortable and knew what they were doing. So I thought.

In conversations with nurse Andi months after Jenny was discharged from Methodist, I was stunned to learn what it was like being one of her nurses. From my perspective, whenever Andi was assigned to Jenny's room during her shift, I knew it would be a good day for *me*. She always appeared so calm and collected; however, Andi told me that she would break into a nervous sweat when she knew she was assigned to Jenny. She was very apprehensive every time she entered Jenny's room and she assured me that all the nurses felt this way. In hindsight, I guess I should have known and now I can see why, but I never noticed it while it was happening, which is a strong testament to them, and how they approached their responsibilities.

While discussing Jenny's rapid changes in behavior, the topic turned to how Andi attempted to describe it to the doctors. She said, "Most times that I paged a doctor, it was more like, 'I don't know, she looks really weird, we gotta do something!!!' Real technical!" Andi was one of the most caring and experienced nurses on the floor. I have no concept of what training nurses receive for the specialties of each area of a hospital they work in, but I highly doubt that they were trained to deal with Jenny's episodes. How could they be when none of them were ever the same? I struggled in dealing with the first one, and I struggled in dealing with the last.

Due to the variations in Jenny's episodes, and how she behaved because of them, perhaps an entire additional book could be written about what each of them were like, how she acted, and how we reacted. However, one key factor that existed in one form or another in most of her episodes was that if whatever was going on in Jenny's head made her do something that was extremely undesirable for any reason, trying to stop her actually made her do it *more*. It was better to let it run its course.

When a new nurse's aide was assigned to care for Jenny, he or she would justifiably work very hard to try to do their job and "help" Jenny, especially if one of the family members was present. Perhaps they felt that we expected them to "do something" to help our daughter. Not only would these efforts fail and cause frustration, but they usually backfired and caused Jenny to get more agitated. Even when we encouraged them to leave Jenny alone if what she was doing was no big deal, I am sure it was a sense of duty to their employer that made them ignore us, but ultimately, the lack of success they would inevitably experience was hard on everyone involved.

Finally, in an effort to not only make Jenny more comfortable, but also to reduce the stress and frustration of the nurses and aides, I sent the following email to the director of the nurses on the floor, which was actually part of an overall and continuing discussion on how to make everyone's time with Jenny easier:

My wife and I have witnessed well over 100 of Jenny's "episodes," so please trust us on this. Although each episode is slightly different, what we know with 100% certainty is that **once they start, there is NOTHING that can be done to mitigate them, and certainly nothing that can be done to stop them.** *I guarantee that you cannot try to reason with Jenny or try to offer her alternatives to distract her once "an episode" has started. You certainly cannot talk her out of whatever it is that is going on in her head. As long as she is not endangering herself or disrupting others, it is actually best to let her do whatever she wants. She may be trying to speak to you, but even when she can talk so that she can be understood it doesn't change anything. She is not actually aware of what she is saying. But above all else, please, please, please stop trying to STOP her from having her episodes, and stop trying to reason with her. It only frightens her and prolongs them. ONLY* **COMFORT** *HER. The "episode" MUST be allowed to run its course, and the less restraint you put on Jenny, the smoother they go. The episodes are no one's fault, there is no external trigger or cause, and there certainly is no trick to stopping them once they start. I know nurses and aides are not used to listening to the loved ones of the patient, but I hope this is a case where, at the very least, this information will be considered valid.*

Thankfully, Lesa Boettcher , the Clinical Nursing Director of the 6th floor, put her faith in what I said and the entire nursing staff was given a copy of the email. As a result, everyone had just a little easier time of it – including Jenny – because everyone stopped struggling with her.

It was not until I was able to slow down and look back on this experience, rather than being in the midst of it, that I was able to determine why we always failed to properly explain Jenny's true condition to anyone. This failure was not due to a lack of effort, not by any means; rather, it had everything to do with "context." People do not have the proper context, or frame of reference, with which to comprehend how Jenny behaved during the depths of her illness.

What may be the best way to describe Jenny's behavior, in a fashion that most people can get their mind around, is something that I read toward the end of Jenny's illness. I do not remember the source, unfortunately, but it was about a doctor who was attempting to explain the devastation this illness can have on a patient to a conference of medical professionals. The doctor making the presentation shared his theory that over the centuries when families called for a priest to perform an exorcism, the illness that Jenny was ultimately diagnosed with was the illness the person actually had. How anyone chooses to translate that description in their own mind for what might be exorcism-worthy behavior, at least we can all agree it would be scary; and surely it is something that none of us wants to be part of, but it is what we saw countless times during Jenny's illness.

The worst of what we witnessed seemed to happen at night. Definitely, my most blood-curdling experience came one night when it was my turn to stay with Jenny. As always, the task was to try to get Jenny to sleep as much as possible. I don't recall the exact time, but it was somewhere around 3 a.m., which is only relevant because it meant that I was trying to stay awake as much as I was trying to get Jenny to sleep. She was lying relatively still in her bed and the room was completely dark due to the door being closed. The only light was that emitted by the pieces of electronic equipment around and above her bed. I was lying as perfectly still as I could in the recliner in the room because if I moved, the chair would squeak and Jenny would pop up to see what was happening. Once again, as had been the case so many times before, in my effort to lie as still as possible, I was losing my battle to fight off sleep, and I began to drift off. The effects of what happened in the following seconds were compounded by my extreme exhaustion and that I had begun drifting off, but the incident would have been disturbing under any circumstances.

I was startled awake by what I initially thought was the sound of an animal attacking Jenny. My shock only lasted a fraction of a second as I knew this wasn't possible and I turned toward Jenny to see what was actually happening. The dim light provided by the various LED indicators located around Jenny, as well as some illumination trickling in the window from streetlights, provided me with essentially only a silhouette of her. I could not believe what I thought I was seeing! I could not comprehend her assuming the posture I saw and could not imagine that the inhuman sound I heard could be coming from her throat.

I got out of the chair as quickly as possible and approached her bed, which was only eight to ten feet away. The only part of Jenny touching her bed was her feet and the very top of her head, almost rolled back to her forehead. Her stomach was toward the ceiling and her back was raised off the bed with her arms reaching up toward the ceiling. I am not afraid to admit that I panicked! I had no idea what to do as my senses were still gathering themselves from having dozed off for just a few minutes and awakening to this.

After a few moments, I moved toward the head of Jenny's bed in an attempt to see her face. (Surely there was no wild animal there, but I needed to be sure.) What I saw still makes the hair on the back of my neck stand on end.

Jenny's face was only partially lit by the equipment indicator lights, so perhaps the shadows distorted what I saw. As best as I could tell, her eyes were wide open, but only one of them was looking at me. The other was looking off in another direction. Even worse was the shape of Jenny's mouth – it was contorted in a way I didn't think was possible and yet her teeth were showing as well. The entire time she was letting out what could only be described as the growl of a wild animal, but I have no idea how any human could make that sound.

I absolutely froze! I stared at my daughter's face for what was likely no more than a few seconds, but the truth is I have no idea how long it was. Because no nurse entered the room, it could not have lasted too long; but by this time they had also grown accustomed to hearing strange noises coming from Jenny's room, so who knows.

As was the case with all of Jenny's odd behaviors and episodes, this one also passed, and eventually she lay back down on her bed as if nothing had happened. I went and turned on the light, and I never sat in total darkness with her again. When I returned to her bed, Jenny stared at me as peacefully as if she had just awakened from a nap on a swaying hammock in front of a lakeside cabin.

"What's wrong Dad?"

"Nothing, Jenny. Just go back to sleep"

She didn't, of course.

But, for anyone who still does not understand what it was like to be with and care for Jenny during her illness, I believe Michelle's very simple description summed it up best, "Scary movies aren't scary anymore. I lived one."

CHAPTER 19

Day 12 – Part 1

Sometimes things do not go as planned. If nothing else, the journey with Jenny has given us that perspective.

Jenny hadn't showered in a few days and her hair, in particular, was messy from the dried glue used for the probes of another continuous EEG over the weekend. Debbie was staying with Jenny for the day again and there was a short time when she seemed to "be there" as Debbie was picking at the bits of glue in her hair. Debbie took this opportunity to ask Jenny if she would like to take a shower, and she said that she would. Debbie paged a nurse to inquire about the shower, and the nurse said she would get it ready.

About 15 minutes later, the nurse came back and said the shower should be ready. Jenny was unable to be left alone for any length of time and certainly could not shower on her own. Debbie guided Jenny down the hall, following the nurse and toting Jenny's set of clean clothes. (Jenny never wore a hospital gown her entire stay at Methodist because of her hyperactivity. God knows who she would have been flashing in the hallways!) Out of our concern that Jenny was still aware of what was going on behind the façade that the demons created, we had developed the practice of having Barb help Jenny in the shower whenever possible, but today the task fell to Debbie.

When they reached the shower, the water was already running. Jenny immediately began to remove her clothes while Debbie was still talking to the nurse. When the nurse left and closed the door, Debbie turned around to find Jenny already naked with one hand under the running water. Jenny stated that the water was cold, and when Debbie tested it, she agreed. Debbie played with the knobs trying to adjust the temperature but was unable to get any warm water to come out.

The dilemma of course was that Debbie couldn't leave Jenny alone but obviously could not take her with to find the assistance they needed either. Additionally, if she were to wait too long to get this shower done Jenny may "go away" or slip into an episode and be unmanageable.

Debbie asked Jenny to wait and not get under the water while she checked to see if there was another shower to use. Not wanting to leave Jenny alone, Debbie opened the door and looked around to see if there was anyone in sight that could help. Seeing no one, Debbie turned to tell Jenny that she should put some clothes on until a warm shower could be found. To Debbie's surprise, Jenny was already under the ice-cold stream of the shower soaping up her hair and body. Jenny was shaking all over but was determined to take that shower. Debbie could not convince Jenny to get out from under the cold water until she felt that she was "clean" and by then she was shaking uncontrollably, so much so that by the time she was done she couldn't even dry herself off or get dressed.

Debbie attempted to dry Jenny off as best she could but because, in Jenny's mind, she was done showering, she was ready to leave the shower room despite the fact that she had no clothes on. Because of the struggle Debbie had between trying to keep Jenny in the room and attempting to dry her off, she gave up drying Jenny and was able to convince her to put on her clean shorts and t-shirt before they went back to the room.

Jenny was still so wet when she got dressed that her clothes became wet as well and stuck to her on the short trip back to the room. Once there, Debbie told Jenny to remove the wet clothes and get into bed. Debbie covered her up with every blanket she could find in the room.

As Jenny lay under blankets, Debbie hoped this would be the perfect situation to trigger a good long nap for Jenny, who, of course, had other ideas. Jenny's fixation switched from the shower to her now wet hair that still had remnants of the glue in it. She sat patiently as Debbie brushed out all of the tangles and then spent about an hour trying to get all the glue out. Debbie managed to get most of the glue removed, but we seldom got all of it out before Jenny was hooked up to Emu, the continuous EEG machine again, which unfortunately happened again that same evening.

Jenny also made an entry into her journal that afternoon. The nonsensical notations serve no purpose other than to show the contrast to her previously orderly writing to demonstrate how much she had deteriorated in the 11 days since the last journal entries she had written:

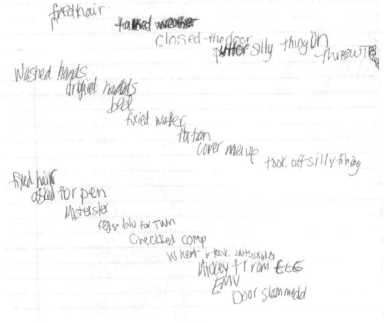

In further contrast, to show how quickly Jenny deteriorated during her illness, the very last note of any kind Jenny wrote before she was totally "gone" is shown below….it was written the very next day after she wrote the notation above:

CHAPTER 20

Day 12 – Part 2

There was still no diagnosis.

Why was it so hard to figure out what was making Jenny sick? Well, of course, it was complicated and I often told people that everything I was learning during this journey might actually have been interesting if it hadn't involved my daughter. The brain is truly an unexplored frontier. I am shocked at how little doctors actually know about it, but what they do know is fascinating.

Adding to my frustration was the fact that even the limited information we received was never clear-cut. There were always a number of layers involved. Even the simplest of issues surrounding Jenny's illness had so many addendums. An example of this was the official term used for Jenny's illness at this point was encephalitis. However, eventually I learned the addendum – that the word means absolutely nothing in terms of how to help the patient that has it. To me, encephalitis is so similar to meningitis – a term people come across more often. The word sounds so official that it must be a precise diagnosis. We may hear something on the news similar to, "An outbreak of meningitis among college kids," and we think "Oh, that's not good. But people get that from time to time and they recover."

In reality, however, the words meningitis and encephalitis don't mean anything by themselves. They are just fancy words that meet the needs of generalizing an illness, but these are just "conditions," not actually illnesses. There is a significant distinction between the two, though anyone with a medical background knows I am oversimplifying the situation. Still, it illustrates how anything we learned seemed to have "yeah, buts" attached to it.

In Jenny's situation, the "yeah, but" was "what is causing the condition?" Meningitis or encephalitis means there is swelling either around or inside the brain, and while that information is helpful, it does not tell us what is happening to the patient who has the inflammation. Again, I am oversimplifying, but my daughter was absolutely convinced that she was seeing two children playing under her hospital bed, so I think the situation was as complicated as it needed to be. Perhaps to some people, it was progress that the doctors knew my daughter had some form of encephalitis, but that didn't get us any closer to helping Jenny to be able to walk in a straight line again.

I was given information that, on the surface, sounded significant, but then I would hear the addendum, and realize that no real progress had been made yet.

I don't want to mislead anyone into thinking that the doctors were not explaining things to us – that was not the case at all. My frustration was no fault of theirs. There was just no escaping the technical side of this situation, and it took more energy than I was able to expend. I was totally focused on Jenny, along with trying to do as much as I could to manage in the other areas of my life. The doctors explained clearly that Jenny was believed to have a viral infection within the interior of her brain with an unknown origin. The medical charts needed to say something, so it was labeled encephalitis, which was technically correct. The doctors were not trying to convince anyone that they had made a great medical discovery – I was still waiting for them to do that. What looked good on paper, perhaps, to some, or more than likely just met the requirement that something needed to be listed on the chart, actually amounted to absolutely nothing in my mind. Since it was not known what the actual infection was, it was not known how to treat it, and hence, Jenny was not getting better. So, the fact that my daughter had encephalitis meant absolutely nothing to me.

The reality of the situation was that the search for a diagnosis of Jenny's illness was a slow process of elimination. From the time the first set of tests on the spinal fluid came back all negative, the doctors worked continuously to check for and eliminate a whole list of possible causes. Hypotheses would be established based on what was known at a specific time, and the proper fluids were drawn and sent to the lab for whatever test was needed. I lost count of the possibilities they eliminated somewhere in the mid-20s.

While I will not even attempt to go down the complicated road of medical explanation as to why the search for the diagnosis was so difficult, I can point out some of the most obvious problems. Every EEG consistently pointed to problems in Jenny's brain, and the spinal fluid continued to show that an infection of some kind was getting worse. Furthermore, by simply standing next to her bed and looking at Jenny, it was obvious something was wrong. However, the results of every MRI showed that the images were "unremarkable," which meant that as far as the MRI was concerned, there was nothing wrong with her.

In addition, as the doctors were trying to focus on finding the cause of Jenny's illness so they could actually make her better, her condition continued to get worse, which meant the doctors had to expend time and energy on two separate fronts. This week was the beginning of a stretch of time in which Jenny showed new symptoms literally every day, and they created new complications as she continued to deteriorate. The use of a drug to treat one symptom triggered another symptom of some kind; and the fact that she couldn't sleep and did not eat continued to challenge her doctors.

The list of challenges is long, but a good example was one day Jenny's blood pressure spiked so dramatically they were forced to start her on blood pressure medication. However, before the drug even had a chance to do what it was supposed to do, her blood pressure plummeted to unheard of levels (one reading was 74/24 – the doctors were hoping for something like 125/80). The doctors scrambled to counteract the dangerous drop, which was complicated by the high blood pressure medication just starting to kick in. It felt like a never-ending cycle requiring a fragile balancing act, and as frustrated as I had become, I was amazed at how the doctors worked together and managed it all. How the doctors and nurses kept track of the changes to medications alone is a medical marvel.

In addition to these fluctuating symptoms, the search for a diagnosis and even the process of running the tests was becoming more complicated. As each test came back negative, the likelihood of a "common" problem decreased. The increasing rarity of the diseases they were testing for had two major consequences: the lab work for the tests was not done at Methodist anymore, and after a while not even in Minnesota. The process of running any single test would take days or even weeks to complete. All we could do was wait and pray while Jenny's continued to deteriorate.

During one of the most intense parts of the search, I repeated a comment to a doctor that was originally made by my business partner, saying, "This seems like a real-life version of the TV show *House*." He did not disagree.

Barb and I were always nervous and often scared, but we never felt that the doctors didn't have a handle on the difficult task in front of them. Although there was no way of knowing it at the time, April 16th would prove to be a monumental day in the search for a diagnosis of Jenny's illness. Six test specimens had been sent out from Methodist Hospital via Federal Express. The specimens for two tests would go to a lab on the east coast, and four would go to a lab in Athens, Georgia. Ultimately, over the coming days and weeks, five of the tests would come back negative. However, although we had no way of knowing it at the time, the one test that would come back positive would take longer than the rest to return; it would be two weeks before those results were received. In the meantime, the doctors kept searching.

Of the hundreds of tests and procedures performed on Jenny, the continuous EEG fascinated me the most. As far as I know, the continuous EEG played almost no direct role in the actual diagnosis of the illness, but it was very significant for a number of other reasons. The information it revealed gave the doctors some insight into what was going on in Jenny's brain, and hence, in part, pointed them in a direction to explore additional possibilities. From my first sit-down meeting with Dr. Freking, the plan had been to perform some tests to help point them in a direction to search, and the continuous EEG was the first step in that process. The EEGs also revealed additional symptoms of the illness, but they could not aid in the interpretation of what was causing it.

Most importantly, the continuous EEG allowed the doctors to see Jenny's behavior firsthand since video and audio were also being recorded and these recordings could be replayed at any time. Thus, in a way, the continuous EEG allowed the doctors to be with her 24 hours a day, which proved to be helpful in a number of ways.

On this day we received some significant, albeit very disturbing, information that was only made possible because of the continuous EEG. Of the hundreds of pieces of news we received during Jenny's illness, this possibly rocked me more than anything else did.

We knew Jenny continued to have seizures because the EEGs had said so. In fact, she was having dozens of them each day, which was a significant sign that she was still getting sicker. Once Jenny was on the anti-seizure medication, I assumed that every time she would "go away" it was because she was experiencing a seizure and the medication was doing its job to prevent any outward signs of the seizure such as the Grand Mal.

The continuous EEG recorded "odd behavior" or episodes as well as when Jenny would "go away," the times I was convinced she was having a seizure. However, when the doctors looked at the EEG and compared it to when we pushed the red button, it was clear to them that none of Jenny's behavior had any relation at all to when the seizures would occur. Perhaps this was interesting and helpful to the doctors, but all it did for me was to provide one more thing to worry about. It felt as if someone was pouring salt into an open wound. Indeed something else was causing all of Jenny's "odd behavior." To the doctors, Jenny's condition continued to get even more complicated and more mysterious. To me it was rather simple – the demons inside Jenny's head had a tighter grip on her than I had ever imagined. Before this information became known, it made sense to me that seizures would cause Jenny to "go away." Now it felt as if the demons were actually just taking her away from me and my helplessness increased.

The bottom line is that the mystery grew and the situation continued to get worse.

Like I said, it was complicated.

CHAPTER 21

My aversion to medical terminology

The fact that this book fails to go into many specific details of the actual medical aspect of Jenny's condition is no accident. What became a source of comic relief for many, and perhaps frustration for some, was my inability and outright lack of effort to comprehend the technical terms surrounding what was happening to my daughter. The best example of this is that I called the doctor of Infectious Diseases, "The Germologist." To this day, I don't really know what their title is, and I sincerely apologize to Dr. Baken and Dr. Baker.

More often than not, it was very easy for me to avoid the use of any technical terms and proper pronunciation of words because I usually only listened to the doctors and nurses talk. I avoided explaining things to people and never attempted to use the proper words when I did. My ability to "put it into layman's terms" was more out of necessity than anything else.

In my defense lest anyone think this was a lack of caring about my daughter's condition, I do this in most areas of my life. Anyone that knows me will attest to the fact that I am not "refined" in any way. I am a very simple person. I don't dress well, I don't eat fancy food, and I most certainly do not speak well. In other words, this was not a phenomenon that occurred only during this medical crisis. It pervades everything I do; the best example of which is in my work as a soccer coach. I will reduce a player's name to a single syllable, by any means necessary, even creating nicknames for some players. It is how my youngest daughter Michelle got the nickname Moe when she was 10 years old, and I still call her that to this day.

The vast majority of conversations where I actually had to speak medical jargon aloud were when I needed to ask questions, and this took place most often with the nurses. I think I was too slow to think of questions while the doctors were present and forgot to ask the questions that my family and friends would ask when I was passing along updates. As a result, the nurses who spent most of their time with Jenny in their rotation were very aware that I didn't even try to pronounce things correctly.

My mispronunciations extended to the various drugs Jenny was taking. While Jenny's day-to-day behavior was the main focus for her family members who had to deal with it, the doctors were very concerned about Jenny not having gotten any proper sleep since the day of her admittance to the hospital. Not only did we all desperately want Jenny to sleep, she desperately needed to do so. It was a strange phenomenon to watch a person whose body physically had very little energy and strength left, being completely overridden by a brain that forced it into continuous action.

One method used to help deal with this issue was a drug called Ativan. It was introduced as a sleeping aid, but that ultimately failed and it began to be used simply to calm Jenny down during her most intense episodes. There was a certain amount of the drug that Jenny could have every day, in total, but the size of the doses could be varied. By the second week of Jenny's hospitalization, her episodes were getting so intense that Barb, John, or I could request a dose be administered if we felt we could no longer manage her until it passed. Due to these circumstances, the word Ativan was, by far, the most commonly used medical term I had to say during Jenny's stay.

However, it was at intense times like the episodes that I began to refer to Ativan as Avatar – I used the word Avatar every time I meant to say Ativan. It was not an attempt to be funny in any way – quite the opposite. I actually started doing it when I was very upset. By the time this drug became a fixture in Jenny's daily medical care, the long-term prognosis of Jenny's situation put my personal stress level well beyond anything I could have predicted and it was certainly more than I believed I could handle. Overall, it seemed rather silly for me to put any effort into pronouncing technical medical words properly. It was just easier for me to use a word I was familiar with, Avatar, rather than that weird unfamiliar term, Ativan. Eventually, Avatar became an engrained part of my vocabulary. When I was thinking about something else and simply used the word in a conversation, with anyone, I would call the drug Avatar without giving it any thought at all.

My family was very used to my language issues, but in yet another testament to the patience and compassion shown to me by the nursing staff that cared for Jenny, they allowed me to talk this way to them as well. Any time I used the word Avatar, virtually 100% of the nursing staff knew what I was talking about, but this did not extend to the doctors. It was never a problem until Jenny's situation had gotten so serious that Barb and I were asked to sit down in a conference room with Dr. Beattie to go over a long-term plan. This meeting resulted in a very long and intense conversation in which Dr. Beattie, bless her heart, listened intently to us, and addressed every question and concern Barb and I could think of.

The conversation got to the topic of Jenny not having had anything resembling a good stretch of sleep since April 2nd. I was recalling an event the previous week when Barb, John, and I (as well as the nursing staff) were particularly desperate for a break from Jenny's behavior and a doctor agreed to give Jenny a relatively large dose of Ativan. After it was administered, I distinctly remember hearing the statement, "There – that will knock her out for a few hours." Unfortunately, six hours later Barb and I were exhausted from wrestling with Jenny – she hadn't slowed down for a minute.

Later, during our conversation with Dr. Beattie, my frustration boiled over and I began an angry rant that ended with the statement, "Even the Avatar isn't working anymore!"

An awkward silence descended upon the room...queue the audio track of the crickets!

Dr Beattie stared at me for a few seconds, and I looked back at her, waiting for a response to "my concern." After a bit she turned to Barb. I too looked over at Barb, having no idea why Dr. Beattie had not responded. Barb was sitting with her head down, shaking it back and forth and finally turned to Dr. Beattie and said, "Avatar is what he calls Ativan."

Stop the crickets but continue the stunned silence by Dr. Beattie as she stared at me for a while longer.

I'm sure she had thought I had finally lost my mind due to the stress. The meeting came to a temporary halt while we explained to her that I have a tendency to not use proper technical terms for things that are relatively complicated by my own personal standards. Like anything more complicated than boiling water or making toast.

CHAPTER 22

Day 13

Barb had spent the night with Jenny and I made my usual stop at the hospital in the morning before going to work. This was an attempt at establishing a routine after getting the help of Debbie to stay with Jenny. As it turned out, Jenny had had a particularly bad night in that she, and Barb, experienced more intense episodes as well as deeper times of "going away."

Barb and I talked for a while and decided we both wanted to spend the day with Jenny; the routine had been abandoned immediately. Our excuse was to hang around and meet with the doctor to discuss the events of the past night with her, but I knew that discussion would not bring any new insights. We had sat with Dr. Beattie for nearly an hour the previous afternoon to establish where we were at and what the plan was, and we knew nothing had changed overnight. The doctors had no idea what was causing Jenny's behavioral issues, nor what to do about it; therefore talking about it seemed pointless.

Truth be told, I believe the real reason Barb and I choose to stay at the hospital that morning was that we both knew in our hearts that we were going to completely lose contact with Jenny very soon. Her physical capabilities and mental capacities were slipping away, and by then it was just a matter of "when," not "if" anymore. The results of any test that would confirm a diagnosis was possibly weeks away, and Jenny was deteriorating more each day. At least, for now, we could still reach her at times and we wanted to spend what little time there may be left with "her."

To be clear, there was no indication at this point that Jenny was in any danger of passing away. It was just that the young woman in front of me was no longer my daughter. To a large degree, although I knew that there was a logical medical explanation, I had gotten to the point that I viewed my daughter as being possessed by another being of some sort. I had no idea what exactly that being was, hence, I called them demons; and I knew I didn't like them at all. I wanted them to give me my Jenny back.

So, we simply wanted to spend time with Jenny. We knew that neither of us was going to able to be with her the coming evening. Michelle and I had a soccer practice to run, and Barb and John each had other appointments to keep. We had already arranged for Jane, Barb's sister-in-law, to take the evening shift for us.

Jane arrived around 3 p.m. and I had already left so Barb gave Jane her initiation and some version of "training" for her evening with Jenny. Jane started by doing one of Jenny's favorite things: playing a game. Our family is very big on playing card and board games together, and Aunt Jane has always enthusiastically joined us. Her family might love them even more than we do, and Jenny and Michelle have spent many weekends at Brad and Jane's house for the sole purpose of playing games. It was natural that Jane and Jenny would play a game together, and they had selected Cribbage.

Cribbage is Jenny's favorite game, but the game did not quite go as planned. While Jenny could speak clearly during Jane's time with her, other parts of her brain were not functioning as well. Jane's email report of the Cribbage game attests to this:

> She was not quite making sense. She wanted to play all her cards down in a row and then I could do the same. I was trying to explain that we wouldn't be able to peg any points if we played that way. We finally gave up that game because, according to her, I just didn't get how the game was to be played.

And in this way, Jane was initiated into Jenny's new world. According to Jane, as the night went on:

> She started to throw her stuffed animals at the door and then looked at me as if I knew what came next. She just kept saying, "See?" I would go pick them up and she would do the same thing again. She was becoming very agitated, and then got on the topic that the covers were shrinking and that I was pulling them off her. I told her they were not shrinking that they were just messy so I straightened them all out and she pulled them way up so her feet were showing and said, "See, they are shrinking!" I fixed them again and that was not to her satisfaction so she called Michelle to let her know that I was not letting her cover up with her blankets.

Michelle and I were in the car together when the phone rang. Michelle told me it was Jenny and that she was very annoyed with Jane. I laughed. Taking care of Jenny was no easy task, but I knew she was in good hands. After a while, Michelle put the phone on speaker, and I laughed even harder. Jenny wasn't angry, really, but I could hear the irritation in her voice as she said, "Jane is being unfair and taking all of the blankets from me when I am cold and just want to cover up." She repeated several times that, "Jane stole all the blankets."

Michelle tried to reason with her.

Michelle: "How many blankets are you supposed to have?"

Jenny: "Just one."

Michelle: "How many blankets does Jane have?"

Jenny: "None."

As Michelle and I tried to stifle our laughter so we wouldn't get Jenny even more upset, we could hear Jane in the background trying to explain to Jenny that she had all the blankets on her bed. Michelle and I were both impressed at how calm Jane sounded.

Jenny suddenly stopped talking about the blankets and moved on to her stuffed animals, claiming that Jane was hiding them. Michelle asked Jenny to name the stuffed animals she had, and she went through and named them all. We knew there were too many for her to name without her actually seeing them. When Michelle asked which ones Jane had, Jenny said, "None," but then repeated that Jane was stealing them.

Michelle, always able to reach Jenny no matter what, told Jenny that Jane was there so she didn't have to be alone and that she wasn't stealing anything from her. Jenny seemed to calm, but kept asking Michelle if she was sure that Jane would not steal her blankets again. Michelle said, "Of course," and Jenny hung up.

I found the exchange amusing because I had been through dozens of incidents much worse than this, so it fell well into the category of being funny. Michelle was laughing along with me because it certainly was odd, but she was also a bit uncomfortable and felt bad for Jane because she didn't understand what was happening. As Michelle would say to me later, "I think I was still in denial, believing there wasn't too much wrong with Jenny."

I could certainly understand that. I had been in her shoes not too long before that.

Perhaps I was insensitive, but it took Michelle expressing concern for Jane to bring me around to finally feeling bad enough to give Jane a call. She told me that she was "working through it" and was just fine. Jane had suggested to Jenny that she should get some sleep. She wrapped Jenny up tightly, rubbed her back, and talked softly until she finally went to sleep.

CHAPTER 23

Day 14

The biggest news of the day was that sometime late the night before or early that morning, Jenny was assigned a full-time nurse's aide to be stationed just outside her hospital room door 24 hours a day. This was good news in the sense that whoever was staying with Jenny now had a bit of support and did not need to stay on high alert every minute. However, it did not mean we could leave Jenny alone without a family member present. In fact, our reasons for constantly staying by her side were more valid now than they had been at any time during her stay in the hospital.

Despite the fact that Jenny was losing more and more of her motor skills each day, her behavior was actually more out of control than she had been before – she was just clumsy about it. Our primary goal that Jenny never be restrained by mechanical means remained in place, which meant that it was best for a family member to be present to avoid forcing hospital staff to make those tough decisions. We never feared that any nurse or aide would actually want to restrain Jenny in such a way, but we didn't want them to have to make that call based on what is and isn't safe and acceptable within their stated protocols.

Unfortunately, having to be assigned an aide was a significant sign of how far Jenny had deteriorated. Jenny wasn't bad enough for intensive care (yet), but she did need more attention than the current patient to nurse ratio allowed. The nurse's aide gave the staff more support to be able to monitor Jenny's condition constantly.

In the meantime, the work continued to find the cause of Jenny's illness.

Debbie was back with Jenny for the day, and two tests were scheduled that would require Jenny's full cooperation. This was a concern as Jenny was either having an episode or was "gone" as much, if not more, than she was "with us" these days. Due to lack of sleep and her complete fatigue, Jenny's body could not function normally, yet her brain kept it in almost constant motion.

Yet, right up to the point that Jenny lost all ability to function, I was always amazed at her ability to do what she was absolutely required to do when asked. In much the same way that she acted as normal as she could be when with strangers early in her illness, she managed to do what relative strangers asked of her now.

The first test of the day was a CT scan of her abdomen, and Jenny was not supposed to eat before the scan. This certainly was not a problem, as by this point we nearly had to force her to eat. However, she was supposed to drink an entire container of contrast before the scan, and that was a problem. We were not always successful forcing her to eat or drink anything, as was the case today. Nonetheless, it was determined that Jenny had consumed enough of the contrast to go through with the scan.

Jenny was argumentative and disagreeable when the hospital staff wanted to put her onto the gurney to transport her downstairs for the CT scan. She didn't actually fight the process; she just had other things that she needed to do first. She needed to use the restroom…twice, and then she needed to pack for the trip. Packing was not unusual, because any time Jenny left her room, with rare exception, she needed to pack up some of her friends for the trip.

Sometime during Jenny's first week after being admitted to the hospital, John brought "Buddy Bear," a stuffed bear who has been with her most of her life, from the apartment to help comfort her. The collection of stuffed animals only grew from there. Many of Jenny's visitors chose to bring her a new "friend," and at least these weren't imaginary like the two kids that Jenny thought were constantly playing under her bed. It seemed that nearly every day a new stuffed animal was added to Jenny's collection. No matter how sick she became, even within the deepest recesses of the abyss to which the demons took her, she never forgot about her stuffed animals. Even in the weeks to come when she could not talk or eat and seemed to barely know we were in the room with her, her stuffed animals were a great source of comfort for her.

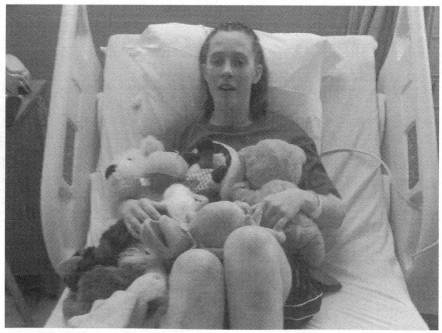

Jenny, with her stuffed animals

Once Jenny was packed for the trip, she reluctantly got onto the gurney to be transported downstairs. On the way there, Jenny appeared to have fallen asleep. I don't recall ever noticing this phenomenon but Debbie pointed out that when Jenny didn't care for what was going on but could not avoid it, sleeping seemed to be a comfortable escape for her. It was amazing to Debbie because of Jenny's nearly complete inability to sleep otherwise. As Debbie saw it, in times of stress Jenny would fall asleep and be limp in the hands of those administering to her.

Jenny proved to be a model patient when she needed to be and the CT scan was completed without incident. She seemed to be asleep as she was wheeled into the room, woke up enough to move from the gurney to the CT scan table, and then appeared to go back to sleep. Debbie had to leave the room at this point, but ten minutes later as they wheeled Jenny out of the lab, she was wide awake, all smiles and happy to see Debbie. The technician said Jenny had done perfectly.

Debbie felt fortunate that the CT scan went well. She knew Jenny was almost always in motion in one way or another so getting through one test without a problem took luck; getting through two would take a miracle. Additionally, the next test created more of a challenge because it was a lumbar puncture. For this, Jenny would need to lie perfectly still, as she did for the CT scan, but for a longer length of time and the consequences were a bit more serious if she chose not to.

Once in the procedure room, Jenny easily transferred to the table from the gurney but was a bit uncomfortable lying on her stomach. She also disliked how far down the technician lowered the top of the basketball shorts she was wearing, which was just below the waist. I am sure it was the location of the waistband that felt odd rather than any modesty issue as nothing potentially embarrassing for her was revealed. The technician would position the shorts where he needed them, and Jenny would reach back and pull them up as he got his equipment ready. The technician would lower them again, and Jenny either would fix them or would ask the technician to fix them. It took a few rounds of this before they were able to convince Jenny that the shorts needed to be in that position to do the test. Eventually she relaxed.

As Debbie was heading out of the room to observe the procedure through a window, she asked Jenny if she needed anything before she left. In yet another sign that my daughter was still in there somewhere, Jenny laughed and requested a shot of tequila. Debbie laughed as well, and was relieved to see that Jenny remained perfectly still during the entire lumbar puncture.

Although the most critical part was over, there still remained one more challenge for Debbie. After a lumbar puncture, the patient is asked to lie flat on their back for at least an hour to avoid headaches. Although Jenny kept trying to get up to do numerous things, Debbie simply had to remind

Jenny that she needed to lie flat so she would not get a headache, and Jenny would respond, "Oh yeah," and lie back down. So as difficult as Jenny could be at times, once again she managed to do exactly what was needed.

We had gotten our miracle that day. It was, admittedly, minor, but we took what we could get and were grateful for it.

CHAPTER 24

Day 15

It seems redundant to say that today Jenny's condition continued to worsen. However, it took on a new feel, and there were various aspects that made it stick out from the previous days, some of which seemed to be related, while some were contradictory.

The most important issue was that Jenny's ability to talk was diminishing. The demons had been attacking her motor skills more and more each day. Her ability to walk on steady legs was of concern, and for a week we had been staying close by her side any time she was out of bed, even aiding her when she used the bathroom. Now the demons seemed to be targeting the one part of her that had allowed us to stay in touch with her – her ability to communicate. Up to this point, at least when she was "with us" we could get an understanding of what she wanted and, more importantly, what she needed, but it had become clear that communication with Jenny was going to be lost any day now.

The demons in her head had a cruel sense of humor, however, because although she couldn't speak clearly, Jenny could sing! Actually it was more was like humming and she would groove to the beat of some unknown music in her head, but at times her humming was so loud that it seemed that the entire 6th floor could hear her. It felt like an extremely odd twist that Jenny was having these short periods of pure happiness. It also felt strange that all of us around her would get some good laughs because of it. While the "singing" was a new development in the previous few days, the timing of it was right before her deterioration was nearly complete. When I look back on it now, I feel like we were actually being teased by the demons in her head with the seemingly happy humming, because in the course of just a few days Jenny was unable to speak at all or even make any intelligible noises such as the humming.

Jenny's appetite had been dwindling every day for over a week, but now the deterioration of her motor skills made eating a laborious task especially without assistance. In part, she had no desire to eat, so there was little motivation for her to work at it. In addition, even when she did try, she had a hard time hitting her mouth with the utensil she was using.

School had let out early because of the weather so Michelle headed home for the weekend in spite of the road conditions and arrived at the hospital ahead of Barb and me that day. Debbie was there with Jenny so the three of them hung out in Jenny's room.

The IV technician showed up to replace yet another IV for Jenny. These typically needed to be replaced every three or four days anyway, but it was rare for Jenny to leave one alone that long. Much of the stress of keeping an eye on her was due to Jenny's propensity to reach for the IV and pull it out, which was another reason that it seemed a good idea to have a family member nearby at all times. The nurses and nurse's aides would do what they could, but even with the one-on-one aide located outside the door there was no way to stay close enough to prevent Jenny from pulling on them.

The job of replacing Jenny's IV took four hands, as Jenny was not being cooperative. Nurse Andi was in the room lending a hand to soothe as well as manage Jenny while the IV tech reattached the line. Even though Jenny was rather irritated with Andi and the IV tech, she was humming loudly and otherwise appeared happy, as if she were out enjoying a beautiful day in the park. Debbie and Michelle had to kind of laugh at the spectacle of Jenny struggling slightly with the nurses but humming in a happy-go-lucky way.

Anyone that knows our family well would attest to the fact that Jenny is too much like her dad in many ways but primarily in that she tends to dress extremely casually. While she can and does know how to dress up when she needs to, she is an athlete through and through and will choose to wear a pair of basketball shorts over a pair of jeans any day of the week. When it came to her hair, Jenny was not too particular. She would comb it, and a simple ponytail was her standard style. A few bobbie-pins would be used to corral the loose pieces up front, but never much more fanfare than that.

In light of Jenny's fashion standards, Debbie's journal about the events of that morning is actually somewhat comical as it shows Jenny's mindset was in sharp contrast to her normal personality; in addition to demonstrating Debbie's patience:

We had an interesting morning after your dad left. Your hair was driving you crazy! We spent almost two hours getting every small piece of hair under control and tied down so that it wasn't bothering you. I'm not much of a "girly" girl, and so carry very little makeup and hair stuff in my purse. You wanted a hair tie, bobby pins, etc. to pull your hair back and up off your face. We found a hair tie and one bobby pin, but because of your haircut, there were MANY loose ends to tie up. I remembered that I had put a headband in my computer bag to use if my hair started to drive me crazy as it had on more than one occasion the past few days while trying to attend to your needs. I gave that to you, which worked wonders, but there were still a few hairs that kept falling on the back of your neck that you needed another bobby pin for. I cleaned out my purse looking for anything that would work, and finally found a barrette that did the job. It was quite the adventure, but you were finally content that your hair was under control and you settled in to watch TV. Shortly after that, you fell asleep. You slept a very short time but woke up when you heard me talking to Michelle. Michelle came around noon-thirty. When you woke up, you were not entirely there, and still bothered by your hair because there was one more small piece tickling your neck. Michelle found another bobby pin and we had it all under control again.

Another portion of her journal also gives a great indication of how Jenny's mind was working…and why it was so heartbreaking for everyone around her to watch what she would go through:

You dozed on and off, and then suddenly you got out of bed, put on a hooded sweatshirt and some sweatpants, gathered up your Nook, a book, your water and a box of tissues and started heading for the door. When I asked where you were going, you said you were going to the living room to read for a while. I said, "Okay, well let me get my book and I'll go with you." Michelle said she would wait for us in the room.

You took me right to the lounge just a few doors down the hall and you settled into a chair and set yourself up to read. I pulled up a chair next to you and we both started our reading. A short while later you started to cry softly, and when I asked you what was wrong you said you were so confused. I asked why, and you said, "Because I'm not at home and this isn't my living room." I asked if you wanted to go back to your room and you said yes. So, we gathered up your things and went back. You, Michelle, and I hung out for the rest of the afternoon. You ate a great lunch and ate almost all of it, which was rare, and around 4:30 p.m., we agreed I should leave and Michelle would stay until your mom, John and/or dad arrived.

Later, when Michelle was getting ready to leave because John had arrived, Jenny looked at Michelle, and kept repeating, "I'm sorry," over and over. Michelle asked Jenny what she was sorry for and Jenny responded that she was sorry that she was in the hospital and all she ever wanted to do was be a good big sister and that she can't do that while in the hospital. It was moments like these that took us to our lowest levels emotionally.

There are times that when we look back and have the perspective created by the time that has passed, our actions at the time speak volumes about where each of our individual mental states were. One event that has really stuck with me was something Debbie reminded me of months after this was over.

On Thursday, April 18th, the neurologist left a note for Barb and me in Jenny's room. I usually stayed to talk to the doctor during their first visit of the day, but that morning I had had to leave the hospital sooner than usual and had missed my usual talk with him. On the note were the technical names of two illnesses, one of which the team of doctors believed Jenny

103

would ultimately be diagnosed with. The tests sent out to the labs two days prior were checking for both illnesses, and ultimately one of them would come back positive.

In light of the fact that the note contained the first semblance of an answer as to what illness might be causing the devastation to my daughter, one might assume that I treasured that piece of paper as if it were The Holy Grail. That, however, was not the case. In fact, it wasn't until Debbie reminded me about the incident, almost a year later, that I distinctly remembered her giving me that note. Ironically, that is the last I remember of it. I know she gave it to me. Barb does not remember me passing it on to her and I have absolutely no recollection of what I did with it. Obviously, the note was not that important to me, which forced me to revisit how I was thinking during that phase, and I believe it says something about this journey.

While my casual treatment of the note might be considered by some as careless, it helps to understand all factors going on during this phase of the process.

First, the names were written in "doctoreze," and I cannot explain how tired I was of trying to decipher all the terminology that had been thrown at me during that time. My daughter was extremely ill and it was getting more serious every day. I was worried about Jenny and the medical terms did nothing for me. However, while I had known that I had become a person who was only interested in the "bottom line" and technical terms clouded my thinking more than anything, I had no idea it had reached that point.

I was also tired of what had come to feel like "guessing" at a possible diagnosis over the previous week and a half. I never doubted the doctors and I understood why the task was so difficult, but I was really tired of the various "possibilities" they presented only to tell me later that the test results had come back negative. Exacerbating the problem, non-medical people outside of the hospital, including my own family members, continually recommended that I "make sure the doctors checked for…" It seemed like everyone who knew Jenny was sick and was aware that the doctors were having a hard time finding the cause had an opinion about what it was. I know everyone meant well, and I truly appreciated their suggestions, but I am not sure why they thought they knew something the doctors didn't when no one had more than about 10% of the information that the doctors had shared with Barb and me. The result of all of these suggestions was that I worked hard at blocking everyone out and apparently, I even started ignoring the "guesses" coming from the doctors themselves. Of course, it should have hit me that this note from the doctor was different, but the complete exhaustion that was setting in, physical and mental, caused me to miss it.

CHAPTER 25

Day 16

Two journal entries by Michelle got me thinking about topics I am sure I would not have considered writing about in this book had I not read them. The first, which I had forgotten about, was the issue of what, when, and how to begin to inform people about Jenny's condition and how my delay to do so became a burden in and of itself.

The second topic was something that I probably chose not to consider, and perhaps even blocked from my mind altogether. It was the literal and figurative price Jenny's illness forced everyone involved to pay. Surprisingly, those "involved" included not only Jenny and her immediate family, as the demons reached far beyond the walls of the hospital to extract a price from people who had never even met Jenny:

Saturday, April 20, 2013
I don't sleep very well. Compared to you, mom, and dad I'm sure I get plenty. I tried to keep dad occupied today. We had soccer and soccer and more soccer. It made him really happy. I know it's his escape during all of this. So many of the parents would come over, talk about you, and ask about you. It's so hard to explain to them that we don't have an answer so we can't give them one. People don't understand how that can be. In my head, I just want to scream, "TRY BEING HER FAMILY!" When we say Jenny isn't doing well, they want to know why. I'm sick of talking to people about it, but I don't know how to be nice about asking people not to ask me about it. You didn't eat much today. You get up and down a lot, mostly going to the bathroom. Now just waiting for the blood tests.

Sunday, April 21, 2013
I had to leave again today. It breaks my heart more than I can say. Dad and I went to church in the morning. I knew dad really didn't want to go because of all the questions people ask. He was right. It was overwhelming. I knew we would get questions but I didn't know so many people knew about what was going on with you. It was truly humbling to hear Pastor Jon pray for you and our family in front of everyone. I got choked up, but I knew everyone would ask again once church was over. We hustled out trying to avoid people. On our way out, I heard so many people whispering about you and looking at us. I felt like I was in middle school again and everyone was talking about me. We had dinner at the hospital, and you slept a lot

of the day, which is good. You are starting to look so tired and exhausted. I know you want to sleep but I think your mind isn't turning off and not allowing you to sleep. They are talking drugs and things to get you some rest. Before I left, we went for a walk in the halls. I took a picture of you and dad walking, and you heard the phone snap the picture, so you insisted on taking a picture, so we took a picture together in the hall. It was the perfect ending to my visit this weekend.

The primary focus of Michelle's journal entry is informing "acquaintances" of the details of Jenny's illness. Truth be told, it never dawned on me that this would become an issue until a few days before the situation at church that Michelle described, but by then it was a bigger issue than I felt prepared to deal with at the time.

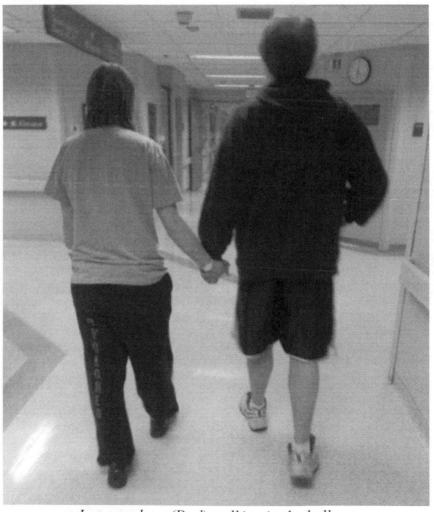

Jenny and me (Dad) walking in the hallway

In the beginning, I was convinced "This will all be over in a couple days," and thought mentioning it to anyone was unnecessary. As time went on and the illness progressed but we continued to lack a diagnosis, I had no idea what to say, or how to say it. We were struggling enough with how to keep close family members up to date. There was a stretch of time that the presumed diagnosis changed even before we could inform everyone about the last one, and it reached a point that I just decided to wait until we knew something for sure. Of course I never dreamed that "knowing for sure" was weeks away.

Beyond close family and friends, the truth of the matter is that it never even dawned on me to inform anyone else. I wasn't keeping it a secret, but I didn't have a Facebook page back then, and neither Barb nor Michelle was heavily involved in any social media. In simple terms, I really didn't know anyone was that interested.

Rockford is small enough and my family's level of community involvement was such that I knew a few people would know who we were and would hear about it. However, I never thought so many people would be so interested in "details," which, of course, we were sorely lacking. Most people who learned of the situation did so through normal everyday activities such as the traveling soccer team I was coaching. Nonetheless, I underestimated how many people wanted to know more than what was "public information" and the number grew every day. Perhaps my inability to grasp this was because most of my energy at the time was focused on Jenny, and what was left was not spent pondering making "public statements." I simply wasn't paying attention.

Debbie, Michelle, and our pastor, Jon Rhodes, had been pushing me to create a page for Jenny on CaringBridge for about a week prior to this, but what finally opened my eyes was when the lack of information started affecting the soccer team. I'm not sure why this triggered a reaction while Michelle and Debbie telling me did not, but the parents had legitimate questions and concerns about Jenny and the only time they saw me to ask was at practices. Eventually a good amount of time at the beginning of every practice was spent giving updates about Jenny rather than helping the girls improve their game.

However, what happened that Sunday at church was what finally forced me to address the issue. The uncomfortable feelings and perhaps even anger that Michelle expressed in her journal was real, but there was no real animosity toward the people around us. I realized that people cared about what was happening and had very fair questions. The problem was that we had no details and no answers. There was nothing to say. I never would have imagined how hard it would be to have this type of conversation with people….over and over again.

All of this added up to the simple fact that at least a general acknowledgment of what was happening and a uniform "public" explanation was necessary. I began seriously considering the CaringBridge page in the car on my way home from church that Sunday. However, the initial mass public statement – if I can call it that – was earlier that week when I decided I would write an email to the soccer team right before each practice. They included the latest news about Jenny, and proved to stop the time-consuming conversations with parents before practices.

When I did the first one, something strange and unexpected happened – I learned that writing about what was happening was very therapeutic for me. To my surprise, I discovered that I not only enjoyed it, I needed it as an outlet.

I was going to proceed cautiously and ponder my next step (and definitely not go to church the next Sunday), but then Michelle posted, "Prayers for Jenny" on her Facebook page later that week and the situation became impossible to ignore. My phone lit up with text messages and my email inbox began to fill up. Once that happened, creating the CaringBridge page saved me time.

Michelle's journal entry also hit me very hard on another front. I began to ponder the price Jenny paid because of this illness, as well as the price I, and those around me, paid.

The "soccer" Michelle referred to was the U14 girls team I was coaching at the time this journey began. It was my first year with the team. I had started with them in February with indoor training and the indoor league in which the team played. Minnesota was experiencing one of the longest, coldest, and wettest springs in recent history, so it seemed to take forever to get to outdoor training. The day Michelle wrote about was our first day outside so everyone was happy to hit the field, especially me. In addition, earlier that day I had run a practice for another team and had coached an indoor game. It really had been a full day of soccer – it was wonderful!

Soccer has always been my escape. I love the game and I love coaching it, as I have for over 20 years. At the same time, I knew that my resignation from the team was inevitable. Perhaps I held on a week too long, but I was selfishly reluctant to give up the little slice of joy I had in my life at the time. It is never a good idea for a team to switch coaches once a season has begun, but it is a worse idea once league play has started, and games were set to begin in a couple of weeks. By this time, it was very clear that Jenny's journey would be a long one. I had already missed enough work and had many responsibilities there, and there really was not room for all of this in my life. My resignation happened a week later.

Thus, Michelle's journal also reminded me that I was forced to walk away from a soccer team that I grew to love very quickly and needed to stop doing what I consider my hobby. Some people go fishing. I coach! It is something I am passionate about and from which I draw a huge amount of personal satisfaction. I enjoy the process of helping a team as well as the individuals develop as players and people. In addition, this was a very special group of girls who were proving to be extremely coachable and they were developing quickly. Jenny's illness was now affecting more than just the people who loved her.

It goes without saying that Jenny's illness extracted a huge price from all of us. Of course, Jenny paid the biggest price, an immeasurable price. However, each and every one of us in my, Barb's, and John's family paid a price because of Jenny's illness. It came in different forms, but we all had to remit something. Of course, as parents, not only does it not matter what the price was, we didn't even think about it, especially as it was happening. Parents are willing to pay any price for their children.

Only a small portion of the price Jenny paid is laid out in the pages of this book, and I can only speak in generalities of the price John and Michelle paid. Barb is a mother, and her pain is likely different from mine, and probably something I cannot fully understand. I know she was the rock through this whole thing, so she had to get some of the tab that I was responsible for as well. Barb paid more than me in many ways.

Now there was proof in Michelle's journal that not only family were affected by Jenny's illness. Other people whom our lives touch also paid, and some of them may not have ever met Jenny. The list of everyone who suffered because of Jenny's illness is as difficult to quantify as it is to determine how much each individual was hurt. I can only speak with any authority about the price I paid. However, I don't need to look far for who else was affected: my business partner was a victim in the added burden she had to carry; and the soccer team in the sense that they lost at least some development in their game with the upheaval of a new coach coming in mid-season. These people did not ask to be involved with Jenny in any way, but they could not walk away from the situation either. I had never thought about this subject before, but once I did, I was forced to multiply it by all of us who are close to Jenny. Truly, the demons in Jenny's head had a very long reach and they were indiscriminate in who they hurt.

CHAPTER 26

Day 18

It was April 22nd, 27 days since Jenny's first seizure.

I didn't realize it at the time, but in hindsight, it was evident the doctors were confident that they had identified Jenny's illness. We were still waiting for the results of the tests on the specimens sent out the week before, but Barb, John, and I expected additional steps to be taken in the meantime. As I review the medical records it is clear that the doctors had essentially stopped looking for any new causes for Jenny's condition. I still do not know if this was because the selection of illnesses to test for had simply been a process of elimination and they had run out of ideas, or because they were confident that one of the latest tests would come back positive.

We probably should have known that we were now simply waiting. The neurologist had left us a note about it on Thursday, but somehow Barb and I missed it. Some of the events of the rest of the week look different now than they did at the time. Some of the conversations with doctors have a different feel now when I consider that perhaps they assumed I had read the note from the neurologist and we knew that they had narrowed the possibilities down to two illnesses.

In reality, not knowing was probably a good thing. My emotions were already shot and although I knew we were waiting for the latest test results to come back and I was somewhat aware the doctors were optimistic, I did not have the same anticipation they did so I was not counting the days until the tests were returned. Instead, I remained focused on the day-to-day, which was easier for me.

Jenny continued to keep us busy. Sometime between Sunday evening and Monday morning, Jenny stopped talking and writing clearly enough to be understood the majority of the time. She continued to work hard to find ways to make her point, but when she talked, she sounded like someone who had just experienced a severe stroke. Episodes lasted longer now, and she was more physical during them. Her diminished ability to talk was attributed to the illness attacking the portion of her brain that controlled her fine motor skills, but despite losing a significant amount of coordination, her strength and determination remained intact. To top it off, Jenny was, once again, hooked up to the continuous EEG, which created the added burden of keeping the probes and tether intact while wrestling with her.

Debbie was back watching Jenny during the day, and one episode got so difficult that she had to have the help of both the nurse and the nurse's aide to keep Jenny from tearing out her EEG probes as well as her IV. A short time later, Jenny "packed up" to go home. Although packing was a fairly common occurrence, on this occasion, despite her lack of motor skills, Jenny was able to gather up all of her stuffed animals, her Nook, a book, some magazines, and all her blankets; then, holding her bundle in her arms, she was ready to head for the door. Another battle ensued, both physical and mental. Jenny was able to communicate enough that Debbie knew Jenny was pleading with her to help her leave the hospital and go home, a plea that would tug at anyone's heart. The results of these events always became a standoff so it was followed by the inevitable physical struggle to keep Jenny in the room once she had decided she was leaving. Whenever Jenny was connected to the continuous EEG, this became even more difficult because of the limited reach of the cable attached to "Emu," and after an extended struggle to get around Debbie and the aide while still holding all of her things, Jenny finally collapsed on her bed in exhaustion.

These were the worst battles, not because of their physical nature but because of Jenny's condition. She was unable to speak clearly enough to request the simplest thing, like help going to the bathroom, but she was always able to make it perfectly clear that she had had enough of the hospital and only wanted to go home. She would look at us, her eyes pleading for help. It was what made me think that despite the outward appearance of her body, Jenny was still inside there somewhere, perfectly aware of what was happening and just wanting to escape. Everyone shared the desire to take Jenny down to the street and run as far away as possible with her, and it felt as if we were holding her captive. The battles to keep her in her room always ended with feelings similar to depression for the person who was the designated warden at the moment.

Sometimes miscommunication led to unintended consequences for Jenny and all of us caring for her. One of the cruelest twists of events was the lack of communication between the family, the EEG technicians, and the neurologists who ordered the continuous EEGs. One thing that remained almost constant throughout Jenny's hospitalization was her desire to walk the hallways, which was related to her desire to leave the hospital in that at least she was able to leave her room. It was rare for Jenny and whoever her caretaker was at any given time to go for longer than an hour without walking the hall. However, because the cable that connected the EEG probes in Jenny's head to the monitoring and recording equipment was only 30-feet long, any time Jenny was connected to it, walks in the hallway were not an option. The vast majority of patients are probably hooked up to this unit for a single stint of a day or two, and quite possibly have the mental reasoning to stay in their room during this relatively short time. But Jenny was attached to the continuous EEG for a total of nearly five weeks during her hospitalization, and she was far from willing to stay in her room.

The very first day that Jenny was hooked up to the device I had asked the EEG technician if there was any way at all to allow Jenny to continue on her hallway walks during these times. As it turned out, the technician is not allowed to inform the patient that the cable can, in fact, be disconnected for short periods of time and the small box on the end of the tether that Jenny would carry with her would go into record mode. For reasons I am not clear on, the technician failed to communicate with us that we could ask the doctor for permission, so none of us ever did.

Thus, it was not until Jenny's fourth week on the 6th floor that we coincidentally fell into a conversation with a doctor about the issue and were told we could disconnect the cable and take Jenny for walks. That very simple lack of communication had a very inconsequential effect on Jenny's medical care, but a dramatic effect on the mental state of both Jenny as well as the people caring for her day in and day out during that stretch. In some small way, it was one of the worst stretches of Jenny's stay in the hospital.

In spite of Jenny's decreased ability to communicate and function, there were various behaviors she would exhibit that made me think that Jenny was actually thinking clearly inside her head. One of those behaviors was how sneaky she could be.

Often, after an extended battle that would end only because she was exhausted, she would fall into her bed and appear to be going to sleep. Of course, since I was as tired as she was if not more, I would go to the recliner to take a break. As much as I wanted to rest, it was times like those that I needed to keep an even closer eye on her and not get distracted or let my attention to what she was doing wander. Jenny would usually roll onto her side with her back to me in what I assumed was a sleeping position, but more often than not, she was simply shielding me from being able to see that she was pulling out her IV or EEG probes. The wrestling match would start all over again.

The danger of Jenny manipulating me like that was almost constant, even at night, yet for some reason it always surprised me. As Jenny's condition got worse, I would feel bad for her and assume she could no longer be sneaky and conniving, but she was able to plot various maneuvers to fool me despite her condition. Perhaps it was the demons in control, trying to disrupt the search for a way to destroy them.

One problem that the doctors at Methodist Hospital never solved during Jenny's entire stay was how to get her to sleep for an extended period of time. The concept of using various drugs as sleeping aids was actually much easier said than done. Jenny's condition required certain medications for her vital organs to function properly, and the drugs that could be used to "knock her out" would counteract or over stimulate the required drugs, causing severe, even life-threatening complications. Therefore, sleep was never an option unless she chose to rest. Ativan was used on a regular basis in an attempt to make her more manageable, but it had a limited effect on her. I often wondered if it had any effect at all; perhaps when we saw her "calm down," it was simply that the episode had run its course or she had just exhausted herself. We'll never know.

Jenny's fixations started to take on a new form. On this Monday, Debbie had to deal with Jenny's obsession with washing her hands so often that her hands were bright pink. Debbie constantly checked the water temperature to make sure it wasn't too hot and relayed this information to me that evening when I returned to the hospital. I realized that I had failed to inform her that the hospital staff had set the water temperature so it couldn't get too hot.

In addition, Jenny woke up from one of her short naps convinced that Debbie had allowed her to fall out of bed. Of course, Debbie assured her that she had not fallen out of bed, but this was a wasted effort. Jenny scolded Debbie for letting her fall out of bed as she began making and unmaking her bed. This particular obsession had become a common occurrence over the past couple of weeks. Jenny would tuck in the sheets and blankets all around the edges, making sure they were all tight. She would then lie down and cover up for a moment before getting out of bed, pulling all the sheets and blankets completely off the bed and starting the routine all over again. On this occasion, it went on for over an hour before Jenny was exhausted and dozed off again for another five-minute nap after which she woke up, looked at Debbie, and said, "Hi! How are you today?" as if Debbie had just arrived.

CHAPTER 27

Day 19 – Part 1

Considering how complicated Jenny's condition was, I always marveled at the doctors' and nurses' ability to keep everything straight. Things changed so rapidly, yet everyone was usually on the same page. Mercifully, the use of computers ensured that the various medications administered were properly managed, and at one point Jenny's medications alone required two and a half pages of notes. Yet, on other fronts, miscommunication took place occasionally.

I believe that, for the most part, my family and I were not difficult for the doctors, nurses and other hospital staff to deal with. We had our moments, to be sure, but we appreciated the work they were doing and did our best to stay out of their way. While Jenny was a patient at Methodist, we witnessed a number of incidences when other patients' family members treated the nurses and staff less than respectfully. I feel confident in saying that we always did our best to never let that happen.

Yet, there were the occasional situations that came about because of miscommunication. Looking back on all of the events now, especially considering how complicated the entire situation was, I am amazed at how rarely miscommunications took place. But another thing that amazed me were the problems that ensued as a result of oftentimes very simple pieces of information being left out of a conversation. One such event took place on the morning of April 23rd. I had spent the night with Jenny and I was tired, which played a factor in my response to the situation, but was in no way the cause of it.

As usual, I had been waiting around for the daily morning visit with the doctor. Jenny had been scheduled for a PET scan that day, and during the night I had gone through some notes and had asked a nurse to answer some questions for me about any other tests Jenny might be scheduled for. The results of my research showed there was very little else planned. A very relevant fact in this story that needs to be understood is that the doctors were relatively sure they had solved the mystery as to the cause of Jenny's illness, and were simply waiting for the test results to come back. However, due to my failure to read the message from the doctor that was given to me by Debbie the day before, I did not know this at the time.

I had heard of a PET scan, and I understood it was a full body scan used most often for cancer patients, but other than that small piece of information, I knew nothing about them. It was very clear by this time that whatever illness Jenny had was located in her brain. There was no doubt in my mind about this, both because of how she was acting and because of some of the medical information the doctors had shared with me. As a result of the many MRIs and CT scans, I was positive Jenny did not have a brain tumor, so I was confused by the decision for a PET scan. That didn't mean I didn't want her to have the test; on the contrary, the doctors could perform all the tests they wanted. I just wanted my kid to get better as fast as possible. And given the lack of anything else on the schedule, I was anxious for something, anything, to be happening. The irony was that although I had absolutely no understanding whatsoever as to why the PET scan was needed, it was very important to me that it be done.

Ultimately, I met with the neurologist, Dr. Worley, in our usual morning meeting. The fact that the PET scan was on the schedule was discussed, but I have no notes from the meeting and have no recollection of the details of "why" it was being done. It may have been discussed, but I had just pulled an all-nighter, so I either misunderstood what was said, or simply didn't remember.

After Dr. Worley departed, I was waiting for Debbie to arrive to take watch over Jenny so I could head home. After a bit a nurse came in and informed me that I was to wait for a meeting with "the hospitalist," which irritated me.

Let me share a bit of my history with hospitalists, whom I didn't even know existed or was a real word before Jenny was a patient at Methodist Hospital. My very first meeting with a hospitalist took place during Jenny's first week in the hospital and did not go well. He arrived in Jenny's room literally two minutes after Dr. Freking had left, and without any greeting, introduction, or explanation whatsoever about who he was or why he was there, he proceeded to repeat, verbatim, what Dr. Freking had just told us. Barb and I were polite and let him have his say. He seemed surprised when we did not have any questions, but Dr. Freking had just answered all of them for us. He left the room, and we had to track down the nurse to have it explained to us who he was.

As Jenny's illness became more and more complicated, the doctors within certain specialties, mainly the various neurologists on Jenny's case, would spend a significant amount of time with us each day going over many details. By the second or third week, the meetings had been moved out of Jenny's room into more private conference areas, and some days lasted an hour or more. Thus, by the time the hospitalist would appear, we were tired, stressed, scared, had already received information overload from the earlier meeting, and simply needed time to digest all that we had heard. However, for some reason we felt obligated to allow the hospitalist to retell us what we already knew. More often than not, whenever we actually did have a question or when something was said by the hospitalist that contradicted what we had been told by a doctor, the hospitalist could not answer our question regarding that contradiction.

I mean no disrespect, but my attitude at this moment in the story needs to be understood, as it plays a key role in what happened on this day. I was driven largely by fatigue and stress, along with concern for the serious condition my daughter was in. I am sure that a hospitalist serves a very important purpose, although it was never really explained to me and, admittedly, I have never pursued an answer to what that is. I am guessing that the idea is so that the specialists can keep moving and see as many patients as possible, while the hospitalist serves as the knowledgeable liaison between the doctor and the patient to spend as much time as needed to answer questions.

It is also very important to point out that by the time this entire journey was over, I would be in great debt to the hospitalists at Methodist and the role they played in our lives. However, on this day, at this point in Jenny's story and my experience with hospitalists, I wasn't there yet.

We were very fortunate during Jenny's hospitalization in that her case was so unique that we were almost always the first stop in the morning and the last stop of the day for the neurologists, the primary doctors on Jenny case. In addition, when the nurses paged a neurologist, they always seemed to answer quickly. This was not the case with the hospitalists – these were the doctors we had to stand and wait for, with no clue as to when they would magically appear.

Since I had met with the neurologist already that morning, I saw no need to meet with the hospitalist, but I honored the request by the nurse to wait for his arrival; it was something I had never been asked to do before so I figured it was for a significant reason. I was tired and stressed out because I seriously needed to get home to shave and shower and then get to work. Debbie had arrived to stay with Jenny, and that was my signal that I could be on my way to try to meet some of the other obligations in my life.

When the hospitalist finally arrived, a major piece of miscommunication occurred. As it turned out, all he had come to tell me was the PET scan had been cancelled. That was it; nothing else. I must admit, at that moment I was most irritated that I had to miss even more work while waiting for news that a nurse could have given me. But as long as he was there, I wanted to know why it had been cancelled. The miscommunication that took place was because the only information that he had as to why was "the insurance company had refused to pay for the test." I went insane!

I would not find out until the next day how incomplete that information was, yet because of my fear of everything going on and the multitude of unknowns surrounding it, I completely overreacted to the situation. My totally inaccurate perception of the situation had two parts to it: The first was that now that this test had been cancelled I had come to believe that the doctors had given up looking for additional causes to Jenny's illness and simply were standing by and doing nothing while waiting for test results to come back. Yet, it was the second incorrect perspective I had of the situation that was the crux of the melt-down that ensued that morning; my belief was that the bill for caring for Jenny was getting too high and the insurance company wanted to wait until the other tests came back before they paid for any additional ones.

Before explaining what happened as a result of this, let's make it clear where the actual miscommunication came in. The first issue was that the PET scan facilities are very expensive to operate, and due to Jenny's condition there was little to no chance of Jenny sitting still long enough for the scan to be performed properly. There had been many cancelled MRIs due to her inability to lie still long enough. The result was that it was, correctly, believed to be a waste of time to even attempt it. In addition, a PET scan requires a patient to drink radioactive material, which requires them to be by themselves during the scan itself, and then for several hours after it is over. Jenny couldn't be by herself for several seconds much less several hours. As a result of these two factors, it actually was the technician who was to perform the scan that made the call to cancel. Once the technician cancelled the procedure for very practical reasons, the insurance request that had originally been granted, also needed to be officially cancelled. But all that the hospitalist saw was the cancellation from the insurance company, which was what he relayed to me.

See, just a simple miscommunication…and, as I said, I went insane!

Jenny had fallen into what appeared to be a deep sleep, possibly her defense mechanism to avoid the stress that clearly existed in the room at the moment, so Debbie quickly asked us to step out of the room as my voice began to rise. We stepped into the hallway, closed the door, and walked about 20-feet down the hall. Debbie could still hear me yelling.

I have to give the hospitalist credit, he was extremely patient with me. He tolerated my screaming, blaming, and tears very well and let me vent. Even the nurses were wonderful. They just closed the doors to all the patients' rooms and let me have my say. No one ever told me to stop or even asked me to move to a lounge. The confrontation in the hallway went on for almost an hour before I calmed down and we moved back into Jenny's room to wrap up the conversation, which included me asking why everyone suddenly appeared to be doing so little for Jenny. I was tired, had lost perspective, and was very wrong in that statement, and his response to my question and what happened next will stick with me for the rest of my life.

As we shook hands he said, "I promise you, everyone in this hospital is aware of Jenny's case and is doing all they can to help her get better." I had enough perspective left to realize that it was very nice of him to say, but although in my heart I knew he was being sincere and truthful, I did not take him literally.

I was running extremely late for a work appointment. On my way down in the elevator, I had legitimate concerns about my ability to stay awake for the drive home so I decided to swing through the cafeteria to pick up a cup of coffee. I hadn't shaved in over five days and hadn't showered in two, so God only knows what I looked and smelled like that morning, but I'm sure I stuck out like a sore thumb.

As I was paying for my coffee, the cashier said, "Do you mind if I ask you a question?"

"No, of course not."

"Aren't you the father of the girl on the 6th floor?"

I was stunned. I am not even sure I responded. I had been positive that the hospitalist was referring to the doctors and nurses within the facility when he said that "everyone" was aware of Jenny's case, but even at that, I hadn't taken him literally. For a brief moment, I felt as if, indeed, everyone knew about Jenny and her case. It was an overwhelming, shocking, and scary feeling as on this day I was not hopeful for a happy ending. Sad news travels as far and as fast as bad news, and in Jenny's case, this was obviously both.

As it turned out, the individuals who staff the hospital cafeteria work side-by-side with all of the individuals in the kitchen that cook the food for the patients, including those who deliver the food to the rooms. Obviously, since food is delivered three times a day and Jenny had been a patient for nearly three weeks by this time, some of the kitchen staff had seen Jenny in the midst of her episodes, so stories about her were shared – even with the cashier in the cafeteria.

CHAPTER 28

Day 19 – Part 2

Debbie had her hands full with Jenny after I left the hospital. The events of this day were not unique, but once again, Debbie's journal offers a clear glimpse of what it was like to care for Jenny during this time.

You were relatively subdued for most of the morning, but kept getting in and out of bed and wandering around the room. When I would ask you if you needed something or where you were going, you would look at me blankly and then get back into bed. You kept trying to use the TV remote but for some reason could not make it do what you wanted it to do. You ran through the channels many, many, MANY times, and then would stop and look at me and say, "See? Do you see that? What is wrong with this thing?" You never stopped at a station long enough for it to "tune in" (digital cable that took a few moments to lock onto the station when you would change the channel) so all I ever saw when you would ask me that question was a black screen. You did this numerous times, and I asked you each time if I could help you find what you were looking for. You refused each time, telling me it was broken. Eventually you got so frustrated you started to cry, rolled onto your side away from me, and said you were tired. I covered you up, and you asked for Horton (one of your stuffed animals) and you curled up around him and appeared to be trying to sleep.

As I mentioned, I had gotten into the habit of watching you incessantly, and was doing that again even though you appeared to be sleeping. You suddenly turned your head, looked at me, and said, "Why are you staring at me?" I told you I was just making sure you were okay. You turned away again and appeared to go to back to sleep. A nurse came in and wanted to take your vitals, and I asked her to come back in a while because you had just gone to sleep. While I was distracted by the nurse, you started to pick at your IV that was currently in your left wrist (it was moved many times during your stay, even more than once a day sometimes). As I turned back to look at you I noticed this and reminded you not to pick at it. You again appeared to go back to sleep. Shortly after that, the aide stepped in and whispered that she was going to take her break, but to just push the call button if I needed help while she was gone.

Shortly after the aide left, you woke up, stood up on the side of the bed opposite of where I was, and appeared to be looking out the window. I walked around the bed to see what you were looking at and saw that you were trying to pull the IV out of your arm. I took your hands in mine and reminded you again that you can't take it out. You said you needed it out because it hurt. I said we will have a nurse come and look at it, and as I let go of one of your hands to push the call button, you immediately tried to get at the IV again with your free hand. I got the button pushed and was able to get a hold on your free hand again before you pulled the IV out. We stood there like that for a short time, you struggling to get your hands free of mine and me trying to convince you that I would let go of your hands if you promised not to try to pull out the IV. The nurse came in, responding to the call button, and helped me get you to lie down on the bed. You appeared to calm down and relax, and when I released your hands, you didn't try to go for the IV again. I was sitting on the edge of the bed with you, and remained there after letting go of your hands. You asked why I was sitting there and I said I just needed to be a little closer to you for a while. You closed your eyes, and after a few minutes, your breathing led me to believe you had fallen asleep. I stayed on the edge of the bed, not wanting to disturb you or get too far away in case you tried to remove the IV again.

The aide came back and checked in, and even though we had a short discussion, you didn't stir, so I got off the bed and moved to the chair next to your bed where I usually sat. As I got off the bed, you turned onto your side but still appeared to be sleeping. After about ten minutes, I noticed you were moving a bit, but couldn't see what you were doing. I said your name, and asked if you were awake. You didn't respond, but I could still see movement under the blanket. I walked around to the other side of the bed and saw that you had pulled one of the EEG contacts off your forehead and were starting on another one. I took your hand and told you that you couldn't pull those off, they were there to help you. You started to try to get at the contact with your other hand so I took that hand in my other hand. You started to struggle and said you wanted them off, that you NEEDED them off. I kept trying to calm you down and tell you that they had to stay on, but you were intent on getting them off and really started to get agitated. You began moaning, softly at first, then gradually getting louder and louder. I was talking to you, asking you to calm down and I would let go of your hands, but you just got more and more agitated and started yelling. The aide came in, saw what was going on, and came over and tried to talk to you.

That just got you even angrier, and your yelling escalated into a scream. You began thrashing your body around, trying to get your hands loose from mine, screaming the whole time. The aide pushed the nurse's call button, but stayed to try to help me. The nurse came in, saw what was going on, and said she'd get the Ativan. She was back a moment later, and another nurse had come with her. It took three of us to hold you still enough for the nurse to administer the Ativan through the IV.

It took a few minutes for the sedative to calm you enough to stop struggling and screaming, and another several minutes for you to become quiet and relax enough for me to release your hands. You immediately rolled over and fell asleep, apparently exhausted from our struggle. We knew well enough at this point, the Ativan only calmed you, and rarely put you to sleep.

The EEG technician was called in to reconnect the contacts you had pulled off. You appeared to sleep right through the checkup and the reattachment of the leads. Your Dad arrived for a short visit on his way from his meeting to the office while the leads were being reattached. I told him about our morning so far, and although he stayed for more than an hour and was reluctant to leave, I convinced him we would be fine and he should carry on with his day. He eventually left with a promise to he back by 6 p.m.

The rest of our day was relatively uneventful, except that "you" never really seemed to be there the rest of the day. You tried to read your book, tried to watch TV, tried to sleep, but nothing lasted more than a few minutes before you would be up again, pacing, lying back down, up again trying to go for a walk, lying back down. Constant motion.

CHAPTER 29

Day 20

Today, everything seemed to take a turn for the worse.

Barb had stayed with Jenny overnight. The plan that day was that I would go to the hospital first thing in the morning, arriving around 6 a.m., and Barb would go home. I would stay to see the doctor and Debbie would arrive around 9 a.m. to take over for the day. We had been trying to institute this plan for about a week but it almost never played out, and Debbie's vacation time was going to be over at the end of this week.

That morning Jenny was completely unreachable, and Barb had informed me she had been that way most of the night. Communication of any kind had ceased to occur, in either direction. The most disturbing part was that her vital signs where extremely unstable. Although Barb had intended to go home and get ready for work or to sleep, she decided to wait with me and attend the morning meeting.

The day shift nurses arrive well before the doctors do on the floor. Nurse Andi was assigned to Jenny, which was always an extra security blanket for all of us, but even Andi was showing signs of stress that morning. In general, she always had a smile and positive things to say, but once she got up to speed on Jenny's current condition, it was obvious she was uncomfortable.

Dr. Worley arrived and was contemplative as usual. At times, he seemed so deeply in thought that we wondered if he had forgotten anyone else was in the room, but today, after talking with Andi and examining Jenny, I could see he was even more serious than usual, and that he was deeply concerned.

In what was a big departure from the nurse's and doctor's usual behavior, very little was said to Barb or me as Dr. Worley, Andi, and a few others came and went from the room over a 15-minute span. Even more unusual was that there seemed to be quite a bit of whispering and meetings in the hallway, clearly excluding us from the conversation. Barb and I sat patiently. Jenny was completing her third week under the care of these people and they had more than proven how much they cared about her. We had complete confidence in what they were doing to help her, but we were concerned and our stress levels were rising as we sat with Jenny and it became clear that something serious was going on.

Dr. Worley finally came into the room and said that a decision had been made to move Jenny downstairs into the Intensive Care Unit. Our hearts skipped a beat or two, but I think we knew it was coming. Jenny had been deteriorating consistently since she arrived on April 5th, and there were quite a few areas in which she was bottoming out. Dr. Worley explained that Jenny's current vital signs dictated that she needed a professional medical staff person closer to her to take care of her, and while an aide had been assigned to Jenny for a week or so, they were not actually in her room. The patient to nurse ratio was four to one on the 6th floor. In the ICU it was closer to two to one, but more importantly they were set up to monitor her vitals from the nurse's station, they would have constant visual contact, and they were physically no more than 20-feet away at all times.

After Dr. Worley had finished giving us the details of what was going to happen and why, Andi entered the room and was very apologetic. Even more than a year later, she brings up that day and feels badly about it. I think she feels bad for scaring Barb and me although she has never used those exact words. We knew it was the right decision. We knew she was looking out for Jenny.

Ironically, I remember feeling very calm once Jenny was down in the ICU. A line I put into many emails and texts that day giving people updates said, "Jenny's condition hasn't really changed that much. They just need to keep a closer eye on her." This development meant people wanted to get information even faster and any doubt about starting the CaringBridge site was gone. I had known it was time to do it; I just wasn't sure when I would get around to it. Now it became a priority.

Jenny was whisked down to the second floor while Barb and I were left to the rather depressing task of taking down all the decorations in Jenny's room, the majority of which were from her birthday party. Then we were forced to say a quick and sudden goodbye to the people we had come to know and trust so well on the 6th floor. So, Barb and I removed the banners and streamers and the handmade cards with wishes of "Get Well Soon" Michelle's students had made for Jenny, and then we headed down to the ICU.

Actually, not a lot changed in how Jenny was being cared for. They simply watched Jenny closer in the ICU. And in what I viewed as an odd twist, despite all of the advantages the ICU unit offered, this was the day that the hospital decided that a nurse's aide needed to be in the room with Jenny, literally right next to her bed at all times. This was an upgrade to the aide that sat outside her room in the hall on the 6th floor who did other short assignments from time to time.

Surprisingly, during the entire time Jenny was a patient at Methodist Hospital, the hospital personnel never discussed or questioned the role Barb, John, Michelle, Debbie and I played in Jenny's treatment. While we were never shunned in any way, no one ever came to us and said, "This is what we need you to do or not do" either. As far as I could tell, they welcomed us but never assumed we were a constant part of Jenny's care. Of course, that makes sense for many reasons. We were family, and given the circumstances, they couldn't really tell us to go away; however, from a liability perspective they had no idea when we might say, "That was your job." Nonetheless, from the purely practical perspective of "everybody wants what is best for Jenny," no one ever complained that we were there or in the way and they respected our input and assistance at all times. Everyone stayed professional and acted as if we weren't there when the time called for it. I think we did a great job of knowing when to step back and get out of the way as well…most of the time. Barb, Michelle, John, and I were allowed to come and go as we pleased. I still have no idea if there is anything resembling "visiting hours" in a hospital anymore, but I do know that when you arrive between 10 p.m. and 6 a.m. you need a security guard to let you in.

Jenny's stay on the second floor lasted all of 23 hours. During this time, from what I could see there were no changes in what was physically done to care for her, but they could keep a closer eye on Jenny. She was moved back to the 6th floor on Thursday, but the 24-hour dedicated one-on-one care of having a nurse's aide sit right next to Jenny's bed at all times remained in place.

So, our little scare was over, in a way. We were out of ICU, which made everyone feel better from a psychological perspective, and Jenny had gained a full-time nurse's aide to keep a closer eye on her. For the rest of Jenny's time at Methodist, rarely was a nurse or nurse's aide not within arm's reach. The doctors remained focused on trying to find ways to get Jenny some quality sleep and address the constantly varying vital signs she presented. Additionally, now the doctors had another dilemma in that Jenny was almost constantly catatonic.

Jenny's condition at this point was clearly the worst yet. She had completely lost her ability to speak. At times, she would be coherent enough to try to do so, but it took minutes or even hours to figure out what she wanted. She still rarely had a truly extended time of restful sleep and 45 minutes was considered a reason to rejoice. Yet, in a sad sort of way, Jenny did stay in her bed much more than she used to up to this point, mostly because she had very little interest in doing much and when she did there was very little coordination left. Jenny was no longer allowed to walk the hallways without a "transfer belt" on to make it easier to catch her if she started to fall, but I refused to use it, and no one ever called me on it. The last bit of dignity Jenny had left right now was to be able to walk the hallways with her Dad in as normal a fashion as possible and there was no way I would ever let her fall.

This day began a weeklong phase in which Jenny ate very little solid food, and she had already lost 20 lbs. since being admitted to the hospital. Additionally, while there had been times that Jenny had lost control of her bladder, she now required a diaper for the remainder of her hospitalization. Jenny continued to experience episodes, but they were no longer defined by her being able to describe what she was seeing nor was she able to vocalize the horrifying cries for help. Now they were just spasmodic sessions in which we stayed close to her out of fear that she knew what was happening. We didn't want her to be alone.

A new "behavior," Jenny sitting in bed and dancing to music that only she could hear, had made small appearances before, but now became established and lasted for weeks. It was clearly a spin-off from the singing and humming she used to do, but now she could barely even hum. It made us smile because Jenny actually looked happy while she was doing it. If this was allowing her to escape, then good for her! We would just sit and watch, wishing that we could join her, and at times, Barb and Michelle actually would.

On top of Jenny's current state, a truly unexpected and sad part of all this was returning to a different room on the 6th floor, which had no decorations and no life. We felt no connection to the room. Surprisingly, it felt like we were starting over in many ways. Perhaps the hardest part was that Jenny really was gone now, and it took a while for us to feel that we were not in the room by ourselves from then on.

CHAPTER 30

Day 21

Although I wouldn't be posting it until the next day, this is the day that the initial CaringBridge entry came together. CaringBridge (www.caringbridge.org) is a free website that provides a source to post updates regarding seriously ill individuals. The initial day was actually three separate postings that started with an edited version of an email I had sent to my soccer team the previous week, combined with a collaboration of input from Barb and Michelle. It gave a two and a half page summary version of Jenny's seizure on March 27th and the first 30 days of her treatment.

The second posting attempted to answer the questions we had received most often: How is Jenny, what is wrong with Jenny, etc. This page was a direct result of the questions the soccer team asked as well as what had occurred at church the Sunday before.

Finding the right words was difficult. I didn't know where to begin or where to end. I also struggled with how much detail to include. Since this form of communication was so new to me, I had no clear idea what I would use it for and what direction it should go. It was difficult finding a focus, as well as a limit.

However, very quickly the CaringBridge site evolved into a valuable tool for me, as well as Barb, Michelle and John on occasion. It was used for two purposes. The first was to give a daily update of Jenny's status to keep everyone informed; this, indeed, did serve the purpose of stopping the questions when moving around town. The other was probably not what it was intended for, and it had not been my intention to use it this way, but it became a vessel for me to vent my pain and frustration. Via the email that I initially wrote for the soccer team, I had discovered the therapeutic qualities of "journaling." Once the CaringBridge site was established, I rarely hesitated to use it as such, although there also were a number of journals that I wrote but never posted.

The biggest problem, as always, verbally or in writing, was describing Jenny's overall condition. Without a diagnosis, it was difficult even knowing where to begin. It felt like a diagnosis would give people a reference point and from there it would be easy; while without a diagnosis, even describing Jenny's symptoms proved difficult, especially in just a few pages. We had come to know that the only way to truly understand what Jenny's condition was at any given time was to actually see her. Of course, that wasn't possible for the vast majority of the people that would read the posts.

Ultimately, we provided a sanitized summary of Jenny's condition in which we attempted to find a balance between showing it was serious without sounding too extreme or unbelievable; which it actually was. We also included a few statements in an attempt to stop readers from analyzing what they were reading and then making recommendations for what the doctors should be looking for, as we had been experiencing more than enough of that during the previous two weeks.

Initially, whether through CaringBridge or just talking to people we saw, all of us attempted to avoid explaining how the symptoms of Jenny's illness would manifest themselves as much as possible to anyone but our closest friends and family; it simply had become our experience that no one would truly understand anyway. However, when a statement has been made that an individual has been sick for 30 days and in the hospital for 21 of them, people understandably don't just settle for basic explanations. We'd had a lot of practice trying various ways to give information that would satisfy people's interest while keeping the conversation reasonable.

It all came back to Jenny's behavior. Anytime anyone would ask what's wrong with Jenny, since there was no diagnosis, it naturally fell to the task of describing her symptoms. Yet, on the one hand we knew whatever we said would come up short and people would use their own frame of reference, more often than not this led to a general lack of understanding and people's perception of the situation fell far short of what was really happening.

As Jenny's illness progressed, and the more people that I attempted to explain Jenny's behavior to, I grew increasingly frustrated with my inability to properly describe to people what she was experiencing. I had always believed that with more practice I would get better at it. Ultimately, I finally resorted to making the statement, "you have to see it to believe it."

In an attempt to clarify what I mean by this, it is helpful to offer the perspective of a visitor who came to see Jenny for the first time. Each of us who saw Jenny every day had at least one individual that we updated regularly and attempted to explain Jenny's condition to most often. Brad, Michelle's boyfriend at the time of Jenny's illness, was that person for Michelle. What Brad saw during Jenny's illness was so powerful, that he also chose to record his experiences in writing. His journal entry below demonstrates how descriptions and words failed to describe what one might witness at any given time.

As Michelle continued to beg me to go up to the hospital with her on the weekend, I put it off as much as I could, trying to avoid the hospital as much as I could (for personal, unrelated reasons). *From looking at the pictures, Jenny didn't look too terrible. The picture that I saw from her birthday with a big smile and all of her Twins gear that she received seemed like she was looking normal. Finally, Michelle got me to come up with her on the weekend. She called me*

127

and said, "Brad, you have to come with me to the hospital. You haven't even seen her since Easter; she isn't the same. She isn't even talking anymore." So what the hell? What could progress so quickly and make someone so dysfunctional that they couldn't even speak or eat on their own. Unaware of what was truly happening, I made the trip up with Michelle. In the car ride up, Michelle continually warned me about Jenny's state and said that she may not even recognize me or know who I was. Michelle also told me that there hadn't really been any visitors yet that had seen her like this. Michelle also told me that she needed to be the strong one in her family and really try to be the one to calm everyone down and take a deep breath. This situation was absolutely bizarre and I will say that what followed, I would not wish on anyone.

When we arrived at the hospital and proceeded up to the sixth floor, Brian and Barb were in the room and looked like they had been up for days. Their voices were cheerful but their faces cried for sleep. Jenny was sitting up in bed and Michelle went over to her, hugged her, and told her that she had a visitor and then asked her if she knew who it was. Quietly Jenny whispered in her ear and told her that it was, "Brad," and then continued to ask Michelle if she was married yet. I went over, said hi to Jenny, and gave her a hug as she tried to talk but was too quiet to hear. Jenny would continue to make inaudible noises and point as if she wanted something. However, the way I would describe Jenny now, it seemed almost autistic. As if whatever she had wrong with her was making her more and more function like an autistic child that was unable to communicate with words, and she looked like she was extremely skinny. Not being present the past few weeks, I realized that this had become the norm of what had to be dealt with. Michelle continued to quiz Jenny on the names of everything in the room that had pictures on it like the Emu and various stuffed animals.

Doctors and nurses proceeded to walk in and run a few tests. That seemed to amuse everyone in the room because it reminded everyone that Jenny was still in there. The doctor asked Jenny if she could raise up each leg. Not responding at first the doctor asked again and Jenny, who seemed almost irritated, proceeded to kick each leg up about 3 feet in the air very fast while the sheets flopped from the sudden movement as everyone giggled.

One nurse also walked in to try to massage Jenny's legs so they didn't atrophy and removed the sheets. I was absolutely shocked. While Jenny outside the sheets looked comfortable, her legs were *soaked in sweat and her feet and toes were locked solid into position. The nurse continued to try to get her to relax her feet and legs but it was a losing battle as the nurse continued to massage her legs as every muscle was locked solid.*

When John arrived, Jenny let up and made a shaky movement to try to kiss him and hug him. She seemed so happy to see him.

Later in the evening after John left, the four of us were in the room and Jenny began to say something. But, it wasn't just once, it was over and over. It started out quiet but it seemed like she kept saying it over and over because no one could understand her. Myself, having not experienced any of these episodes, had only heard them described. But Barb, Brian, and Michelle continued to her bed to try to comfort her and try to get her to lay down, but she was locked solid. Jenny then began to scream what she was saying over and over the same phrase. However, it wasn't Jenny's voice. It was much higher pitched, and almost didn't sound anything like her. After about a minute or so it was almost like every muscle in her body was so tired that she finally laid down but continued to mumble the same phrase until finally her eyes were closed but her lips were still moving in the same phrase trying to get it out. I was sitting dumbfounded not knowing what to do. It appeared as though the episode was over.

What happened next was even worse. With whatever energy Jenny had, she popped up her legs locked at a 90 degree and tilted her head up and then screamed as loud as she could to the sky. It was as if her body was on fire but there was no way to put out the flames. Michelle burst into tears and ran out of the room crying. I can't imagine what my face looked like but I am sure it was absolute shock and I froze in my chair not knowing what to do, until finally Barb gave me a head nod to go out and be with Michelle. As I held Michelle she told me, "This is what happens. A person's body should not be able to do that." Then I understood the mood of the room when I arrived because these episodes are a hundred times worse to experience.

Another event that took place a full five months after Jenny's hospitalization had been completed is shared here to drive the point home that Jenny's behavior was so incomprehensible that even actually seeing her was not enough.

In December of 2013, all of Barb's family was gathered together. Those in attendance were Barb's parents, siblings, nieces, and nephews.

These were all people closest to us on Barb's side of the family. All of the adults in the room had seen Jenny on a number of occasions at the hospital, and these were also the people getting the most detailed and accurate explanations of what was wrong with Jenny and what caused the "behavior" they all saw.

At one point in the evening, I was talking with one of Barb's brothers while Barb was engaged in conversation with her father and sister on the other side of the room. Brad and I were discussing the fact that we had a hard time explaining to people what Jenny's behavior was really like. He agreed, saying he was still surprised by what he saw and couldn't find the words to properly explain it to anyone. At that very moment, we heard Barb's father ask the question, "So was it the medication making her act that way?" to which, in anticipation of Barb's answer, her sister replied, "Well, at least part of it was." I looked at Brad and said, "See? No one gets it." He smiled and nodded his agreement.

What all of us saw was so horrifying that we couldn't even explain it to ourselves. We now have all of the medical details available, and we still can't comprehend what the body could do to itself, and what it did to Jenny.

The fact is that none of Jenny's "behavior" was caused by the medication. If the medication had any effect on Jenny's behavior at all, it was that the anti-seizure medication and drugs such as Ativan worked to inhibit or at least subdue some of Jenny's outward symptoms of the illness. Perhaps, because of the medication, we were only seeing a portion of what was truly happening to Jenny; and the thought of that means that what Jenny suffered was that much more tragic.

CHAPTER 31

Day 22

Thursday night marked the first time that Jenny was in the hospital without a family member with her.

Jenny had been assigned a nurse's aide who was stationed next to her bed 24 hours a day. Over the previous three weeks, Barb and I had gotten to know all of the nurses on the 6th floor and had become comfortable with most of the aides that came and went. In fact, by this time a few of the aides had been assigned to "Jenny duty" more often than others because of their willingness to accept the tall task of managing her as well as their innate ability to make Jenny feel comfortable with their presence. This was not due to anything that a particular aide did or didn't do, it was just the nature of Jenny's illness – either she was comfortable with a person's particular manner or she wasn't, but she made it clear when she wasn't.

Jenny's condition had deteriorated to the point that she was easier to deal with, even when she was having episodes. There were also longer periods of time that, although she still didn't really sleep, Jenny was in a catatonic state in her bed.

Seeing all of these factors as, perhaps, a cruel opportunity, Barb and I finally succumbed to the fatigue that had overtaken us both and went home and slept in our own bed at the same time, something we hadn't done very often for nearly a month. We desperately needed some quality rest or we were going to end up in the hospital right next to Jenny.

There was also the very serious need to meet some of the other responsibilities in our lives, most importantly that of earning a living. Both my business partner and Barb's employer had been more than patient in allowing us to focus solely on Jenny as much as possible.

Perhaps, with some rest, we could also avoid some of the unobservant and incoherent things we had done, such as when Barb backed the car out of the garage and scraped it against the side of Michelle's car in the driveway. Or the time when I went down to the cafeteria to grab a bagel and I smothered it with cream cheese, taking it back to Jenny's room to eat, and only then discovering I had covered it with vanilla yogurt! (I was so hungry and too tired to go back downstairs, so I ate it anyway.)

Michelle had come home from school early that weekend and was actually looking forward to spending the day with her sister while Barb and I went to work. When Jenny saw Michelle walk into her room, she managed to communicate that she wanted to play cards. It was a positive sign that Jenny was "with it" enough to recognize Michelle and recall a favorite pastime. However, it was a great disappointment that not much of the carload of stuff hauled out of her first room when she went down to ICU had made it back into the hospital yet, including the playing cards.

After engaging in an extensive search for the cards simply because it gave Jenny something to do and there was really no point in trying to explain to her that many things had not yet been moved back into her new room, Jenny settled back into her bed. After a short time, she "went away" again.

Jenny had not been eating much, to the point of serious concern for yet another aspect of her health. However, as Michelle was sitting next to her bed, Jenny began moving her mouth as if she was chewing food. Michelle began to push grapes into Jenny's mouth, and although Jenny didn't even seem to realize it, she actually ate a few.

The biggest surprise of the weekend was when Jenny and Michelle's cousin Drew arrived unexpectedly for a visit. He brought with him a bouquet of flowers and a vase that he had purchased for Jenny. Drew filled the vase with water, pulled out his pocketknife, cut the stems on the flowers, and created his own arrangement for Jenny. He even incorporated the paper that had been wrapped around the bouquet into the arrangement. He worked so hard at it and it had so much love in it, that Michelle left it exactly like it was.

Michelle and Drew also took Jenny outside of the hospital for the first time since Jenny's arrival three weeks ago. In a sign of how brutal the Minnesota spring had been that year, Michelle's journal that day read, "It is 63 degrees out today, which is the warmest it's been all year, so it feels more like 75!"

Michelle and Drew situated Jenny in a wheelchair with the help of the nurse's aide assigned to Jenny for this shift. The three of them took Jenny down to the main floor and out the front entrance of the hospital. The sun was bright and Jenny was definitely not used to the rather cool breeze blowing on her. She looked a bit uncomfortable and Michelle remembered that Jenny hadn't liked cold of any kind when she was healthy, so she asked Jenny many times if she wanted to go back inside. Every time, Jenny shook her head no, but after about 20 minutes, Jenny fell asleep in the chair so they wheeled her back to her room.

Given the circumstances and all that had happened since March 27th, this amounted to a banner day and was the most positive experience Jenny had had since her birthday.

Michelle gave Barb, John and me the reports of the day when we arrived that evening. All of us were a bit more relaxed than we had been in weeks. We finally understood that all we could really do for Jenny at this point was to wait for the return of the blood work that had been sent out. The doctors had made it clear that the search for additional possible causes of Jenny's illness had ceased, and we were finally okay with that. Surprisingly, it allowed us to relax a bit. The doctors were confident they had it narrowed down to two possibilities, and we had faith in them.

Four of the six separate tests sent out on April 16th had come back negative, and the results of the last two tests were not expected for several more days. I had conversed at length with the neurologist the day before about possible treatments. Regardless of which illness it proved to be, it would be rare, so the treatments still had to be researched and confirmed with doctors from other parts of the world.

All of this gave Barb and me some hope that we willingly grabbed onto because we needed something positive to dwell on. Regardless of what illness Jenny proved to have, it would not be good news in and of itself, and we had watched it take our daughter away already. At least when we had a diagnosis, the doctors would know what to do about it. All of this provided an odd sense of peace that led to a quiet and enjoyable evening.

CHAPTER 32

Day 23

Thank God for the weekend! How often has every one of us said that? I am fortunate in that I like what I do for a living. Every day is different, I really like whom I work with, and I am able to move around most of the time. However, I have to be honest, I still love my weekends.

While Jenny was sick, weekends took on a new meaning for me. They were easier in so many ways, mostly because Michelle was usually around. She has always had a very calming effect on me, but she was also extra help with Jenny and she was so good with her. Yet, more than anything else, the weekends were easier because there was no pressure to be in more than one place at a time.

During the week, although there was hardly ever a question of where I needed to be and my business partner put no pressure on me at all to do anything different, my ethical obligation still gnawed at me in the back of my mind. I always found myself torn between the need to be at work to meet my responsibilities there and being at the hospital to do everything possible for Jenny. The trouble was, whichever one I chose, I felt I should be doing the other. Saturday was the beginning of a break from five days of making that choice, so Saturdays always felt better to me.

This particular Saturday was rather busy. Michelle and I ran errands for things that needed to be done. Some were for Jenny, some for Michelle, others for me, and taking care of needs for the house. However, we also had some other key things to do as well.

That morning started with what would prove to be my final soccer practice with the team I was coaching. I firmly believe that to be a good coach, more work is done away from the field than on it in terms of practice planning and preparation. Between my need to be with Jenny and what little bit I worked and slept, I had not done any of the necessary prep work for the soccer team.

In part, because I was not prepared, and in part, because I knew it was my last practice with the girls although I had not yet informed anyone other than Barb and Michelle, the entire practice consisted of a loose scrimmage. I simply wanted to spend time on the field, enjoy the game, and see the girls have some fun. We were on an outdoor field for only the second time this spring, so I used the excuse that the team needed to get used to longer passes than they had been using in the gym. However, the truth is that this type of practice in no way helped the team develop. I knew I was not doing my job properly and so in an email to the club president and coaching director, I made the statement, "Since Jenny has been sick, I have not been proud of my performance as a coach. I hold myself to a very strict standard, I have repeatedly failed to reach that standard in the past few weeks, and I see no reason that won't continue. The emotional distraction I constantly feel interferes with my practice planning, and I am "slow on my toes" at practice with making adjustments. I feel I have become short-tempered with the girls, which in my opinion, is a mortal sin of coaches. The girls deserve better."

This decision was hard and painful, but I was very confident that it was the right one for everyone involved. Yet, I was very thankful at the end of practice when one of my players came up to me and said, "We aren't doing anything to help us get better." That comment removed any doubt I might have had and convinced me that I was doing the right thing. I have always encouraged my players to speak their mind and give feedback, and this statement wasn't made just because of what we did and didn't do on that day. It was rooted in the previous three weeks of practices. The demons in Jenny's head had extracted their toll on the soccer team.

After leaving the soccer field, the next errand was to run and pick up some very special visitors for Jenny. Michelle and I went home and loaded our two dogs into the car to go to the hospital for a visit. Since the weather was providing us with another beautiful day, we wanted to get Jenny outside again.

As soon as we arrived at the hospital, Barb and a nurse's aide brought Jenny down to the front of the hospital, where there are benches to sit and visit. It was a very sunny day and the sidewalks reflected the sun, so everyone was squinting as they stepped outside. The sun was so bright that Jenny removed the hat she was wearing to cover her entire face. This may sound like an insignificant comment, but it was a very big deal to me because regardless of Jenny's condition throughout her entire illness, I was always looking for any sign that Jenny was actually "in there" despite appearances. Especially now that Jenny was catatonic so much of the time, I desperately needed to see some sign of normal brain function. Jenny had lost almost all "fine motor skills," which included speaking. The doctors told me it was only her motor skills and not her overall brain function, but I continued to need to see some sign of recognizable brain function for myself to confirm it. The very simple act of removing her cap to block the sun, thereby showing common reasoning skills, was reason enough for me to celebrate.

Jenny seemed very happy to be outside again, but I can't say the visit from the dogs was a banner success. The dogs were wild from the car ride and a collection of new people to see. Rossi, our Beagle, accidentally scratched Jenny while saying hello, and Jenny disliked it when I let Maya, our Pit Bull, lick her face. There wasn't a lot of "visiting" going on as I spent much of the time managing the dogs while everyone else spent the time trying to determine what Jenny wanted and if she was comfortable. We were outside together for about 20 minutes, and then Barb and the aide went back inside with Jenny while Michelle and I took the dogs home.

Jenny must have enjoyed being outside, however, because according to Barb, she was very agitated for quite a while once back inside and she was able to communicate that she wanted to leave the hospital.

Despite her ability to convey that she still wanted nothing more than to go home, Jenny was having a terrible time with any form of communication. What came through loud and clear, however, was her frustration as she attempted to tell us what she needed or wanted. We spent a significant amount of time trying to guess what Jenny was trying to say. Barb and Michelle were always better than I was at this task. I'm not sure what was more heartbreaking; the fact that we couldn't figure out what Jenny needed or that we knew she was disappointed that we didn't understand.

Jenny started to refuse medications today as well. The list of medications Jenny was taking on any given day was long, but it also changed often. Some of them were administered via IV bags or transferred from a syringe directly into her IV. However, some of them could only be administered in pill form. This morning Jenny was refusing to take her pills, so Barb and the nurses had to resort to good old fashioned motherly techniques to accomplish the task. The first tactic was to sneak the pills into applesauce, which proved problematic for a number of reasons. First, Jenny wasn't willing to eat much of anything, so it didn't matter what the pills were hidden in, but, additionally, as this battle ensued, the pills began to dissolve. I'm pretty sure that there isn't a food that tastes good with medication dissolved in it. Even when they finally got the pills into Jenny's mouth, her gag reflex kicked in, a form of communication that is universal. The best results came from putting the pills into Gummi Bears, which have been a favorite of Jenny's for most of her life.

This was another moment in Jenny's new life that made her appear to be regressing back to when she was a baby. She couldn't talk, she couldn't walk, she couldn't eat by herself, and she was wearing a diaper. Now her mother had to trick her into taking medicine. I was losing my child, a bit more every day.

I am sure all of us were looking for signs that Jenny's mind was still intact despite all of this, and at least a portion of Michelle's journal that day shows that she was looking for it as hard as I was:

> *When I give you water and you drink too much, you give me this look like I just did something stupid. I can't help but smile because it's the look you always give me before you make fun of me, or say I did something stupid. I just wonder now what you are really thinking and what smart comment you want to make to me. We can still see you among all the IVs and drugs. You are still Jenny, and that is what keeps me going.*

I was fortunate enough to have some quality moments with Jenny on that day as well. At one point, she gave me a simple wave from the hip that is exclusive to her personality. Additionally, during a return trip to her bed from a bathroom run, I stood in front of her with my arms out for a hug. It appeared she was just going to walk past me to her bed and ignore me, but then she got a small smile on her face and turned to hug me. She was playing a trick on me! Later, as Barb was helping Jenny in the bathroom where things didn't go exactly as planned, Jenny let out a frustrated, "Oh Crap!" as she is known to do from time to time. That inappropriate comment put the biggest smile on my face because it showed more strongly than most things that Jenny was in there somewhere.

Still, I continued to struggle with the double-sided coin that Jenny's condition had become. I could never make up my mind if seeing the small signs of her true personality were good or bad. They gave me hope that I would have my daughter back again someday, but they also horrified me by making me consider that she might actually be trapped inside her body, desperate to escape, begging us to help and able to see that we did nothing for her.

Jenny was not the only one who had changed. Barb and I had adjusted our standards for what we considered a reason to celebrate our child's successes. We had taken pride in watching Jenny take her first step as a baby all the way through to walking across the stage with a college diploma in hand, and on that day in the hospital, as parents, we shared a small success together via a text Barb sent me later that evening:

> *Jenny ate all her fruit, all the Jell-O, all her yogurt, a banana, drank half of a can of Sprite, and she took her pills with ice cream. Granted we had a little episode in there where she was trying to move the bed, but hey, I thought it was a good evening. She is settled into bed now. Whohoo!*

That constituted a banner ending to the day and showed how significantly life had changed in a short amount of time.

CHAPTER 33

Day 24

Mercifully, Jenny had a relatively quiet day. We learned very early on in this journey that Jenny didn't care for strangers seeing her in the condition the illness had created for her. Today there was a steady stream of visitors, and as Debbie had pointed out to me a couple of weeks prior to this, Jenny tended to fall asleep if she didn't like what was happening when she had no other defense. She slept quite a bit that day, and I felt it was a result of her discomfort of having visitors. However, her body was so exhausted that perhaps it was just time.

What was interesting for me were the consistent reactions of all the friends and family that saw Jenny for the first time that day. Even if they were only there while Jenny was sleeping and did not interact with her, it was clear that Jenny was very ill. She had lost quite a bit of weight and even her face had changed significantly. Without exception, first time visitors were, at least temporarily, taken aback, especially if Jenny was awake when they were there. It was very easy to understand why most visitors would be uncomfortable with the way Jenny behaved, but some were even surprised by her physical changes, as it was such a dramatic difference from the strong young woman she had been.

Jenny did have one severe episode during the day that a few visitors, unfortunately, had to witness. She sat in her bed for the entire time, but the panic clearly showed on her face. Her expression was pleading with anyone in the room to help her. She did not speak a word throughout the episode, and Michelle stayed by Jenny's side and comforted her as best she could while Jenny gripped Michelle's hand tightly the entire time.

Nonetheless, when compared to the previous three weeks, this was a good day. There were even a few good laughs that included Jenny when she was awake. In addition, for the first time in three weeks, Jenny ate her entire dinner. The use of a feeding tube was being discussed mid-week, and almost on cue, Jenny began to eat. It began slowly, but this was a big step forward in that department.

When awake, we were all pleased to see Jenny's face light up at times during the conversations. At one point there were some serious bouts of teasing me going on by everybody in the room, and she joined in with that laughter at Dad. It was so great to see. As we were leaving for the night, Jenny gave us all big hugs. When she got to Michelle, Jenny said very clearly, "I love you," and they looked at each other for a long time. I took this exchange as an indication Jenny knew it was Michelle that stayed with her during the episode.

We came home that night to a house that was probably cleaner than it had been in a few years. While we were gone that day, Barb's sister and sisters-in-law had come and given the house a thorough cleaning top to bottom. We certainly enjoyed the clean, but the biggest reason it was such a treat was that when we got home that night, we could actually sit down and relax without feeling there was something else we should be doing. That night Barb received an email that let us know that the three women also realized I had cleaned a few hours the night before because I knew they were coming and was uncomfortable with it.

In some ways, it is funny that no matter what crisis is going on in our lives, there are some things that just don't change. Many people are surprised to hear that one of the hardest aspects of Jenny's illness for me was to accept help from friends, and even family. Ironically, I accept it from strangers easier than friends. I have never been one to reach out and ask for help for things I need. I don't hesitate to ask for help with the soccer program in Rockford or other community or school related things, but the truth is I hate feeling I am in debt to anyone, that I owe them because of what they unselfishly gave to me. It's silly, I know, and I'm not claiming I never do it, but I can say that I am never comfortable with it. It may have been part of the reason it took so long for me to inform people of Jenny's illness – perhaps I was afraid of what would come after that.

However, my family was in the deepest levels of helplessness that I can ever remember us being. We needed help, and thankfully, we discovered a whole community of people who wanted to give it. I will be forever grateful, and I will never be able to repay any of it, which, of course, was my problem to begin with.

There is a very long list of things we learned during Jenny's illness. Most were obviously directly related to Jenny, the hospital, and her condition, but we learned some other interesting and unexpected lessons as well. Perhaps no lesson was more surprising than what a person in need really requires.

All of us, I imagine, have made the comment, "Please let me know if there is anything I can do." I know I have said it countless times. While the statement is sincere, sometimes it is offered at times when we don't know what else to say. A person is feeling deep pain, there is a very real desire to help, but we have no idea how to do so. Before Jenny's illness, I never needed much help, but after this experience, my eyes were opened to a completely new perspective.

Throughout the entire summer Jenny was sick, literally dozens of people did hundreds of different things for us. The list of what people did varies greatly, but we are so grateful to all of them in that they were willing to use what resources they had for our benefit. One friend gathered terrific items for the silent auction for a benefit held on Jenny's behalf, while another friend invited me to a restaurant to chat about sports one night. The gestures have nothing in common, but each was exactly what I needed when they were offered. Honestly, nothing that any one person did for my family and me was more valuable than any other. At the time of each offering, it was the most important thing we needed, and ultimately, we needed all of it.

With all that said, there is one lesson I can pass along that I learned from this experience. Almost every time that anyone did something for us, I was unaware that I had needed that help until it had been done, so I didn't ever think to ask someone to do it for me. In our situation that summer, it was better that someone just went ahead and did something without asking us or waiting for us to ask them. Three of my neighbors took care of mowing the lawn for me that summer. I never asked them to do it, but each time I came home and saw that it was done, I almost broke down in tears in my relief at not having to worry about it. One day I was talking to a friend and commented that Barb had made an appointment for me to take both dogs to the vet at the same time. The next thing I knew, that friend was accompanying me to the vet because she knew it is tough to handle two dogs alone in a vet's office. It had never crossed my mind that I would need help because I was so tired. I was aware I needed to do it without Barb's help, but she recognized it and stepped up without me needing to think about asking for the help.

Close family members usually stepped in to take care of the "must do" stuff. More often than not, it was the things that didn't seem important when looking at the big picture that were such a relief to have help with. Every time this happened, I was grateful that people cared.

My universal recommendation for anyone that wants to help someone going through a tough time similar to ours, but has no idea what to do is to buy them gift cards, especially to a popular local chain of gas stations. Gift cards to gas stations removed concern at moments when I didn't realize my gas tank was empty until the light on the dashboard turned on. Eventually I left the gas station gift cards in my car so when I suddenly realized that I hadn't eaten for nearly a day, and had also left my wallet...somewhere...I could swing into a gas station and grab something.

The greatest gift my family received was given to us by whomever it was that created the website called "Meal Train (www.mealtrain.com)." This website can be used by families, friends and even entire communities to organize and work together to schedule regular meals to be delivered to families experiencing a variety of crises. In early May, Michelle was discussing with Brad, her boyfriend, how she felt desperate to help Barb and me out on more than just the weekends. He pointed out that his family had experience with Meal Train and introduced her to the website. Michelle knew that it still needed to be managed by someone in Rockford, as people would need access to our house in order to deliver meals since we did not know what our schedule would be. Michelle contacted two former soccer moms whose daughters her and I had coached and asked them to take charge. It was a Godsend. We no longer needed to plan what we were going to eat and we were able to back off on all the fast food we were consuming.

As a tip for anyone participating in this, although the hot, home-cooked meals are wonderful, it was helpful from time to time to have received the type of premade and individually wrapped sandwiches one family provided us with. They were in tortillas and contained ingredients that didn't get all soggy sitting in the fridge. There were many of them, each with different ingredients. They sat in the fridge just waiting for us to grab on the go as needed, while the other prepared meals that were delivered allowed us to sit down as three-quarters of a family and eat together with very little prep time.

In the future, I will let people know that I care when they go through a rough time. I will tell them that I am there for them and I will undoubtedly ask if they need anything, but more importantly, I will look for ways to help them without their having to ask. I will find ways to help with the "little things" that we forget to consider in the midst of a crisis.

CHAPTER 34

Day 25

I will forever remember this day as the worst day of Jenny's illness and the day that I had lost all hope.

After what had turned out to be a relatively relaxing weekend where I even got a bit of quality sleep, I was driving toward the hospital that morning in time for the usual meeting with the doctor. During the drive, it hit me that this week was going to be another period of waiting and seemingly doing nothing. Based on my understanding of everything that had happened last week, all we were doing was sitting around and waiting for the blood tests to come back to confirm which illness Jenny had. My understanding was that this was still several days away. The doctors seemed to believe they knew what it was, but they were doing nothing about it and I struggled to understand why they couldn't do anything preemptively, the way that people are put on amoxicillin before the strep culture comes back during a sore throat.

Meanwhile, Jenny was into her fourth week of hospitalization and continued to get worse daily. As I drove, I realized that I was in no way prepared for another week like the previous one.

Jenny had clearly bottomed out; at least I was praying that she had. In almost every way, she had returned to the state of infancy. Any form of communication was difficult and slow at best and because she was seldom coherent, even her attempts to communicate were rare. While I don't recall ever fearing she was going to die or of even having a conversation about the possibility with anyone, Jenny had reached a point that I couldn't see any other alternative if further deterioration took place.

Jenny's physical appearance had also changed dramatically. She had lost over 20 pounds and appeared to be a small child in the seemingly oversized clothes that she wore. Her face had developed a "droop" that is common with stroke victims and she had developed something of a "tic" disorder of her mouth. It was a minor condition in the big picture of everything else going on and we didn't know if it was dysarthria, a disorder caused when the nerves that control the mouth become disorganized when brain damage occurs, or a side effect of the various medications she was on. Regardless, to anyone visiting Jenny who did not have a medical background or any understanding of what was going on with her, it may have been the predominate feature they noticed when they first saw her. The motion varied, but for someone who didn't know better it appeared as if Jenny was exaggerating the motion of someone trying to silently mouth words, using her teeth and tongue to play with her lips, or that she had a dry mouth or had just eaten something sour. Her lips were also extremely chapped, so much so that it looked painful, yet, Jenny seemed unaware.

I had been pondering all of these facts as I drove to the hospital and discovered that I got increasingly depressed and frustrated. Part of my frustration was that this would be my first sit-down meeting with yet another new neurologist to work with Jenny and I could not fathom that a another change of doctors was necessary on Jenny's case. At the time, I imagined that the previous three doctors were on a beach in St. Thomas somewhere, unreachable and uninterested in what was going on with Jenny. In reality, nothing could have been further from the truth.

What I did not understand was that most, if not all hospitals, use a rotation system within certain specialties and it is actually very logical. In this case, all of the neurologists that rotate through Methodist Hospital work together in the same office, each taking a weeklong rotation in the hospital and the rest of the time seeing their individual patients in their office. On extensive cases, such as Jenny's, all of the doctors consult each other and compare notes daily. The result was that even though we would see a new doctor, that person was not coming in cold nor were the other doctors on an island with no cell phone service.

I did not know this at the time because none of the doctors had explained it to me. The average stay for a patient on the 6th floor was something like 51 hours, so I suppose very few patients see more than two neurologists during their stay. Additionally, by the time the second doctor comes around, the diagnosis and treatment plan is in place and it has very little impact on the patient to suddenly have a change in doctors. Thus, the process does not need to be explained to patients or their families on a regular basis, so I am sure the doctors either thought I understood this or it just never dawned on them how the system appeared from my perspective.

In Jenny's case, we were now on the fourth doctor that we would see on a daily basis, and I was losing my patience. I'm not really sure where my frustration was coming from. I was never disappointed in how any of them treated Jenny. On the contrary, I appreciated the new perspective and additional ideas that appeared to come to the table with each additional neurologist. Had I looked at it cynically, I might have likened it to Ron Gardenhire, the Twins manager, calling to the bullpen when his starting pitcher was struggling. The starting pitcher did well for a few innings, but now it was time for a fresh arm.

At the time, I was unaware of how closely the doctors were working together. Yes, new perspectives were undoubtedly being introduced, but I now believe the progress had more to do with the processing of more information than it was that a new doctor was seeing Jenny and had new ideas. I now know that all of the neurologists at the hospital were constantly comparing notes and in addition were consulting with doctors from other hospitals. Research was continually being conducted and further analysis of

143

the information available was happening constantly. The situation was evolving and everyone was up to speed.

I can see now how difficult the problem before the doctors was and how it was being addressed as a collaborative effort. More importantly, progress *was* being made. I just didn't understand any of that as I was driving to the hospital that day.

I had met Dr. Tran the previous Friday, as the doctors' rotations run from Friday through Thursday. However, this was our first "sit down." Much to my surprise and despite the mood I had worked myself into on the drive in, Dr. Tran and I connected right away. While I had appreciated and learned from the other doctors, I found that I was able to communicate with Dr. Tran better than with any of them. She spoke frankly, which I appreciated, but she was also able to "go with" the sarcastic sense of humor that I employ when I am under extreme stress. When it was all said and done, Dr. Tran had a way about her that put me at ease.

As it turned out, it appeared that the doctors and I were on the same page. Dr. Tran agreed that more needed to be done for Jenny while we were waiting for the test results although it was not clear just yet what that would be. At the conclusion of the meeting I was assured that I would hear from her very soon about a plan of action. I came out of the meeting feeling a bit better, convinced that the doctors were going to begin addressing Jenny's symptoms head on. However, Dr. Tran had also explained that this was not strep throat. Even if the doctors guessed correctly about what illness was affecting Jenny, treatment had serious ramifications. There was more to consider than simply jumping in and treating an unofficially diagnosed illness.

After I finished meeting with the doctor, I went and spent some time with Jenny. Although I was feeling better about the approach the doctors were taking, there was still the immediate issue that Jenny was sick. Debbie had no more vacation time available so she was unable to spend the days with Jenny, Michelle was back at school, and Barb, John, and I had to spend as much time at work as possible. We were already a month into this and the electric bill still needed to be paid.

I decided I just wanted to sit with Jenny for a while before I "left her alone" for the day. Yes, she had the 24-hour one-on-one aide with her, but that just didn't feel the same. The truth was that I just missed my kid and felt so helpless that I couldn't do more for her.

As I sat with Jenny, it was apparent to me that she was more "aware" than I had seen her in quite a few days, maybe even a week. I remember trying to fabricate my own, baseless, clinical explanations, all of it designed to give me hope that Jenny was coming out of it, getting better somehow. However, this thought process would come back to bite me as well. Although Jenny was more aware this morning, it didn't mean she could talk or even walk; it just seemed that she was somehow aware of what was happening to her. This thought horrified me to the point of tears on an almost daily basis and it hit me particularly hard on this day.

When Barb, Michelle, John, or I were present, the one-on-one aide would leave the room if we asked them to so we could spend some time alone with Jenny. I told the aide that I would let her know when I was ready to leave and she checked Jenny's vitals before she left. That meant that unless I pushed the nurse's call button, there would be no reason to check on Jenny as long as I was there.

I sat with Jenny for about a half-hour. During this time, the "aware" Jenny had a few things she was trying to get across to me. None of it seemed to be of monumental importance, yet, as her dad, I wanted to do what I could for her. The problem was that Jenny had lost almost all ability to communicate in terms of actually getting across what was on her mind or specifically what she needed at the moment. It is impossible to explain the frustration that was clearly being communicated on Jenny's face as she tried to tell me something. We "talked" about why she wouldn't eat her breakfast, what was or wasn't on TV, and how the Twins did the day before. For our entire "talk," I understood none of what she had to say and she knew it. We were both very sad and frustrated.

When it was time for me to say goodbye for the day and head to my business appointments that morning, Jenny managed to let me know that she wanted one more thing before I left. I did all I could to grasp what she was trying to tell me. She kept repeating something over and over but I could not understand it. She could not clearly point out the issue or do anything to fix it herself, and I made guess after guess, running around the room and grabbing everything I could find to see if that was what she wanted. All of my guesses were wrong. Jenny cried from time to time as this went on. I was doing the best I could but it wasn't good enough, not even close.

After what seemed like forever, Jenny finally stood up and made a motion around her waist that made me believe that she wanted a different pair of shorts on. I went through all of the clothes that we had brought to the hospital, but that wasn't the issue. I kept saying that I had to go because I was late for an appointment, but Jenny made it clear that she knew I had to leave and wanted me to fix one thing for her before I left. I was sweating because I was working so hard at figuring it out. To the casual observer it probably would have looked like a horrible game of charades as Jenny would make the same motion over and over and I made wild guess after wild guess. Each time Jenny would show me her disapproval with her body language.

I finally became exasperated. I had already missed so many business appointments in the past four weeks and while all of my customers understood, they had people they had to answer to as well. I finally told Jenny that I could not stand there any longer trying to figure out what she needed and that I truly needed to leave. She plopped back down onto her bed and began to sob. I kissed her and hugged her goodbye, and it took everything in me not to join her in tears.

As I went to the door to leave her room, I needed to push the bathroom door closed as the layout of the room meant the bathroom and hallway doors slightly overlapped. As I pushed the bathroom door closed, my eye caught a momentary flash of what was on the shelf above the sink in the bathroom. I pulled the door back open, went in, and grabbed one of the diapers that was on the shelf, and showed it to Jenny.

That was what she had wanted, but I still didn't quite understand what was happening. Throughout Jenny's entire illness I never helped with any of her...private moments. Ever since Jenny was a young child, she had wanted those boundaries respected and being in this condition had not changed that. We respected her boundaries, especially since we always believed she was aware of what was happening. We would not take that level of dignity from her.

At least I knew it was something having to do with her diaper, so I called in the aide. While I was waiting for her to come back, I asked Jenny to show me the diaper she had on and I could see it was the style that was provided by the hospital. Barb and I had determined the previous week that the hospital diapers were very uncomfortable for Jenny, so we had purchased our own and brought them in for her. The aide today was new and was not aware of this, so she had used the hospital-issue diaper, as was her job. I asked the aide to help Jenny change, and then waited until Jenny came out of the bathroom and I got her settled into bed. She was happy now and okay that I had to leave.

This entire process took more than two hours. I did all I could to hold myself together until I got to my car where I cried like a baby for over 10 minutes.

We had all bottomed out. Jenny was like a newborn child in so many ways and I was dealing with it worse than a brand new father. It all seemed so simple, after the fact. All she had wanted was to be a bit more comfortable while she waited for...whatever was next, and I was the bumbling buffoon of a father who took nearly two and a half hours before stumbling across the answer totally by accident.

If she hadn't been so "aware" she would not have even cared. If she could have functioned on her own, she could have fixed it herself. If she hadn't been so sick, none of this ever would have happened. The frustrations kept mounting, for all of us, and it seemed that no end was in sight.

Part 3

Diagnosis

April 30 to May 23, 2013

CHAPTER 35

Day 26 – Part 1

This chapter of the story actually began the night before.

I was sitting in my office that evening around 6 p.m. when my cell phone rang. It was Dr. Tran. She said she had been "thinking about this case most of the day" and wanted to meet the next morning at 7 a.m. with both Barb and me to discuss a possible plan of action.

During our conversation, it was clear that she had done quite a bit of research, all based on the illness the doctors believed Jenny had. My understanding was that she had spoken to doctors in various parts of the country about possible treatments. Dr. Tran was considering beginning a "very mild treatment" (relative to the other options) of steroids, which is sometimes done prior to an actual diagnosis. She wanted to meet to go over all of the risks and side effects, which included agitation and insomnia. Since we were already dealing with both of those issues, there was no down side as far as I could see.

Dr. Tran wanted to start right away but stated that it would "only be for five days, just to see what results we get." Hopefully, by that point the blood test results might be back. It sounded like a long shot to me. I couldn't see how steroids had anything to do with what might be wrong with Jenny, but then again at least we would be doing something, so I was on board immediately.

The meeting on Tuesday morning would prove to be monumental.

Barb and I had arrived at the hospital about 6 a.m. It was not our first sit-down meeting with doctors, and they tended to last an hour or more. We both had busy days planned at work so we wanted to spend some time with Jenny beforehand. Usually we joined the doctor in the room with Jenny and then moved elsewhere for the meeting, but this time a nurse came and escorted us to a conference room on the 6th floor, the same room where we had met with doctors many times before.

There was no one in the room and we were asked to wait. This was not the protocol we were accustomed to, but we knew that Jenny wasn't the only patient in the hospital, so we really didn't think much of it. We were excited about the possibility of finally doing something positive for Jenny though we knew nothing was definitive until the tests came back from the lab.

15 minutes later, Dr. Tran entered the room. The room was longer than it was wide, and Barb and I had taken a seat near the back, so Dr. Tran needed to take quite a few steps to get to us. She said nothing as she walked toward me, looking me squarely in the eye, and I remember glancing over

her right shoulder and seeing the faces of a couple of nurses that I had come to know very well peering through the narrow window in the conference room door. One was smiling and the other had a look of anticipation on her face. My heart kind of stopped, as I knew something different was going on, but I didn't even have a moment to process what it might be before Dr. Tran reached me and handed me some sheets of paper without saying a word.

I took the papers from her, glanced at them quickly, and could see they were a medical report. I didn't even attempt to read it; I just wanted the bottom line from the doctor. Experience had taught me that this doctor would cut to the chase and put it in terms I could easily understand.

"What's this?" I asked as Barb sat silently next to me.

"The results of the blood test came in 10 minutes ago."

35 days after Jenny's first seizure, and 26 days in the hospital later, we finally had a confirmed diagnosis.

We were stunned and relieved.

As little as 13 hours prior to this moment I was told by this same doctor that we were possibly days away from getting the results that I was now holding in my hands. I had prepared myself to be patient until the results arrived and to be receptive to anything that happened in the meantime. Now, suddenly, we could look and move forward. The results were here!

Over the next couple of hours, Dr. Tran explained the illness to us, and what the treatment plan would be. After she left the room, Barb and I sat there alone for a short time to gather our thoughts and emotions. Then I sent a text to Michelle and to my business partner before calling John.

Michelle was at school. Usually I hesitated to interrupt her during class, but because of the situation with her sister I knew that her phone would be on her desk, and while she wouldn't be able answer it she would see the text very quickly. I simply wrote, "Call me ASAP."

Because all we had been getting for 35 days was bad news, that text froze Michelle. She left her classroom as quickly as possible and called me back. However, I was on the phone with John so she had to hang up and call Barb's phone. The entire time, she was positive something devastating had happened. Since that day, we have all learned to be very specific in our texts.

There were still a billion questions swirling in my head, and in fact, later that night when I tried to create a CaringBridge post with as many details as possible, Barb and I discovered that each of us remembered different things that the doctor had said, but neither of us recalled all of it.

Jenny was diagnosed with something called Anti-NMDA Receptor Encephalitis. My family simply refers to it as NMDA. Technically speaking, NMDA is a "Subcategory of a Paraneoplastic Syndrome," so it is one of a number of related illnesses. However, NMDA is classified as one of the most devastating. Medically speaking, it is an autoimmune "reaction," which means NMDA is actually caused by something else occurring within the body. Statistically, the root of the illness usually lies in a tumor of some kind (most often a teratoma in the ovaries of women younger than 30).

All of that was way over my head. Here is my summary of the illness in non-technical language that I know a doctor would laugh at, but is essentially accurate if one accepts the lack of proper medical terminology as well as some over simplification.

Jenny had a cancer somewhere in her body that ultimately caused the NMDA. Through some of the tests doctors performed over the extended time Jenny was in their care, no actual tumor or any sign of tumors was found, so it was presumed that the cancer was "on the cellular level" (this is common and happens in everyone from time to time, but the body attacks and destroys it in most cases). Regardless, at some point Jenny had some form of cancer. These cancer cells, rather than growing more cancer cells and forming a tumor grew otherwise healthy cells that were released into Jenny's body. Appearing to be normal and healthy cells, they were not attacked by the white blood cells but were allowed to exist in Jenny's blood. However, these cells are not normal or healthy cells at all, and exist with the sole purpose of creating antibodies, which are supposed to be healthy and acceptable for the human body, but these antibodies are unique. For reasons that doctors do not understand (as of the last time I read the latest research), these antibodies are allowed to penetrate the brain, something that no other antibody in the body can do. They are then able to attach themselves to the nerve endings in the brain and block the signals (synapses) between receptors in the brain, thus making an individual act as if the devil himself has possessed the patient.

The most accurate summary of the illness that I have seen is, "The body's own immune system attacks the brain." As long as the illness goes unchecked and undiagnosed, more antibodies are allowed to attack the brain, and the result is the deterioration we witnessed in Jenny. NMDA can kill its victim, and does so in about 6% of the cases (based on the latest research I have read).

The bottom line is that it's complicated. I am not aware of another illness that has so many steps in the process of making someone sick. When we consider the fact that the MRI showed nothing and the numerous other negative test results, the challenges the doctors had faced for several weeks are easier to understand.

There are multiple resources available for more detailed and specific information on this disease. The intent of this book was not to be a medically accurate reference about the illness itself, it is only meant to relay our reaction to it. In reality, I have no medical background and admittedly made no effort to understand the medically defined details of this illness. The fact that it is so complicated and is rarely diagnosed dictates that I not even try to speak to the medical aspects of Jenny's diagnosis.

While I am not aware of reliable numbers available anywhere, some of the estimates that I recall having seen at the time Jenny was diagnosed in 2013 were that fewer than 1,500 people in the world had ever been diagnosed with the illness. This statement comes with a gigantic asterisk attached to it however because the disease was not "identified" until 2007. In other words, no one could be diagnosed with the illness before that time. It is an absolute certainty that this illness existed long before that, there simply wasn't the technology available to identify it.

It absolutely freezes the hair on the back of my neck when I think of the thousands of people who have or have had this disease and were either unable to be diagnosed or, worse, have been misdiagnosed. My sincere hope is that, if nothing else, this book can play a role in the efforts to raise awareness among doctors about this and other related Paraneoplastic illnesses. Even since 2013, great strides have been made in this area. The number of diagnoses is up dramatically, not because the illness is occurring more often, but proper diagnosis is happening sooner. Thankfully, not all patients experience what Jenny experienced, but even a mild version of the illness can be life-altering. However, doctors need to be aware of what to look for and testing for the disease needs to be made easier, quicker, and less expensive.

What scares me more than a delayed diagnosis is misdiagnosis. I am aware that there was a brief conversation between the doctors during Jenny's stay in the hospital, as ideas for what was making her act the way she did were running out, in which some speculated that the problem was just in Jenny's head – that Jenny was actually schizophrenic or psychotic. Essentially, it was suggested she was making it up, willingly or unwillingly. I laugh at that prospect when I think back to some of the things Jenny did during her illness – Stephen King couldn't have made some of that stuff up. I thank God for Dr. Heidi Joos who would not allow the focus of the search to sway from a clinical cause.

Although it has little or no direct impact on the overall story, I love to tell the small tale of when Dr. Joos was explaining to me how rare NMDA is. She told me that in medical school, the students are taught that "when you hear the hoof beat of horses, look for zebras." The point is that doctors are taught to look beyond the obvious diagnosis of symptoms. More often than not, the noise of the hoof beats are indeed caused by horses, but one should not rule out that they could be zebras. She went on to tell me that NMDA was not only zebras, but zebras with orange strips.

I do realize how lucky Jenny was to have contracted this illness in 2013, when a diagnosis and help was available. It moves me to tears at times when I imagine all of the parents over the decades who have watched their children suffer the same way Jenny did, only to have them end up being institutionalized because no one could figure out what was wrong with them, much less how to help them.

In so many ways, Jenny was actually very lucky.

CHAPTER 36

Day 26 – Part 2

When Barb I walked out of the conference room that morning, I remember wanting to tell all of the staff that we finally had a diagnosis, but almost everyone on the 6th floor already knew. Everyone was going about their business as normal, but the room we were in was very close to the main nurses' station so we ran into a few of the nurses as we walked out and were greeted with smiles, hugs, and even a few cheers. It seemed that everyone was as happy as Barb and I were.

In spite of the good news, we could not ignore that we still had quite a battle in front of us. The news had not been all good. Dr. Tran explained that the treatment for the illness was actually surprisingly simple given the devastation that the disease caused. The issue was the recovery time. Ultimately, the result of Jenny having had this illness was that she was left with what amounted to a severe brain injury. Although it was not caused by physical trauma such as in a car accident, the damage to Jenny's brain was significant and the brain is the slowest part of the body to heal. Jenny had months of recovery in front of her before she could do the daily activities that all of us take for granted and it could be years before she fully recovered.

However, that wasn't as bad as it sounds, at least not from the perspective of potential recovery. Jenny's brain was not physically damaged in any way, which is why the MRIs never found anything. Apparently, in the non-medical terms I like to translate things into, the antibodies in Jenny's head were just a bunch of "goop" clogging things up. Dr. Tran explained that over time, things would slowly clear and Jenny's brain would function again; although it was not clear how close to 100% she would get back to. I saw all of this as good news once it was all summed up. It meant that a full recovery was very possible for Jenny but that recovery would take lots of work, patience, and time. I could live with that. All I wanted was to have my kid back. After everything I had witnessed, I could accept the diagnosis as Dr. Tran laid it out.

So ultimately, Barb and I felt somewhat elated that day, which felt funny, even back then. Essentially we were told, "Your child has a rare disease that could take months to recover from," and we felt a type of relief that we had never felt before. Before this whole thing began, I never could have imagined what "not knowing" could feel like, but now that we knew exactly what to expect and what additional hurdles we needed to cross, I wouldn't say it got easier, it just became bearable.

The natural reaction for everyone when they learn about an illness they or a loved one has is to begin to learn all you can about it. I didn't go that route, before or after diagnosis (I think some parents have a hard time with that, especially mothers). Contrary to my stance the previous two weeks of ignoring all speculation about what illness Jenny may have had until I heard the official diagnosis, Barb, Michelle, Debbie and a few others close to us had already researched the remaining possibilities of the tests were waiting on, so a basic understanding of NMDA already existed. Yet, after the diagnosis, everyone around us began to study in earnest and compare notes. While I listened to all of the talk and did do a very limited Google search, I really wasn't interested in too many details. As far as I was concerned, by watching what it did to Jenny over the previous month I had learned firsthand what the illness was and what it could do. The doctors told me what the treatment plan was, so I already knew all that I needed to know. The doctors told me they could make her better, all we had to do was ride out the storm in the meantime, which I believed would be easy on that morning. That was all I felt I needed to know, and I knew Barb and Michelle would fill me in on any additional details I was missing.

I also felt like everyone else was sort of wasting their time. The fact is, the information available about NMDA, especially in early 2013, was very spotty at best. The illness was so rare that even the few people considered experts did not have much definitive information about treatment of the illness. The four or five cases we could get detailed information on had each treated the disease differently, so really, what did we know? I have no idea if the degree of the illness was different in each person or if the knowledge of how to treat it was changing. The good news is that additional knowledge has been gained very rapidly in the past year and hopefully others will benefit from this.

What truly surprised me about the treatment plan that Dr. Tran had laid out was how simple it was. It was done in three phases and had started even before Barb and I had contacted everyone about the fact that we had the diagnosis.

The first step was a series of steroid doses, one each day for five days, the same treatment Dr. Tran had been proposing we start when she called and scheduled the meeting with us the night before. The role of the steroids was to stop the antibodies from attacking the brain, thereby allowing Jenny to begin the healing process.

The second step, performed at the same time as step one, was a drug called IVIG. Honestly, this is one drug that I actually tried to learn a bit about, but still don't understand it. The doctors said that this drug would allow Jenny to start talking, walking, and eating on her own again.

Dr. Tran repeatedly warned us about the side effects of these first two phases of the treatment. She said Jenny "would be uncomfortable" specifically experiencing agitation, aggressiveness, and severe insomnia, which I found hilarious. As Barb, Michelle, John, and I can attest, Jenny had been suffering from these "side effects" until about a week ago.

The final phase of Jenny's treatment would be a series of chemotherapy treatments to kill the cells that had created the antibodies in the first place. The chemotherapy would not address any cancer Jenny may potentially have, only the cells that were presently causing Jenny's illness. The chemo treatments would not take place until sometime later, after the first two phases were complete.

Ultimately, Jenny's treatment was very straightforward and relatively free of serious risks. The downside to all of this was that Dr. Tran told us it could still be up to a month before real improvement would be seen. I chose to cling to the "up to" part of her statement. I needed to believe Jenny would start coming back sooner. The fact remained that she would have to come back through the hell she had already gone into in order to get better. I had no idea how long it would be until the demons in Jenny's head would really let her go so I could take my daughter home.

By the end of the day I knew we still had a long and scary road ahead of us, but at least I knew which road we were going to travel. Jenny would have all of us with her for the journey. I never allowed myself to doubt that Jenny would make it back. Even with what little was known about the illness and the treatments, the statistics that were available were in Jenny's favor. Additionally, I knew I could see Jenny "in there" almost every single day. I knew she was still whole; there was just some junk in her head getting in the way.

An interesting thing happened after we received the diagnosis. We went from difficulty explaining what Jenny was experiencing while we were waiting for the illness to be diagnosed, to difficulty explaining what the illness with which she had been diagnosed was. It didn't really matter or change anything as far as we were concerned; it just struck me as kind of funny. Not really having given it much thought beforehand, I had believed that once we had the diagnosis it would be easier to explain to people what was going on. I believe it is natural for people to resort to their own experiences, frame of reference, and expectations of what an illness is; or more accurately, what it is capable of doing to the human body. When we hear that someone has been diagnosed with diabetes, we may have follow-up questions, but in general, we understand what is involved. NMDA is so rare that there is no way for individuals to understand what is involved and what Jenny went through. While this certainly isn't a major issue when we are discussing things with our neighbor, we were very surprised to find the same to be true among many medical professionals as Jenny went through her rehab.

Even the rarity of the illness is hard to grasp if one doesn't slow down to ponder it for a moment. I remember a conversation in which I was talking about what NMDA was and brought up how rare the illness is. I made the statement, "No real numbers are available to us, but a few of the estimates are that less than 1,500 people have been diagnosed with the illness." The person I was speaking with responded, "Oh, that's nothing. The cancer I had was so rare that less than 800 people in the United States are diagnosed with it every year." I didn't bother explaining that I had meant that fewer than 1,500 people in the *world* have *ever* been diagnosed with the illness.

The majority of the time, when a person asks, "How's Jenny?" all most people were interested in was finding out if she was getting better. Therefore these conversations rarely needed to focus on the true nature of her illness, that is, what the illness actually did to her. However, Jenny's current condition was difficult to explain unless a person understood what she had been through and how bad her past condition had been, so most of the time I avoided that portion of the topic anyway. Once the diagnosis was received, my view of Jenny's status was based on how far she had come since the worst of it as much as how she functioned on a day-to-day basis.

In my opinion, the name NMDA Encephalitis is what leads to much of the misunderstanding, or rather, underestimation of what it is, and more importantly, what it can do to its victims. About a week after we received the diagnosis, I crossed paths with an acquaintance who had heard Jenny was sick who asked, "Did they figure out what she had yet?" I said, "Yeah, she has encephalitis," leaving it simple for the purposes of that particular conversation. He meant well and was trying to be positive when he said, "Encephalitis, oh yeah, my aunt had that. Bad for a few days, but she was fine after a couple weeks." He walked away, I believe, convinced he had put me at ease that Jenny would be fine. That is a very understandable response from anyone without any medical background; however, we even had a nurse at the rehab facility Jenny went to tell Barb and me, "We have dealt with hundreds of encephalitis cases," though I knew that Jenny was their first case of NMDA Encephalitis.

Yes, I have no medical background at all, but it seems to me that encephalitis is a very generic term. What needs to be known is what is causing the condition. So, while these are medically accepted terms, if one doctor says to another doctor, "The patient has encephalitis," the conversation doesn't stop there, as it is the cause and the severity of the situation that is relevant. The word encephalitis, by itself, means nothing.

Actually, I don't think that the word encephalitis should be part of the name of this illness because NMDA basically hides in the brain. It doesn't cause any swelling or actual physical damage (in most patients) that can be seen by any medical technology available today. All of Jenny's CT scans and MRIs came out perfectly clear for the duration of her illness, a fact that played a very large role in why her illness was so difficult to diagnose.

157

Even if one Googles the name of the illness and reads up on it, the effects sound generic in print: "…resulting in hallucinations, paranoia, and psychosis." While definitely true, it just sounds so clinical, and while none of those things are good, most people have a rather simplistic image of what the results of having such an illness is. At the very least, I think, most people believe once it is identified, some medication is given, and the road to recovery is smooth.

That was not the case for Jenny.

CHAPTER 37

Day 27

Contrary to the previous week, things got very busy around Jenny once the diagnosis was in.

The second day of the steroid and IVIG treatments had been completed. Both treatments were administered via an IV bag, which took a total of about six hours each day. Jenny simply needed to lie there, which mercifully was much easier for her than it had been even a week earlier. However, I already found myself wishing she were more difficult about it and wanted to get up out of bed, because that would have meant she was "with us" more. I found that I was already watching her closely, looking for any sign of improvement. I knew it was unrealistic, but held out hope.

Jenny was also put back on the continuous EEG. It was started after the diagnosis came in and run for 48 hours to establish a benchmark for the status of her brain activity as the treatment began, so it could be compared as the treatment progressed.

Finally, speech, occupational, and physical therapists began working with Jenny on this day, and would continue to do so on a daily basis for "as long as possible," which is how it was listed at the time. The primary goal was to "try to keep Jenny as strong as possible for as long as possible." It was discussed this way because during these very early stages of Jenny's treatment no one knew exactly what all would be done over the long haul.

While the doctors were able to make some decisions and plans early on, they continued to consult with other doctors outside of Methodist to determine Jenny's full treatment regimen. Although I certainly was not involved in any of those discussions, my understanding was that the University of Pennsylvania was the nationwide leader in the field at the time simply by merit of having dealt with the most cases. However, treating this disease was so new that everyone was simply comparing notes and making judgment calls about the next step. Essentially, they were making it up as they went along. I don't mean that as criticism, it is simply a testament to how rare the illness was and how new the treatment protocols were. The fact is there were no protocols, part of which may have stemmed from the varying degrees to which patients had the illness.

Ultimately, Jenny's treatment stopped after the three phases that were laid out on the day we received the diagnosis (steroids, IVIG & chemo), but the doctors always kept the door open while they were being completed to add treatments if Jenny did not respond to the initial phases. These additional treatments may have subjected Jenny to much more aggressive approaches, which could have left her in pretty rough shape or even without any energy to be active. Thus, the speech, occupational, and physical therapies were being utilized as a preemptive move to avoid muscle atrophy and other side effects resulting from inactivity, if that were to happen.

By all accounts, Jenny worked hard in her therapies. However, I have to believe the therapists were being positive and generous with her parents because when I saw Jenny working with the occupational therapist one day, it looked as though she was auditioning for a role as an extra on the TV show, *The Walking Dead*. As the therapist led Jenny down the hall for a simple walk, she didn't even open her eyes. However, the therapies did wear Jenny out and she slept soundly for a relatively long time that evening.

While all of these positives were occurring, however, Jenny felt the need to add a couple of new problems to the list of things the doctors had to deal with. Perhaps she was just making sure that none of us relaxed too much and began to think that the coming days would be a cakewalk. She began experiencing severely low potassium levels as well as high blood pressure. I remember Dr. Tran explaining all the possibilities that could result from this, but when I went to Barb to explain it to her later that evening, I fumbled the explanation, saying, "It was a sign of…something. I didn't really get it, but it is minor compared to everything else." Sadly, this type of explanation was pretty much what she got from me the entire time Jenny was sick.

Of course, more tests were ordered because of these developments. I was told that this marked the day that Jenny went over the century mark for the number of tests they had run on her for different ailments she had experienced since her arrival. The potassium and blood pressure problems proved to be only the first of quite a few complications that would occur in the coming weeks.

In addition, Jenny had begun developing a rash on various parts of her body a few days before which now covered the majority of her body. At the time, it was considered a "medicine rash," which sounds simple enough, but when nearly a dozen different medicines arc being administered it was exceedingly difficult to discover exactly which one was causing the problem. The rash would be an ongoing issue in the coming days.

Although all of us were exhausted due to the stress and lack of sleep, Barb, Michelle, John, and I were just bystanders. All we had to do was watch as the nurses and doctors kept track of about a dozen medicines, which changed each day, and everything else that went into giving Jenny the proper care that she required. It was amazing to watch.

Yet, lest anyone think that all I had to do was sit back and relax while all of this was going on, I did have a couple of crosses of my own to bear. While it is clear that I didn't work very hard at paying attention to details or even trying to process any information in a way that I could relay it back to Barb, I actually did have to deal with a few issues all on my own.

Even though Jenny was catatonic a fair amount of the time by this stage of her illness, she still experienced episodes and was still adamantly determined to remove her IV as well as the EEG probes when they were in. The reattachment of the continuous EEG for another 48 hours meant that this was going to be an ongoing issue once again. Now that there was an aide assigned to Jenny on a 24-hour basis, I felt bad that they would have to deal with this. I also knew that a new aide would probably be caught off guard by how fast Jenny could manage to do this, as well as how sneaky she could be in hiding what she was doing. With the NMDA treatment and the new problems popping up, I knew the entire staff had their hands full and adding errant EEG probes into the mix just didn't seem fair.

I sat with Jenny most of the afternoon the probes were attached and stayed at her side in case she reached up to pull any off. Although she was sleeping, she would reach up to scratch her head from time to time and then almost instinctively start to pull the probes out, seemingly as she slept or in a new and even more clandestine method than those she usually employed. The EEG techs had long abandoned any attempt to wrap Jenny's head to protect the probes. It was actually easier to rely on us to prevent her from pulling them off and not have any obstructions to deal with when they came to the room to fix them when we inevitably failed. Barb and I had talked about both of us going home again that night, so I knew the aides would be on their own, and as I sat next to Jenny's bed, all I thought about were ways to solve this problem once and for all.

After maybe 30 minutes of just staring at Jenny's head and not thinking of much, the solution came to me. As is often the case, the solution was so easy that I was mad that I hadn't thought of it a few weeks ago.

Ironically, however, I could not remember what my solution was actually called. I could see it in my mind, but I could not think of the name. I knew where to go buy one, but I didn't want to walk into a store and not know the name since I knew I'd have to ask for one because I had no idea where they would be located. I am going to blame this particular lapse in memory on the fact that I was tired, but I called a friend who is a high school teacher and basketball coach.

"Hey, Mike! What do you call those things that athletes wear on their heads?"

"I have no idea what you are talking about. What kind of a description is that, you dope." (Okay, these were not his exact words; his was much crueler and more descriptive.)

"You know, the nylons that football players wear under their helmets."

Mike had a good laugh and I was quickly off to the sporting goods store to buy Jenny her very first Do-Rag! My daughter was now hip and modern, officially the first patient on the 6th floor with her own Do-Rag. Jenny's new fashion accessory almost completely eliminated her ability to rip off the EEG probes. If nothing else, it bought time for whoever was watching her to stop her from getting a good grip on them. The problem was finally solved.

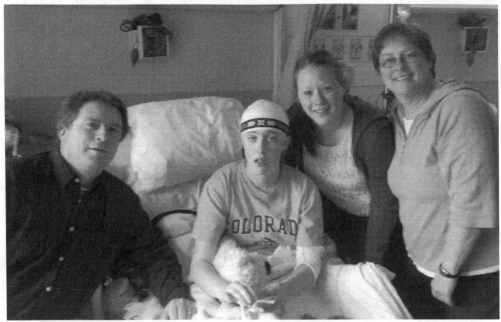

Brian, Jenny, Michelle and Barb – Jenny sporting her new Do-Rag

Another issue surfaced that was caused by Jenny's condition. It had nothing to do with anyone in the hospital, but it did create an extremely awkward moment.

As is often the case when someone is in the hospital, our pastor came to visit Jenny on a number of occasions. Pastor Jon is a very laid-back person who proved to be extremely versatile with regard to his visits with Jenny. I suppose as a pastor he witnesses many tough situations, but I was very impressed with how he handled seeing Jenny the first couple of times, which was always the toughest for most visitors. Pastor Jon had come to visit Jenny on the first day that it was clear that this was going to be a very long and difficult journey. Late the first morning that Debbie stayed with Jenny, Jon arrived before I left for work so the four of us visited. Jenny was a bit out of it as she had just settled down after an episode, but Jon managed to act as if everything was fine as we visited.

As is the case, I imagine, when pastors visit members of their congregation in a time of need, the visit ended with a prayer over the patient. Jenny sat still, even respectfully while Pastor Jon said his prayer as Debbie and I stood by his side. Shortly afterward, Jon said his farewells and left the room. Unfortunately, immediately after he walked out the door, Jenny began to repeat over and over, "I'm going to die, I'm going to die" and became very fearful and sad. She then went into a minor episode in which the theme was that she was going to die (not for the first time). Obviously, it was very sad and I knew there was a connection to Jon praying over Jenny before he left, but I didn't think much of it and had completely forgotten about it a couple of hours later.

However, the next day Debbie was with Jenny again when Pastor Jon made a second visit. Debbie called me after he left to tell me that Jenny had once again gone into a panic attack after Pastor Jon departed and was convinced that she was going to die. Debbie asked me to ask the pastor to please not visit again in order to spare Jenny.

I could never have even imagined telling a pastor that he couldn't come and visit a patient in a hospital. In fact, I believe I might be the first person to have ever *banned* a pastor from comforting a patient.

At times during the course of doing business, it is necessary to call a customer and deliver bad news. I take a lot of pride in the fact that, unless it is completely unavoidable, I never deliver bad or uncomfortable news by any means other than in person or at least with a phone call. I don't use e-mail or any other electronic means unless absolutely necessary. I feel it is disrespectful and kind of a cop-out to do so. If I make a tough decision, I should have the guts to deliver it "in person," rather than hiding behind a computer screen.

This time I wimped out.

I am horribly embarrassed to say that I e-mailed my pastor to ask him not to visit my seriously ill daughter in the hospital. Over a year later I still turn red thinking about it. Of course, Jon was very understanding and agreed to stay away until he heard from me. When Jenny went into the ICU, I let Jon know and he came right back to see her.

On the afternoon of the day Jenny was first sent to intensive care, Jon returned from exile. I had been expecting him, and he was already much later than I had anticipated. I was in the hallway around the corner from the ICU when suddenly Pastor Jon was in front of me looking a bit shaken. I had already seen him with Jenny on previous visits, and that didn't shake him, so I was very curious what the issue was. Jon proceeded to tell me that he had just spent the past 20 minutes stuck in the elevator with three other people. I laughed pretty hard. He probably didn't see the situation as funny yet, but it was the funniest thing that I had heard in a few weeks and while he didn't laugh with me, he allowed me to have a good belly laugh at his expense. It also crossed my mind that there were, indeed, demons in Jenny's head and they were doing all they could to keep the man of God away, but that may have been the result of a few too many horror movies as a kid.

I am very grateful for Jon, his understanding and patience, as well as the relationship he has had with Jenny. Moreover, I am grateful that neither he nor God struck me down for exiling him from the hospital.

CHAPTER 38

Day 28

 Barb and I had taken our first "full night off" the night before. Thanks to John going straight from work to spend the evening with Jenny, Barb and I were able to leave work and spend the evening together. Bonnie, my business partner, had planned a "date night" for us, however, neither Barb nor I had any energy to put into a date.

 Due to our sheer exhaustion, Barb and I made a quick trip to *Buffalo Wild Wings* and then went home to sleep. It was time for some serious rest. I think we were both experiencing a bit of the "come down" that occurs after a long stretch of high stress. Receiving the diagnosis Tuesday had been a major turning point in the situation and the drop in adrenaline sent our bodies into shutdown. So much for romance.

 Jenny's medical treatment continued. She had a pelvic MRI, which was the first step in the process to see if the cancer that had probably caused the NMDA encephalitis could be found. The majority of women who had been diagnosed with the illness were found to have had a tumor (teratoma) in the pelvic region of the body, usually in the ovaries. I was glad they had started the search, but we were not expecting much as there had been a few ultrasounds of the same area previously and nothing had been found. There was actually a high likelihood that the NMDA was triggered simply by cancerous *cells*, not anything that had actually formed into a tumor yet.

 There was a lot of uncertainty about Jenny's total treatment plan at this point, and the doctors were not very clear about how the potential for cancer was going to fit into it all. It was considered a minor issue, and while this seemed logical, I knew the cancer was going to be an issue at some point, so I was glad they had started looking. Of course, the immediate issue was the NMDA itself, and on that day there were many unknowns and the chance existed that the treatment would have to be adjusted to include steps that would leave Jenny too weak to tolerate too much in terms of additional testing.

 The issue of the potential for cancer was an interesting phenomenon. I still have never gained a great understanding of how the science of all this worked inside Jenny's body, but I did know that the NMDA was caused or "triggered" by something and I knew the doctors were not directly dealing with that issue yet. That decision actually made sense to me, but it was always in the back of my mind. I still get chills when I recall that, on that day, I actually said a short prayer that the doctors would find cancer in my daughter. I knew they were dealing with the NMDA, but as long as the source of the illness potentially lurked somewhere in her body, I was afraid of a relapse. Although I don't regret the prayer and have even repeated it since then, it is a chilling thought to know that anyone would wish for that. However, the fact was that right then the NMDA was much worse than any cancer they might have found.

I was well aware of the oddity of such thought, as can be seen in the text message exchange that Michelle and I had that afternoon:

Dad: Jenny just went down for the MRI.
Michelle: I hope they find something.
Dad: Ha! I agree COMPLETELY but I find it funny that we are essentially saying, "I hope they find cancer! Have a super sparkly day!"

In any other situation we would have been horrified by the idea of Jenny having cancer, but what we had witnessed with the NMDA was so horrific that cancer felt like a better alternative.

Unfortunately, we were still dealing with the NMDA. Over the previous four weeks, Barb and I had been forced to watch our daughter deteriorate from the woman we knew into a mere shell of herself. I clung to the hope that Jenny was still "there" behind the garbage in her head, but she had been a bit distant the past couple of days. I hoped that the worst was behind us now that the treatments had begun and I was constantly looking for even the tiniest sign of it. Jenny had been mostly catatonic in recent days, so any sign of life would have satisfied me. She still had episodes and at times needed to be comforted and helped through them, but I was looking for something that showed that she had an *opinion*, that she had some "reason" left in her. I was looking for some of the fight that I knew had been inside of her.

When I arrived at the hospital that day at 5:45 a.m., I got my wish, in a very strange way.

Jenny had been reattached to the continuous EEG two days earlier so she had the 25 wires attached to her head. It was easy to understand why these irritated her: they limited her movement, they caused pain with pulled hair, slight pricks to the scalp when they were tugged, and they itched like crazy. On that Tuesday when the tech attached the probes, I was extremely concerned because Jenny slept through it. She didn't seem to care at all. As happy as I was about getting the diagnosis, it made me so sad to see her lack of reaction to reattaching the probes. I wondered if we were too late with the treatment to save her.

As I walked into her hospital room that morning, I was greeted by the most wonderful sight! Jenny was in a wrestling match with the nurse's aide that had been assigned to her for the night. The aide was holding Jenny's arms down as she did all she could to reach up to her head for the probes. We had been in dozens of these "wrestling matches" with Jenny; they could get intense at times, especially if they were accompanied by an episode. Due to the just rising sun and a sliver of light from the ajar bathroom door along with the fact that my eyes hadn't adjusted after walking in from the bright hallway, there was enough light for me to make my way through the room but not nearly enough to make out details. I immediately stepped into the fray, replaced the aide, and took over the task of keeping Jenny's hands away from her Do-Rag; which I am pleased to say successfully protected the probes through all of this because, previously, even Jenny just squirming in her bed could dislodge a probe or two before she had it on. As I took hold of Jenny, I very quickly realized that she was soaked in sweat. I looked over to the aide and asked her how long this had been going on. I was stunned when I heard her reply, "About two hours!"

I had never struggled with Jenny anywhere near that long the entire time she was sick. In spite of my sympathy for the aide, I was thrilled that I had gotten my sign of life. Not surprisingly, I never saw that aide again, but I will forever be grateful that she did not call security and choose to use mechanical restraints.

In addition to the good sign of Jenny being an uncooperative brat, John had sent a couple of text messages that seemed to indicate that at least some form of communication was going on while he sat with Jenny the evening before: "She thinks she has been discharged and wants to go home." Her thought process obviously wasn't clear, but she had *communicated* a *thought process*. At that point, I was truly grasping at straws and looking for anything that I could take as a good sign.

I had to make an effort to find positives in Jenny's situation while the negatives seemed to jump out and ambush us from every angle. The rash Jenny was experiencing had continued to spread and got thicker with each passing day. For this reason, the doctors ordered a "punch biopsy" taken from Jenny's back in which they removed a piece of the rash to determine its cause. The results of that would come back the next day. They were not good, and would signify the next crisis Jenny would have to face.

CHAPTER 39

Day 29

Jenny had her good days and her bad days. In turn, each of us close to Jenny had to deal with the highs and lows of our own emotions because of what she was experiencing at the time. Some days we handled things better than other days. It was directly related to what was going on right in front of us at the time, rather than the overall situation. It was depressing to watch Jenny struggle as she came and went from being "with us" or "going away," and all of us suffered if we were present during a string of bad episodes. They were hard to shake, and while up to this point I felt I had dealt with everything reasonably well, no better or worse than anyone else, everything started catching up to me about that time and I went into a six or seven day stretch of my own version of depression.

Michelle was coming home again for the weekend, but she had to finish her day at school first. Usually she was my first phone call of the day after the daily meeting with the doctors, even before Barb if she was not present. However, the journal entry Michelle wrote to Jenny that day rather summed it up:

> *Dad was pretty depressed today. He usually calls me every morning before I go to work and he sent me a text and told me to read CaringBridge instead. It broke my heart, and I knew he was sad. I later learned you didn't greet him with that big smile of yours when he got there...*

Once again, I wondered if Jenny was "in there," but it was actually just me reacting to how Jenny greeted me when I arrived at the hospital that morning and taking it very personally. Up until that day, even if Jenny was out of it or in the midst of an episode, whenever I arrived in her hospital room she would greet me with a smile. It may not have been much of a smile some days, perhaps just a slight reaction that acknowledged that she knew I was there, but at least it felt like I was cheering her up by being there, and her knowing I was there and showing her appreciation of that always cheered me up.

Today, there was nothing. She was sitting up in bed being attended to by the nurse. When I walked in, she turned and looked at me, gave me a long stare, then looked away without a reaction. My heart sank.

The meeting with the doctor occurred almost immediately after my arrival that morning, giving me no time to recover from the surprising emotional blow of Jenny's failure to greet me, so the relatively minor news the doctor delivered hit me much harder than it should have.

The results of the pelvic MRI performed the day before had come back "unremarkable." In other words, nothing was found to narrow the search for the cause of the NMDA. Absolutely no one, including me, was surprised by this, so my reaction could only be attributed to the fact that I was tired and had lost control of my emotions. My emotional state was clear in my sarcastic posting on CaringBridge that morning: *They didn't find cancer in my kid, darn! God - that statement and this whole thing is so absurd. See, you gotta laugh to stop from crying.* I had truly lost perspective. Decisions about if and where within her body to continue the cancer search were saved for another day.

The much more relevant news that morning was an update about the rash on Jenny's body. It was just an update and not definitive information so my reaction to it seemed extreme. Now I wonder if it was a premonition.

The rash covered nearly half of Jenny's body by this point, and the areas where it initially appeared were covered with layers of it. Some areas on Jenny's legs had turned a dark brown, almost like a grotesque bruise. For the previous few days the doctors had been reducing or adjusting the less critical drugs as best they could to determine which medication was causing the rash. However, despite these actions, it continued to get noticeably worse even over a few hours. Dr. Tran informed me that they were concerned that the anti-seizure medicines were causing the rash. The results of the biopsy from the day before had not come back yet, but the rash was so bad and spreading so quickly that they feared Jenny would have to be completely removed from the anti-seizure medicine.

The terror that went through my body at hearing that news froze me. It was clear that the NMDA had been the cause of the seizures, and although the treatments had been started, I had been told they would take up to a month to begin to take effect. I had been looking for any sign of improvement since the first minute after the treatment had started, but it had only been four days so it was beyond unreasonable to expect that Jenny had actually improved yet. However, given the way she failed to greet me that morning, I was convinced that she was actually getting worse.

The cumulative effect of the negative greeting by Jenny and this news about the rash and the anti-seizure medication within a few minutes swung my emotions to thinking the worst. By late that afternoon, I felt the worst was actually happening. The results of the biopsy came in showing that the anti-seizure medicines were indeed the cause of the rash and the decision was made to remove Jenny from all of her anti-seizure medicine cold turkey. The risks posed by the rash outweighed the risks of not taking the medicine.

Jenny had originally been placed on Keppra after her second seizure on March 27th. A week later, well before NMDA was even in the vocabulary of the doctors, an allergic reaction to the Keppra was considered a possible cause of Jenny's "odd behavior," and Jenny was switched from

Keppra to Dilantin. Later doses of Depakote were added to the Dilantin because Jenny's seizures were not controlled by the Dilantin alone.

More than a year later the irony of this situation still blows my mind: on speculation that Jenny was having an allergic reaction to one drug, she was switched to a drug that she was, in fact, allergic to.

As I look back on it now, the combination of thinking the worst and misinterpreting at least some of what the doctors were telling me, both of which had to be a reaction to the fatigue, really had me overreacting to the situation. It certainly wasn't a good scenario that was playing out, but I don't know if it was as bad as I had made it out to be. As I look back, I was the only one panicked over it. I have a vivid image of Dr. Tran telling me this news and the only question I remember asking is, "What do we do if the seizures return?" Dr. Tran shrugged her shoulders and said, "I don't know," then turned and walked away. That cannot be what actually happened because that was not Dr. Tran's style, not at all. She may have, in fact, told me that there were more questions than answers at the time, but she wouldn't have handled it like that. My "memory" is clear evidence to me that I was having a really bad day emotionally and that I was interpreting everything very badly.

Regardless of the reality of the seriousness of the situation, the truth is that there was something of a race going on in Jenny's body, and at the time, I felt it was the worst thing that had ever happened to my daughter. A crazy illness had taken control of her brain, literally, and was causing seizures, among other things. Those seizures were kept under control with a combination of two drugs, which her body had now rejected. Treatment for the illness had begun, but not long enough ago that it really had any positive effect yet, and now the anti-seizure medicines were being removed. It would take a few days for the medicine to clear out of Jenny's body, so the race was on for the NMDA treatments to work fast enough to stop the seizures before the medicine designed to do the same thing wore off.

My head was spinning.

CHAPTER 40

Let's Go Shopping

As the rash was developing, the doctors were taking note, adjusting medications, and making suggestions as to what could be causing it. One of the first places the rash appeared was around Jenny's neck and rib cage. Up to this point Jenny had been wearing any one of her various sports bras day in and day out as part of the street clothes that she wore instead of the usual hospital gown. Her sports bras were made of nylon or a very similar material, and one of the doctors suggested removing the bras, believing that they may have been the cause of the rash. Jenny was very warm much of the time, and the theory was that her skin was getting irritated from the perspiration and the skin not being able to "breathe" due to the bra's material.

Jenny was losing her ability to communicate clearly, but it quickly became apparent that she was not comfortable with the new dress code.

Almost any time that Jenny was up out of bed or even just sitting up, she would hold up her breasts with her hands and say, "my boobs are sticky." It was clear that along with the disappearance of her fine motor skills, she was also losing the concept of proper public decorum. We had a good laugh the first few times it happened, but once she started doing it as she was walking the hallways of the hospital, it became a bit more serious, and something had to be done.

To this day, I am not sure how I was elected to take care of this issue. I am not clear on what day it happened, but I distinctly remember Barb being at the hospital with me. My hunch is that Barb was taking Jenny down to help with her shower and my job was to come up with a bra before she was done drying off. I'm unclear on the details, but I do know that I suddenly became a man on a mission to buy a bra...and for some reason I was in a hurry to get it done.

Now, it must be understood that I have been surrounded by women my entire life. For the majority of the formative years of my youth, I was raised by my mother as a single parent and surrounded by older sisters. I married and had only daughters. I am a girls' soccer coach and my business partner is a woman. Heck, even my favorite dog is a female. I'm not ashamed of doing things that some men won't do. I willingly go and pick up feminine products and other things and I don't really think twice when I am in line at the register. In fact, many of my high school soccer players have discovered that I keep an "emergency pack" in the very bottom of my coach's bag. I am very comfortable with my role as a man and with the things that women need on a regular basis.

However, picture this, if you will: I hadn't shaved or showered in a couple days and didn't even have a hat on to cover my rats-nest of hair. I entered Kohl's department store probably looking somewhat like what most people may interpret as a homeless person...needing to buy a bra...in a hurry.

The only good thing that happened that day was that I got lucky and walked into the store right next to the women's sports apparel, so at least I found the right department. I had to walk up and down the aisles for only a minute or so before I found the sports bras, but there were more different types than I had ever imagined possible. I was in too much of a hurry to ponder this for very long, so without hesitation I stopped the first female salesperson I could find (yes, I let the first male salesperson I saw walk past) and said, "Excuse me; can you help me find a bra?"

I have to give the young woman credit; she didn't miss a beat. (How many homeless men buy bras?) She asked me a few questions, which I didn't really pay attention to as I didn't even want to try to process what the possible answers would be. I quickly made up a story that my daughter forgot her sports bra for a soccer game and I was sent to retrieve one before kick-off, which was only minutes away. I had one criterion for the bra; it had to be made of cotton. I got a bit of a strange look, but only for a moment.

Then she asked a question that I could not avoid; what size? All I knew for sure was 100% cotton. As a married man, I have occasionally needed to describe the size of my wife to a salesperson. However, that was very different from describing the size of my daughter. The experience had reached a new low.

Refusing to panic, I said, "Give me a medium and a large!" as I prayed that sports bras came in the same sizes as t-shirts and that I would not have to discuss cup size with this young woman.

Thank God, she handed me two bras without further inquiry, I got in line to pay, and this portion of the living hell that was my daughter's illness was over.

CHAPTER 41

Day 30 & 31

True to the trend of the previous three weeks, the weekend was quieter. Less hospital staff was around and, for reasons I never understood, it seemed that fewer patients were around as well; it was enough to lead one to ask whether some people schedule their strokes and other neurological problems. There was also less pressure to deal with customers and other business issues. Basically, the only thing to do this weekend was sit around with Jenny and a few family members and friends to wait for the treatment to work.

That weekend had a different type of urgency to it. I sat watching Jenny waiting for a Grand Mal seizure to take over her body at any minute, but that never happened. I had not recovered from the day before and its continuous string of bad news. By the end of the day, Jenny was doing better than she had been that morning, but it did little to offset my mood.

Even the CaringBridge entries that weekend were less intense than the previous week, which had covered the receipt of the diagnosis. However, given what was actually happening with Jenny, this lack of sharing was a little surprising. Jenny was at a critical juncture of her care, but we could only sit and wait. There was really nothing else to do.

Sunday, the 5th, marked exactly one-month since Jenny had been admitted to the hospital. Michelle and I had been discussing that off and on since she had arrived on Friday. The conversation actually centered on how crazy it was that Jenny had been in the hospital for so long. We knew it wasn't any kind of a record as we have a friend who had once been in for 80 days, but we also knew it was extremely rare. We did the best we could to be positive, and Michelle spent a lot of time doing all she could to make me laugh that weekend because of how low my mood had gotten.

We began to list the fun things that came with being in the hospital so long, and deciding that we would have some fun with everyone, posted that list as the CaringBridge posting Sunday. All of these items have at least an element of truth to them and all were a direct result of our experiences over the previous 30 days.

YOU KNOW YOU HAVE BEEN IN THE HOSPITAL TOO LONG WHEN...
...you know which lounges have the best puzzles.
...you know which parking lot cashiers are fastest...and which ones tell the best jokes.
...you are able to step in and give breaks to the nurse's aides.

...the hospital staff knows the occupation, daily schedule, and first name of each family member.

...your room is known as being the brightest and most festive on the floor (and nurses from others floors stop by just to see it).

...the nurses wear birthday party hats the entire day just because you offered them one.

...you know each of the IV nurses and EEG techs by name.

...you notice that the gift shop changes their window displays.

...you stop addressing the doctors as "doctor" and call them by their first names, and they are not insulted.

...you start to give human names to the machines used by the nurses and doctors.

...you know which plants are real and which are fake throughout the hospital.

...you know that the button for the first floor doesn't light up in the elevator on the left.

...the workers in the first floor cafeteria know "you are the father of the girl on the 6th floor" even though you have never spoken a word to any of them.

Despite the fact that all of us were simply sitting around and watching Jenny as we waited to witness the results of the NMDA treatments while fearing the worst because of the removal of the anti-seizure medicine, nothing came to a standstill for Jenny. The NMDA did not take the weekend off even though the doctors had started to attack it.

Outwardly, Jenny continued to be in rough shape. She was catatonic or "gone" much of the time and couldn't even walk herself the 20-feet from her bed to the bathroom anymore, so a wheelchair became a permanent fixture in her room. She could eat very little on her own and her ability to communicate continued to be limited at best.

An odd twist to Jenny's illness was that occasionally she could speak clearly enough to deliver a short, appropriate-for-the-moment statement, right in the middle of being unable to effectively form any other words to communicate properly.

A great example of how this would occur when we least expected it was during an episode Jenny was having a few days earlier. Her sole mission was to leave the room at any cost. It took place during a phase of her illness when it was common for us to need to engage in rather extreme and physical confrontations to stop her from doing something she shouldn't. Jenny would never get violent, but controlling her usually involved what amounted to a wrestling match between her and me.

During one such episode, I had managed to get Jenny to the bed and forced her to lie down. This was a deliberate tactic I had employed many times because it gave me a distinct advantage as she had less leverage with which to use her strength. On this occasion I was becoming tired and was running the risk of losing control of her, so I resorted to lying on top of her using my entire body weight to restrain her. In Jenny's efforts to get up out of bed, she had managed to roll onto her side, and we were positioned so I was looking at the side of her head. With my arms on either side of her body, my strategy was to use my arm strength to hold myself up off her body to allow her to be comfortable as I continued to try to talk her into agreeing to stay in the room. Any time she would fight to get up, I simply relaxed my arms and my body weight would hold her in place on the bed.

Our confrontation had been going on for about ten minutes, during which time I had used my body weight to stop her from getting up anywhere from 12 to 15 times. Jenny was having a difficult time with any verbal communication, and her attempts at repeating the same statement of unrecognizable words seemed to be her trying to explain why it was so urgent that she leave the room. What was very clear was that Jenny's frustration level was climbing, but she was also getting tired.

During a short break in her struggle to get away, Jenny suddenly turned her head so we were nose to nose, and with almost a smile in her voice, she said to me with absolute clarity, "You have a horrible bedside manner." After a moment of stunned silence, everyone in the room had a good laugh, and then Jenny and I went back to struggling for several more minutes. She never said another intelligible word for days.

Although the incident was humorous at the time, my perspective of it changed during my drive home that evening.

It was odd that Jenny couldn't speak clearly the majority of the time, but then she would easily blurt out something like that during an episode. It wasn't only that she could suddenly speak so clearly, it was that usually the comments were so witty. For me, this only served to support my theory that Jenny had demons in her head. If the illness was causing the speech problems, why wasn't her inability to speak consistent? I came to think of incidents like this as the demons releasing her long enough for her to make a statement, or worse; they were making the statement for her.

This thought process made the incident more disturbing than funny for me. I began to fear that the demons were not releasing her simply to let me know Jenny was still in there; it was to let me know that Jenny was trapped, they had control, and there was nothing I could do about it. God, how I hated the demons that I believed were in Jenny's head.

Although they had ceased being the outward explosions of fear and activity of even a week ago, unfortunately, the episodes continued. This is clear in one of Michelle's journal entries from that day:

When I got there today, you were sitting in the wheelchair. I bent down to say hello and give you a hug, and you grabbed the collar on my sweatshirt really hard. You were looking at me as if you were scared, and I couldn't tell what you wanted. You were pulling me

174

down close but I couldn't figure out what you wanted. I hope one day you can explain to me what it was that you were doing. You wouldn't let go for a long time and I felt bad I couldn't figure out what you needed.

I often wondered how many episodes Jenny still had despite the fact that we didn't actually see the outward physical manifestations of the previous weeks. At their peak, Jenny had about 10 to 12 serious episodes a day, but that was when Jenny was relatively coherent and had not lost a majority of her motors skills, particularly in her upper body, as she had by now. I had no idea if the episodes were occurring less often or if they just remained internal. A journal entry from Michelle on Sunday was stark evidence that Jenny was still experiencing the terror that we could see when she was active, regardless of what little body movement she had now:

Got there today and you were chatting away with mom. Of course, we couldn't understand a word you were saying. You laid down and were mumbling for a while. Then you started to get more and more agitated. You locked your body up. I was sitting on your bed and I tried to pull your legs down. You are so strong I couldn't get them to move. You were also pushing your nails down into my hand and it was hurting pretty bad. After I finally got my hand out from under yours, I had marks in my hand. I'm still blown away at how strong you can get during this whole thing. Things started to get worse, and you were getting louder and louder. The look on your face was unforgettable, even though I wish I could forget it. You looked terrified. I can't even describe what your face expression looked like. You were yelling and sounded so scared. Mom and I were there trying to calm you down. Nurse Kathy was getting you some drugs, and the aide Leah was massaging your legs to try to get them to relax. I saw the tears in mom's eyes as we were holding you. After I saw that, I started crying.

Other than her ability to communicate, in a horrific fashion, that she was still experiencing some intense episodes, Jenny had to work very hard at any form of "normal" communication such as letting us know that she had to use the restroom, or she wanted to change the channel on the TV, etc. She could not speak a single intelligible word.

Despite Jenny's current condition, all three disciplines of therapy continued to work with her each day, even over the weekends. While I am not clear how much was the therapists pushing Jenny, or how much of it was Jenny simply wanting more to do than lay in bed, she appeared to always be working very hard; and the reports from the therapists supported this.

When Jenny was healthy, she was known to "show attitude" from time to time when asked to do things she was not in favor of doing. So even though Jenny appeared to be working hard during most of her therapy sessions, that didn't mean she was always excited about it. Despite her condition, Jenny was still able to communicate that there were things she liked and disliked, as can be seen in Michelle's journal:

A speech therapist came in to work with you today and you weren't having anything to do with it. I can't tell if you really can't get your hand up to touch your nose, or if you were too mad that someone was asking you to do that. You looked mad on your face and you wouldn't do what she was asking you.

Jenny could also "cop an attitude" with the doctors:

...when I came back from a walk a doctor had just woken you up to do his check up on you. Mom said he just walked in, saw you were sleeping so just used his fingers to pry opened your eyelids, and woke you up. I could tell you were upset from it and you were repeating things over and over again. We couldn't tell if you were singing or if it was something you were trying to get us to get for you. It sounded like "wake up" or "pick up." I'm thinking you were so mad he woke you up. When he was making you do stuff, like lift up your legs, you kept doing it over and over, it really looked like you were so angry he woke you up, so you were doing things way more than what he was asking. Mom and I were laughing so hard, because we know your personality and figured that was your way of calling him a jerk.

As a father I would normally be upset at Jenny's behavior and be ashamed of Jenny's disrespect. However, I don't believe anyone can deny the bedside manner of this doctor left something to be desired. Still, given the situation, I was always ecstatic when Jenny showed any kind of attitude at this point. It was just another sign that the real Jenny was still in there.

Jenny didn't limit her displays of attitude to the hospital staff. She also showed it to family members as well:

When we mentioned the word pills to you, you got upset and kept saying "NO" really loud and shaking your head. We crushed them and fed them to you in ice cream. I think you knew that, but ate it anyway.

So ultimately, the weekend was a period of waiting; mostly waiting for the treatment of the NMDA to kick in so that Jenny could begin to come back to us. But we also had the issue of the anti-seizure medication being removed because of the rash, which had already begun to show improvement. This meant that the medicine that had caused it was wearing off, which then, of course, only increased my concern that Jenny would begin to have seizures again. This was actually my primary concern during these few days, despite everything else going on. The doctors could not give us any indication as to what was going to happen, or even what steps would be taken if certain scenarios played out. So all any of us could do was stay by her side, give Jenny comfort when needed, pray and hope for the best. Of all the unknowns we faced during this journey, in an odd way, this weekend was one of the worst. My CaringBridge note that day sums up my attitude: *"I have always been worried since this started on March 27th...for the first time I am truly scared."*

CHAPTER 42

Day 32

My depression of the previous Friday hadn't lightened at all by Monday morning, and there were still a couple of shots to the gut I had to take. Barb had spent the night with Jenny, but I was up most of the night as well, just "missing" her. It was probably the night that I struggled the most throughout the whole journey.

After this rough night, I arrived at the hospital in time for Barb and me to meet with Dr. Tran for an update. There was actually some good news in that the rash was clearing up, but I didn't really need the doctor to tell me that; I could see it for myself. The rest of the report, however, seemed to be bad news, or at least not what I wanted to hear.

For the most part, we had entered a phase of "wait and see." It shouldn't have been a big deal, but this had been going on long enough as far as I was concerned. I wanted answers about the seizure activity now that the anti-seizure medicine had been stopped. I was told there was a slight uptick in seizure activity, but according to the doctor, it was nothing to be concerned about as it could be anything. I learned that steroids can serve as a mild anti-seizure medication and was comforted that Jenny had some form of medication for the seizures.

The most disturbing news that morning was very subtle. I doubt the doctor even realized she said it. From a conversation the week before, I had understood that Jenny could possibly go to a Transitional Care Unit as early as Wednesday; however, that morning the doctor wanted to see where Jenny was at on Friday or Saturday and go from there. This change hit me extremely hard, but I laugh at myself now. The date for what I had viewed as progress had been moved, but Jenny could literally not do anything on her own and had a 24-hour nurse's aide. I was truly lying to myself if I couldn't figure out that two or three additional days in the hospital made very little difference.

Barb and I both left the hospital after the meeting and I went to the office for the day. I worked the longest day that I had since early April, getting almost eight hours in. I remember actually enjoying it and I accomplished quite a bit. It felt good to contribute something to the company again.

I have to admit that I had one eye on the clock the whole day as I was looking forward to the evening. Mollie Bjelland, a dear friend of Jenny and Michelle's from Jenny's JO volleyball days, was coming for a visit that evening! We have many happy memories of when Mollie, Jenny, and Michelle spent time together when they were younger and not so busy.

We're always happy when Mollie is around, so I was sure the evening would be uplifting and a nice change of pace.

I had no idea how great it would be.

After meeting for dinner, Barb, Mollie, and I arrived at the hospital about 7 p.m. Initially, it was an average evening. Jenny was "distant" when we arrived and one was left to wonder if she even knew we were there. The conversation turned to sports, mainly volleyball, the initial bond between Jenny and Mollie. After a while, it became clear that Jenny was coming around and making an effort to be part of the conversation. She still could not talk at all and was barely moving her eyes to look at each person in the room, but she was clearly laughing at jokes and smiling the familiar huge toothy smile of hers.

Much of our discussion that night revolved around which sport was better, volleyball or soccer. I had become the Rockford High School Girls Varsity Soccer coach the year Jenny entered seventh grade and I remained the coach throughout her high school years and three years of her college volleyball career. This rivalry of two sports that are played in the same season naturally has been a source of banter between Jenny and me through the years, and Mollie joins in when she is present.

More often than not, I am ridiculed when the topic of volleyball comes up because I can never remember the proper terms used in the game. At one point, we were discussing if the term was "pass" or "bump" when talking about the first portion in the sequence of the volleyball routine "pass, set, spike." I turned toward Jenny and asked her to show me a "bump," using the incorrect term purposely to reitcrate my opinion vollcyball isn't really a sport, and just to get under both girls' skin. At first, Jenny didn't react and the conversation kept going. Yet, Jenny was laughing at appropriate moments, a clear sign that she was comprehending what was being said. Then, about 30 seconds after I had asked Jenny to show me how to do a "bump," her arms started very slowly to come together and straighten out with the inside of the forearms facing up. It took her at least five and maybe as much as 10 seconds to get her arms there, but she was clearly showing me how to do a "bump."

It was a stunning moment! It is not that Jenny could not be coaxed into doing specific motions at times. In fact, high-fives were part of her regular speech therapy. However, this was only a single request for a particular motion and then the conversation moved on without additional prompting. She had processed the conversation and the request, was working at being an active part of the conversation, and wanted to show her dad something about volleyball.

This single, simple, albeit late motion was the happiest moment Barb and I had experienced in quite a long time – for sure since March – and maybe since Jenny's very first step as a baby, because after all the deterioration we had witnessed, in a way this was exactly the same thing.

179

Barb and I had watched Jenny deteriorate from an intelligent and happy young woman to something resembling an angry two-year old over the previous month. The experience and the emotions that went along with it are indescribable, unthinkable. I pray that none of you will ever have to watch a loved one, much less your child, go through that. It defines the word helpless. Now after all of that, we had perhaps witnessed a turning point. It was very much like Jenny had taken her first step. In fact, I don't recall being as happy when that happened.

Then, Jenny assumed the proper pose for the volleyball "pass" and held it for a moment. Barb and I stared at Jenny and then at each other in shock, and then we went crazy! With tears in our eyes and both of us fighting the urge to burst into outright sobs of joy, we began to high-five each other as well as Mollie and Jenny. It took Mollie a bit to grasp the significance of what had just occurred, but Jenny was all smiles as we repeatedly gave each other high-fives, cheered, and hugged. I have no idea if Jenny actually knew the significance of what she had done, but it was clear that she was enjoying the celebration, regardless of the reason.

I love my kid. I had been clinging to hope that I would get her back someday and this was the first truly significant sign in over a week that it might actually happen. The simple performance of a sports technique that Jenny had done maybe a million times before was hope that she was on her way back.

As much as it would have been great to end the evening on that most amazing high note, reality hit again as we were preparing to leave. Less than 30 minutes after Jenny was clearly alert and part of the conversation, she suffered another rather extreme episode that lasted nearly an hour and we were reminded that Jenny still had a long way to go. The demons had forced us to watch her deteriorate and by the previous week, when there wasn't much left, we had hoped she had finally reached the bottom of the depths to which she would descend.

Perhaps the diagnosis arrived just in time, but the demons were not ready to let go of her yet. Her episodes would get more powerful, more real, and more horrifying, but along the way, "Jenny" would make an appearance or two as well.

CHAPTER 43

Day 33

The day started with some rather disturbing news. Jenny was still attached to the continuous EEG and it showed a spike in her seizure activity overnight. According to the doctor, it wasn't dramatic, but obviously, this news disturbed me. I was relieved to hear that the doctor had decided to put Jenny back on Keppra, the original anti-seizure medicine she had been taking when this whole thing began in March.

Tuesday evening we began The Meal Train. When I got home from work, I was greeted by Jolene, a soccer mom whose two daughters I had coached over the years, who provided Barb and me with a home-cooked meal with all the fixings. It was wonderful! Barb and I had not eaten a delicious hot home-cooked meal together in over a month that hadn't come out of a microwave.

For the next month, we received a Meal Train daily delivery, all organized by Jolene and another soccer mom, Karen, aided by the website. This wonderful gift by so many people throughout the month played a huge role in keeping us healthy and sane during what was yet to come.

That evening Barb went to the hospital to be with Jenny, and I let loose and got together with one of my closest friends for a wild night out on town. After more than four weeks of near constant vigil over a hospital bed, it was time to bust out and release some steam. I deserved a night out with the boys. It was going to be a testosterone-filled night with unadulterated debauchery. Actually, I don't even know what debauchery is, but if it is going to Culver's and sitting in a booth eating custard and engaging in pointless debates about sports, then I absolutely engaged in it.

In the midst of my wild night out my cell phone rang. I could see it was Barb by the caller ID, and as much as a wife should never disturb her husband when he is tearing up the town and committing who knows what sins, given the circumstances, I figured it best that I answer the phone. It wasn't Barb calling.

I am nowhere near the type of writer that it would take to aptly describe what I heard when I answered the phone. I also cannot describe how my heart simultaneously stopped and leapt out of my chest when I heard Jenny on the other end.

The sound was immediately identifiable as being Jenny because of the breathy attempts at speaking. They were essentially quiet grunts with more air than noise, and she repeated the same sound, as if she was excitedly repeating a word.

In yet another display of my 26-year-old daughter's regression to infancy, I began to speak into the phone as if I was speaking to a baby, complete with the high-pitched voice most of us use when we talk to babies and repeating myself. "Hi, Jenny! How are you? Hi Jenny, how are you?" I instantly forgot where I was and who was with me. I didn't care who heard or what they thought. I was facing the wall so only Mike could actually see me when all of a sudden I heard Jenny say "Dad!" Mike was the only one who could see me tear up. It was the first intelligible word I had heard Jenny speak in 10 days. Just as the volleyball gesture the night before was reminiscent of her first baby step, this felt better than I remember it feeling when she had spoken her first words more than two decades ago. First volleyball and now speaking; progress was definitely being made.

It only got better after that. After a few more "grunts," Jenny began to repeat "Dad" over and over again. "Dad, Dad, Dad." I just sat and listened for a bit. Then she went silent, and I struggled to find something to say. I wanted the "conversation" to keep going. I could hear her breathing so I knew that she hadn't hung up, but I as I searched for something, anything, to say Barb's voice came onto the line and told me that Jenny was done talking.

Jenny had spoken. "Dad." I needed a napkin to dry my eyes. Barb told me that it was Jenny's idea to call and she was actually able to say what she wanted to do.

The day suddenly became wonderful!!!!!

CHAPTER 44

Day 34

Looking back on it now, Wednesday, May 8th, was a very odd day given what had happened the two days prior. We had been very lucky. We had seen some remarkable signs of awareness and function in Jenny the past two days, the first when she was able to follow the volleyball conversation during Mollie's visit, and then the very deliberate attempts at talking the night before. There was great reason for optimism!

Yet, as it turned out, I was about as low as I had ever been at most anytime during Jenny's illness on this day. So with everything good that was happening, why was I so focused on the negative?

The fact was, not everything was going smoothly. There continued to be more low points than high. Perhaps the positive events of the previous two nights just felt, to me, as if we were being teased. Barb and I were physically and emotionally exhausted, and we were at the point that we just wanted it to be over. We were smart enough to know better, but I think subconsciously we wanted to get in the car to take Jenny home, stop for a chocolate shake on the way, and pretend none of this ever happened.

It had only been eight days since we had received the NMDA diagnosis and the treatment had started. It was not realistic to expect dramatic improvement in such a short time period. The doctors had been very conservative in their estimates as to when things would begin to turn in the right direction for Jenny. The NMDA had had more than 35 days to inflict its damage; there was no reason anyone should believe it would get better in any less time than that.

What I had come to learn that morning, and what I didn't anticipate happening, was that with each positive step Jenny took forward, so too did the intensity of the episodes. In fact, despite how great the night before had been, I was greeted with a rather intense episode on my arrival at the hospital that morning. Because I had to watch my daughter tortured yet again, I was extremely negative the rest of the day.

The problem was the episodes. It was always the episodes. There is no way any of it would have ever been pleasant, but what made it all so hard to deal with was the episodes. Although over the previous week or two we had had a short reprieve from being forced to witness the terror they could inflict on Jenny, we were still just so darn tired of the episodes…and now they were starting up again.

I will never know what Jenny experienced during any of her episodes (thank God), but they were still very difficult for me to deal with, especially when I looked into her eyes. It is a natural response when trying to comfort someone, but on the really bad days, it was best not to look into Jenny's eyes during an episode. Despite the fact that other forces had a grip on and control of her behavior, even during the worst of it, her eyes showed that the real Jenny was trapped in there and wanted to get out. When her eyes would lock with mine, I was sure I could see the pain and fear in them – that she was screaming for me to help her. Yet, all I could do was stand by and watch. I was sure she could see that I was doing nothing for her, and I was convinced that fact tortured her even more – Dad wasn't willing to make it all better for her.

Another part that was so unnerving was that there never was any indication as to when the episodes would begin or how long they would last. Part of preparing for any difficult task is mental. In most situations one can prepare based on knowing when the event will occur, its cause, what must be done and, maybe most importantly, how to pace oneself in order to endure it. Jenny's situation offered us none of those luxuries, and both her family and the nursing staff were forced to deal with it multiple times a day. The result was an attempt to be on high alert at all times, which was very exhausting for everyone. Certainly watching Jenny go through them was scary at times, but I think the biggest emotional toll was that they caused the deepest feelings of helplessness for the onlookers and caregivers

I was so reluctant to accept the fact that the process of Jenny getting better would include helping her through the episodes again, that I needed to clarify it in my own mind: "Jenny has to come back through the hell she traveled into in order to make her way back to us." It makes perfect sense actually. As the NMDA retreated, and as the demons were forced to release their grip on my little girl, not only would her motor skills come back, but so too would whatever triggered the episodes. The demons were not going down without a fight and they were going to be sure they left a lasting impression…as if they hadn't already. Once I realized this fact on that morning, I believe I became scared more than anything. I didn't know if I had the endurance left in me to go through any more of it.

So, on what should have been such a positive day, because, indeed, everything was pointing to the fact that Jenny was coming back to me, that morning I was focused on the negative. The demons still had their grip on me too.

As I look back on the series of events of that day, I honestly am not sure what all the fuss was about. All the change that had come about recently was for the better, I just didn't see it that way at the time. The only thing I can say for sure is that I had lost it. I was unhappy and I was letting everyone know it. I ranted and raved that morning and ultimately triggered many discussions with several of the different doctors involved in Jenny's case. In hindsight, I am very impressed with how everyone tolerated and listened to my rants, the focus of which was that I wanted the doctors to do something about the episodes. For some reason, watching the doctors do all they could the past four weeks apparently wasn't enough for me to understand there was nothing they could do, but they listened to me anyway.

In what proved to be an odd twist that day, a plan for one final attempt at mitigating the episodes in any way possible was conceived and implemented. The plan was a sincere effort to make life easier on everyone involved, because, indeed, everyone involved suffered through Jenny's episodes. Yet, in a cynical way, I look back on this plan as an unintended consequence of my negativity and rants.

One of the doctors decided that all of the nurse's aides assigned to Jenny 24 hours a day would begin to take notes on all of Jenny's behavior. The goal was to find "patterns" and, much more importantly, "triggers" to the episodes. The theory was if a pattern could be identified, not only could they then be predicted, but the physical care could be prescribed for all of the nurses and nurse's aides. More specifically, by concentrating on the triggers, the doctor hoped that we could discover what not to do or what situations to prevent, thereby ending the undesirable behavior.

I still laugh at the thought of this. I did express my opinion that I thought it was a pointless exercise, but I appreciated the thought and effort. If the doctor that suggested it turned out to be right, it would be better for everyone involved; Jenny, her family, and the nurses. But I felt bad for the nurse's aides even before they heard about what it was they were going to be asked to do.

Unfortunately, as I suspected, this task only served to frustrate the aides. They wanted a clear explanation about, "What are we supposed to write down?" As it was, the plan was for them to write down that if Jenny did "X," they would note the time. If she did "Y," they would note the time. However, it very quickly became clear that were unable to quantify what was worth noting and what was not.

At 10:03 p.m., Jenny began what appeared to be her scratching the back of her neck. Is that worth noting? No, it was just an itch. However, by 10:18 p.m., the scratch had turned into a "behavior" as it had been repeated over and over and it was now obvious that she was trying to brush something off the back of her neck, not scratch it. And by 10:34 p.m. she was mad and yelling at the imaginary person who was standing behind her constantly putting Gummi Bears on her neck. The innocent scratch was actually the beginning of a simple episode, but ultimately the poor nurse's aide had no idea what to write, or even when to start describing what she saw. And God only knew what actually triggered it in the first place.

Any individual who had not seen more than a couple of episodes simply could not understand that each and every one was something new, so it was difficult to explain that there wasn't anything specific to look for. The result was that the aides never knew what was significant, and what was actually just an itch on the back of Jenny's neck. It meant watching her literally every second and trying to determine what was real and what were the beginnings of an episode. This was really an impossible task. Even Barb and I, who had spent the most time with Jenny by far, could not predict when one was coming with any accuracy.

After about a week of this effort, it was mercifully stopped. Not a single usable note was obtained.

CHAPTER 45

Day 35

The best way to sum up what went on today is to present the post that Michelle wrote for the CaringBridge that night:

I heard my Big Sister
Written May 9, 2013 7:34 p.m.

Hi, it's Michelle. Sorry to disappoint most of you who come on to read my dad's journals. I'm nowhere near as clever or funny as my dad. We have always said Jenny was always more like my dad than me. But, I have some info I wanted to share.

First and most important: JENNY IS TALKING! Well, sort of. Today when I called my dad, he was walking into the hospital and as usual, I always ask how Jenny is and how her night was. But today my dad said to me, "Why don't I hold up the phone to Jenny's ear and you talk to her." At first, I got nervous, not knowing how she would react to it. But after I was talking for a while, I heard a very quiet "Hi." My breath literally got taken away. THEN, I hear "How are you doing?" I was so shocked I didn't know what to say! I continued to talk, and then I hear my dad laughing in the background saying Jenny was now looking at the phone as if she were about to text.

That truly made my day. I went to school on such a cloud and some tears in my eyes. It was the first time I have heard Jenny talk to me in what seems like forever. All I kept thinking about all day was Friday night and how I get to spend my evening with my Big Sister and maybe even be able to hold a conversation with her again! I can't wait!

John also said she was talking some tonight with him and some people who came to visit. Nothing makes me smile more than knowing she is making progress. Being away from my family during this whole thing has been the hardest thing I have ever gone thru in my life. I look forward to my weekends now more than ever. That 2-hour drive home always takes 4 hours (at least it feels like it) and I can never get there soon enough.

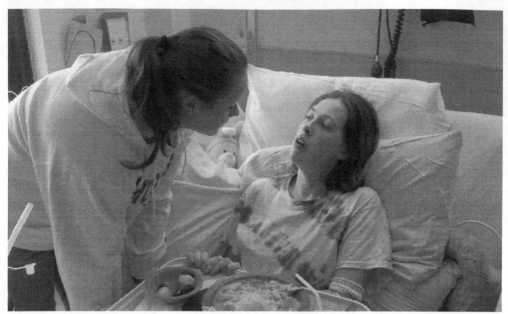
Michelle and Jenny

Michelle and I had spoken for a bit after her conversation with Jenny and then I hung up the phone. As soon as I hung up, Jenny looked at me and said, "I want to call Mom." It came out so smooth and clear. I was so surprised that I was shaking as I tried to push the right buttons on my phone. Jenny was not only able to communicate, she was processing things and able to articulate them.

I was so excited and running through all of the implications of what was happening that I have no recollection of what was said between Jenny and Barb. The call didn't last long, in part because Jenny tired so quickly at that point and she had already been in the hallway with an aide for quite a while when I arrived.

After Jenny was done talking with Barb, she said that she wanted to nap. A nurse was in to give meds and a few other things, but then the nurse, the aide, and I helped Jenny get settled into bed. Although not able to articulate the words at all, Jenny made it clear that she wanted to watch TV and wanted a specific channel on. We struggled to determine what channel she wanted, but with lots of time and work, I was finally able to satisfy her and she settled in for a short nap.

Later that evening I was at my office when I received a call from Dr. Tran to schedule our meeting for the next morning. The conversation continued and Dr. Tran relayed her experience with Jenny when she stopped in to see her after I had left the hospital for the day. Dr. Tran said that Jenny was able to speak clearly enough that she described the greeting cards hanging on the wall in the room, and that "Moe" (Michelle) was her sister and that she was a teacher. As Dr. Tran was telling the story her voice grew more and more excited, and I could hear she was getting emotional.

Jenny was still hooked up to the continuous EEG, which meant that this entire event was also caught on the video and audio being recorded in the room. As our phone conversation continued, Dr. Tran told me that the techs were in the control room as this was happening and could see all of this going on. Dr. Tran said that even the techs were excited about what they were seeing, "You have no idea how many people behind the scenes are cheering for Jenny."

I got a bit emotional too.

It had always been very clear how deeply the nurses and doctors cared about Jenny, but for the most part, I never assumed it was any more than the passion each of them had for their jobs. I certainly never doubted the doctors' sincerity in wanting to see Jenny get better, but again I believed it was on a professional level. The emotion I heard in Dr. Tran's voice during that phone conversation made it clear to me that I had underestimated how all of the medical professionals at Methodist felt about Jenny. Jenny truly was in the right place.

CHAPTER 46

Day 36

Jenny was making some dramatic improvements but there were still some major hurdles to get over.

On the medical side of things, at least one major decision was made that day. Plans were put in place to perform the third phase of Jenny's treatment of the NMDA, and on the upcoming Monday, Jenny would receive a dose of a drug called Rituximab. The easiest way to describe the treatment is a one-time dose of chemotherapy. My understanding was that this drug has many uses, but in this case, it was to target the specific cells making the antibodies responsible for attacking Jenny's brain rather than attacking the possible cancer itself. In other words, it was killing the NMDA but not the cause of it.

Over the previous 35 days, there had been countless hours of meetings with multiple doctors, in which I grasped maybe 10% of what they told me. Despite my lack of understanding most of the medical details of what was going on, for some reason I really wanted to understand how this drug worked. Dr. Tran attempted to explain it to me, but it very quickly became clear that this would need to be filed under the category of amazing-things-that-people-much-smarter-than-me-developed-and-thank-God-they-did. This treatment was another piece of information that would have been really cool to understand if I wasn't learning it because of what was happening to my kid. I did come out of this event much smarter than when I went in.

Beyond the fact that I can't get my mind around how a drug knows which cells to attack, I could not understand why this drug was "a long-term solution that will take up to a month to actually work." More often than not, I very quickly let the technical details of what the doctors told me go in one ear and out the other, but for some reason I couldn't let this one go. I repeatedly asked that it be explained again, but each time the results were the same…I was a deer in the headlights. In the end, I knew it really didn't matter that I was lost. I just wanted my kid back.

As much as the NMDA itself kept things in a constant state of change, Jenny's desire to go home was also constant. I can still see her lying in bed on the very first day she was admitted to the hospital with only one question for Dr. Freking after he went through all of the details and plans: "When can I go home."

She repeated this question whenever she was coherent with the doctors.

Further into Jenny's illness, as she began to deteriorate into the demons' abyss, she repeatedly became frustrated with those of us in the room. Either we could not comprehend that the word "Wild" had 4 letters in it and that "Blue Jackets" had 11 or, more often than not, we had stopped her from leaving her room to go into the hallway. While "going for walks" was common, many times it just couldn't happen, and there came a point that Jenny failed to or chose not to comprehend any reason for it, instead becoming frustrated with whoever was restricting her.

Her frustration led to an interesting habit that developed very early in Jenny's stay at Methodist and persisted all the way through. Whenever she could not get the person in the room with her to comply with her wishes, regardless of what they were, she would press the nurse's "call button." It didn't matter if it was the nurse that was standing in front of her and the problem at hand was not finding the correct channel on the TV she wanted to watch – if Jenny wasn't pleased with the person there at the moment, she would press the button to summon a nurse.

I was always amazed that no matter how sick she was, even when she wasn't coordinated enough to feed herself, she could hit that little button on either the hand-held unit, the two on the control panel on either side of her bed or even the main one on the wall behind her bed.

Although this had become a habit for Jenny and usually she didn't really need anything, there was no way the nurses could ignore the request. Therefore, the nurses repeatedly came in to see what the problem was only to find us wrestling with Jenny during an episode or keeping her from pulling out her IV line or even just debating the color of the flowers on the ledge. Each time, they patiently shut off the light and went about their business, only to return seconds later because one of us let Jenny's hand slip away and she pushed the button again. Each time the nurses came to see if, in fact, this time she actually needed something.

Both the urge to walk the hallways and to press the call button when she was frustrated came to a head one day. Barb, Michelle, and I were all at the hospital that day, and this coincided with an odd day when almost all of the nurses and aides on the floor were relatively new to Jenny.

Jenny was extremely determined to leave the room that afternoon, but Barb, Michelle, and I would not let her and were easily able to overpower her if she made a break for the door, which was a very common occurrence at times like these. However, what also became common was to let Jenny attempt to burn off her frustration by allowing her to wander freely around the room while we guarded the door. This tactic however gave Jenny free access to the call button, which she pushed. The nurse's aide for that shift had stepped out of the room for a bit since three family members were present but quickly reappeared when the call light came on. At this point, Michelle and I were guarding the door while Barb consoled Jenny. The aide took up position by Barb and Jenny.

After a bit of conversation, Jenny again pushed the call button. Another aide appeared and joined Barb and the aide next to Jenny. I am sure the two aides were just following Barb's lead and trying to verbally coax Jenny back into bed without actually touching her in any way, which, unfortunately, allowed Jenny to press the call button yet again. This time a nurse appeared. Like the aides, the nurse took up post next to Jenny, but decided to take charge and physically lead Jenny back to the bed while Barb moved closer to Michelle and I who were simply serving as sentries at the door.

So here we were, six grown adults trying to get one person back into bed. This time Jenny had three people standing around her in a united front that were not going to let her press that call button again, so something of a stalemate ensued. Jenny refused to walk back to her bed but did not make a break for the door either. She could not speak at all during this incident, but Jenny made her displeasure with all of us very clear with grunting, facial expressions and body language.

Finally, Jenny's frustration boiled over. She did not want to go back to bed, but she couldn't leave the room and there was no way to summon yet another nurse who, I believe, Jenny was sure would talk reason into all of these other six stupid people in the room. The three nurses were closely encircling Jenny, using more and more force to push her toward the bed while Barb, Michelle, and I stood back to observe. There wasn't anything we could do, and all three of them were new to us, and to Jenny, so we respected that they had a job to do and let them do it.

That is when Jenny squeezed her eyes shut tight, made her hands into fists, and curled her arms up into her chest. None of us knew what would happen next and all six of us froze, waiting to see what Jenny was about to do. I remember the first aide looking straight at me because Jenny looked like she was about to get violent, but other than one very minor episode a couple of weeks before, Jenny had never done that, so I wasn't too concerned.

As we stood there, Jenny began to repeatedly take long, deep breaths. Her hands were still in fists and her arms were held close to her chest as it rose and fell with each exaggerated breath. After about five or six breaths Jenny inhaled a large one and held it. All of us held our breath as well, wondering what would come next. Certainly the three brand new hospital staff had no idea what was about to happen, but neither did Barb, Michelle or I. It was probably only a fraction of a second, but I remember the moment as if time had stopped. Everyone watched Jenny. Here, yet again, was something new that we hadn't experienced.

Suddenly Jenny let out a loud, long, and extremely high-pitched scream. It hurt the ears. It lasted for many seconds. It had to have been heard in the farthest reaches of the 6th floor, and maybe even portions of the fifth and seventh floors.

At first, we stood in shock. Then Barb, Michelle, and I did the last thing that the other three healthy people in the room expected of us...we began to laugh hysterically. I'm sure Barb and Michelle tried to hold it in as much as I did, but one of us gave that little snort that is released when a person tries not laugh at something but can't fight it off, at which point there was no stopping us. I know I was laughing at much more than Jenny's scream. I was laughing at the complete absurdity of everything that had happened the past month, letting off steam as much as laughing. I am sure Barb and Michelle were doing the same thing.

The three medical professionals looked at us as if we were crazy. It is not surprising that they couldn't see the humor in the situation. I am sure they were wondering how the family members of an uncooperative patient could react this way to such an odd outburst. Perhaps the surprise is that Barb, Michelle and I actually could find the humor in such a situation, but we had been through too much and seen far too many horrific scenes. Whether we just needed release or the situation was truly hilarious compared to everything else we had been through, we laughed until tears came to our eyes.

CHAPTER 47

Day 38

Jenny began sleeping a bit more than what had been "usual" during the previous few weeks, still nowhere near enough, but like everything else, it was an improvement. The sleep she was getting also appeared to be "deeper" and more restful. The healthy Jenny talks in her sleep, and I thought I heard that happening again, a hopeful sign that her dreams might be happy. The hospital also had Jenny working hard with occupational, physical and speech therapy every day, which may have been a factor in her being able to sleep.

We celebrated Mother's Day as a family, but Michelle signed Jenny's name on the card she gave Barb. Since the weather was nice, Barb asked Jenny if she wanted to go for a walk outside and she popped up instantly and went for her shoes. We felt that she might be bit cold outside, but when we handed her some sweatpants to put on, she threw them to the floor and headed for the door. Her sweatshirt met a similar fate.

It was the first time she had been outside in over two weeks. Jenny walked for 15 to 20 minutes, with Barb and Michelle guiding and assisting her on either side. Michelle and Jenny even made a wish and threw coins into the fountain. Michelle cried as she did it, and I tried to imagine what her wish was. I knew Michelle struggled with being so far away and only able to be here on the weekends, and I saw the toll it was taking on her. I believe that Michelle's wish was for her sister to get better, and over the next three weeks and as the summer would continue, perhaps no one would play a larger role in that than Michelle.

Barb, Jenny and Michelle

The biggest news was that Jenny was able to feed herself for the first time in about two weeks. Jenny was not always successful at hitting her mouth (in fact one time Jenny fed the bed sheets), and the bib was put to good use, but obviously this was a sign of progress and a testament to the therapist's work. Some "processing" issues were still going on as a couple of times Jenny would fill her mouth with three or four spoonfuls before deciding to chew. It still seemed as though we were celebrating the efforts of a two-year old, but the feelings of hope were still somewhat new and any improvement felt momentous and welcome.

In the coming week we dared to have brief conversations about what the next step was for Jenny. As ecstatic as we were about the "improvement" that weekend, the distance still left to travel seemed daunting. My concern was how much of Jenny's knowledge and ability would come back as she began to heal, and how much she would have to relearn. Jenny showed more and more evidence that her "mind" was still intact, recognizing people who would come and go and speaking more clearly each day, which encouraged us, but questions remained.

In the midst of our focus on improvement, we *enjoyed* an episode Jenny had that day. Barb, Michelle, and I even had a few laughs out of pure joy as the appearance of episodes, though they are not pleasant, meant that Jenny was starting to come back. She had a rather intense episode in which, for some reason, she wanted to leave the room because "I am a patient here," which went on for almost 20 minutes. I was impressed with the two nurses who decided to take Jenny out in the hallway without any family members along. They guided Jenny, preventing her from getting hurt or causing any damage, and they worked through the episode by allowing her to act as a nurse. Jenny repeatedly scanned her wristband using the nurse's scanner to prove that "I'm a patient here." They allowed Jenny to walk behind the nurse's desk and, as Michelle told Jenny later, "You got to touch stuff that only the nurses get to touch."

The final positive sign of the day was when Michelle was saying goodbye to Jenny for the week before she headed back to school. Jenny had developed quite a collection of stuffed animals during her stay and each one of them had been given a name. Michelle asked Jenny the names of each of her stuffed animals every Friday when she arrived, as there always was at least one new one, usually more, and she had always been impressed that Jenny always remembered all of their names. However, it had been a couple of weeks since Jenny was able to talk and Michelle wondered if she could still remember the names of each of the stuffed animals, so she began quizzing Jenny. It was a bit of a struggle to be sure but after some time and coaxing, Jenny was able to recall the correct name of each.

Jenny's ability to recall those names after so many days of not being able to speak showed us that her memory was still intact and gave us hope that she would continue to improve and manage to travel the long road back to a "normal" life.

CHAPTER 48

Day 39

As Jenny improved step-by-step, Barb and I felt like the parents of a toddler as we watched our child make new strides and discoveries every day. Due to some car trouble that forced Barb and I to rely on one car, our time spent at the hospital was together rather than separate that week. As much as the hassle of the breakdown was something we certainly didn't need, the result was that we were able to share a few happy moments with Jenny together as parents.

Jenny was sleeping when we arrived at the hospital that morning for our usual morning meeting with Dr. Tran. We watched Jenny wake in slight confusion as she scanned the room. Then, she saw both of us and smiled, and I was immediately struck by what a simple gift that could be. I asked Jenny how she was doing and got an enthusiastic Jenny-style exclusive thumbs-up. Then without saying a word, she went to get out of bed. Barb asked if she was headed to the bathroom and Jenny nodded her second response to a question in 15 seconds. This was already turning into a good day, just like that. Barb and I got into our "ready" position, one of us on each side of her to aid Jenny as she walked, which had become standard about two weeks previously, but Jenny got up unaided and walked directly to the bathroom. After two weeks of stumbling and wandering, Jenny was able to walk purposefully to accomplish a goal and remain focused until she did so. Barb accompanied her, but Jenny essentially took care of business all on her own. As she started back toward the bed, she gave big hugs to Mom and Dad, another uplifting gift.

In those three minutes, we experienced what we had come to see as a full day's quota of positives, and we were just getting started!

Jenny settled into bed again and pointed to the food tray across the room that had been delivered earlier. She still had not spoken, but she was clearly communicating. Once the tray was in front of her, Jenny began to dig in without hesitation. I frantically cut up her eggs and fruit, just as one would for a toddler, trying to keep up as Jenny began to feed herself, even more easily than yesterday. We ignored her rejection of "manners" as she skipped using the utensils and were rewarded when she was able to open her own yogurt container, a huge accomplishment. Additionally, for the first time in a long time she ate almost all of her food.

Barb and I watched all of this in awe. These were gigantic steps from where she had been five or six days earlier. Jenny was the most functional she had been since April 13th, exactly one month earlier.

Of course, as parents, we felt as if we were floating, but the doctors and nurses who took all of this in that morning were also excited. Dr. Tran arrived for the meeting and was so happy to see Jenny's current condition that she simply stood and watched with a smile on her face. Later in the day, after I had left the hospital, a nurse called me on the phone and was telling me how happy she was to see "the real Jenny." She also told me that the occupational therapist had said that it was by far Jenny's best day. She had performed all of the tasks assigned to her, and even more remarkable, she was able to do things on that day that she had been shown a few days earlier without being reinstructed, which showed that she had absorbed the information given to her days before, even though her body could not perform the task at that time. This may have been the greatest sign of the day that healing and improvement really was taking place and that even better days were on the horizon.

CHAPTER 49

Day 42

When I arrived at the hospital that morning, Jenny looked at me for a long time but gave no real response to my presence. There was no way to sugarcoat it: she looked very depressed. John had arrived before me and said that she had been asking to go home again. My heart sank. I lied to John saying that I would leave them alone and go to the lounge to work. I went to the lounge, but it was to shed a few tears. Barb and I hadn't been doing very well the previous couple of days, and John didn't look his usual self either – clearly by this point the whole situation was taking its toll on everyone involved, directly or by association. It isn't that the previous few days were bad in any way. It just felt as though we had been here doing this forever.

Jenny had suffered another sleepless night and was pretty tired. After walking John to the elevator, we walked back to her room and she fell into a light sleep at about 8:15 a.m. When the nurses came in an hour later to do their jobs and woke Jenny up, I asked Jenny if she wanted to go for a walk, as it was beautiful outside. Again, she gave no response.

Jenny drifted in and out of sleep, so I packed up to leave. Suddenly, with no warning or additional prompting, Jenny popped up out of bed and walked across the room to her shoes. Since she had the tendency to become focused on one thing and I was afraid she would get upset and act out if I had to stop her from going to the elevator, I quickly called for Janet, the aide, and asked her to grab a wheelchair. It was sunny outside and we were going to get Jenny some vitamin D and make this a better day.

The campus of Methodist Hospital is actually two buildings standing next to each other, with the other building, Meadowbrook Clinic, housing multiple offices for outpatient visits. Each building has a large parking ramp. The two buildings are connected by an enclosed walkway with a patio on one side for people who wish to sit at tables to eat or relax. The other side of the walkway has a small garden with benches and paths that lead to a short alleyway behind the hospital and the parking ramp for the Meadowbrook building. The walk around both buildings, including the parking ramps and a small portion of the boardwalk is just over three-quarters of a mile.

After taking the elevator down to the main level, Jenny and I walked side by side toward the walkway that connects the two buildings while Janet pushed the empty wheelchair behind us just in case Jenny got tired. As the walkway runs adjacent to the patio area on the right, the enclosure is made up of a series of floor to ceiling windows and a set of double doors for access to the patio.

I let Jenny dictate where we were going. She knew this part of the hospital from previous walks, but I was not aware if she had been down this particular hallway since her arrival. The patio was her first actual glimpse of "outside," so that is where she wanted to go. Jenny had not spoken a word yet. She suddenly turned to go outside onto the patio, by attempting to walk through one of the floor to ceiling windows…yeah, she did. My bad.

I redirected her to the door, and she proceeded to walk across the patio toward some stairs that led up to the road that fronts the hospital. I had no idea if she knew where she was going, but it was clear she was enjoying her walk, so I didn't stop her, although I was a bit concerned because she always wanted to "go home" and she was walking with a certain amount of determination that made me wonder if she was up to something. However, I was caught up in the fact that the sun was shining on her face and she seemed to be enjoying it; but I did feel sorry for Janet pushing the wheelchair, as Jenny did not pick the ideal path for her to navigate.

One of the wonderful features of the area surrounding Methodist Hospital is the boardwalk that intersects in a few places with the pedestrian walkways around the buildings. It is actually part of a larger path system in this part of the Twin Cities that was built over a portion of Minnehaha Creek. The section of the creek that is directly behind the hospital is extremely wide, and the water moves very slowly. It actually looks more like a swamp than a creek. The boardwalk is accessible at either end of the hospital and extends 50 to 60 yards out from the back of the building. It is probably two or three hundred yards to walk the whole thing. It has high railings on both sides and is approximately four feet wide.

Jenny walked all the way down to one end of the hospital campus, around the parking lot to behind the hospital, and onto the section of the boardwalk that connects the walkways to the rest of the hospital grounds without incident. She was already looking tired by this point and I asked her how she was doing. She had not spoken a word yet that day, but she gave me two thumbs up, holding them above her head for a good 10 seconds, causing me to get a bit emotional.

The walk continued along the back of the hospital until the boardwalk ended, then we crossed the alleyway and through the small garden until we came to the same enclosed walkway in between the two buildings where Jenny had first stepped outside. We had walked approximately a half mile, which is not bad for someone who hadn't walked more than a few hundred yards at a time in the past month. Jenny had also allowed me to hold her hand for the vast majority of the time we walked. On top of everything else this may have been the best part of the day; the gesture made me feel as if I had my kid back. At least in a small way.

Upon our return inside the walkway, Jenny began to tremble and sway and she was starting to sweat as we stood waiting for the elevator to take us back upstairs. The walk had taken its toll. Janet moved the wheelchair behind Jenny and we urged her to sit down. She glared at us and gave me a very soft push to make her point as she stepped away from the wheelchair. She still had yet to actually speak a word the entire morning. When the elevator arrived, Jenny entered and immediately leaned against the wall, showing more and more signs of fatigue. Another nurse who boarded the elevator also encouraged Jenny to sit down during the ride, but Jenny closed her eyes, got a very determined look on her face, and turned away from the chair to face the wall at the back of the elevator. The door finally opened at the 6th floor, after stopping at almost every floor, and Jenny nudged us out of the way to walk as quickly as she could to her room. She went straight to her bed where she fell asleep almost instantly. She hadn't even taken the time to remove her shoes.

This walk was an unmistakable and clear indication that Jenny was in control and taking some autonomy back. She had decided where she was going to walk and she was going to complete the entire walk under her own power. She refused to let anyone take that away from her. It was a monumental morning. The day had started with all of us feeling a deep level of sadness about everything that had occurred to this point and even despair over how much longer it was going to last, but it had turned into one of the most beautiful mornings in a long time.

CHAPTER 50

Day 44

Barb went ahead to the hospital early that Saturday morning while I stayed home to get some chores done and take care of a few things. She arrived to find Jenny more active than usual and much more aware of her surroundings, demonstrating a marked improvement in her ability and willingness to follow instructions compared to the day before, but she still could not speak clearly. The difference in Jenny's condition between the previous night and that morning might have been the most dramatic and positive improvement since she had been admitted to the hospital and the relatively "new Jenny" seemed to excite and reenergize both Barb and the staff.

The physical and emotional struggles over the previous five weeks to keep Jenny safe and secure were made more difficult by the obvious frustration she showed, as well as how it made her visibly sad. While it had clearly been necessary for Jenny to be in the hospital, it had been equally obvious that she did not want to be there. There was nothing her family and the caregivers at the hospital wanted more than to grant Jenny's wish to get on the elevator at the end of the hall.

The combination of the excitement created by a seemingly improved Jenny, the pent up frustrations of everyone involved, and finally having a decent stretch of weather created the perfect situation where everyone wanted to take Jenny outside for a walk. Neither Barb nor any of the people on staff that day were part of the walk Janet and I had taken Jenny on the previous Thursday, and my excitement in telling the story of that walk made everyone else want to share and enjoy that experience with Jenny as well.

A plan was made for an exciting adventure outside. Despite having been in the hospital for the past 44 days, Jenny was not as weak as one would have imagined. I was best suited to physically manage her, so it had been determined that I needed to be present before she could go outside.

I was expected at the hospital no later than noon. Usually I arrived on time, so Barb and the nurses had every reason to believe that I would be there. To help keep Jenny calm and focused, as well as giving her something to look forward to, Barb told her that she would be going outside for a walk as soon as I arrived. Unfortunately I was held up at home far past the agreed upon time. As was often the case with Jenny while she was sick, she became increasingly uncooperative when forced to wait for something. In Jenny's mind, it was time to go, whether I was present or not.

By 1:30 p.m., Jenny was trying to head for the elevator regardless of what others thought about it, which created an unfortunate situation that was even more stressful than normal. Everyone was disappointed because they had gotten Jenny excited about going outside and now they had to deny what she clearly believed she was able to do. It took multiple people working together to manage her, and everyone was anxiously awaiting my arrival.

I finally arrived at around 2:30 p.m. As I rode up in the elevator, I noted my usual feelings of apprehension. I hadn't talked to Barb since she left the house that morning beyond the usual text update upon her arrival. Though I knew Barb had been there all morning and Jenny's recent improvement gave us every reason for confidence, there was still the familiar "what now" feeling as the elevator took me closer to the 6th floor. My body had formed some habits over the past month and half, and one of those was to get my adrenaline flowing to be prepared for anything when the doors slid open.

As passengers exit the elevators onto the 6th floor, it was a left hand turn and then a few steps before the need to turn right into the main hallway. That first hallway was fairly long, with the first significant location being the nurse's station at a halfway point where the hallway continues straight ahead, as well as opens to the right and left leading to patient's rooms. It is unusual to see anyone immediately upon entering that first hallway, but today Jenny was there, facing me, along with three or four other people standing by the nurse's station.

Initially, none of the identities of the other people nor what they were doing with Jenny registered with me as I heard someone say, "There he is!" Jenny lit up and headed toward me at a very brisk pace, just short of running. My heart kind of leapt at the thought that my daughter had been waiting for me and couldn't wait to see me. It had been a long time since I had been able to enjoy that feeling. If it were a Hollywood movie, the scene would have been in slow motion with some emotionally charged music playing in the background!

Of course, just as it had been for the past seven weeks, nothing was as it seemed. I walked toward her with my arms extended to give her a hug only to have her head right past me (stop the music, return the film speed to normal) as she put her arms out to push me away while I was reaching for her. Jenny had no interest in seeing me. All she was interested in was going for a walk outside of the hospital "as soon as Dad arrived." There was no time to waste as far as she was concerned. Dad's here, let's go!

Without further delay, Jenny, Barb, a nurse's aide, Laurie, and I headed down in the elevator. Laurie was pushing a wheelchair, just as Janet had, for Jenny to sit in if and when she needed a break. Once again, we could go pretty much anywhere on the hospital grounds without worrying about Jenny running out of energy.

As we descended, Barb and I began to discuss where we would go on this walk though we might have saved ourselves the trouble, as the

203

choice was obvious. Way back in early April when Jenny first arrived at the hospital and was still aware of her surroundings, she had expressed a desire to take a walk on the boardwalk. However, not only was Jenny not healthy enough to leave the hospital for even a short walk until just recently, the Twin Cities was experiencing what had to be one of the coldest and wettest springs on record. The result was that the gates allowing access to the boardwalk had been locked until the past couple of days. It had become a primary goal of Barb, Michelle, and I to make sure Jenny had the opportunity to walk on the boardwalk as soon as she could.

As far as Barb and I were concerned, today was the day we would be able to snatch a small piece of normalcy for all of us. Our victories over this illness were measured in small and otherwise insignificant events. A walk on the boardwalk would be symbolic as much as it would be a welcomed change of scenery.

We went to the ground floor and exited by way of the enclosed walkway between the two buildings into the small garden area, then took the path through the garden to the alleyway that led to the boardwalk. It was beautiful outside and it was such a pleasure to see Jenny walk with some determination as she worked her way toward the long-awaited stroll on the boardwalk. It was clear that she had comprehended what was being discussed in the elevator and that she knew where we were headed.

Throughout this entire experience, even though there were so many tragic and even horrifying events, seemingly minor and non-medically related setbacks were much more heartbreaking than they otherwise would have been. At times there seemed to be an unexpected hurdle that would deprive us of some small respite from the reality of the situation, and we took them much harder than we should have. I was convinced that nothing of the sort would happen today, sure that we had paid enough of a price by now to deserve a slow, relaxing stroll outside as a family on one of the first truly beautiful weekend days of the spring.

Nope. Apparently not.

Once we navigated the walkway and emerged onto the alleyway behind the hospital, the boardwalk came into view about 30 yards away. The access gate was locked! I had wanted this walk so badly that I refused to believe my eyes and continued to walk to the gate with Jenny as Barb and Laurie walked a bit slower behind us. Sure enough, the gate to the boardwalk was locked.

Who knew a locked gate could be so heartbreaking? I'm not sure who felt worse, Jenny, Barb, or myself. Jenny began to fight with the gate trying to get it open. While fighting back tears, I tried to explain that it was locked and we couldn't go for our walk there. Without any expression on her face, she began trying to climb the gate and I had to physically hold her back. I looked toward Barb at one point and the pain she felt was evident on her face. As symbolic as the walk on the boardwalk would have been, that locked gate basically summed up our lives over the past seven weeks.

There are so many things surrounding Jenny's illness that cannot be accurately explained. Most of these things surround her behavior and personality when she was in the deepest recesses of the illness and the pain it inflicted on everyone involved; however, another thing that can never be adequately explained is the compassion extended to Jenny by the staff throughout Methodist Hospital, especially the nursing staff on the 6th floor. As uncomfortable as I believe Laurie was on that day taking Jenny out on this excursion, she was another example of how each of them always did what they could to give Jenny some comfort whenever possible.

It would have been easy for Laurie to just say, "Okay, let's move on," or "Let's head back in," and relieve herself of this duty. Instead, she pulled out her cell phone and said, "I'm going to try calling security."

This is what I heard on one side of that phone conversation, or at least my best recollection of it.

"Hi. This is Laurie, a nurse from 6Neuro. I have a patient here that wanted to take a walk on the boardwalk, but the gate is locked."

"It's beautiful outside."

"Oh, it's going to rain later?" She repeated what the security guard said for our benefit.

"Do you think you can open it for just a little bit? I have a patient that really wants to go for a walk."

"Yes, I'm a nurse from Neurology."

"Yes, I have the girl from the 6th floor."

"Okay. Thank you so much."

She disconnected the call and looked at us. "They are coming to open it up for Jenny."

Wow! I could have hugged her at that moment. She went the extra mile and made things happen just for Jenny.

There is no way to explain how much we relied on the nurses and nurse's aides while Jenny was at Methodist. Of course, the doctors were vital, but the support staff, such as the security guard, did countless little things in an effort to ease the pain and suffering of our entire family. This gesture remains in our hearts as one of the greatest.

As we waited for someone to come and open the gate, the four of us walked around the small garden. Jenny remained extremely agitated and seemed to be trying to find a new way out of the garden. I presumed she was attempting to find a different way to get on the boardwalk. We had tried to explain that someone was coming to open the gate for us, but that it would take some time. It was impossible to determine if she didn't comprehend, was just anxious to get on the boardwalk, or if something else was going on.

I had already forgotten that I was meeting Debbie that day. She was stopping by the hospital on her way out of town and would have to maintain a tight timeline. She arrived after we had headed outside and thus found Jenny's room empty. Thankfully, one of the nurses, Andi, discovered Debbie waiting in the room and told her we had gone out for a walk. Andi was aware that we had intended to go to the boardwalk and although it was only partially visible from the window in Jenny's room, what was visible included the locked gate that we were waiting at for the security guard to come and open.

After ten minutes or so, security arrived to open the gate. Jenny had gotten a bit tired and was sitting in the wheelchair. As the security guard unlocked the gate, I approached him to say thank you. However, it was clear that the gentleman was more interested in greeting Jenny once the gate was open; he walked right over to Jenny and said, "It is a pleasure to meet you," and turned to Barb and said, "It was my pleasure," as she thanked him.

Finally, our stroll on the boardwalk began! A little bit of happiness for Jenny, and a chance for all of us to enjoy some new scenery on a gorgeous Minnesota spring afternoon.

Jenny immediately got out of the wheelchair and walked onto the boardwalk. She walked very quickly and I stayed with her while Barb and Laurie walked at a more leisurely pace. I had imagined this day for quite a few weeks. While Jenny and I had been on the boardwalk two days earlier, that was unexpected, and at the time it was simply to see how far she could go. If anything, that walk made me look forward to this one even more, as we were doing it as a family. I had pictured it as a slow stroll, taking our time to look at the plants and birds, taking in the sky without having to view it through a window, exploring the entire maze of walkways the boardwalk had to offer, and the simple pleasure of feeling the wind blow through our hair. I would even have welcomed a little sunburn.

However, similarly to her running toward me in the hallway when I arrived at the hospital, those images are for the movies and this was real life.

I kept encouraging Jenny to relax and walk more slowly, but she made it clear that she had other plans. It soon became obvious that Jenny wanted to run. Yes, run! Less than two weeks ago she could barely walk and now she was running!

And we did, much to the dismay of both Barb and Laurie. Barb was soon yelling for me to stop Jenny from running, but I decided to just stay close and run with my daughter. I have to admit, there was a bit of that same feeling of teaching Jenny to ride a bike for the first time. Her face was as bright as it had been in weeks, and I imagined that she felt free for just a bit. I know I did. I enjoyed running with her, looking at her face while I ran.

Up in the window on the 6th floor, Andi had joined Debbie in the room and they witnessed this scene as it unfolded. As Jenny began to run, Debbie and Andi began to cheer, which drew the attention of two additional nurses on the floor that came to see what all the fuss was about.

Jenny wasn't moving too fast, but Barb's concern was well founded because Jenny wasn't that steady. Apparently, Debbie and Andi were yelling for me to keep up as well (as if I could hear them). As much as I was aware of what Barb was saying and I understood the dangers, I made the conscious decision to let her go. It was too beautiful watching her run. The railings on the boardwalk are very high so there was no danger of her going over them and I have never been too concerned about my kids falling and scraping a knee. They heal. At this moment, the excitement of the run outweighed everything in my mind.

I was feeling so much joy as Jenny and I ran and I wanted to share it with everyone. That portion of the boardwalk is visible from dozens, if not hundreds, of the windows on one side of the hospital, including many of the rooms on the 6th floor. I had a hunch that at least a couple of the nurses that had been caring for Jenny may have been watching for us, as they all knew we wanted to get Jenny on the boardwalk. Playing my hunch, I said to Jenny, "Wave to all of the nurses on the 6th floor" and I looked up and waved enthusiastically. Jenny did not.

One of the nurses with Debbie said, "Oh my gosh! Can he see us? I have always told everyone that no one can see into these rooms from outside!" Indeed, I could not see anyone at all, a fact that the nurse made sure to verify once we returned.

Back down on the boardwalk, we were soon out of sight of the rooms on the 6th floor, and the tone of the day began to take a turn.

At what point this "walk" transformed from a leisurely time outside to another escape attempt for Jenny, I cannot say with any certainty. I don't believe that is what it was when we started, but I will never know for sure. At some point, I suppose, Jenny realized that once the walk was over she would have to return to the same four walls she had been staring at for the past 44 days, and at this point, we still had no indication as to when she would be discharged or where she would go from here. I can understand how trapped she must have felt. Heck, all of us felt trapped, and we got to go home at least once every day or two.

Throughout this entire journey, I have always wondered what Jenny actually understood on any given day. Although Jenny tells us now that she does not remember anything during her time at Methodist, including this day, that does not change the fact that she did experience it and there was at least some comprehension of what was going on around her the entire time. When she could talk, there was not a single day that she didn't ask, "When can I go home?" and even when she had a hard time communicating, she was able to express this wish loud and clear. I am still brought to tears at the thought of how trapped she must have felt through this phase. Even if the long-term memory of those months is lost, I can't bear the thought that she may have been conscious of what was happening, and how helpless she must have felt.

I was right next to Jenny the entire time she was running. If she had fallen, as Barb feared, I knew I was there to at least break her fall. However, after a couple hundred feet or so I also began to feel concerned. Her speed increased and she became even more unstable as she ran the fastest she had moved in nearly two months. A combination of the damage the illness did to her motor skills, combined with pure lack of exercise for several weeks caused us to reach a point at which the running was dangerous. It was clear she was getting winded and I knew it was time to stop. And, let's be honest, I'm no world-class athlete by any stretch of the imagination. I was ready to stop running too.

At first, I simply asked her to slow down. If anything, she sped up. Then I reached out and put my arm across her body to hold her back while I slowed down, and it was at this moment that I knew we were in serious trouble as she immediately began to fight me. She tried to push my arm away and leaned into her run. At the time I couldn't decide if the look on her face was determination or anger, but I believe now that it was a combination of both.

We neared the point on the boardwalk where there was a turn to the right that went directly away from the hospital, and although originally I had been looking forward to walking farther out onto the boardwalk, now there was no way I could let her go in that direction. It would have required that at some point I would have needed to convince her to turn around, or we would have had to make the entire trip around the swamp back to the walkways leading us to the hospital doors. Therefore, I needed to keep her going in the direction we were headed because it took us to a back entrance of the hospital. I managed to get her past the potential turn as she continued straight ahead. That was the first battle I managed to win.

Jenny had momentum going in the sense that her adrenaline was flowing and her determination was building. If there was one thing we had learned over the past seven weeks, it was that once she got fixated on something, there was no letting go of it, which was especially true when it came to what she believed was an opportunity to leave the hospital. Luckily, the boardwalk severely limited her options. She had a choice of only two directions and one of them was back toward Barb and Laurie. Additionally, the high railings combined with the narrow walkway made it easy for me to keep her within my reach.

While some of the times that I had had to restrain Jenny were tense and certainly sad, I had never been frightened while doing what I had to do to keep her safe. That all changed on the boardwalk that day.

Jenny's determination and resistance had reached a new level and she could get very physical when she was in that state of mind. It was rare for her to actually get violent, but it was certainly not unheard of. She was very strong and while I was stronger, the wrestling matches could get fairly intense at times, and it was clear to anyone watching that it was a serious issue and not just people fooling around. Until now, every time we had had to get physical with her was within the confines of the 6th floor. More often than not, physical confrontations took place in her room, but even when it was elsewhere in the hospital, everyone present knew the situation or at least it was clear that everyone involved was supposed to be doing what they were doing.

But now, all of this was happening within view of roughly 150 windows through which people within the hospital could be watching this scene, and I wasn't sure what they would think. It crossed my mind that 30 or 40 people might dial 911 to report a horrible man trying to abduct a young woman on the boardwalk. The combination of Jenny's ferocity and the very serious thought that the police may get involved made me truly frightened of the situation for the first time.

The first thing I did when I realized what was happening and what this whole episode was about to turn into was to ask Laurie and Barb to get close to me. Laurie was dressed like hospital staff and she had a wheelchair so at least anybody watching through the windows or passing by on the street would know that I was not some random crazy man.

After doing what I could to influence public perception, I turned my full attention back to Jenny and getting her back into the hospital. The trick during these episodes was to take advantage of Jenny's momentum as much as possible. She needed to be convinced to go the direction we wanted her to go on her own but not so fast that she couldn't be redirected when necessary. It was a balancing act between being in control and letting her think that she was.

The boardwalk made the first part of this very easy as there really was only one direction to go, so we both wanted the same thing in that sense. However, the boardwalk ended at a sidewalk that ran alongside a parking ramp for the hospital, essentially creating a "T" in the path where it ended. I assumed that once we got there Jenny would want to go right toward a major road with lots of traffic about 100 yards away. I needed her to go left, to an entrance to the hospital 15 or 20 feet away. I had a physical strength advantage, but it proved to be the longest 20 feet that I can ever remember walking.

An added advantage for Jenny was that once we got off the boardwalk her options increased. There was only one way I wanted to go, and because her ultimate goal was to get away from the hospital, she had several options. She could go over the short concrete barrier into the parking ramp, down into a shallow gully, or toward the street itself, which I believed was her ultimate goal. There was no doubt in my mind that she would not hesitate to go in any one of these directions and anything off the sidewalk would severely reduce my ability to control her. I needed Jenny to, at the very least, stay on the sidewalk.

What ensued was a test of strength, determination, and will. While I physically restrained Jenny, Barb and Laurie tried to reason with her, attempting to talk to her while Laurie used the wheelchair to help block her path.

Jenny could not talk clearly, but was repeating something over and over again, clearly pleading with us, which was evident in her facial expression and, worst of all, her eyes. These were the times that looking into her eyes was the most painful thing to do.

Jenny was more insistent that day than she had ever been since getting sick. I am sure that if I had not known the whole situation and had come upon the scene as a stranger, I would have been sure that Jenny knew exactly what she wanted and that it was imperative that she get her way. That was actually true, but the urgency with which she was doing it this time would have convinced anyone else that we, indeed, needed to let her go.

Much of the scene took place on a ten-foot section of sidewalk. Any step Jenny took toward the door we wanted her to go into we allowed, while I restrained her from any movement deviating from that path. Often I didn't grip her firmly enough and she would manage three or four steps in the direction she wanted to go. At times, she tried to go over the concrete barrier, but mercifully, I don't recall her making any serious attempt to get down into the gully.

There were never any punches thrown or any violence beyond the pushing, shoving, and physical restraint of wrapping my arms around her and holding her as tightly as I could while she struggled to get out of my grasp. She would push on my arms and even try to pinch or scratch me, but although there were a few close calls, neither of us ever went to the ground. While each of them did what they could to help hold Jenny at times, the role Barb and Laurie played most of the time was to be physical barriers with their bodies and the wheelchair and try to verbally reason with Jenny.

This struggle clearly was the biggest test of wills that Jenny and I had ever experienced in our entire relationship. I have no idea how long our battle lasted. It felt like an hour or more but was probably 20 minutes at the most.

As painful as it was to have to physically force my daughter to do something she didn't want to do, that type of engagement took place between Jenny and I multiple times over the weeks of her illness. However, what made this situation so much worse than all of the others were the added elements that came from not being within the secure confines of the hospital and the 6th floor.

As is the case with many of the more traumatic events of Jenny's illness, many of the minor details of the incident are gone or blocked from memory. I don't recall any singular significant turning point in this confrontation. I remember the almost static battle going on for what seemed like forever, but eventually Jenny walked into the hospital under her own power. Barb and I were on either side of her holding her arms, but I seem to recall her going willingly. More than likely, the three of us had simply out lasted Jenny and her will and she returned to being the sweet and cooperative woman that was her true personality.

This event summed up Jenny's situation in so many ways. The pain that was suffered during the confrontation was real and symbolic at the same time. There were strained muscles as well as the torment we saw in Jenny's eyes as she pleaded with us to let her go. This event was a clear reminder of how trapped she had been for the past seven weeks, not just physically trapped within the walls of the hospital, but emotionally and psychologically trapped within the confines of her mind that she was forced to share with the demons that appeared to be controlling it. I suppose I will never have a clear understanding of the times that her behavior was driven by the NMDA, or by an actual conscious thought process on her part as a result of the situation the illness put her into.

CHAPTER 51

Day 46

When I arrived on this Monday morning, I was greeted with a wonderful smile and a long, tight hug. Jenny was very bright, aware and actually seemed happy. It felt as though the demons were losing their control and Jenny would come out from time to time.

By this time, we knew Jenny was going to go from Methodist into a rehab facility of some kind, but we hadn't even begun to discuss where. The previous Friday, when I met with Dr. Tran, I specifically asked for a probable discharge date but the answer was that there was no way to tell at that point as certain criteria had to be met and it was anybody's guess when that would happen. The two primary questions were what facility would be able to handle the specific needs Jenny would have and when Jenny would be able to be removed from constant medical care. Although the doctors were not doing much anymore, the nurses were still administering various drugs on a regular basis and she still had the 24-hour one-on-one aide. Jenny was doing much better relative to where she had been even a week ago but she wasn't ready to sit unattended anywhere.

One doctor explained that the two conditions would have to come together. In other words, Methodist would need to be willing to sign off on the fact that she no longer needed clinical medical care and the rehab facility would need to agree that Jenny was in a condition that they were equipped to handle. As recently as that Monday, I had been told that the two sides were far from connecting.

In spite of the distance we had yet to travel, the treatment of the NMDA was essentially finished. Jenny had received an additional dose of Rituximab, and the doctors were going to keep a very close eye on things to be sure a relapse did not occur. However, all there was to do at that point was to wait for Jenny to recover from the damage done. Her recovery would be a two-step process: first Jenny needed to function on her own, and then the goal would be "full-recovery" where Jenny's life would return as "back to normal" as possible.

Everyone knew that the second step could be years away, if it ever occurred at all. At that point, our goal simply was to get Jenny home again. Then we could start to think about her going back to work. The good news was that the latest MRI still showed no damage to the brain so there was a great probability that Jenny would be fine. For now, it would simply take time for the NMDA to be destroyed and then more time for her brain to heal.

The conclusion of the NMDA treatment was just one step of many before Jenny could be discharged from Methodist. We needed to temper our excitement when considering how much work was still in front of her and all of us that loved her. Her recovery was going to be a marathon, not a sprint.

Jenny's motor skills were coming back fairly rapidly. She could now walk without assistance, and perform other basic tasks like feeding herself and performing personal hygiene, although she remained in a diaper. Motions that were more intricate, however, such as operating a remote control for a TV, were still a struggle for Jenny. We could see that she knew what she was trying to do, which meant that her brain was functioning properly, but she was just unable to execute those motions. The other very good sign in terms of her ability to work through the hard times that lay ahead was that although Jenny would look very frustrated at times, she seldom quit or even asked for help.

Yet, the most intricate of fine motor skills is talking, and while that was improving and those who knew Jenny well could communicate with her, she still lacked the speaking abilities that would be required for her to function on her own.

Yet, in a perfect example of how confusing this issue could be, one day during that week Dr. Tran walked in just to check on Jenny while I was sitting next to her bed, helping her through a very mild episode. Dr. Tran stood at the foot of Jenny's bed and we gave each other the usual greetings but Jenny never moved. She continued to stare toward the floor and to her left, away from me. I let Dr. Tran know that she wasn't going to get much during this visit by saying, "Jenny is just going through an episode." Without missing a beat Jenny turned, looked straight at me, and in the clearest and brattiest possible voice said, "I'm not having an episode, you're having an episode." She immediately turned back to exactly where she had been looking two seconds before and "went away" again. Dr. Tran and I looked at each other in amazement for about five seconds and Jenny remained "away" until long after Dr. Tran had left.

Other concerns also existed. Jenny needed to continue to eat ample amounts of food all day, every day, and work at gaining back some of the more than 20 pounds she had lost over the past seven weeks. In addition, while improving, Jenny still had a few issues with things like her potassium level and, at that time, extremely *low* blood pressure.

An immediate concern was that Jenny was still experiencing periods of catatonia as well as "episodes" of agitated catatonia. While difficult to quantify, our belief was that they seemed to be tapering off. The doctors believed the seizures were under control with the Keppra she was taking, but they continued to closely monitor her medication and adjust it almost daily.

Jenny's medical summary at the time meant very little to me. I knew the medical professionals controlled many if not all of the decisions that were to come, but I still tended to look at Jenny to draw my own conclusions about the only fact I was interested in: was my daughter any closer to coming back to me. The medical jargon and measurements meant nothing to me. Could Jenny and I go to a Twins game – that was the measure of progress I would use.

Over the previous three days, while I saw small improvements in Jenny, there were some mixed signals about what was going on in her head. One day Debbie stopped in for a quick visit and Jenny and the nurse's aide were the only ones in the room. Debbie had been hearing very good reports and was anxious to see Jenny after not seeing her for a few days; however, she could tell that Jenny wasn't all "there" as soon as she entered the room. Debbie greeted Jenny and gave her a hug, which Jenny returned, but she got no response when she started to ask Jenny questions. Jenny was sitting in bed with the head of the bed raised. Her hands were limp on her lap and she was staring at something (or nothing) at the foot of the bed. Suddenly she started making eating motions, appearing to pick something up between her thumb and forefinger and place it in her mouth. She did this several times and Debbie asked Jenny what she was eating. She said, "Cheerios." Debbie felt bad that she was eating imaginary food and asked her if she was hungry, but instead of answering the question, Jenny turned to her and said, "You shouldn't poop in public, it's rude and gross."

Obviously, Jenny was not ready for any public appearances yet. I knew that the demons still possessed Jenny's brain at least a bit and the NMDA was not dead yet.

This encounter was in sharp contrast to when Jenny allowed Michelle to do her hair, a moment that brought me back to their high school days when Michelle would do Jenny's hair before volleyball and soccer games. Jenny sat perfectly still, and when it was finished, she gave Michelle a hug and said, as clear as she could, "Thank you. I love you."

Yet, the most significant event that had taken place that indicated we were definitely on the right track was when Michelle arrived that evening. She had discovered two plush toy cupcakes Jenny had received during the week as a gift from her coworkers at Barnes and Noble. Michelle began to play with them. They were just a bit larger than a baseball and the softest toys imaginable. Michelle admits that her first thought was to throw them at Jenny as she would have done as a kid just to make Jenny mad. Instead, thankfully, she simply tossed one of the cupcakes to Jenny in a high arc so that the toy landed in her lap. Jenny smiled, grabbed the cupcake, and tossed it perfectly back to Michelle. Barb, Michelle, Brad, and I were all shocked. After waiting for a moment, Jenny put out her arms and made it clear that she wanted to play catch. Michelle moved to the foot of Jenny's bed so she was directly facing her and tossed the cupcake back in the same high arc. It landed in Jenny's lap as Jenny swung her arms and clasped her hands together too late to catch the toy. Jenny picked it back up, continued to smile, and made another perfect toss back to Michelle. This continued for three or four tosses until Jenny actually caught the cupcake out of the air. The toss from Michelle was not perfect and Jenny had to adjust her hands to get in line with the path of the toy. Our smiles got bigger as we watched the "casual" game, but no one said a word as the two tossed the cupcake back and forth, each making more direct and faster throws each time. Jenny's motions got more fluid with each toss, and after a very short amount of time, Jenny began to catch the cupcake one handed. Right before our eyes Jenny was showing signs of improvement in her condition from minute to minute.

Then, Jenny began to give some nonverbal instructions, indicating that Michelle should sit in a chair that was to Jenny's left and further away from the bed. Michelle's position would be lower than Jenny's, effectively making the target much more difficult to hit. Jenny pointed to Brad, then Barb, and then me. Jenny wanted all of us to play catch.

At first, we each tossed the cupcake to Jenny and she tossed it to another person. Then Jenny created a sequence she wanted us to follow with each of the tosses so that each of us got "a touch" (soccer term) before anyone got it a second time. The sequence, however, wasn't a simple circle, it was a deliberate pattern designed to create the longest tosses possible. At first, she got mad and stopped the game if we went in the incorrect order, adamantly pointing out the correct sequence with her arm, but after a while, she allowed random tosses where each of us tried to fake all of the other participants out, including Jenny. It was not long before Jenny caught on and was able to keep up with the ball. She rarely dropped a pass, even from Barb who was standing about five feet to Jenny's left and positioned just a bit behind her. We watched Jenny in amazement as we also tried to keep track of the toy.

After five minutes, Jenny added another element to the game, clapping her hands to a steady beat and chanting as she waited for the cupcake's return." Each time she released the toy she would clap and chant "Hey to, hey to, hey to," seven or eight times before the ball was returned to her. Of course Michelle joined in and phones came out to record the moment. Eventually, Jenny insisted that we all join in, and pretty soon, all five of us were tossing, catching, clapping, and chanting, "Hey to, hey to, hey to," together.

It was not a quiet affair, but I am quite sure that none of us gave a hoot about who could hear us. I have a booming voice and while I wasn't actually yelling I wasn't holding back and using my indoor voice either, although I am not sure who was actually the loudest in the room.

We were celebrating an extremely happy moment in our lives that hadn't seemed possible just a week ago, or even 20 minutes ago.

It did not take long for several nurses on the floor to stop in to see the cause of all the commotion. Apparently, we hadn't broken any rules yet because each of them smiled, watched for a while, and then left without ever asking us to keep it down. I am sure they understood the significance of what was happening at that moment, but I am equally sure any visitors to other patients on the floor wondered what the deal was with the lunatics in that room; it was the neurology floor after all. Michelle said later, as she was in the best position to see the door during all of this, that she had noticed a few people pass by very slowly three or four times trying to see in the room while making it appear they were simply walking past.

Our game lasted for almost 20 minutes. Jenny even stood up for a while when the tosses were getting faster and more direct so that she could adjust better and make the catches. She had her huge toothy smile on her face the whole time, which may have been the best part. When we were done, we were all very tired – I wasn't the only one sweating and needing to sit down with a bottle of water – and all of us grasped the beauty of something as simple as a stuffed cupcake providing us with the most wonderful evening we had enjoyed in a very long time.

I can't say I thought of it at that moment, but a few weeks later, I would refer back to that evening as confirmation that Jenny didn't actually have to "relearn" everything as the therapists had told us. In my own interpretation of things, there was just "junk" stuck in Jenny's head and she needed to push it aside for the synapses in her brain to function properly. In what would later become the greatest irony of this entire story, Michelle would prove to be Jenny's best therapist. Many of Jenny's leaps forward were triggered by something Michelle did. At times, it seemed to me, the professionals felt they had to stick to "the book" and do things the clinical way. Their checklist told them that Jenny had to be able to grab a ball and then squeeze it before they would even consider tossing it. They predetermined what Jenny was ready for and believed certain checks had to be in place before additional steps were taken.

Jenny's favorite coaches over the years were the ones that yelled a lot and pushed her for more, and Michelle was the natural person to step into that role at this time. She did not have the parental instinct to coddle when things were tough and there was no one else in the world that combined wanting what was best for Jenny along with mercilessly pushing for her to go after it herself. Whereas a medical professional might be reprimanded for throwing an object at an individual who very possibly could get hurt, once Jenny tossed the stuffed cupcake back to Michelle, it was natural for the evening to progress the way that it had. Michelle didn't have a checklist to follow and this would be the case for the next three months as she helped Jenny recover.

CHAPTER 52

Jenny's Impending Discharge from Methodist

Due to the nature of NMDA, Jenny's story of the previous 56 days since her first seizure had been a continuing series of short events; things seemed to evolve so rapidly day-by-day, even hour-by-hour. Unlike someone with a more common and predictable illness, it was never possible to say, "Moving forward, first this will happen, then that will happen and from there we go on to the next thing."

Not everything went perfect during our stay at Methodist Hospital, but in terms of our direct interaction with the staff, given the complexities of Jenny's illness and the multitude of facets required for her care, I am amazed at how relatively smoothly things went. When miscommunications did occur, they happened for different reasons and, more often than not, it was no one's fault. Circumstances would create a scenario where there was a difference in what we knew, what we thought we knew, what we were told, what we understood, and what was really happening.

Never did communication go as badly as it did surrounding the issue of moving Jenny from Methodist to a rehab facility. The long process of miscommunication, confusion, extreme emotion, frustration, and even fear was as much about the reaction we had, as a family, to Jenny leaving the relatively known entity and comfort of Methodist and the people that had cared for her for eight weeks as it was about how it happened.

By Tuesday, May 21st, we were well aware that the next step for Jenny would be to move her to a rehab facility, but our understanding that morning was not only was Jenny not ready to go, but there was no facility that was ready to take her.

Friday, May 17, 2013

The story actually began the previous Friday, a full four days before Barb and I were told that we should start to consider moving Jenny to a rehab facility. Although I would not know any of this until the following Wednesday, my understanding of the situation was that on this date, Methodist Hospital notified the insurance company that the treatment of the NMDA was complete. Based on what I have been told, because of the nature of Jenny's illness the insurance company had stayed relatively uninvolved up to this point because there were no protocols in place for treating NMDA. I can only speculate that after receiving news that Jenny had completed treatment for an illness the insurance company knew nothing about, they assumed that Jenny was ready to leave the hospital, which triggered a series of events that began to expedite the process of finding a suitable facility, or at least the insurance company's definition of suitable. Once the insurance company was involved, something we had experienced very little of up to that point, much of what happened was out of our control and even out of the control of the medical professionals at Methodist.

Ultimately, the insurance company sent out the request for an open bed at a facility that would "accept a patient who has the condition described in the attached report." Methodist was essentially out of the loop.

The issue was that there was a significant difference between the treatment of the NMDA being completed, and the reality of the fact that Jenny still required constant medical care. What still held true was Methodist would have to get Jenny to a point that her medical care requirements matched what a specific rehab facility could offer before Methodist would officially release her. As I understood it, the issue of the one-on-one 24-hour care was the sticking point in that no rehab facility would willingly offer that. The issue I had no grasp of was the "elopement risk" Jenny presented (her constant desire to "go home" and attempts at getting on the elevator). The truth of the matter was that I had never even heard the term. It was ignorance on my part, of course, but my daughter just wanted to go home, and I struggled to see her as a patient who was an elopement risk. I had no concept that it was even a medical term.

Tuesday, May 21, 2013

Fast forward to 8 a.m. that morning when I met with Dr. Tran and was told, "Jenny is at least a week away from being ready to leave." The meeting was concluded by saying that we would not be discussing Jenny's possible release from Methodist until at least the following Monday.

Jenny still needed constant care. She was in no way ready to be left alone for a minute, much less able to begin the process of starting to return to a normal life. In our minds, based not only on what we saw, but also on what we had been told, Jenny was days, if not weeks, away from being finished with the care she was receiving.

At 9:30 a.m. that same Tuesday morning, Barb was summoned to the hospital from work at the very last minute so that she and I could meet with two social workers from Methodist. Our understanding of the meeting, which was corroborated by what was actually discussed, was to educate and begin to prepare us for Jenny's transition. A rough plan was put into place, but it was made clear that we should start making arrangements for tours of possible facilities immediately. We were even given a list of facilities to consider.

Barb and I left the meeting feeling very comfortable with everything based on two things we had been told: 1) We had at least a week to decide where Jenny should go; and 2) we would have the choice of where Jenny went.

The social workers gave us two primary suggestions: The Courage Center in Golden Valley (now called Courage Kenny Rehabilitation Institute) and Bethesda Hospital in St. Paul. Both were highly regarded. Barb and I immediately raised questions about who knew *anything* about dealing with NMDA although we were confident the answer was that nobody in our local area had any experience. Naturally, the follow-up question was which facility had the type of staff that would do the most research to learn and adapt to the challenges that Jenny would present them. Of course, as expected, the two social workers were unable to answer either question. Because we had time, we felt that we could try to get an honest answer and a feel for that during the tours we were going to take.

We left the meeting with a plan to tour both Courage Center and Bethesda and then meet again to discuss what we had learned, ask any questions, and decide the next step. I had a lot to digest after the meeting and wanted to contemplate the questions I had. Ultimately I left feeling no pressure to rush into any decision, and all of the information that I had received that morning supported this.

My goal turned to figuring out how to adequately scrutinize any facility we would visit. My intention was to put all of my time into doing all I could to find the best place for Jenny no matter where it was.

As I left the meeting, I was already devising a plan to accomplish my goal. Despite all the time I had already missed from work, my very first call was to my business partner to inform her that I would not be available for much of the week due to my impending search. As always, I had her full support. My second call was to Dr. Joos, a neuropsychiatrist I had grown to trust in our time at Methodist to ask her to meet with me. She was never afraid to tell me what I *didn't* want to hear, but she had a way of breaking everything down into terms I could understand. She made herself available but was quick to admit that she didn't have the answers to any of my questions. However, she agreed to spend time with me to develop a plan for how to get the answers I needed and said that she would go over some things with me that would give me background knowledge to figure out how to analyze what facility would be best for Jenny.

However, even before I had a chance to meet with her, the process took on a life of its own.

I have no recollection of ever talking with any facility other than Bethesda. I am certain I called Courage Center for an appointment because that was our first choice based solely on its location, which was all we had to go on initially. However, by that afternoon the only facility that mattered and that I remember speaking to was Bethesda, and not for any of the right reasons.

Around noon, I called Bethesda to set up an appointment. The individual I needed to talk to was on vacation, but I was told someone would call me. I left a message that my wife and I wanted to come out on Thursday for a tour if that was possible.

About 2:30 p.m., I received a call back from someone at Bethesda. "You wanted to come out on Thursday?"

"Yes."

"That doesn't make sense because Jenny is scheduled to be admitted tomorrow."

I was stunned. I had to take a moment to be sure I heard her right, and then I asked her to repeat what she had just said. Then I asked her to clarify it.

"The paperwork I see here says that everything is approved for her to be admitted tomorrow."

I could not believe what I had heard, no matter how hard I tried. What had I missed? Why wasn't I informed? What happened to the fact that it was supposed to be our choice? And, most importantly, how was it possible that I was informed of it in this manner?

I held my temper for as long as I could, but ultimately I took out my confusion and frustration on the woman on the phone. I was so upset that I honestly don't remember anything I said, or any details of the rest of that day. All I know for sure is three things happened in the following hour or two:

1. I made many phone calls and successfully delayed Jenny's transfer from Methodist to Bethesda until at least Thursday.
2. Barb and I had an appointment for a tour of Bethesda the next morning (Wednesday).
3. I learned we had absolutely no choice in the matter – Jenny was going to Bethesda eventually, no matter how we felt about it, and it was going to happen very fast.

I wasn't actually able to piece together what had happened, and more importantly, why it happened, until late the following day. By that evening, all I knew was that I had been as angry and upset as I had been the entire time Jenny was ill – honestly perhaps in my entire life.

Now, more than a year later, I can say that if all of this had been communicated to me properly, I would have understood and made the best of it. However, to find out that my daughter was scheduled to be transferred in the manner that I did was incredibly shocking and even painful. It felt as if complete strangers were taking my daughter away.

Wednesday, May 22, 2013

By Wednesday morning, I had calmed down – I really had – and so had Barb. We had given it a lot of thought the evening before as well as during the night. Although I still felt insulted by the callousness of the process and whoever allowed the communication to fail to the extent that we learned about the transfer the way we did, I came around to the fact that ultimately this was great news because it meant Jenny was another step closer to coming home. I still didn't understand what had happened to suddenly deny us any choice in where Jenny was going, as we had been promised, but now there were bigger issues to which I needed to direct my time and energy. We would go on the tour at Bethesda to get comfortable with the situation and then move on.

Unfortunately, not much went well in terms of Barb and me getting comfortable with Bethesda.

We arrived for the tour at the scheduled time and were asked to wait in an area resembling a museum that depicted the full history of the hospital as well as many of what they considered their greatest accomplishments. I'm assuming this was a deliberate and strategic move on their part, to give us a chance to browse and see for ourselves the rich history of the hospital. Unfortunately, the only effect it had on us was to reinforce the antiquated feel of the entire facility. I decided to give Bethesda the benefit of the doubt and hope that maybe I was wrong in my initial assessment of their facility (but I was also a father who was naturally being very protective of my child).

However, Barb and I both knew we were dealing with uncharted territory, for us as well as for Bethesda. In order to learn all we could in what little time we had to react, we had made quite a few calls and heard nothing but absolutely rave reviews of the facility and the work they did. Although we knew this was nothing to base final decisions on, the initial impression that we had received from the facility left us with doubts that it was progressive enough to deal with the issues presented by our daughter. The reality of the situation was that NMDA was a relatively new illness for the medical community. Of course, tried and true principles had been applied to the treatment of the illness, but we had learned at Methodist that dealing with the day-to-day issues the illness caused was tough, to put it mildly. I doubted very much that the rehab process for such a patient would follow tried and true principles; maybe it would, but no one actually knew for sure so our goal was to find a facility that was open to the fact that they were also going off into uncharted territory for their facility.

I needed to know that the facility my daughter ended up in would take the time to get to know her and her situation, not just follow a book of protocols that determined how patients were treated. Medically speaking, I had no idea how Jenny's situation might be different from others, but I was very confident that it was. I did not believe that my daughter was worse off than all the other patients were. That was not even remotely true. In no way am I trying to imply that Jenny deserved special treatment, but I knew she

222

needed personal treatment and I needed to see that the facility she ended up in would provide that.

My desires can be simply stated: I needed the people who worked with Jenny to be able and willing to research, learn, and be flexible.

Barb and I waited for the person that would give us the tour for several minutes. She appeared from the hallway, and walking straight toward me extended her hand and said, "Good to meet you Mr. Nichols and I am so sorry to hear about your sister."

Oops.

However, I had learned the day before that she had been on vacation and this was her first morning back. It was early in the day, and I was sure that she was busy with voicemails and emails. Besides, she was simply the person showing us around. The doctors would treat Jenny, not a tour guide.

After we recovered from that awkward moment, we moved on to some basic information about the facility. During this portion of her presentation, we were still standing in the museum, but she eventually came to describe the specifics of their fourth floor, which was where they housed the patients recovering from brain injuries. Since many patients on the floor were "elopement risks" like Jenny, there were measures in place to deal with this issue. The entire floor was a secure floor, meaning that access to the elevators was restricted so that no patients could wander off the floor and visitors were required to have a nurse or security guard use a special key to allow the elevator to stop at that floor. In addition, many patients, including Jenny, would have mechanisms on their wrists that would sound an alarm if they got too close to the elevators or stairwells. All of this made sense and we were comfortable with that aspect.

The tour guide went on to tell us that in addition to these safety measures there were two separate sections of the floor. "4 South" was the main portion of the floor and housed a majority of the patients while "4 West" was a smaller ward with only 12 beds. This ward was unique from the other in that it was a locked ward where the patients were secured in a smaller and more tightly restricted area. In fairness to Bethesda, I need to be clear that my descriptions are based solely on my recollections. I did not take good notes at this point in our meeting and the details of this area of their hospital were not discussed on their website. My understanding was that these 12 beds were for patients who either were extremely high elopement risks or were a danger to themselves or others. The patient to nurse ratio is much lower in this section and everyone is in close proximity to one centralized common area outside each room.

The tour guide went on to describe the key features of the fourth floor that help patients recover from their injuries. In all honesty, I was very tired from all that had occurred the previous eight weeks and much of what she said about the facility that was meant to impress me went in one ear and out the other. It had been made clear to me that we had no other choice than

223

for Jenny to come here, so all I was interested in was to learn how they were going to deal with Jenny's specific needs, I didn't need to be sold on the place. The tour guide was only doing her job and trying to make us feel comfortable, and it was not her fault that I had no focus or desire to absorb any unnecessary information.

I was listening; I was just choosing which information to process. However, I did hear her when she said, "The west side is where Jenny's bed is." Everything came to a screeching halt in my brain and I asked that she repeat what she had just said. She stammered a bit, as I hadn't been particularly nice about my question, she opened her file, and told me that the only open bed they had on the fourth floor was on the west side. I didn't hide my concern as I asked why Jenny was going to be in a restricted ward. She stuck to the position that it was the only bed they had available, but also correctly pointed out that I had yet to see the area and assured me it wasn't as bad as it may have sounded. I understood both points and agreed to wait to pass further judgment until I saw it.

The tour guide finished her verbal description of the facility and we proceeded toward the elevators to work our way up to the fourth floor. Along the way, she pointed out a few key features she wanted us to see.

In fairness to Bethesda, I was not in a good place emotionally on that day. The way I heard about the transfer, my initial impression of the facility, and the introduction error of the tour guide had combined to make me uncomfortable with the whole situation, though most of it was not Bethesda's fault.

Additionally, I had never in my life seen any place that even remotely resembled what I saw on the fourth floor. It must be remembered that Bethesda is considered an excellent facility, and over the previous 15 hours or so I had spoken to many people who said that it had saved their lives. However, I cannot express how shaken I was that day as we stepped onto the fourth floor. I believe Barb felt similarly, and considering all we had witnessed the past eight weeks, that's saying something, although it is probably the only portion of our experience that she and I have never discussed.

As we got off the elevator, we went through a security door that was the key element of the system to ensure that no patients wandered off. I wasn't comfortable with it, but it made sense in terms of what it was designed to accomplish. I definitely wanted to know Jenny would be safe, as I knew we wouldn't be present in the same capacity that we had been at Methodist.

After passing through the first security door, we were in a wide hallway that went right and left. Clearly most of the activity was to the right; however, the tour guide took us to the left, where we encountered a set of double doors that led to what I came to call "the west wing" where they intended to house Jenny. Each door had a window in it and I could see another set of double doors about 10 feet beyond that. I very quickly realized that only one set of doors would open at a time. We passed through the first set of doors, waited for them to close and lock behind us, and then proceeded through the next set of doors to enter the west wing.

Once we passed through the second set of doors and I had a clear view of the large room we had entered, I was astonished by what I saw; the room resembled what I imagine when I think of what a prison looks like. The facility may have been instrumental for many people and I am positive that Bethesda has done some great work there, but there was no way I could see Jenny in this place. It was a large room, roughly oval shaped, and I am guessing it was about 150-feet wide and no more than 50-feet deep. By design, every inch of the room we were standing in, as well as the 12 small rooms for the patients, was visible from where we were standing. The 12 rooms each held an individual bed and doors with large windows so that all activity inside the room could be seen even when the doors were closed. I understood the reason for this, but again, I could not see Jenny being housed in this place. The room had a center counter that was 30- or 40-feet long and served multiple purposes as I recall – from a nurse's station to a dining room table. The room was crowded and cramped with people, chairs, tables, and medical equipment.

Although I did not say anything right then, I had already made up my mind that Jenny would never stay in this portion of the facility. However, my biggest problem with this area was not what one might think. Throughout everything that Jenny had gone through in the previous eight weeks, one of the few things that had remained constant was her inability to sit still. It went away for a bit more than a week when she bottomed out, but her need to take long walks in the hallway of Methodist had since returned. I understood that Jenny was an elopement risk, but the very nature of the illness she had dictated that she needed to be in a place where she could walk. The only option that Jenny would have in this ward of the hospital would be to walk in a circle and that was only if she was capable of navigating around the many obstacles that would block her way. There was open space, just not long stretches of it, and there was absolutely no doubt in my mind that Jenny would feel like she actually was in prison. Any hope of rehab would be lost simply because of where this area would take her emotionally.

I remained relatively silent as the tour guide showed us some details of the area. As we made the short walk through, the lead neurologist of the facility walked out of one of the offices. He would be responsible for Jenny's care whether she was on "4 South" or "4 West." We spoke briefly and he assured me that Jenny would be in great hands. I did not doubt the sincerity of his words.

After about five minutes, we exited the locked ward and proceeded to the other side of the fourth floor, which was much more like any other hospital that I am familiar with and what I believed was appropriate for Jenny, especially considering it had the secured exit. What was most important to me was that there were two hallways, each of which were twice as long as the single circle Jenny would have to navigate on the locked side. Additionally, there was a very large common area with many comfortable tables and chairs, along with a large birdcage and aquarium that I knew Jenny would enjoy. This side would provide a much more comfortable environment for Jenny, one I felt would be more conducive to her emotional recovery. As far as I was concerned, this environment was what she needed in order to regain any semblance of "normal."

As the tour guide took Barb and me through this part of the facility, I was actually impressed with its potential to help Jenny. Each of the staff members we watched interact with the patients clearly cared about what they were doing. Most of the patients were in tough physical condition compared to Jenny, as many had been victims of an accident of some kind, and all but a few seemed very comfortable with their surroundings. In my mind as long as I could change their intention of where "Jenny's bed" would be, I could be comfortable with the facility.

Toward the end of the tour, we stopped in a hallway that was close to the nurse's station and were introduced to the head nurse on the floor. Barb and I started peppering both the nurse and the tour guide with questions about how Jenny would be challenged in terms of rehab. Neither of us had enough background to know the correct way to phrase our questions or what key words to listen for in the answers, but we were impressed with what we heard. Toward the end of the discussion, we made it clear that Jenny's personality was such that she would want to be challenged as much as possible. The response from the head nurse is what clinched it for us. "This place is like a boot camp." That is what we knew Jenny needed.

I finally broached the subject of which side of the floor Jenny would reside on. I chose my words carefully and explained why I thought Jenny would be more successful on the south side rather than the west side. As if I was intending to try to stress my point, I suddenly lost control and broke down and cried as I stated why I was against her being placed in the west wing – the thought of Jenny being locked up in that confined area was overwhelming to me. The tour guide reminded me that there were no open beds on this side but said she would talk to the doctor to see what could be done.

In her defense, I was not aware of the report that Methodist had submitted to the insurance company on Friday. I would learn about the report later that afternoon, but I could tell at the time that she was only telling me what I wanted to hear in order to end the discussion. I dropped the subject but knew what my next step would be. We concluded the tour, and Barb and I left the building. The tour guide said she would be getting back to me about which side Jenny would be housed on, but she assumed she would be admitting Jenny the next day.

I had other intentions. After working so hard and exerting so much energy to ensure that Jenny never had any version of mechanical restraint used on her and having had the complete cooperation of the Methodist staff in that regard, there was absolutely no chance that I would put Jenny into the situation that I believed the west wing represented. No chance at all.

CHAPTER 53

Day 48…continued

As soon as we were out of earshot of all hospital personnel, I told Barb, "There is no way I am allowing Jenny to be in that west wing." The tears in Barb's eyes were all the confirmation I needed that she agreed with me.

Early on in Jenny's stay at Methodist, we had worked with a hospitalist on a daily basis whose role was to improve communication between the patient and hospital staff. Once it was clear that Jenny's illness was a bit more complicated than most were used to, we saw less and less of the hospitalist, but they were still involved and overall proved to be helpful. Once the miscommunication issues the previous day came to light and it was clear we had to make a very quick decision, I received a call from the hospitalist offering his services in any way possible. I dialed his number that day before I even had the car started in the Bethesda Hospital parking lot.

Briefly, I said "no way" to what Bethesda had in mind and that I wanted a very clear understanding of how we had gotten to this point so that I could develop a plan regarding what to do next. After listening to me summarize my concerns – very loudly – the hospitalist was clear that much of what Bethesda did was out of his control but he would do all he could. Due to the deadlines and the urgency, we quickly decided that the best way to find the underlying cause of everything was to get everyone into the same room and set up a meeting with everyone involved for that afternoon.

Later that afternoon, a large group of people sat in a family lounge at the end of a quiet hallway on the sixth floor. Barb, John, and I were there, as were the two social workers, the lead nurse for the 6th floor, the hospitalist, and the neuropsychiatrist that had been involved in the case, Dr. Joos. I made it clear that there was no way Jenny was going to be placed on the west side of Bethesda Hospital's fourth floor, and in order to prevent this from happening I needed a clear understanding of how the events of the day before took place. I also made it clear that I was not interested in blame I just needed to understand. I explained that Barb and I were not being unreasonable. We were okay with Jenny going to Bethesda, just not to the west side.

One of the social workers gave us a crash course in Insurance 101. In this meeting, we finally heard about all that had gone on the previous Friday, which was the result of the insurance company's understanding that Jenny was no longer being treated for the NMDA, and therefore their belief that Jenny was ready to be discharged. We received a lesson on the procedural, literal, and legal process of an insurance claim as well as the relationship between the providing hospital and the potential rehab facility. The bottom line was that the insurance company wanted Jenny out of the hospital because it was less expensive for them and Bethesda wanted to fill the bed they had open. From my cynical perspective, although I do not feel I was wrong in thinking: no one really cared what Jenny was actually ready for or needed.

I decided that my job was to give everyone in the room my own crash course on the west wing of Bethesda Hospital since none of them had seen it before. Once again, I lost control and began to cry as I begged for help finding a way to stop Jenny from being placed there.

In what had become the norm for everyone at Methodist, led by the very direct Dr. Joos, everyone in the room asked pointed questions of each other to get all of the details, and ideas were tossed around. Through this process, it was determined that there were two key issues from Bethesda's perspective. The first was that Jenny did in fact still need the one-on-one care and Bethesda was not in a position to provide that. The second was that they were working off the medical report submitted to the insurance company the previous Friday. The summary of Jenny's situation at that time very well may have been the real trigger in placing Jenny in the west wing. However, it was an indisputable fact that Jenny had shown tremendous improvement since Friday morning when the report was written. It now was Wednesday, a full five days later, which in Jenny's case was an eternity in terms of the changes she would experience from a medical perspective. Through everyone in the room working together to find the best solution for Jenny, it was determined that Bethesda was making a determination for placement based on outdated information.

As written here, this may not sound as monumental as it was. Everyone in the room wanted what was best for Jenny. It would have been so easy for anyone of those other five people to say, "This meeting was called at the last minute and I have somewhere else to be. It is what it is," gotten up out of their chair, and never given Jenny a second thought. The gratitude I feel today, more than a year later, still moves me to tears. If any one of them had walked out perhaps the whole meeting would have come to an end, but five very busy people gave Jenny nearly two hours of their time to figure out the details of how we got to this point and, more importantly, figure out a solution.

The solution was not as simple as someone just telling me what to do. Basically Barb, John, and I ended up doing nothing. A plan was put in place and each of the other people in the room had a role. The overall plan involved one person who knew someone at Bethesda calling and asking them to look closer at the facts and reconsider Jenny's placement. Another would rewrite the report of Jenny's current condition for submission to the insurance company and thereby to Bethesda. Since there were other forces involved in terms of the insurance company, some compliance issues had to be addressed so that Jenny would not be forced to take the current open bed to not lose benefits altogether. Finally, a call was to be placed to officially decline the bed and ask Bethesda to find room for Jenny on the other side of the floor.

Nothing was definite yet, but all of these actions were a unified front to attempt to change decisions that other organizations had already made. I left the meeting feeling both encouraged and energized. I was encouraged by the confidence displayed by the people in the room that knew better than I did. Moreover, I was energized by the caring and compassion of all the people in front of me who were willing to take the time and energy to benefit my daughter who, regardless of what happened the next day, was going to be out of their lives forever. That feeling is overwhelming, even today.

Part 4

Rehabilitation

May 23 to June 17, 2013

CHAPTER 54

Day 49

After all the drama and trauma of the previous 48 hours, it is ironic that I have no recollection of receiving the call that everyone's efforts had paid off. Exactly what occurred, I don't know, but the bottom line was that Bethesda reconsidered Jenny's placement and agreed to house her on "4 South," the side with fewer restrictions and more room, but reserved the right to move Jenny to the west side if they determined that she was not doing well on the south side. A bed would be available that afternoon so we still had to get Jenny packed up and ready to go in a hurry.

It had been 58 days since Jenny suffered her first seizure and was found lying in a snow bank outside of a store in Minnetonka on March 27th. It was 49 days since she walked into Methodist Hospital in a confused state on April 5th. We hadn't known at the time that our journey would be so long or so traumatic. However, now a clear new chapter had begun and it felt like the trend was going the right direction. We were moving toward getting Jenny home.

Earlier that morning it was not clear if the bed at Bethesda would be ready that afternoon or the next morning, but I tried to prepare Jenny for the move by telling her what was happening. Although I wasn't sure if Jenny had a full understanding as I explained it to her, she did appear very excited and happy about it. I said a small prayer that she didn't believe that she was going home. Barb and I were also excited about the move. We still had heard nothing but positive reviews of the hospital as we continued to inquire with everyone we could think of and, quite frankly, we were really hanging on the promise that the place was "like a boot camp."

The therapists at Methodist had been working with Jenny every day for nearly three weeks and we had seen good improvement, especially over the past six days. Although it was just "playing catch," we had seen how Jenny reacted to the stimuli of Michelle throwing the stuffed cupcake to her, so we knew she was ready for more. We were all excited about the prospect of Jenny getting into a facility whose sole purpose was to help patients recover from a serious injury or illness.

When I arrived at Jenny's room that afternoon to pick her up, she was on the edge of her bed with the nurse's aide. When she saw me, her face lit up and she began to clap excitedly, saying clearly, "Do I get to go to rehab today?" I was relieved that she understood that she was leaving the hospital but *not* going home and was excited about it.

The entire time we waited to leave, Jenny spoke in full sentences. What she was saying was not always clear, but it was obvious that she was

233

making rational statements about what was going on around her. She and I actually had a conversation for the first time in many weeks. It was an ongoing exchange back and forth about various things such as the Twins' losing streak – I had never felt such joy in discussing a disappointing season! At one point, Michelle called and I handed the phone to Jenny. She was speaking so clearly that she and Michelle were able to have a brief exchange. Jenny started by saying, "Hi, what's up?" Her personality was there in that simple greeting. I hadn't heard her say those words in so long and I could see on her face that she thought it was a regular phone conversation with her sister. In other words, in her mind this was normal.

There were so many things that Jenny did that day that she couldn't do four days before. Earlier that morning, I asked if she wanted to eat breakfast in the chair rather than in bed. "Yeah, that'd be good," she replied and immediately moved to the chair without forgetting where she was going during the five seconds it took her to get there. I was proud. In addition, even though breakfast didn't actually arrive for another 35 minutes, she continued to sit and wait. I do not believe she had willingly sat still in a chair for that long since she had arrived at the hospital. People would come and go from her room and she would explain that she was hungry and waiting for breakfast.

While she waited, the aide came in to take her vitals. Jenny put her arm out and got it in the proper position for a good reading without needing to be given instructions. When the IV nurse came in, Jenny not only got her opposite arm ready for the nurse to have easy access, she also reached over to turn off the TV and hit the correct button on the first try, all without prompting. These actions may sound simple but they are light years from where she had been.

Not everything went perfectly of course. While she was eating, I asked her why she was chewing her food so funny and she replied that she had a hard time chewing because of the braces on her teeth (no, she didn't have any). Later, she asked me to get the people out of her hair on the back of her head – you read that right – and then complained about the music coming out of her mouth. Clearly, Jenny was still experiencing hallucinations but at least these "episodes" were just mild irritations, not completely controlling her mind and body. So, as weird as it sounds... braces on her teeth was a good thing!

The original plan had been for a medical transport to transfer Jenny to Bethesda. However, as the time to depart arrived, I was pleasantly surprised when it was suggested and approved that Barb and I drive her there ourselves. This concession meant that others recognized that Jenny's condition had improved dramatically over the past three or four days. In a show of further independence and stubbornness, Jenny refused the traditional, and maybe mandatory, wheelchair ride to the car when leaving the hospital.

234

I have to admit that when I dreamt of this day over the weeks that preceded it, I had imagined Jenny leaving the hospital with a huge smile on her face. After all, this was a monumental day! She had overcome a terrible setback in her life and had triumphed! I looked at her departure as the first step toward coming home, but my imagined scene did not play out.

I had gone ahead to pull the car around to the front of the hospital as Barb and a nurse escorted Jenny down to the lobby. I got out of the car to go around to the passenger side and open the car door for her. While I waited, I decided to pull out my phone to record the monumental moment as I expected Jenny to come out with a big victorious smile on her face. It was not to be. As I aimed my phone at the door Jenny would exit from and hit record, Jenny walked out of the hospital in tears. As it turned out, despite how clearly Jenny was thinking, she was having a hard time understanding that John knew she was moving and she was worried that he would be unable to find her at the new place. We got her settled down from that crisis and tucked her into the back seat of the car.

In one final throwback to the years of being young parents raising a young child, I helped Jenny get settled into the backseat of the car and made sure she buckled in properly. Then, of course, since Mom's always think of everything, Barb had me engage the child safety lock on the back car door to ensure that Jenny couldn't open it while we were driving. That was a great idea I never would have thought of.

I must admit that I took great pride in being the one to take my daughter for her first car ride in 49 days. The sun was shining, the window was open, and Jenny had her head out enjoying the breeze in her face…oh wait, no. Turns out that was another image in my head that was not to be.

At this point in the dialogue, it would be helpful to point out that the helicopter landing pad for the hospital could be seen from some of the windows on the 6th floor of Methodist Hospital, and while we were waiting for Jenny to be discharged, Barb, Jenny, and I sat and watched as a helicopter came in. So now, instead of Jenny enjoying the car ride as I had imagined she would, she sat in the back seat with a pained look on her face, and at one point said, "This sure is a rough helicopter ride."

My stomach was in a knot as we pulled into the entrance at Bethesda. There was no way to tell how Jenny was going to react to this new experience. She was greeted at the door by the same person who had given us the tour of the facility the day before. Barb stayed with Jenny, and they had a few minutes to talk while I parked the car.

Once on the fourth floor, Jenny was introduced to a few people and had a pleasant exchange with each of them. Then, literally 10 seconds after she walked into her room, she took off her shoes and headed for the bed. She was very tired of course. She had had an exciting morning, an hour and a half of therapy, the busy afternoon of packing up her room at Methodist, and the move over. However, it was still a relief to see how easily she settled in.

In a somewhat comical side note, very early during the tour of the floor the day before, I had asked if ESPN was available in the rooms. The tour guide looked at me strangely and I believe she thought I was kidding. I explained that both Jenny and I were ESPN junkies and Methodist did not have that channel. After Jenny had jumped into bed, the tour guide left the room for about 15 minutes, and when she came back to check on Jenny, she laughed when she noticed that Jenny was watching ESPN.

Miraculously – to Jenny – John was able to figure out that she had moved and he managed to find her! The look and excitement on Jenny's face when John walked in was priceless. Jenny was then truly relaxed and ready to settle in for the long haul. There were a couple of conversations about what the future held and a couple of tears about the unknown, but overall Jenny demonstrated a determination to get through this chapter of the story as quickly as possible. As I stood and waited for the nurses to complete the busy work necessary to admit a new patient, I watched Jenny very closely. At that moment, I predicted she would be out of there in less than a month in contrast to the unofficial timetable I saw on an insurance form that day: "Minimum of five weeks."

Jenny settled in and appeared comfortable. We had come through some turmoil to get to that point, and although I was comfortable with everything, it was now time for Bethesda to get busy. We had gotten off to a rough start due to some miscommunication, but now here we were, and it was time for them to do the job they said they could do. I still needed to see that they could adapt to the truly unique situation I knew they had before them. I had hoped that the "old school" way of doing things was just an impression I had gotten from the museum downstairs. I prayed they were, indeed, flexible if not progressive. I knew that they had never seen a case of NMDA Encephalitis in their hospital and wondered if they were up for the task or if they would take the time to learn. In a few words, we needed the people who worked with Jenny to be able and willing to research, learn, and be flexible. At this point in the day, I had confidence that the doctors would.

Later that evening, as Barb, John, and I were getting ready to leave for the night, I suddenly realized that Jenny did not have the one-on-one nurse that she had been assigned at Methodist and that I knew had been listed in her transfer orders.

That's when it all became clear to me. That was why they were going to put Jenny on the west side, in the restricted area. That was their answer to the one-on-one, and here was the compromise: they agreed to the south side of the floor but removed the one-on-one.

As I drove home from Bethesda that night, I was even more aware that our treatment at Methodist was not how all hospitals accommodated patients and their families. Yet I still clung to the statement that "This place is like a boot camp," and I wanted to believe Jenny was in the right place.

CHAPTER 55

Day 50

Initially it appeared that Jenny's transition into the new facility was going smoothly. I believe the ease with which she adapted was a combination of her understanding that this was the next step toward going home and her determination to get there, as well as her flexibility and adaptability. I am also sure that part of it was that she was still not fully aware of what was going on at all times.

Bethesda was set up in a way that made them better equipped to deal with Jenny's specific issues, but they also had a much larger population demanding the attention of the staff. As with anything, there was good and bad but we remained confident that Jenny was in a good place that would help her get better.

What had not changed for me from Jenny's time at Methodist was I still felt the apprehension on the first elevator ride up to her room each morning. Standing in the elevator as it ascended to the fourth floor was nerve-wracking. So much could change with Jenny in such a short amount of time and sometimes a night felt like an eternity. Before the elevator doors opened, adrenaline would begin flowing through my body in preparation for what I would find on the other side.

On that first morning after Jenny had been admitted to Bethesda it was no different, but I had a talk with myself as I arrived. "Jenny was as aware as she's been in weeks yesterday, and this is a new place and a new situation. All is fine." I had to remind myself of this many times on my way up in the elevator. I had calmed myself down really well as I exited, passed through the security door and turned right to head down the hall to Jenny's room…just in time to see Jenny walk into the room of another patient across the hall from hers.

Okay, not a great start.

By the time I got down the hall, a nurse had retrieved Jenny from the room and was escorting her back to her room as Jenny repeatedly told her that this wasn't her room. I only could assume she had slipped a bit during the night and was looking for her room at Methodist. This was not good. It was clear that the nurse was a bit taken aback by the way Jenny was acting, but she handled it well.

I had not forgotten that the hospital had reserved the right to move Jenny over to the west wing if it did not work out well on the south side and I have to admit that my heart was beating hard and fast as the nurse began to explain that Jenny did not have a good night. From her description, I knew it wasn't bad at all by Jenny's standards…so I lied…and said it was unusual for her, hoping the nurse would let it go and not report it to anyone that might make the decision to move Jenny to the west wing.

In all honesty, I still felt that Jenny deserved the true one-on-one aide that was listed on her transfer orders, but I dared not broach the subject in case they resorted to moving her to the west side. Now that Jenny was actually here, if they made that move, I had no idea what recourse I would have. For quite a few days after that morning, every time my phone rang I'd grab it and check the caller ID, fearing that it was someone from Bethesda on the other end informing me that Jenny had been moved.

The first day was spent doing evaluations of Jenny's status, planning, and helping her adjust to a new routine. I was hopeful that these introductory procedures would help the staff develop an understanding of Jenny's illness and help them learn how to manage and deal with her as well. Unfortunately, Jenny was not as coherent as she had been the previous few days. In hindsight, I believe this was a defensive response by Jenny resulting from the stress of the move and change; similar to how she would simply go to sleep if she didn't like something occurring at Methodist. It was not clear what she understood and what she didn't. For their part, the nursing staff showed a great deal of patience with Jenny. Although a couple of sessions of therapy took place, it wasn't as intense or as long as what had been done at Methodist leading up to Jenny's discharge. I assumed that this was a transition period in an attempt to become familiar with Jenny's condition, in addition to the fact that it was Memorial Day weekend, so there was a smaller staff on duty. "Boot camp" would have to wait a few days.

Later that evening Michelle made her first visit to see Jenny since she had been admitted to Bethesda. All of the news that Michelle had heard the past three or four days had been positive and she had even had a brief phone conversation with Jenny the day before so she was very excited to see her and the progress she had made since the last time they were together.

Unfortunately, Jenny had been regressing at a slow yet steady pace since the previous evening, and I think Michelle's hopes and expectations had risen to an unrealistic level, so she was taken back a bit by what she saw that evening. Here is a portion of the journal entry Michelle wrote to Jenny after the visit that night:

So, when we came to see you I was ready to see more of the real you. When we turned the corner, I saw about eight people that are on the fourth floor with you all eating and staring at this tiny TV. I kept walking and there you were. You were sitting all alone in a chair, and you looked so little in the big chair. You got so excited to see us you jumped out of your chair, ran up to me, and gave me a hug. You hugged dad, led us to your chair, and pointed to the TV where the Twins were on. Then, you started crying. It broke my heart.

Jenny recovered and settled down after a few minutes and began to give her sister the full tour. The two made their way around the floor and I just stood back and watched the siblings interact. The scene took me back to when they were younger and one was excited to share something new with the other. Now they were both adults and their time together was less frequent, especially times when I could just sit back, observe, and take it in. I hated the circumstances, of course, but the times like these became a bit of an escape for me in which I could watch my daughters enjoying each other's company and I realized that I had taken it for granted when they were younger and we all had so much more time together.

CHAPTER 56

Day 51

Throughout the three most intense months of Jenny's illness, it seemed that we were on an emotional roller coaster ride. Sometimes we would be crying nearly uncontrollably due to news we received or something Jenny did, only to be laughing hysterically within hours or even minutes of that news because of something one of us did. At times, we would even laugh at the things Jenny did even though the cause of it was very sad and we knew that the illness had actually caused those actions. The only thing that was common about both of these emotions is that the trigger was never predictable.

Two days earlier, we were all excited about Jenny's arrival at Bethesda and the promise of intense therapy that was sure to put Jenny on the road to recovery. She had been showing good progress in many little ways since the treatment of the NMDA had begun, but I was very anxious for more significant signs that "the real Jenny" would soon be back with us. We had been told she would be part of a "boot camp" environment, and we were more than ready to do our part.

The greatest blessing God bestowed on Jenny is her younger sister, Michelle. She had been a wonderful sister for Jenny her entire life and although they were different in almost every way imaginable, Michelle was always Jenny's biggest fan whenever she needed one. There could hardly be a time that Jenny would need her sister more than now, and Michelle stepped up in countless ways. Ultimately, Michelle proved to be the most important person in Jenny's life over the next two months.

On this particular day, Barb was in Alexandria, Minnesota at a family reunion that had been planned months before in celebration of her parents' 60th wedding anniversary. Jenny was alone all day as Michelle, John, and I had spent the earlier part of the day away from the hospital making plans and arrangements for the upcoming fundraising benefit that Michelle and John were planning for Jenny. After accomplishing all we needed to that afternoon, Michelle and I went to the hospital to spend the evening with Jenny.

We had always believed that Jenny grasped some of what was going on around her throughout this ordeal and never more so than during the past few days as Jenny showed some true signs of boredom. Her restlessness had become more than just the desire to escape the confines of the hospital that she had demonstrated since her first day after being admitted. For this visit, we were determined to give Jenny something new and fun to do.

Jenny and Michelle have always enjoyed assembling puzzles together. On the way to the hospital, Michelle and I stopped to pick up a "Skip-Bo" card game, one of Jenny's favorites, and at the last minute decided to pick up a simple Winnie-the-Pooh puzzle.

We arrived around 5 p.m., which we knew was dinnertime at the hospital. After getting off the elevator and passing through the security door, the hallway leads directly into an entryway near the nurse's station that also serves as the main dining room for the patients. As Michelle and I turned the corner, we saw Jenny in this area among the rest of the patients. However, I never could have prepared myself for what I saw, nor would I have predicted that it would have caused the deep emotional pain I felt that evening.

Jenny was sitting alone in an area down a short, narrow hallway that ran off to the side of the main room, facing a small TV that was mounted so high on the wall that she had to crane her neck to look up at it. Her posture, combined with the fact that she had lost so much weight that her clothes hung on her loosely, gave Jenny the appearance of a young child sitting in a chair that was too big for her. What topped it off was the incredibly sad look on her face. She looked so alone, helpless, scared, and hopeless, and despite everything we had seen the past eight weeks, or maybe because of all that we had seen, this moment sticks out in my mind as one of my saddest and lowest points. Throughout her illness, as much as I would have given anything to grant Jenny's wish to take her home, I had always known she was exactly where she needed to be until this moment. This scene was the first time I began questioning whether Jenny was where she belonged.

It didn't get any better once Jenny saw us. She instantly started to cry, got out of the chair and headed for us as quickly as she could. While she wanted and accepted our hugs, she was adamant about something. She still could not speak clearly, but she appeared very agitated, moving her hands a lot as she tried to communicate something. When Jenny went to Michelle, I could see in Michelle's eyes that she felt the same pain that I did.

As was the case so many times during the past few weeks when we failed to understand what Jenny was trying to say, we forced the "conversation" to move another direction. Once again, whatever Jenny was trying to communicate would go unfulfilled and that just added to the pain I felt.

We moved to Jenny's room and sat with her while she finished her dinner and watched the rest of the Twins game. She seemed excited to see the Skip-Bo card game but was not interested in playing. As the evening progressed, Michelle started working on the Winnie-the-Pooh puzzle on the small table in Jenny's room. Jenny seemed to want to participate, but initially only removed pieces from the table and put them back in the box. It appeared that Jenny was having a good time. Despite the loss of control of many of her facial muscles that impaired even basic facial expressions, I was sure I saw a small smile on Jenny's face many times.

Michelle, ever the teacher, showed no frustration with Jenny and began a series of maneuvers to redirect Jenny's efforts to actually help with the puzzle. Once Michelle had Jenny's focus on assembly rather than tossing pieces into the box, she began to find ways to allow Jenny to help despite her limited motor skills.

Initially Michelle started setting two puzzle pieces that she knew went together directly in front of Jenny so she only had to focus on those two pieces. Michelle set them down lined up so that all Jenny had to do was to lift one piece and set it into the other. At first, Jenny tried to slide the pieces across the surface of the table and squeeze them together. Michelle showed Jenny the proper way to assemble the pieces, but Jenny had to slide the piece to the edge of the table to pick it up. Michelle continued to put two pieces in front of Jenny, each time reminding her that she needed to lift one piece up to be able to connect them. Eventually Jenny began to put the pieces together properly, one pair at a time, still needing to slide each piece to the edge of the table to pick it up but no longer needing to be reminded of the proper process each time. While Michelle was still locating the matching pieces for Jenny, Jenny was showing the ability to interpret and react to instructions. A significant sign of improvement had occurred right in front of us, and our own private Nichols family therapy session had begun.

For the first time in weeks I was able to witness Jenny taking instruction, processing the information, and demonstrating the ability to change and control what she was doing. It may have been the most beautiful sight I have ever seen; this became more than the two sisters interacting, this was Michelle helping her sister in a way no one else had in her most critical time of need.

After a while, the puzzle began to outgrow the size of Jenny's bedside table. Truth be told, Michelle and I hadn't held out much hope for success when this project began, but now we were anxious for it to continue, so we asked Jenny if she wanted to go down to the family room to a larger table. Jenny got up and was out of the room on her way down the hall before we could gather up the puzzle.

After getting situated on a table in the family visiting area, Michelle was as patient as I have ever seen her with her sister, but she also appeared to have a clear mission in mind. Jenny had mastered the process of picking up one puzzle piece without sliding it to the edge of the table, so Michelle began a progression of increasing the challenge for Jenny in a way that I never would have considered, nor would I have had the patience to do it. She started by turning one of the puzzle pieces so that Jenny had to figure out which way to spin the piece so that it would fit with the other piece. After a few successes, Michelle turned both pieces. Later, she began pointing to pieces without moving them next to each other, and finally she just pointed to a general area where matching pieces could be found. The progress was slow, but it became easier with each piece. After an hour or so, Jenny found a couple of pieces all by herself. In some ways it was like watching a child mature right before my eyes.

Jenny was as focused as she had ever been during her illness. The three of us stood around the table that held the puzzle, and Jenny's head was down as she worked hard at each task Michelle presented her. Not only was she enjoying putting the puzzle together, it was clear that her natural competitiveness and determination to succeed were coming through. It had turned into a challenge as much as entertainment, and Michelle and I had accomplished our goal of giving Jenny something new to think about and on which to focus. Even if for just a little while, Jenny's mind was on something positive for longer than a few minutes.

I only pretended to work on the puzzle. In reality I watched in awe what my two daughters were accomplishing together. Michelle was showing immense patience as well as ingenuity in her rapid thought process of increasing a challenge appropriately at just the right time. I felt so lucky to witness this.

Just after 8 p.m., Jenny appeared to be getting tired. We talked about stopping for the evening, but Jenny was so focused that Michelle and I didn't have the heart to force her to stop. I'm not sure if we were motivated by Jenny having a good time, or our own enjoyment at having some version of a normal evening together as a family again. This may have been the happiest I'd felt in weeks and I selfishly didn't want it to end.

Then things started to turn.

At first, the change in Jenny was small. She was still standing next to the table, but she had stopped focusing on the puzzle and she was not moving. Then I noticed that Jenny was having an unexpected bowel movement, evidenced by what had run down her leg and onto the floor. For a moment, Michelle and I stood and looked at each other with "what now" expressions on our faces.

I guess it should have been odd to watch my 26-year-old daughter have "an accident" such as this, but given everything else that had happened during the previous eight weeks, this became just another "oh well" kind of moment. This experience was another first for Michelle and me and we had to figure out how to deal with it, just as we had with a hundred other situations involving Jenny during her illness. Within a couple of seconds, Michelle and I were responding to the situation as if we had done it any number of times. We didn't even exchange any words as we reacted.

I went to get help to clean up while Michelle made sure Jenny didn't do anything that made the mess any worse. A couple of nurses came and took Jenny back to her room while a third nurse cleaned up the floor.

Once the event was over, Michelle and I did what we had so many other times – we discussed what had just happened, what it meant, and how we should move forward. All of the things we had witnessed and experienced so far in this journey helped to make this a minor event in the scheme of things.

I have no idea if Jenny had no control, if her mind could only focus on one thing at a time, or if it was simply that she was so focused on the puzzle it didn't dawn on her to stop, even for that. The reality was that our lives were at a point that these unanswerable questions instantly became moot points. It was all about moving forward.

The question now was if we were going to continue with the puzzle when Jenny returned or if we would call it a night. We both knew in our hearts we should probably call it a night, but we decided to let Jenny make the decision. We moved a few puzzle pieces around to try to make it easier for Jenny when she got back, but we didn't do any assembly.

Eventually, Jenny was guided back into the area by a nurse. She had showered and her hair was wet and freshly combed. She barely seemed to notice we were there as she turned the corner from the hallway into the area of tables where the puzzle was and bee-lined straight to it. It was as if she had tunnel-vision focus on the puzzle and was ready to get back to work. Jenny refused to sit down and returned to standing in the same spot she had occupied before to continue working on the puzzle.

Only a few minutes later, it was obvious that Jenny was tiring, and I was questioning our decision to continue working on the puzzle rather than putting her to bed. Michelle and I both began to work to finish the puzzle as quickly as possible. Although Jenny was wavering as she stood there, her continued focus on the puzzle made it obvious there was no way we could ask her to stop working on it.

Twenty minutes later, Jenny suddenly bent forward over the table and made a pretty awful sound that sounded like a painful grunt, moan, and scream all at the same time. I quickly reached out and wrapped my arms around her to keep her from falling. It was instantly obvious that Jenny's body had gone fully rigid from head to toe. I was able to get my head around to look at Jenny's face and I could she had gone into a seizure and I lowered her slowly to the floor. I distinctly remember being shocked that the rigidity of her body made it easy to prevent Jenny from falling. However, most astonishing to me at the time was realizing how much weight Jenny had lost. She had always remained strong enough to fight with me during her episodes, and this was the first time that I had held her when she was completely submissive.

Once I laid her on the floor, I held her head while she had a Grand Mal seizure, which lasted 45 seconds to a minute. Michelle retrieved the nursing staff and the crew from Bethesda took over. This was her first known seizure in about three weeks and the first Grand Mal since March. After such a monumental day in her recovery, we now appeared to have had a monumental setback.

Ten minutes later, Jenny was in her bed and had regained most of her awareness. In fact she was able to talk just enough to be clear. Michelle went over and hugged her. Jenny could tell that Michelle had been crying so she asked, "Is everything okay?" Michelle said that everything was fine and asked Jenny how she felt. Jenny said that she was tired and wanted to go to sleep. She had no recollection of the seizure.

Michelle and I drove home, and I was left to wonder which part of the evening I would remember with more clarity in the future. It was a tremendously fun evening, but it had both started and ended on such amazingly low notes. It was uplifting in so many ways because I had confirmation that "the real" Jenny was indeed in there somewhere and was just waiting to get out. However, I was clearly reminded that the NMDA still owned her. Was the seizure a sign that she wasn't ready for the type of intense therapy the evening proved to be or had she had just gone beyond the limit of her endurance at the time?

In hindsight, a year removed from that day and after everything that has happened since, we know that the seizure was serious but was not a huge setback. However, that day proved to be the beginning of Jenny being able to follow instructions as well as improve motor skills within the timeframe of a single therapy session. Our family night seemed to prime the pump toward recovery.

It took Michelle a while to come around to doing puzzles again, especially when Jenny was around. Thank goodness she got over that, and it is one of her favorite pastimes once again.

CHAPTER 57

Day 53

For the first time since Jenny began this odyssey in March, Barb and I were away from her for more than 24 hours. Actually, until this point, I am not sure there was ever a 12-hour period in which at least one of us was not with Jenny.

Barb actually departed on Friday. Barb's parents were celebrating their 60th wedding anniversary, and to honor the occasion Barb and her three siblings had planned a family gathering over the long Memorial Day weekend at a resort in Alexandria, Minnesota, located about 200 miles northwest of Minneapolis. When I think about that now, I am still surprised that she actually went, but all of us were glad that she did. The planning for the gathering had begun months before Jenny got ill, and it was truly a significant event that needed to be recognized.

Michelle and I stayed in town until Sunday morning and then we joined everyone else at the resort. John stayed with Jenny the entire time we were gone, staying at the hospital 32 hours straight until Barb, Michelle, and I made it back there on Monday.

There were no two ways about it, and no way to sugar coat it, Jenny was not doing well. She had another Grand Mal seizure on Sunday morning, the second in a 12-hour span, after having had the seizures completely under control for weeks. Jenny was also having a hard time communicating and the episodes had increased in intensity again. According to what I wrote in the CaringBridge journal after that weekend, I estimated that Jenny had regressed about three weeks. My hunch is that my discouragement and frustration added about a week to that estimate, but it was a significant slide.

The good news was that there were some significant periods in which Jenny would "come back" and we could see the real her. Additionally, she had started receiving some very short periods of therapy and the reports were that she was able to focus during those times. She was essentially able to perform the tasks assigned to her, but the sessions comprised only a few minutes each day. We anxiously awaited the "boot camp environment" we had been promised as Jenny had always enjoyed being challenged and having a clear objective to accomplish.

The alarm attached to Jenny's wrist sounded every time she walked toward the elevator, something she couldn't seem to stop herself from doing. The alarm was a constant reminder to her that she wasn't going home. What had seemed like a positive transition that first day may only have been her reaction to what we had portrayed to her as the first step to going home. Perhaps now the reality of the situation was settling in. By the end of that long weekend, not only did I not believe Jenny was adjusting to Bethesda, I also did not believe Bethesda was adjusting to Jenny.

NMDA was still an unknown entity to most doctors. People who have not actually witnessed the illness with their own eyes have no concept of what it is truly like. I don't blame Bethesda at all for the fact that they did not comprehend what they were dealing with, but that did not change the fact that I desperately needed them to help me get my daughter back. When I was initially told that we had a choice of what rehab facility Jenny would go to, my goal was to choose a facility that I knew would work with us and spend some time learning about NMDA to understand the unique challenges Jenny presented.

Although the "treatment" aspect of Jenny's illness was completed at Methodist, she was still a very sick woman. The doctors had done all they could for her from a clinical perspective, but that didn't mean she was ready for a rehab environment and the type of care those facilities had to offer. In fairness to Bethesda, Jenny's current condition made her difficult to work with and I am not sure they were fully prepared to deal with it. Yet, the fact was, she was there and it was Bethesda's decision to accept her. Due to Jenny arriving at Bethesda just before a long holiday weekend, I was holding out hope that things would improve.

As has often been the case, the day-to-day journaling by Michelle is the best way to clarify Jenny's condition on this particular day, as well as how it was affecting all of us:

I went to Alexandria Sunday morning, so we didn't come see you. I know Dad and I felt guilty. But anyways, I looked like poop, I cried a lot over the weekend. Grandpa even cried when we talked about you too...everyone missed you there and wished you were there. I wish you were there too because I was the only one that is too old to hang out with the cousins, but too young to be with parents. The usual situation but I always have you there. Not this time...We got thru it and then came to see you Monday.

When we got there, you were at therapy. When you walked back, you got a huge smile on your face to see us. You laid down in your bed and John said he was going to go. You got so sad he was leaving. Once again, I began to cry. I'm tired of seeing you sad. I'm tired of seeing you not yourself. I miss you...You cried a lot and I tried to calm you down, which worked most of the time, but your stuffed animals were talking to you. I could tell you were getting so mad at them. You were holding them up to your ears trying to hear them. You ended up throwing them all across the room; you said they were too loud.

Then, you brought up the two boys that hang out in your room. You used to mention them and two little girls who bother you in your room. You are hallucinating again. It's been a while since you have been seeing things, and I don't know if that is a good thing or a bad thing, but the parents of these boys were also in the room, or so you were saying. I could tell they were behind you because you were talking to them and you kept turning around. You cried more because they wouldn't stop and you were annoyed. I still can't imagine what it is like to see something, and be convinced it's there when it's really not.

Later in the night we asked if you wanted to play cards and you jumped out of bed and we went down to the bigger table. I asked which game you wanted to play and you said Skip-Bo. We were playing for a while and you looked really confused. You weren't playing right, so I tried to help you. Then at one point, you said you don't get this game. So we switched to Uno. I know you love Skip-Bo and you know how to play. It hurt knowing your brain isn't ready for that game yet.

CHAPTER 58

Day 54

After a very stressful weekend – the combination of dealing with Jenny's seizure, seeing her regress, and the guilt of being away at a lakeside resort for about 20 hours – things felt a bit better that day. Perhaps a bit of rest helped, and it provided me with a chance to slow down, think, and get some perspective. Actually gaining perspective was a recurring theme the entire time Jenny was sick. It was too easy to become a permanent passenger on the roller coaster ride of emotions. Something good would happen, and I so desperately wanted it to be a sign of permanent improvement that I allowed my emotions to carry me to believing that it was *the* sign, but then something bad would happen and the stress and fatigue would allow my emotions to convince me it was a sign of impending doom.

I entered the day with a new perspective and reminded myself not to let the highs take me so high and the lows take me so low. It certainly helped that Jenny had had a remarkable turnaround and was much closer to how she had been the week before. When I arrived at the hospital that afternoon, Barb had been there ahead of me for quite a while and was engaged in a very good conversation with Jenny – at least the current version of a conversation. Feeling the weight lift from my shoulders and the loosening of the knot in my stomach was remarkable.

Jenny ate her entire dinner and was even able to unscrew the cap on a water bottle, take a drink without a single drop of water spilling, and recap the bottle tightly. Some of the ground that seemed to have been lost, even the day before, had now been taken back. I had to keep reminding myself that this would be a gradual process with peaks and valleys and resist the temptation to ride along with them.

This day was the first "care meeting" with the heads of each of the departments that were responsible for Jenny's care. Although today was the fifth full day of Jenny having been a patient at Bethesda, three of those days were a holiday weekend so there really wasn't much to discuss. We spent the time becoming familiar with each other and getting the answers to a few basic questions as the head of each therapy department laid out their plan. None of it sounded very aggressive to me, but I remained patient, as it was still early. I decided there was no need to get myself all wound up before they really had a chance to do something.

During the meeting, Barb and I each attempted to broach the subject of the lack of a one-on-one nurse's aide; however, as a team, they successfully ignored our question. I had the distinct impression that they had collaborated to avoid talking about it. Admittedly, I was also afraid to push the issue hard because I didn't want them to use it as an excuse to move Jenny to the west side. The staff expressed no concerns about Jenny's behavior, so that was good, and Barb and I decided to let a sleeping dog lie for the time being.

Later in the evening, I overheard some nurses in the hall say that all of the beds in both wings on the floor were full. This information relieved some of my apprehension about pressing Bethesda about the one-on-one aide issue since they probably couldn't move Jenny to the west side even if they wanted to unless they did a swap, which I imagined would be unlikely.

It was not long after hearing that conversation that I made a comment about the one-on-one aide to a nurse who was frustrated with Jenny's behavior. She was very surprised by my comment and I got the impression that she wanted to talk to her supervisor about it.

The next morning the report from the nurse on duty with Jenny overnight reported that Jenny had "stood on her bed and touched the ceiling" and at one point during the night, "she was weepy." I knew these were both the result of "episodes" Jenny was having, but the doctors and nurses had yet to listen to any of us when we tried to broach the subject about how to deal with Jenny's episodes. The only thing the nurse said about it was "she can't do that because it is not safe." I wasn't entirely sure if the comment was just part of the conversation or if I was supposed to do something with the information, like scold Jenny about having done that. I mentioned the one-on-one aide again.

In a completely separate incident later that day, I was having a conversation with one of the lead nurses who informed me that all of the nurses were under orders to try to find a pattern to Jenny's behavior. I couldn't help but laugh. She gave me an odd look, so I told her the story of the Neuropsychiatrist from Methodist trying to do the same thing and I said, "Good luck with that." I explained that we had seen dozens, if not hundreds of "behaviors" and had actually named them "episodes."

The timing was perfect because Jenny had a small episode right at the end of the conversation. The nurse could see that nothing triggered it and it came out of nowhere. Jenny got up on the bed again, similar to what was reported from this morning, which actually surprised me because it suggested a possible repeated behavior. Since I was present this time, I could see that Jenny was trying to open the access panel above her bed. I'm not sure if she had done that during the prior incident or not, but it presented an opportunity to demonstrate how to deal with Jenny during these times. She saw that it was easier to allow Jenny to finish what she was doing rather than try to get her down. Of course, she expressed concern about the danger if Jenny did that while no one was with her and I had my chance! I not only mentioned the one-on-one aide, but also said that it was in the transfer orders. The nurse was very surprised to hear that. Minutes after she left the room, I overheard a conversation in which the nurse was demanding the one-on-one aide for Jenny. She must have at least gotten a discussion about it started because it happened two days later.

The conversation with the nurse prompted me to resend the email discussing how to handle Jenny's "episodes" that I had sent to the lead nurse at Methodist weeks before, and what our experience was with them. I also included what we knew about them after two months of dealing with them. The next day, my email was posted in Jenny's room with a large print note for all nurses to read before they cared for Jenny.

Perhaps we were making some progress, in that Bethesda was starting to listen to some of our input.

CHAPTER 59

Day 57

Jenny finally began to fall into and grow comfortable with the routine that was being established during the week and she seemed to be doing a bit better. Therapy was progressing, but it was nowhere near the boot camp pace we had imagined. Maybe our definition of "intense" was different from theirs – I had no idea. Although we tried to watch what went on with the other patients, it was an impossible and unfair task because we were not around enough and each patient was in a different physical condition.

Jenny received another MRI and an EEG. The MRI required her to be lightly sedated as it was still impossible for her to lie perfectly still for the required amount of time. I often wondered if it was that she couldn't, wouldn't, or if she simply didn't understand the instructions she was given.

The trip from our home in Rockford to the hospital in St Paul was a 37-mile drive, and although most of it was on an Interstate, it took me directly through Minneapolis and to the edge of downtown St. Paul. For this reason, I had developed the habit of getting to the hospital between 5 and 6 a.m. and staying until about 9 a.m. or so, which allowed me to avoid all of the rush hour traffic and made it possible for me to have breakfast with Jenny. That morning Jenny and I had a very nice time together. It was good to spend some time with her that felt somewhat normal.

Another habit I had formed since Jenny was first admitted to Methodist was I used that time in the mornings to text updates to Michelle before she went to work. Sometimes detailed exchanges took place, and I would tell her everything that Jenny was doing, even including pictures from time to time. The main topic of discussion that week had been Jenny's ability to feed herself, which seemed to come and go, but it also served as a barometer of Jenny's condition for us. Once it was determined that Jenny was able to feed herself on a particular day, the question would then become whether Jenny was using utensils and employing proper manners and etiquette. Not that it really mattered, but, again, it was simply a barometer of how she was doing at any given time. Jenny had been feeding herself most of the week but had been using her fingers each time and even had a phase of difficulty hitting her mouth. That morning I was very pleased with Jenny's ability and reported it to Michelle during our text message exchange:

> Dad: "She ate her whole breakfast again this morning!"
> Michelle: "Good. But did she use a fork?"
> Dad: "I am pleased to report that she did..."

Then I sent a follow-up text: "...the only problem was that she was eating a breakfast sandwich!"

We debated whether this was a good sign or a not so good sign...but Michelle and I both laughed a lot. That definitely was a good sign.

The day before, I had met with the lead neurologist for quite a long time to talk about Jenny's lack of quality sleep. While there constantly seemed to be bigger concerns, Jenny's inability to sleep was an issue from the day of her first seizure. It was very plain to see that her body was exhausted and it was yet another manifestation of "the garbage in her head" being in control. One doctor guessed that some of the antibodies had lodged in the adrenal gland. However, there was no way to know if this was the true cause or not. Often, it seemed as though Jenny's brain and body were in a physical battle over who was going to win, and almost without fail, the brain did. All of us agreed that true and deep healing would not begin until she got some quality sleep.

The doctors at Methodist tried to address it many times but always needed to be careful with what and how much medication they gave Jenny because of all the other issues going on at that time. Now that the NMDA had been treated and she was somewhat stabilized, the neurologist essentially asked permission to get more aggressive. We talked about the pros and cons of his plan, including the potential side effects; however, the overriding factor was that Jenny's lack of sleep was now becoming her biggest problem. Thus, the decision was made to begin giving Jenny some heavy sleep aids at night.

My understanding and recollection of the first night was that Jenny received a combination of four different drugs. The score after round one: Drugs 0, Jenny's brain 1. No sleep, at all, that first night. The second night was also unsuccessful.

Each morning I met with the doctor and he would formulate a new plan. Finally, on night three, the score read: Drugs 1, Jenny's brain 2! Although Jenny only slept an estimated 65% of the time, she stayed in bed the whole night and that was considered a great success.

Now that the doctor was able to make sleep one of Jenny's priorities, we believed that her rate of recovery would improve. Even that first morning with Jenny after she stayed in bed all night, she was as "aware" as I had seen her since early April. More often than not since Jenny had deteriorated to the point of her not being aware, it had always been a challenge to get and hold her attention. She was rarely able to absorb and/or participate in even just two things going on in the room at the same time. At times, it seemed that while she was doing one thing, a gun could have gone off behind her and she wouldn't have noticed. However, today she was aware of and acknowledging almost all the distractions going on around her. Even when a nurse simply entered the room, Jenny would turn and look. Any form of multitasking would remain a problem for Jenny for months, but at least we were finally seeing some progress and it appeared that the sleep was already paying dividends. Thankfully, it was a trend that would continue. We were very thankful to the doctor for getting Jenny over that hurdle.

CHAPTER 60

The Benefit

On June 1, 2013, a benefit was held on Jenny's behalf.

In early May, Michelle and John had proposed putting one together. I was initially against the idea and, frankly, thought they were more than a little loopy for even contemplating it with everything else that was going on. I had been so focused on the day-to-day of what was happening to Jenny that I had never given the financial side of things a moment's thought. I also failed to realize that this was very important to Michelle and John, serving as a way for them to contribute in any way they could. By the end of May, I was more clear-headed about everything that was going on, and what the future was going to hold for all of us in terms of Jenny's medical expenses. I was very grateful they had taken on the task.

Part of my new clarity was the CaringBridge site had started about a week before the idea came up and it was becoming clear to me how many people cared about what was happening to Jenny. Between CaringBridge, the Meal Train, and many other avenues, the outpouring of support from the entire community, including the people that Barb, Michelle, John, and I worked with and the organizations we were involved in was amazing and completely unexpected. I knew there were people who cared and would be concerned, but I had no idea that so many people would step up to help in so many ways. I also realized that the benefit would offer a terrific opportunity to say thank you to so many people that there just was no time to see on a regular basis, as well as a chance to see people with whom I otherwise may not cross paths.

By mid-May, I was very nervous about the amount of work that it was clearly going to take but I was also very excited about what Michelle and John had put together. They did a great job of formulating and building ideas for the event and getting other people involved. They had the usual items that benefits include: a silent auction, t-shirt sales, and a spaghetti dinner. However, as the planning continued, it grew into a very large affair. Soon there were wristbands, a musical group, and an updated version of a good old-fashioned bake sale. In addition, John's family came up with a way to use a beanbag toss game to generate money, but it also turned into another form of entertainment at the benefit. In fact, it turned into an intense event itself. It was held in a separate room and often very loud cheers could be heard coming from the room. John's sister did a great job of attracting people to the room and encouraging participation.

Michelle worked with a family friend and former soccer mom to create a scrapbooking center so that people could give Jenny something to see since she could not attend the event. One of Barb's sister-in-laws took a picture of individuals or families and then it was printed for them to create a scrapbook page at one of four different tables that had been set up with a plethora of scrapbooking supplies. Barb Myers and her family worked behind the tables keeping the printer going, the tables stocked, and assisting people who were hesitant to get creative with their page. The scrapbooking was my favorite idea of the whole event; I felt it would give Jenny a connection to the party that the event ultimately became, because I knew she would be upset that she missed it.

People from various areas of our lives stepped up to help with the benefit. Many people from Barnes and Noble, where Jenny worked, got involved and they were the source of the musical group that volunteered to entertain the crowd that day. A company that catered events for the school completely managed the food. My entire family, as well as Barb's and John's families and many of John's huge circle of friends all played a role in making the event the success it turned out to be.

The silent auction was the most stunning aspect of the whole affair. When I first heard about the idea, I had pictured maybe 20 to 30 items that would include a few handmade products and maybe a pair of Twins tickets donated by my business partner. Never in my wildest dreams would I have imagined the volume of donations that came in, nor the variety of sources that contributed. Suppliers to my business made donations and t-shirt purchases. A neighbor got his employer involved and donated a huge variety of professional sports memorabilia, and a family friend of John's donated a large collection of "gift baskets" that were each unique and extremely creative. Thanks to John's networking and the efforts of a former high school teacher of Jenny's, a variety of businesses got involved.

Saturday, May 18th was the first date for people who wished to donate items to drop them off at the house. I had put a 4 x 8 sheet of plywood over an air hockey table to place the donations on so whoever was going to organize the auction could work without needing to bend over or work on the floor. Donations could be brought any time after 9 a.m. and at 8:59, there was a knock on the door. The father of a former soccer player I had coached had put together an amazing "party cooler" as well as a gift package from the horse track in Minnesota. I had never expected a person with that type of connection to my life to donate, nor had I expected such great and extravagant donations. I didn't even know if they had ever met Jenny.

I placed the cooler on a corner of the plywood tabletop and found a basket for the gift certificates. An hour later, another "gift basket" that someone had taken the time to put together was dropped off. I had no idea people would go so far out of their way. I looked at the air hockey table and thought, "Those two baskets are cool and will look really good on the table at the auction. Maybe I can make a couple myself to fill up the table a little more," but before I had time to do more than consider the idea, people were coming up my driveway one after another. Two hours later, I had placed a second sheet of plywood over the foosball table, created a barrier to keep the dogs away from what I had set on the floor in the basement, and had begun to move things upstairs to the living room. Items continued to arrive over the next couple of weeks, even on the day of the benefit itself. There ended up being more than 230 items in the auction! Once I looked at the big picture and realized the enormity of organizing all of it, it felt like an overwhelming task. Thank God, my sister Debbie volunteered to manage that aspect of the project.

When the idea first came up, the plan was to hold the event in one of the meeting rooms of the Rockford Community Center, but about two weeks before the event, Michelle told me that the benefit was being moved to the commons of the Rockford Elementary School. I was stunned, and actually a bit concerned. I still pictured the event being Barb, Michelle, John, and I standing in the meeting room for four hours with a few people occasionally swinging in, grabbing a quick bite to eat, giving their well wishes, and heading out. I felt it would be a bit embarrassing to stand in such a large area of the school hearing the echoes off the wall as 10 or 15 people stood around and chitchatted.

Michelle asked me to come to the first meeting at the school with Christa Larson, who worked with Rockford Community Education. I had known Christa for years due to my family's involvement in the various activities that were run through the Community Center. I also knew Scott, Christa's husband, very well. It didn't take long to grasp how much work Christa and Scott were putting into the benefit. Christa was carrying a folder with multiple sheets of paper in it, clearly keeping a long checklist. Scott walked around with Michelle asking how many tables were needed and where to put them. I heard them talking about hauling tables over from the high school. Holy cow! I was stunned by the amount of work, time, and labor, and wondered where exactly Michelle and John were going with "this little get together" they had planned.

Later I realized how little I knew about the event and what was going into it. I knew the facilities were being rented, but I also knew an organization pays for the custodian that is required to be on duty during any event held at the school. I took Michelle aside and asked what rate the school was charging for Christa and Scott. "Nothing! They are volunteering their time!" This was ultimately my first clue as to how many people were getting involved and what they were sacrificing on Jenny's behalf. Again, I was stunned.

I mentioned my concerns about the size of the venue when I heard Christa and Michelle talking about how many cafeteria-style tables were being set up for people to eat. I had heard something about enough spaghetti for 300 people earlier in the week, but when I heard "we need more food" I started to panic a little bit, imagining that not only would we have echoes as we talked, but there would be dozens of empty tables and tons of food going to waste. When I asked Christa about all of this she said, "I am not sure we will have enough room for everyone." I was shocked. What would make her think that? She continued by saying, "People have been calling the Community Center all week asking how they can help." I was speechless and wasn't really prepared to believe her. I braced myself for a horribly embarrassing situation as the day drew closer. Apparently, the stacks of auction items in various rooms in my house were not enough evidence for me.

As with any undertaking of this type, there were problems, and Michelle asked me to get involved in a few of them. I was a fatigue-ridden and overly stressed father/business owner/soccer coach/control freak, and unfortunately, I stepped way over my boundaries by attempting to get more involved than either of them wanted. Three days before the event, Michelle and John were furious with me and I owed each of them an apology.

The benefit was scheduled to begin at 4 p.m. That morning was chaotic, mostly because of the sheer number of silent auction items. My sister Debbie and Karen Nielsen, the soccer mom who had helped organize the Meal Train, had been working on organizing the silent auction items since the Thursday before while John, his friends and Scott Larson took care of setup. Dozens of tables needed to be moved and set up. Signs and decorations were hung and many specific locations around the commons area in the school had to be set-up, including a stage for the band. The volume of people involved blew my mind. I had no idea so many details had been attended to as Barb and I essentially did nothing in terms of planning.

Barb had gone to spend the morning and afternoon with Jenny while I was at the house with Debbie, Karen, Michelle, and Brad working on cataloging the silent auction items, making sign-up sheets for each item, and then moving them to the school and setting up. What I had pictured as a table or two turned into more than three dozen banquet tables set against the walls that ran the full length of a long hallway at the end of the commons area and started its way back on the other side.

I was the last of our family to arrive at the benefit as I was bringing some things from home over to the school. I arrived a few minutes before the designated start time, but had received multiple texts from Michelle telling me to hurry up as people were starting to arrive. I had no idea what she was talking about until I got about 15-feet inside the door and ran into some of the first people coming to the benefit. They wanted to share their concern, ask for an update about Jenny, and get a few questions answered. From that moment on, for the next four hours, there was hardly a moment that I did not have someone who wanted to talk with me. Initially I was so focused on whatever conversation I was having, that I didn't see that the room was already almost full. When I finally noticed, I was overwhelmed. I would love to be able to share stories about what everyone else experienced during the evening, but I have no idea. Other than the one time I snuck off to the restroom and the time I grabbed a microphone to address the crowd, I never had more than a few seconds between conversations. At one point, I rushed over to the food area because I noticed that they were shutting down and a plate of spaghetti was put together for me. A couple of hours later, as clean up was taking place, someone yelled across the room asking who the untouched plate of food belonged to. It was mine. I hadn't had a chance to take a single bite.

The memories of that evening will warm my heart for the rest of my life. So many people from so many different aspects of my family's life were there. At one point, I was told the school parking lot was full and the cars overflowed into the street. I never would have dared to imagine the outpouring of love and support on Jenny's behalf. I know I didn't talk to even a fraction of the people I knew, let alone everyone on John's side. Of course, no one came to see just me. The circumstances of the gathering were unfortunate, but it served as a bit of a reunion for some friends to meet up again as well and I witnessed many people catching up with old friends they had not seen in some time. That was fantastic and fun to see.

We were all very blessed, and I felt extremely grateful for everyone who took time out of a gorgeous summer weekend night to come to the benefit. I was deeply touched and comforted by everyone that was there and I hope everyone whose name I forgot has forgiven me. I was very overwhelmed.

Some of Jenny's teammates from her college volleyball and basketball teams were there. Many players and parents from the soccer team that I coached for only a few weeks earlier in the spring attended. Customers of my business attended. Actually, there were too many people there for me to keep track, but I was thankful for every single one.

What really touched my heart was that five of the nurses from Methodist came and stayed for a long time. It was a pleasure to introduce them to everyone via the public address system. I was sorry that I could not introduce my business partner to everyone. She had done more for Jenny and me than anyone outside the family. I saw her for maybe 30 seconds at one point, but she had already left by the time I addressed the crowd.

The nurses presented us with a gift for Jenny, a t-shirt with a ferocious tiger and "6Neuro Track Team" on the front. I was so tired that day I missed the connection at first. "6Neuro" is what the 6th floor is called by the people that work there. The track team, of course, refers to the fact that Jenny was constantly on the move in the hallways of the 6th floor and even ran away from some of the nurses from time to time. The gift was absolutely perfect, and hilarious... and I cried, in front of God and everyone once I got the joke. The best part was that all of the nurses and aides on the floor had signed the back of the shirt around the "Nichols" that was printed there.

The evening was a wild success in terms of being able to see so many people who had helped in so many ways, as well as those who cared for Jenny and wanted to reach out. However, it would not be until weeks later that I would realize how important the benefit was in terms of our financial survival as we worked to get through all of this.

It hit me on the day that I picked up the first batch of prescriptions after Jenny was released from the hospital and the bill came to $687! That was my wakeup call as to what was to come. Jenny could not work, of course, and her disability benefits at Barnes and Noble had run out, yet there were months of medical care in front of her so it was important to keep her insured. The proceeds of the benefit were used to curtail Jenny's medical and insurance costs. Barb, Jenny, and I will forever be grateful to Michelle and John for organizing the benefit, and to the hundreds of people who donated in various ways.

CHAPTER 61

Day 59

The day after the benefit, everyone was very tired. It had been an extremely long day, starting at around 6 a.m., and it was just about midnight before all of us were in bed. Since John did not make it to the hospital at all the day of the benefit, he was going to spend the morning with Jenny and Barb, Michelle, and I would follow later that evening.

Although there were many things that needed attention around the house, we all decided that we needed a break. The weather was forecast to be beautiful and sunny and I knew the soccer team that I had been coaching was in a tournament nearby along with another team coached by a friend of Michelle's, so we decided to take in a couple of games and enjoy the great outdoors for a while.

I must have taken full advantage of the situation because I honestly have little recollection of the day, and since I did not do a CaringBridge update that day, I have no notes about it. Michelle did the CaringBridge entry for the day and gave a good summary of what we did as well as what was going on with Jenny:

> We went to see Jenny on Sunday after what my dad claims was *"sitting in a patch of grass catching some rays."* (We really went to watch some soccer.) Oh, on a side note: watching the team my dad coached for six weeks and I had met about three times, it really made us miss coaching and miss those girls. It was good to see you girls coming along, and to come running up to my dad after the game really made his day. We are going to try our best to get to more games. Anyway, we went to see Jenny after that. I was so excited to see her because the stories I was getting from John and my parents all week made it sound like Jenny was doing better. When I walked into the room, Jenny was eating dinner, she looked up at me and said, *"OH HEYYYYYYY!"* and if you know Jenny, you can hear her say this exactly. I laughed so hard. That was the first welcome I got from her that wasn't a wave or a simple hello. She explained to us she was having a taco for dinner and it was really messy. She was talking very clear and was aware of everything going on.
>
> After she finished eating, we asked if she wanted to go play a game or do a puzzle. She said she wanted to play Sequence. I jumped up to grab the game – I was so excited to play a family game. We were ready to head down to the family room and Jenny said to me, "We

262

aren't playing Yahtzee." I told her I knew that and that I heard her say Sequence. Then she gives me this "you're stupid" look and pointed at the game I had in my hand. Of course, I grabbed the wrong game and was holding Yahtzee in my hand. In a typical world, this would be a story about how stupid I was. However, in our world now, this was a sign that Jenny was aware of what was going on around her.

We went and played I think 18 games of Sequence. I was on a team with my mom, and Jenny and dad were on a team. This next part is hard to say... but Jenny and my dad won 15 of those games; mom and I only won three. Even given Jenny's situation, we don't go easy on her (maybe John did once), but no way do I let my sister beat me. But she kicked our butts so bad! She was so into the game and aware of it. She was making silly comments when she got a Sequence, she was laughing at our jokes, and it really felt like family time we used to have back in our living room at home. We all laughed a lot, made fun of each other, and enjoyed being a family. It felt normal.

We saw Jenny was getting tired, so we went back to her room and got her ready for bed. Before I left, I explained to her how I will be moving home for the summer to be with her and that she has to put up with me being with her all day, every day. She rolled her eyes at me, then smiled and said, "I suppose," then gave me a great big hug and told me she loved me. It was really the perfect ending to a wonderful weekend.

CHAPTER 62

Day 60

I arrived at the hospital that morning still energized from the terrific weekend that had included the benefit, relaxing in the sun, seeing the soccer team, and most importantly the best visit with Jenny yet. Things were looking up. I knew there were still hurdles to get over, but I was feeling about as good as I had since early April. For quite possibly the first time since this whole nightmare began, I was feeling optimistic about the long-term prospects for Jenny's recovery.

As I said, hurdles remained.

That morning I arrived to find the aide assigned to Jenny for the night bandaging the back of Jenny's hand after she had pulled out yet another IV. I inquired about what I had missed and the report I received was not all bad news. Jenny had slept 85% of the night and had only gotten up to go to the bathroom. The work the doctor had been doing to get her to sleep was working. Nonetheless, about a half-hour before I arrived, Jenny went into an episode that started with her making "a run down the hall." The image of the nurses chasing after her made me smile that morning, but the nurse didn't seem to see the comedy in it. When they got Jenny back into her room, she pulled out the IV. Jenny was still coming back from the episode and I could see that she was scared. With the aide at our side, Jenny and I walked the halls for a while, which sometimes had a calming effect on her and it seemed to help that morning.

The good news that morning was that Jenny ate 100% of her breakfast and was able to cut the French toast herself using a fork and knife. She didn't use her hands to eat anything.

However, Jenny did tell me that there was screaming in her head and coming from her bed. I didn't give the comment much thought at the time because she had made so many other "strange" statements during or right after episodes in the past. I asked the nurses to give her Tylenol, a treatment that had worked at Methodist when she claimed there was ringing in her ears, and within 15 minutes, she was calm and took a quick nap. However, as it would turn out, this complaint was the beginning of an issue that Jenny would have in one form or another for months to come.

In addition to "the screaming" in her head, Jenny began to show signs of depression and started repeating more often that she wanted to go home. Depression would be another issue Jenny would need to deal with for the foreseeable future, and is very common in patients with any form of brain injury. I initially attributed it to the fact that she was getting even sharper from a cognitive perspective so she was more aware of the fact that

264

she was staring at the same four walls all day, every day. She was not trying to "escape" the way she used to; perhaps she was simply more aware that it was a pointless effort. Jenny's depression affected all of us, as we all started to suffer with her and for her.

Regarding her day-to-day recovery, Jenny continued to do well on all fronts that week. She was talking as clearly as she had since she lost that ability. However, part of her clarity was attributable to the fact that we were used to her speech and could make out more of what she was trying to say. At times, it still took repeated efforts to get it right, and a stranger would still find it nearly impossible to understand her. When we would question what she was trying to say, she was now able to reword her statement to help us understand better. That was in contrast to a week or more prior when she would just continue to repeat the exact same words she had spoken previously. Her thoughts were not always clear enough for extended conversations, but it was a great comfort to be able to determine exactly what she needed with much less effort than in the past.

Jenny was staying "with us" more than she was "away" and her memory was showing the biggest improvement. Although far from perfect, she began sleeping most nights. Her overall motor skills continued to improve at a faster pace than her ability to speak and the number and length of her hallucinations and "episodes" continued to diminish. She had not had any visible seizures in over a week, although the latest EEG "was not normal" (although that was all the doctor was willing to tell me for some reason).

Overall, Jenny was progressing and I sat for a long time that week and pondered what might have been the trigger of this improvement. It had been exactly one month since the treatment for the NMDA had been completed, which is when the doctors at Methodist told us would be the latest we would start to see improvement, so I'm sure that was a large factor. Yet, in my mind, the NMDA had done its damage and all that needed to be done now was clean up the mess, which of course took time. Yet, my thoughts constantly went back to the day that Michelle tossed the stuffed cupcake at Jenny and how she had helped Jenny participate in putting a puzzle together, a skill that she had not possessed at the beginning of that evening. Other times Michelle would play various card or board games with Jenny. Each time Jenny had started with absolutely no ability to participate effectively in the activity, yet, with Michelle's insistence and persistence, Jenny was able to develop the necessary skills in a rather short time span. Because I knew that the NMDA had caused no actual brain damage but had just left some junk behind, I believed this progress was different from a typical brain injury rehabilitation because she wasn't "relearning" anything. Jenny's skill set improved while Michelle worked with her and it had happened so clearly and quickly that I was absolutely convinced that she was just pushing the "junk" to the side.

What became perfectly clear to me was that Jenny did, in fact, need to be encouraged to work at something, but as she was doing it she did not need *instructions*, she simply needed *encouragement*. With only a couple of exceptions while doing the puzzle, Jenny wasn't actually being taught to do anything so much as just responding to the challenge of doing something she knew she should be able to do.

Of course, the success of the doctor at Bethesda to get Jenny to sleep properly played a large role. I knew the importance of rest to the human body. Almost all of my high school soccer players could recall me telling them that sleep was the only time that they recovered from the rigors of "hell week," as I pleaded with them to get to bed early even though school was not in session yet. Jenny was indeed sleeping more and I knew that had helped in her improvement.

We never "let" anyone win in our family, even when the girls were little. Barb and I believed that competition, not winning, made people better. Furthermore, throughout Jenny's entire illness, hardly a day went by that we couldn't see that Jenny was "in there" somewhere, and a flash of her personality would show itself. Part of Jenny's personality was determination. As I considered all of these factors that day, I realized that Michelle was as responsible for Jenny's improvement as anything else was. Michelle and Jenny always challenged each other. They were each other's biggest fans, but they also hated when the other one beat them.

To this day, I believe that as Michelle was desperately trying to help her sister get better in any way possible, Jenny was making sure her sister did not beat her. When Michelle tossed the cupcake, she laughed at Jenny after she missed the catch, not out of any spite, but because Jenny had swung her arms after the cupcake had already passed. Jenny was not going to stand for Michelle laughing at her; while it may not have been a conscious thought that she would have articulated even if she could speak, Jenny was going to prove she actually could catch the ball. In the same way, when Michelle wanted Jenny to put the pieces of the puzzle together, Jenny didn't feel that Michelle was teaching her something, she felt Michelle was challenging her and she was not going to let her sister down, in a competitive sense, by not completing the task.

All of this led me to understand that Jenny just needed to be pushed harder and more consistently. However, there was no way for Michelle to be with Jenny all of the time. Therapy seemed to be continuing at a snail's pace. It was barely outpacing what Methodist was doing when Jenny was barely coherent, and it hadn't changed or intensified at all since she had started to improve over the weekend. I also didn't feel like it resembled anything close to our definition of "boot camp."

Due to the hospital's distance from my home and office, I was unable to adjust my schedule often enough to be able to see any of the individuals in charge of Jenny's care. Therefore, one day early that week, I made a point of saying to a nurse, "What happened to the 'boot camp environment' we were promised she would receive?" The nurse was completely surprised and asked where I had gotten that phrase. After I relayed the story of it to her, she left the room. A bit later she came back to confirm a few details of my story, and then left again. At that moment I held out hope that something would change.

CHAPTER 63

Day 65

The days had started to fall into a positive routine in that there were no major surprises or setbacks. In fact, there were signs that the worst was behind us. A good example was when Jenny woke up on Wednesday of that week. I had already arrived and was sitting in the chair next to her bed reading emails. She looked at me as she sat up in bed, then looked around and saw that the board in her room still read, "Tuesday, June 4th." She quickly looked back at me and asked, "Isn't it Wednesday today?" I just smiled. Her immediate awareness upon waking was a huge step, as this type of brain function was what we feared would be lost because of the NMDA. While her "thinking" was still far from perfect, I began to have some confidence that those skills were still intact, which allowed me to hold out hope for her long-term, full recovery.

In a sign that the doctors had acknowledged how dramatic Jenny's improvements were, Jenny was finally allowed to leave the fourth floor as long as she was with a family member. I had been pestering the staff to allow us to take her outside, and while initially they would not allow us to leave the building, that only lasted about a day. Soon the only rule was that we had to stay on hospital grounds.

Perhaps the most significant change was that on Friday of that week the full-time, one-on-one nurse's aide was removed. This decision was driven by Bethesda and made them happier than us, as they were never pleased with the added demands it placed on their staff. I wasn't completely comfortable, but in my mind this confirmed that there was no need to move Jenny to the west side of the floor anymore, finally completely removing that fear. It was actually a monumental sign of how far Jenny had come from the deepest recesses of the illness. However, we were still nervous because not all of Jenny's decisions were good ones and there was still some impulsive behavior in addition to small episodes and confusion from time to time.

I was in a good mood driving home from the hospital that Saturday evening for the first time since this had all started. I was surprised, but I realized that it was a sign of my confidence in Jenny's improvement. To be sure, I was still afraid of what the future held, but I had decided that I could enjoy the moment, which also got me thinking about how far Jenny had progressed in the past week.

By the end of the week, Jenny could speak coherently almost constantly, which made every aspect of her situation easier, particularly for those caring for her. From a selfish perspective, I once again had the simple pleasure of sitting and talking with my kid. Our conversations were not "deep" in any way but Jenny could initiate conversations that went beyond, "How are you." I could ask simple questions and get answers, and more importantly, she could ask questions and respond to the answers given. We talked about what the weather had been like that spring, and how the Twins were doing. At times even her "sassiness" came back.

Jenny also began to ask questions about what had happened to her. She was aware of the date, which also meant she realized that she had been ill for a significant amount of time. Earlier that week, I thought she was remembering things about the previous two months, but ultimately it became evident that she had no recollection of anything after March 27th, which was both a blessing and a very sad realization. I was glad that she didn't have to deal with the aftermath of the hallucinations, but I recognized how difficult it would be to deal with the big hole in her life and I was surprised to learn that there was no help or support available for someone experiencing that.

By late in the week Jenny was eating on her own 100% of the time and consuming all of the food put in front of her. She had even reached the point that she would get upset when people tried to help her if she struggled. Jenny had lost more than 20 pounds since her arrival at Methodist in early April and we started bringing in additional food and snacks to keep in her room.

Quality sleep was still only obtainable with the use of drugs, but at least she was sleeping. Over the previous two months, even heavily medicated, sleep of any kind would elude Jenny and during that long stretch of sleep deprivation, her body was so physically exhausted that she would walk without even opening her eyes. Her entire body wanted to sleep but something in her brain refused to allow it, keeping her up for days at a time without more than a few broken hours of sleep.

An added benefit to Jenny getting a significant amount of rest was that she looked much more like herself. Actually, I thought she looked wonderful. Her eyes were wide open for the first time in weeks and we saw her big toothy smile on a more regular basis, along with a full range of facial expressions.

Jenny had always talked in her sleep before she got sick, and while she did from time to time throughout the illness, it began to return at a rapid pace that week. It was clear that she was dreaming very vividly about a variety of things, and the good news was that most of it was pleasant as often she had a smile on her face as she slept. That was a welcome change, and a sharp contrast to a good portion of the previous two months when the look on her face made it clear that monsters of some kind were haunting her dreams.

Still, at times, when Jenny woke, it could take her quite a few minutes to decipher reality from a dream. On Thursday of that week when she woke, she asked me if I had received the change I was supposed to get. Later that same day she asked Michelle if she had won the game of Yahtzee, even though they hadn't played yet. These concerns seemed minor, however, when compared to the fact that Jenny now easily played Uno, Sequence, and Yahtzee, and wanted to play whenever possible.

The following Monday she turned and asked me "where the coloring stuff went" immediately after she awoke. I sat and waited for a few moments, staring at her without saying anything. I wanted to hear where she went with her thoughts. After a few seconds of sitting in bed and thinking she said, "I must have been dreaming and now I am awake." Her awareness was a good sign of improvement; corroborated when, right before she got out of bed to use the bathroom she said, "Oh shoot, I'm going to set off all kinds of alarms" and stopped moving. As part of the "one-on-one" nurse being removed, the nurses set the alarm on her bed to trigger if Jenny got out of bed with no one in the room. She had remembered the alarms, and as minor as this may sound to an outsider, it was actually a big deal.

Of course, Jenny had not accomplished a complete victory over the NMDA, not by any means.

For example, during that week of many dramatic improvements, Jenny didn't understand that her food was preordered, and she couldn't be convinced that the exact food she liked didn't just "magically appear." This is just one example of a list of other minor symptoms she still experienced.

That week Jenny appeared to begin "hearing things" more often, usually music of some kind, but at times it was "many people screaming." There was also an element of not being able to hear some things as well. The last day of that week, Jenny had been listening to music on her Nook but could not hear the vocals in the song. It was weird at the time, and I had a hard time understanding what she was trying to explain to me. She was telling me that something was wrong with the music player she was using. It sounded just fine to me. As it turned out, it would be months before Jenny could hear the vocals of any music she listened to or even the voices on something like a Twins broadcast. If she could not see the person speaking then she could not hear the voices, even if she knew they were there. It was odd, and I never received a clinical explanation for why it happened.

Mercifully, it appeared that the days of Jenny's "episodes," in which very detailed and overwhelming hallucinations took place, were over. Thank God. They had caused the most fear in Jenny and made those of us around her feel so helpless. The "episodes" contained countless horrifying scenes that seemed to go on endlessly so we were obviously relieved to be finished with them.

The doctors at Methodist had warned us repeatedly that the brain is the slowest part of the body to heal and to temper our expectations of the future, as there was no way of knowing what the future would hold. We were well aware of the fact that despite this amazing week of improvement,

Jenny would still hit various plateaus where improvement would seem to stop from time to time.

All of us were losing our patience with the need to deal with the emotions and other effects of having to stay at the hospital. On Wednesday of that week, Jenny said, "I want to go home and do normal things." All of us had been searching for ways to make Jenny as comfortable as possible to help combat the boredom she so clearly was experiencing, so I asked what kind of things she would do if she were at home. Her answer was, "I want to go to work at Barnes and Noble!" I regretted bringing the topic up. Jenny wanted a normal life, not just to do normal things. The most significant sign of "normal" to Jenny was to go back to work. She wanted to return to her friends almost as much as she wanted to go home. I didn't know how to respond to her comment, so we just ended up hugging and crying together for a couple minutes.

Despite everything else Jenny was up against, she seemed to have reached a point where she was fully aware of her situation, and although she was not happy about it, she stopped fighting it and began to fully participate in it. This attitude really amazed, impressed, and inspired me. She cooperated with the staff at all times and was determined to work hard to get "all the way better." She would tear up many times, but I never heard her complain during the previous week.

Jenny would jump up immediately when the therapists arrived, put on her shoes and head directly for the door. She even seemed to get frustrated if the therapists stopped to talk to a nurse.

There was no doubt that Jenny hadn't lost focus of her real goal, as earlier in the day when she was taking a nap she repeated over and over in her sleep, "I want to go home, I want to go home." She even appeared to begin crying before rolling over and settling down again, which made me even more impressed and proud of her in that she did not allow those feelings to interfere with what she needed to do when she was awake. Perhaps she was using it as motivation to work hard instead. I could never imagine being as brave as she was during that phase of her life.

Although we were not clear as to what the criteria was for Jenny to actually go home for good, and indications from the doctors were that it was still "a few weeks from happening," I had allowed myself to start dreaming of the day.

The one caveat to all of this was that an appointment had been made for Jenny to go to The Mayo Clinic in Rochester, Minnesota (about 80 miles south of Minneapolis) on June 17th. The appointment had been set up while Jenny was still at Methodist and was essentially a follow up to their contributions and consultation regarding the actual treatment of the NMDA.

Barb and I had been a bit puzzled by this appointment. We knew Jenny would be only the 11th NMDA patient they would see so they were hardly experts, but they had vastly more background than anyone in the surrounding area. We were unaware whether we were taking Jenny to Mayo in order to help in her recovery, or to help the medical community learn about the illness. We had no idea how many of the other 10 cases were actually treated at Mayo or were simply consulted on – nor did we really care. We realized that the more patients a facility saw, the more they would learn about the illness in order to help others in the future.

We had received very few details about what was going to go on during our visit to Mayo. In fact, when we asked how long Jenny would be there, we were told that more than likely she would just be there for the day, but to be prepared to stay five. Huh? Let me be clear, while we were more than happy to make the trip and have the doctors at Mayo look at Jenny, as we knew it would only help and certainly couldn't hurt to have her examined there, more detailed information would have been helpful.

The biggest problem that Barb and I faced was that the appointment completely ignored the fact that Jenny remained admitted to a separate and independent hospital with no connection to either Mayo or Methodist. We didn't know how Jenny was going to get there and wondered whether we could take her or if she had to be transported. We also didn't know whether her bed at Bethesda would be waiting for her when she returned, and neither Mayo nor Bethesda answered these questions. The appointment was more than a week away at this point, so we didn't push too hard for answers yet. There was a "care meeting" scheduled for the following Monday at which we intended to clear up any questions and put a plan in place.

Over the previous month or so, Barb, Michelle, and I began to have many conversations about the various factors that would be required in order for Jenny to come home. We knew much of it was out of our control, but we had learned enough at that point to understand that the day-to-day conditions of where Jenny would be living were a primary factor. Once I knew that, I was even happier that Michelle had become a teacher and had her summers free. It was clear that Michelle was Jenny's ticket home sooner rather than later because we could say that Jenny would have someone with her at all times. In my opinion, Michelle had already proven to be the best therapist Jenny had anyway and she was more than willing to play that role. In fact, Michelle had cancelled most of her summer plans to focus on Jenny and her needs.

That Friday Michelle packed up her apartment in Wabasso and headed "home" for the summer. She drove straight to the hospital and, as it turned out, arrived in time to join Jenny for her therapy session, which was something Barb and I had not managed to be able to do. I was very curious as to what happened during these 20-minute sessions, so I was very anxious to hear Michelle's report.

The session was occupational therapy and the entire time was spent asking Jenny to identify "safe and unsafe conditions" on a series of 40 cards. She was correct on 37 out of 40. Of the three she got wrong, one was a pill bottle in the trash with the label still on it. I had no idea that that was unsafe, and have been breaking that rule my entire life. The next portion of the session was identifying unsafe conditions in a kitchen: a toaster cord in the sink, the stove left on, a broom on the floor, and a cupboard door left open. Those two exercises made up the entirety of Jenny's therapy that day.

I understood that we all needed to know that Jenny wouldn't burn the house down when she got home. While I know absolutely nothing about therapy, I was growing increasingly frustrated with what I considered to be a lack of intensity. I couldn't wait for the care meeting the following Monday so we could discuss the issue, and hopefully develop an understanding of what the people at Bethesda were thinking.

CHAPTER 64

Day 67

Jenny continued to do very well throughout the weekend and into Monday. The care meeting with the heads of all the departments caring for Jenny was at 1:30 that afternoon. Barb and I had planned and prepared for the meeting for days and were ready to push for answers to quite a few questions.

Michelle was home for the summer and wanted to play an active role from now on, so she also attended the meeting. In part this was because she had missed so much the previous two months but also because she wanted to know exactly what Jenny's status was, since she would play the role of primary caregiver once Jenny was discharged from Bethesda. Representing Bethesda were the occupational and speech therapists, the care manager as well as the lead doctor caring for Jenny. There was also an additional attendee…Jenny.

It may sound funny, but apparently it is rare for the patient themselves to attend these meetings. Sometimes they are physically unable to attend, but more often than not, they are not coherent enough to comprehend them, as Jenny had not been up to this point. I was the first to arrive at the hospital that day and when I looked at the schedule, I saw that Jenny had a speech therapy session at the same time as our meeting, so I told Jenny where we would be during that time. She asked, "Why don't I get to come to meetings when I am the person everyone is talking about?" Then she added, "I want to know what is going on too."

It was a great point. Barb and I had talked about this previously, as we knew the healthy Jenny would feel this way. However, it had been a couple of weeks since we had a meeting like this and she clearly wasn't able to actively participate or even to sit still long enough to listen until now. Jenny attended the meeting with us and it was good to have her there even though all she did was sit quietly and observe.

As all of these types of meetings do, it started with everyone summarizing what they had done up to that point. The therapists went first and their reports reflected what we already knew – they hadn't worked very hard with Jenny. We very politely questioned them about this, and the conversation immediately turned to Jenny's dramatic and exceptional turnaround the past seven days. The lead doctor actually said that in his 20-some years of working at this facility he rarely had seen that type of progress in such a short amount of time and was "astonished" by it. He acknowledged that he never would have predicted this for Jenny two weeks ago.

The therapists acknowledged that Jenny had caught them off guard and that they had not kept up with her recovery. The fact is that the pace of Jenny's recovery was extremely unusual, so it would be difficult to plan for. They stated they understood that they needed to push her harder, and promised to do so.

The discussion then turned to the following week when Jenny was scheduled to go to Mayo for her follow up appointment. The situation was ridiculous. Mayo either couldn't or wouldn't give us any indication as to whether Jenny would be there for a few hours or a few days, which caused difficulty regarding planning. The issue for Bethesda, from an insurance perspective, which was very logical as well, was that if Jenny stayed even one night at Mayo she would lose her bed at Bethesda. It raised the question of what we would do after Jenny was done at Mayo, as at that point, we had no indication that Jenny was actually ready to go home.

And this is where the meeting took a surprising turn.

I can't recall exactly who, but someone made the point that Jenny's progress over the next week would be critical, and very frankly pointed out that the doctors and therapists were expecting a "plateau at some point soon." The key point was that assuming Jenny could continue the progress she had made during the previous week, she could possibly leave Bethesda for good when she departed for Mayo.

It was not a final decision of any kind, but it was the first time since Jenny was admitted to the hospital on April 5th that anyone had set anything resembling an actual discharge date for her. I almost jumped out of my chair!

It also did not mean that Jenny was necessarily coming home. There were actually a couple of other options that included a less acute care inpatient facility or a transitional care facility. The conversation continued over what arrangements were in place for Jenny when she did go home, as a big part of that would be based on what the situation was when she got there. It was a very sweet moment for Barb and I, as parents, when the care manager said, "Am I remembering correctly that you will be able to provide a 24-hour-a-day safe environment for Jenny at home?" Michelle leapt from her chair and her arm popped up like she was in school as she yelled, "THAT'S ME!"

Words could not express how happy, grateful and proud Barb and I were that Michelle changed many of her summer plans to be home with and for her sister that summer to help with her recovery. She willingly made those changes in plans as soon as she heard the advantages for Jenny if she were to be available and with her at all times, as well as the ability to transport her to the outpatient therapy she would need to attend. Thus, Jenny coming home became a serious possibility. Thank God!

No decisions were made that day. Everyone understood that Jenny still had to show improvement over the next seven days for her *not* to come back to Bethesda after Mayo. We also knew this was predicated on whether there would be a bed for her at Bethesda after her Mayo visit, yet there was no clarification of what would happen if there was not. However, it was still amazing to actually hear that there was even a possibility that Jenny would be coming home...way ahead of schedule.

CHAPTER 65

Day 69

Jenny continued the relatively quiet routine of therapy during the day and visitors in the evening. The only major difference was that Michelle was able to spend the entire day with Jenny a couple of days during the week when she wasn't busy making final arrangements and getting settled in for the summer.

Jenny was still battling a few nasty symptoms leftover from the NMDA, but boredom was becoming a serious issue in its own right. By all accounts, Jenny seemed to be doing well with occupational therapy, but she was struggling a bit with speech. She seemed to have difficulty when she was tired, speaking clearer in the morning than she could after a long day.

We were very pleased that both therapists did turn it up a notch, but honestly, only a notch. Still, it was an improvement. Barb and I attended an occupational therapy session during the week and the focus was still on relatively simple skills that Jenny would need to function on her own such as making a piece of toast and buttering it. Jenny appeared bored, but did what she was asked without complaint. Later the therapist did ask Jenny to do some basic searches on the Internet, which challenged her. It was good to see that she struggled because that was the only way she would improve, but she also showed determination in accomplishing the task. At one point the therapist invited Jenny to take a break, but she refused.

We were very impressed with the speech therapist that worked with Jenny. Jenny always wanted to attend, which meant she was challenged and she showed good signs of improvement. Michelle attended two of the sessions, in part, as a way to learn what she would need to do during the summer, and came away very impressed with how he pushed Jenny.

I also was very pleased to hear that Jenny and Michelle spent an entire day assembling a relatively large puzzle. Jenny handled it well, as did Michelle, showing that she had recovered from the seizure incident on Memorial Day weekend. In many ways, that weekend already seemed like a long time ago.

All of us hoped for the continued improvement Jenny needed to show by Monday before her trip down to Mayo. Our goal was for her to be able to leave Bethesda for the rest of her life. There certainly were no setbacks in the two days after the care meeting, but I can't say I saw dramatic improvement either.

I was in my car that afternoon when my cell phone rang and everything took a strange and unexpected twist. The caller was the care manager assigned to Jenny and she very enthusiastically informed me that Jenny could be released as early as that Friday.

Shocked, I asked her to repeat what she had just said, really just trying to gather my thoughts.

We talked about details for a while, but as much as I had wanted to hear this news for nearly two weeks for a variety of reasons, she caught me so off guard that I had to say that I would call her back. I needed time to think, to process this new information, and as I always did when my mind was blown and I couldn't make a decision…I called Barb and then Bonnie, my business partner, to talk it through, sort out the facts, and clarify some questions.

Only 48 hours earlier, we had been discussing the possibility of Jenny being discharged by the following Monday, with no guarantee that she would be ready at that point, and now she would be ready to go home in two days. Really? A whole range of emotions went through my head. Suddenly it felt like things were happening so fast. We hadn't even finished getting Jenny's bedroom set up again after converting it to a craft room when she had moved out three years earlier.

After careful consideration of all the factors involved, I called the care manager back and made a very strange request given how badly I had wanted Jenny to leave Bethesda just two days earlier: I asked if they could keep Jenny until Monday.

There were some very practical reasons for this request. Most importantly was that we were unaware of how long Jenny would be at Mayo, with an outside prediction of a five-day stay. Regardless of how Jenny was acting outwardly, she still wanted desperately to go home and I worried about taking Jenny there for two or three days only to go to the unfamiliar surroundings of Mayo for up to five days. Given Jenny's current level of depression, I felt this would essentially be teasing her and could be a very serious emotional mistake. The care manager did not disagree at all.

We also needed time to set up Jenny's outpatient therapy sessions, and it was obviously a bad idea to interrupt the current work going on. Finally, certain drugs that Jenny was on could only be administered under professional care, so she had to be converted to doses that could be taken orally.

All of these factors led to the extremely ironic decision of leaving Jenny at Bethesda for three days longer than she otherwise would have had to be. I still wonder how her discharge from Bethesda came about so suddenly.

However, we had a date, and I was ecstatic! Jenny would be leaving Bethesda Hospital. Regardless of what happened at Mayo, by the end of the following week, my kid would be *home*!

CHAPTER 66

Day 70

Since there had been nothing but good news the past few days, it seemed to be time for a barbeque!

The plans for this day had been in the works for about a week, but with Jenny improving so rapidly and the added news that she was to be discharged that coming Monday, the event took on a completely new feel. We had repeatedly told Jenny that she hadn't missed anything in terms of weather that spring, as it had mainly been wet and cold, but we were lucky enough to take full advantage of an absolutely beautiful day.

Bethesda Hospital has a wonderful garden on the grounds that includes a large gazebo, a built-in gas grill and food service area, as well as lots and lots of grass with something of a sculpture garden around the edges. Michelle and Barb planned a barbeque as a way to give our family and John's family, along with a few close friends that had helped us organize and put the benefit together back on June 1st, a chance to see Jenny in better surroundings than a hospital ward. More importantly, it also gave Jenny a chance to see more than two or three people at a time. Additionally, now that we knew Jenny was to be discharged the following week, it was a great way to start easing her back into real life. We had no idea if Jenny would be overwhelmed or not, but this was a nice controlled environment in which to find out.

Jenny enjoyed a few hours outside with Michelle that afternoon before the barbeque was scheduled to start. I am pleased to say that she broke all the rules, walking much further than hospital policy allowed and ultimately leaving hospital grounds. I admit that I was not even a little bit disappointed in Jenny's younger sister who was supposed to be "in charge" and take good care of her. Michelle allowed Jenny to go wherever she wanted and was a co-conspirator in the horrible disregard for the safety protocols put in place for Jenny's safety. Jenny made her own decisions and enjoyed a little bit of freedom, and Michelle was very pleased to report that no one from hospital security tackled them as they crossed the street that took them off hospital property.

Later that evening about 30 of us gathered for a fantastic dinner put together by Barb, which included a few yard games and good conversation. Jenny got her first look at the scrapbook that had been compiled as part of the benefit. Barb Myers had bound it together in a neat little book with a custom cover. It is a priceless reminder of the wonderful friends we have and the terrific community in which we live.

Everyone was overwhelmed by Jenny's outpouring of emotion as she greeted each person that came to see her that day. It was the first time that Jenny had seen anyone new in nearly 80 days. It was truly a terrific evening, and Jenny handled all of it well. She "talked" as best she could with everyone and enjoyed a good hour or more of different yard games out on the grass.

There was one terrible moment, however, though I'm sure it was nothing more than a misunderstanding. I'm confident Jenny didn't mean to do it, but she didn't want to hurt anyone's feelings by correcting the mistake. At one point, someone asked Jenny if she wanted John or her Dad as her partner for one of the games. She chose John. I'm sure it was just because he was standing closer to her and she knew I needed to get the grill started, or she was being polite and didn't want to hurt John's feelings. It may even have been that she just wasn't speaking clearly and everyone else simply misunderstood. I was going to push John down and flick his ear, but I chose not to make a scene.

It really was a wonderful evening!

CHAPTER 67

We are LUCKY!

I felt it appropriate to insert an edited portion of the journal posted on CaringBridge on Saturday, June 15, 2013.

Clearly, we have reached a milestone in this long journey. Although she is still residing at Bethesda, and perhaps I am presuming no major setbacks (or a relapse) will occur, the past week has shown that Jenny has made her way back through a major portion of the version of hell she is experiencing. We have all done our best to hold her hand and go through it with her, trying to ease her burden as best we can. However, the fact remains she has had to experience the majority of this on her own.

I will not consider this journey complete until the day that Jenny comes full circle and parks her car in the parking lot at Ridgehaven on her own, completes the walk across the parking lot, and walks into Barnes and Noble to work her shift. This was her destination on March 27th when she fell into a snow bank during a seizure, and was found unconscious.

Nonetheless, we have reached a point where we want to stop and reflect on how far Jenny has come. Honestly, weekends do that to me, because I get a chance to slow down for a few moments. I also know next week is going to be a whirlwind of activity that we will all be swept away in. However, given the fact that the plan right now is for Jenny to be released for outpatient therapy after the trip to Mayo, this is clearly the end of a major chapter of this story.

Of course there were many key moments the past two and a half months, but it was during a conversation earlier this week that I realized that we actually have some very strange reasons to feel LUCKY. Barb and I discussed if we wanted to say, "We are lucky," or "We are thankful for." I think both are correct.

Yes, if Jenny was going to have to go through this anyway, there were actually some things that happened that were real blessings in disguise...mostly in hindsight. (The "We" by the way, is Jenny and all of those that love her.)

1. *We are LUCKY that all of this started with a seizure!*

   Among Barb, Michelle, John, and I, without a doubt I am the one that has done the least amount of reading about NMDA Encephalitis. What I do know is that very few victims of this illness have had their symptoms begin with a seizure. Most had the behavioral issues that Jenny experienced manifest themselves prior to the seizures.

   Unless you were one of the few that were at the hospital and actually saw the way Jenny acted through the entire month of April and into May, you can't understand how indescribable the behavior is. Seeing the behavior firsthand makes it clear as to how many people stricken with this illness are treated for any number of mental illnesses before the search for the true cause begins. It appears, from what little is known, that Jenny's case was severe in that it lasted longer and did more damage than most documented cases, and although we are not aware of another individual that had complete loss of the ability to speak, it has more than likely happened to others. The fact remains, Jenny may have suffered even longer if her symptoms had not started with a seizure that grabbed everyone's attention.

2. *We are LUCKY her first two seizures happened where they happened.*

   We are so lucky that Jenny was taken to Methodist Hospital. I don't know that any other hospital would not have done as well as Methodist, but I have a hard time imagining any place handling the overall situation better than they did.

   If Jenny had had her first seizure somewhere other than Ridgehaven, some other hospital may have been closer and the ambulance would have taken Jenny there. We are lucky Jenny lived with John and that she went to the apartment that first night rather than come "home" with Barb and I, as we wanted, or again the ambulance would have taken her somewhere other than back to Methodist.

   Methodist would have been our first choice anyway, but I don't know that we would have had her moved once this all got started. We are so lucky it all happened in a place that made Methodist the logical choice. The entire collection of doctors, nurses, and staff made this journey much easier than it otherwise would have been...even if they are not mentioned by name below.

3. *We are LUCKY Dr. Freking was the neurologist on staff April 5, 2013, and the following week.*

Although the entire neurology staff at Methodist proved to be stellar, we are lucky that Dr. Freking is a focused and stubborn man. He kept refusing to believe what the tests were telling him, and knew that something else needed to be done. Although it was not Dr. Freking who discovered the true cause of Jenny's illness, he was the one who raised all the red flags so that no one rested until the true cause was found.

4. *We are LUCKY Dr. Joos is not afraid to speak her mind.*

I'm not sure Dr. Joos would approve of how I am verbalizing her role in this, but she was a key element in Jenny's treatment. Because Dr. Joos is not afraid to step on the toes of doctors in other specialties, Jenny's treatment stayed focused and moving forward at a rapid pace. I believe the entire system at Methodist encourages doctors to share ideas, and at the very least, all of them were heavily involved in Jenny's case.

5. *We are LUCKY Dr. Tran has no ego.*

Again, I'm not sure she would approve of me putting it that way, but I know that it is not true for all doctors, as has been proven to us since we left Methodist.

Jenny is so very lucky Dr. Tran came along when she did for many reasons. The fact that she is aggressive, and willingly listens to and seeks out input from other doctors, are two key reasons Jenny was so fortunate. I believe Dr. Tran was the one who helped to create the environment where many doctors from many specialties from within and outside Methodist consulted on Jenny's case. She also agreed to stay on as the lead neurologist once her cycle was over to ensure Jenny's continuity of care.

6. *We are LUCKY Michelle became a teacher.*

Michelle having the summer off did more for Jenny than can possibly be explained in this journal. Michelle's love and commitment to Jenny is stronger than I ever knew it could have been.

7. *We are LUCKY John wandered into "Chops" one day, and was drunk enough to ask Jenny for her phone number.*

    I'm not sure how true that statement is, although I do know it is part of the story...

    Okay, this is the mandatory levity that I try to bring to the journal, combined with my desire to admit publicly that John is a good person. John and his family, along with his long list of fiercely loyal friends, have played more than a monumental role in this whole journey for Jenny and her family.

8. *We are LUCKY that the parking attendant at Methodist told the stupidest joke ever!*

    "What do you call a fish with no eye? A fsssssh."

    It was on a day that everything was going badly, and we were beginning to understand that this was a huge problem that was going to be a long haul. It had been a long day of tears and fears, and we felt drained of energy. Michelle and I were leaving the parking ramp to go pick up some food for everyone when the parking attendant taking our fee greeted me with the opening line to that joke. Honestly, it took all the self-control I had not to tell him that I didn't give a hoot. However, I politely said, "What do you call a fish with no eye?" He delivered the punch line as he handed me the change.

    Yes, the joke is as stupid as it sounds. Nonetheless, as I drove away, Michelle gave a small snort, trying not to laugh. We both started laughing so hard I could barely drive and we continued to laugh for five to ten minutes.

    I never did find out that man's name, but I did stop long enough one day to tell him our side of what he did for us that day, and to thank him. Since then we have tried to find a reason to laugh every step of the way.

9. *We are LUCKY Jenny played sports the vast majority of her life.*

The time, expense, energy and hours behind the wheel of a car have all been worth it...tenfold. Sports has engrained in Jenny a determination and work ethic that helped her fight back from the grips this illness had on her brain and mind. I truly believe the recovery phase of this illness would have been longer and more painful had it not been for all that Jenny learned through sports. The doctors were "astonished" at the speed of her recovery, one saying that he had never witnessed anything like it. I believe sports played a huge role.

10. We are LUCKY Jenny likes card and board games.

This one may sound silly, and I certainly can never prove this and will never know for sure. While I know the sleep that the doctors at Bethesda were able to bring about for Jenny played a huge role in her recovery, I also KNOW it was the games she played that opened up her mind to be able to fight through the garbage in her head. We used them only as a means to fight boredom, because we know Jenny understood her situation deep inside despite outward appearances. However, in hindsight, it was the games that proved to be great additional therapy for Jenny and accelerated her recovery. I believe this with all my heart.

11. We are LUCKY Jenny likes to drink water.

This may sound sillier than the one about board games, however, Jenny went through a phase of her illness where she was hours away from a feeding tube. This would have been necessary much sooner if dehydration had occurred (it became an issue only once for about a half a day). Jenny has never been much of a pop drinker, nor anything other than water as part of her athletic commitment. That engrained habit paid off big time as Jenny almost constantly had a bottle of water in her hand, even during the deepest depths of her illness.

12. We are LUCKY that we live where we do.

Between Jenny's family, John's family, and the communities of Rockford, Delano, Buffalo, and beyond, there is no way we could have made it through this without the extended support system that Jenny has around her. Thank you to all of you.

13. Finally, we are LUCKY they "identified" this antibody in 2007.

It is impossible to explain the chill that I get down my spine every time I think about what would have happened to Jenny if she had gotten this illness before the medical field knew what it was. We know that there have been undocumented numbers of people who have suffered from this illness without any diagnosis, or years of misdiagnosis. I pray for them, and wish this illness on no one. However, we are so very LUCKY Jenny had it when she did.

"13" was Jenny's jersey number for most of the sports teams she has ever played on. Because I firmly believe her involvement in sports was one of the more powerful forces throughout this whole journey, how appropriate that this is where this stops.

CHAPTER 68

Day 73

I consider Sunday, June 16, 2013 the greatest day of my life!

It was better than the day I was married, and even better than either of the days that my daughters were born. I guess in part, this day had come about because those other three days all happened, but no other day in my life has ever been so enjoyable and so special. It was a day that I laughed as hard as I ever could have imagined was possible and it was the first day in more than two months that I cried only tears of joy with no fear that something would happen minutes later to snap me back to reality. I will forever cherish the memories of that day.

Ironically, it was also Father's Day. I could never imagine a better one.

When the sun rose that day, I actually never gave it a thought that it was Father's Day. The most important thing on my mind that morning as I rose was that it was Michelle's birthday. Now, Michelle wasn't a 10-year-old that would get jealous of a sibling that overshadowed her birthday, but the fact was that just about 99% of the thoughts Barb and I had had for the previous two months were of Jenny. It didn't surprise Barb and me, but it makes a parent proud when we have the opportunity to see how mature our children have become, and it was amazing to see how Michelle stepped up and went above and beyond what a sister might be expected to do to help her sibling. I was so very proud of Michelle and wanted to do my best to make at least a portion of her birthday special.

As it turned out, the only thing I actually did right for Michelle's birthday was going over budget to get her a bike rack for her car.

Barb had gotten up to make everyone breakfast and Michelle slept as late as possible, as usual, only waking when I called her to eat. The plan for the day, specifically because it was Father's Day, was to spend the day with Jenny as a family. We planned for the four of us to have lunch together and then help Jenny do some of the packing needed to check out of Bethesda the next day.

As we were wrapping up our breakfast, Michelle went to her bedroom for a moment and I went to put her bike rack on the dining room table for her to see as she came back. That is when it hit me – not only did we not have a cake for Michelle, I hadn't even thought about wrapping the gift. Great birthday. Sure, we may have gotten her a nice gift, but we couldn't even find time to bake a cake or give her the pleasure of unwrapping a gift.

But wait! Am I one to be deterred by a minor setback? I say no! I am quick on my toes and think fast in moments of adversity! There was still time to make this right! Michelle was going to enjoy her birthday.

I quickly grabbed a portion of the Sunday paper that was lying out on the dining room table and draped a couple of pages over the box, covering just enough of it that would face Michelle as she walked into the room so the whole box looked wrapped. I did use a couple pieces of tape to hold it in place, partly because I got lucky and a role of tape was in the kitchen. But, I was not done yet, because then I recalled that we had some leftover bite-size cupcakes from the barbeque that previous Thursday. I quickly grabbed one off of the counter and set it on top of the box. But, what about candles? What kind of birthday cake…er…bite-size cupcake is complete without candles – but there was no time! I knew what cupboard had old candles in it, but I had no idea which shelf they were on, and Michelle would be back any second. Never one to crumble under pressure I grabbed a match (yes, a match) and lit it before sticking it into the cupcake. Then, instead of waiting for her to return, I called Michelle to hurry up before the match burned out.

The truth is I was desperate. I really wanted to make Michelle's birthday special for at least a few minutes. She would know that I had failed miserably, but I had hoped she would see I tried…sort of.

To my astonishment, Michelle thought it was the greatest thing Barb and I had ever done, or at least she put up a great act. She loved the gift, as it really was all she wanted, but she seemed to genuinely enjoy the way I presented it. She immediately took a picture and posted it to Facebook. It was the perfect start to my Father's Day because it showed me the type of person Barb and I had raised. We all knew that there was nothing whatsoever special about our presentation, but Michelle has always found pleasure in the simple things in life and humor in almost any situation. She had every right to complain, or at the very least show some disappointment, but whether she is the type of person that could find joy in this situation, or just nice enough to act as if she did, I was an extremely proud father at that moment.

Moe's birthday present, "birthday cake" and "candle"

After our celebration, we drove over to Bethesda and put the plans for the rest of our day in motion. We had told Jenny we were going to spend the day together, just the four of us, and she specifically asked us to bring her lunch from McDonald's. She hadn't had that kind of junk food in months and she wanted to taste some of the finer things in a "normal" life.

During our drive to the hospital, we noticed what a beautiful day it was outside. We decided to take Jenny over to the large and plushy grass that make up the grounds in front of the Minnesota State Capitol Building, about a three or four block walk from Bethesda Hospital. I dropped Barb and Michelle off at the hospital and then went to the nearest McDonald's. Barb and Michelle went up, signed Jenny out, and started to walk over to the Capitol. I got the food, parked the car, and met them at the agreed upon spot.

It was a perfect day already. The story could stop there and it would be just about perfect, but it wasn't done yet.

We sat down to eat our lunch. The meal was relaxed and slow and we talked about the next day and all that had to be done in order to be ready to make the trip down to Mayo, which included packing clothes in case we had to stay there for a few days.

Part of the decorations we hung in Jenny's room at Bethesda included some greeting cards cut out of construction paper in the shape of sport balls. These had various, and hilarious, greetings written on them from some of the students at Wabasso. Michelle commented that we needed to take those all down and that it was something that we could do today before we left.

At that moment something happened that will forever be the funniest moment of this entire journey and I don't believe I am exaggerating when I say I laughed as hard as I ever have in my life.

The sport ball greeting cards were taped to the walls of Jenny's hospital room at the ceiling level and obviously needed to be removed before Jenny left the hospital. It took quite a bit of time to hang them, so Michelle was correct in suggesting that we take them down that day, as we needed to leave at 9:30 in the morning to be sure to get to Mayo in time for the first appointment.

As we were lying on a blanket on the grass in front of the State Capitol, Jenny began telling us how she was so bored that morning that she started to take down the paper balls and got yelled at by the nurse.

"Why did you get yelled at?"

"Cause I was trying to reach the high ones."

"Were you standing on a chair?"

"No, I was standing on that ledge in front of the window cause that is the only way I could get up that high, and it seemed like a good place to stand until the nurse came in and yelled at me to get down."

There is no way of telling this story that properly captures that moment, but it will forever be one of the great moments for Barb, Michelle, Jenny, and me. We laughed so hard, for so long, and so loud that I'm sure the few people around the area that saw and heard us must have wondered what was wrong with us. We laughed hysterically for better than five minutes. I was sore when I was done laughing.

Of course, Jenny standing on the window ledge was dangerous. It was a typically designed building for its era in which the window creates a cantilever out from the room a bit and, as was usually the case back then, the radiator to heat the room was built into the resulting cove below the window.

These days, the spaces below the window have been built up to create a ledge or windowsill, but it extended out beyond the walls around the window. This design created a situation in which Jenny was standing on the ledge, leaning out over the floor below her, and reaching back toward the wall to reach the greeting cards. The nurse was correct in yelling at her to get down.

Jenny's tone of voice was a large part of why the story was so funny. She still couldn't speak clearly, but she told the story as if she didn't understand why she had gotten yelled at. Additionally we had the visual image of her getting caught standing where she was and the fact that she actually thought that was a good plan when 14 days ago she couldn't have thought any plan through whatsoever, and it all amounted to the funniest moment I can ever remember.

The laugh was long, hard, and most importantly, refreshing. Two months of fearing that I would never get my kid back came rushing out. We were together as a family and sharing a moment that could have been shared by any family, anywhere, at any time. We deserved that moment, and I will never forget it or the feelings I had during it.

We spent the next three hours playing Frisbee as we ran around on the grass and then settled in for a round of the card game "Phase 10," where I mounted the greatest comeback in the history of the game. It was the most wonderful afternoon I can remember having with my family. There was absolutely nothing wrong in that entire day. Nothing. It was the best Father's Day ever.

To top it off for Michelle, Jenny remembered her birthday too. She had made a card for Michelle and had John pick her up a gift. As Michelle posted in the final line of the final journal entry she wrote to Jenny, *"It was unforgettable and probably the best birthday ever."*

In the "I'm a bigger brat than my kids" department, the icing on the cake for the day was a nurse scolding us for being gone so long. She said there was a time limit for patients to be gone, although she couldn't say what that limit was and it wasn't posted anywhere. I'm assuming no one came looking for us since no mention was made that we could not be found "on the hospital grounds." I sarcastically said that she could "kick us out at 9 a.m. tomorrow morning." I was really just trying to be funny and lighten the mood, but I can see why she wasn't impressed with my humor and wasn't laughing as she left the room. (My sincere apologies for being such a brat.)

I wouldn't trade this day for anything.

Part 5

Coming Home

June 17, 2013

CHAPTER 69

Day 74

June 17, 2013 was the day that Jenny finally came home!

Barb, Michelle, and I arrived at Bethesda Hospital early that morning, as we did not want to risk hitting rush hour traffic as we drove through both of the Twin Cities. Jenny was excited and ready to go. I suspected everyone, except maybe the speech therapist and one nurse, was glad to see us leave as well, beyond the usual desire they have for all of their patients to leave after a successful rehab. We spent the morning packing things up and sorting what needed to come to Mayo in case we had to stay and what we could send home in Michelle's car as Michelle was staying behind to finish getting Jenny's bedroom ready for her.

Jenny had stopped wearing diapers for about two weeks, but there were still a few left in a package that had gotten pushed to the back of a cabinet since they weren't being used. In the process of cleaning out that cabinet, Michelle pulled them out and showed them to me asking, "What should I do with these?" At that moment it hit us both that we had just revealed an aspect of her illness to Jenny that she had no way of knowing about, as she had no recollection. We both stopped and looked at Jenny, who was sitting on the bed. The look on Jenny's face was a combination of amusement, shock, and embarrassment.

"Were those for me?" she asked.

"Yup! You had to wear them for a little bit a while ago." I attempted to make it sound as matter of fact as I could and in almost the same breath turned to Michelle and told her to toss them, deliberately saying, "We won't be needing those anymore." In a small way, I was hoping it would sound like no big deal to Jenny as well as to bring some closure to the subject.

In reality, within the big picture of everything else that had happened, the diapers were, indeed, barely a footnote in the story. However, Jenny was a bit mortified for a moment. Exactly what emotion she felt, I am not sure because she didn't say anything at first. In part, while Jenny had already asked a few questions about her illness by that time, we had answered them in very general terms. Besides the significant length of time that she knew had passed, I believe this was her first realization that something major had happened to her. We talked about the diapers very briefly and then the subject went away, for more than a year.

As time passed, none of us purposely broached any aspect of the subject of what had happened to her during those two and half months. If we were together, say, having dinner or for any other reason just sitting and talking, we would not shy away from any subject that triggered a memory for Barb, Michelle or me, but we have never, to this day, forced any information on Jenny. There are very few occasions when Jenny brings any of it up on her own, but there are times when she does something silly and she will say, "Don't blame me, I have NMDA" to get us all to laugh. We printed all of the CaringBridge daily journals and Guestbook entries for her, put them in a 3-ring binder, and even collated both sets of journals in chronological order. More than six months would pass before she eventually sat down to read any of them. As I type these words into my computer, she has yet to read past Mother's Day of that year although she has read all of the journals Michelle and Debbie wrote. She knows this book is being written, and in the only version of encouragement we are giving her, she knows that we believe she needs to read it before we publish it. In fact, if you are reading this page, Jenny has in fact read the book in its entirety because it will not be published until she does.

When compared to all that had happened in the 83 days prior to this one, the day Jenny was discharged from Bethesda was a very simple day. The only thing that made it special was that Jenny came home. Our exit from the hospital was quiet as was the 80-mile drive south to Rochester.

Neither Barb nor I had ever even seen Mayo Clinic before. I had no idea where it was, exactly, nor what to expect. It was quite the experience. I have to admit, when I hear the word "Clinic" I think of a small building with few floors. Ha! Not even close. Mayo is a huge complex with blocks of 15 to 20 story buildings.

What blew me away the most was the sheer number of patients that went through there. All of Jenny's appointments were on the eighth floor of just one of the buildings, yet I am sure we saw four or five hundred patients coming and going throughout the day. I have no idea if this happens on all floors or not. The only reason I mention this, because it has no real point to Jenny's story, is that it put into perspective how rare NMDA Encephalitis was. People come to the Mayo Clinic from all over the world for a whole host of illnesses, and after making multiple visits there in the year since Jenny's recovery began, I know the pace and volume of patients is the same every day- at least on the Neurology floor. Out of the tens of thousands, if not hundreds of thousands, of people that have visited the Neurology department alone, Mayo had only seen 11 patients with NMDA.

Ultimately, we were at the Mayo Clinic two days, but we came home after the first visit that Monday and went back on Wednesday. While we were very glad to have made the visit, and listened carefully to what the doctors there had to say, the main conclusion of those visits was that Methodist had completed all of the treatment very well and there was nothing else to be done at that time. However, there were additional follow up visits scheduled, the first in three months and every six months from then on.

The only significant difference in Mayo from Methodist and Bethesda was that this was the first time we were in the room with doctors that had a full understanding of NMDA and what it was capable of doing to its victims. It was an amazing relief to know that we were with people that weren't going to underestimate the help Jenny needed. These doctors knew that this was not just another case of encephalitis.

The only disturbing revelation that came from the trip to Mayo was that they were confident that Methodist did a great job of searching for the cause of the NMDA in Jenny, and they did not recommend any more of it. We knew this was a possibility, as the cause of the illness is not found in 25% of the documented cases. (Jenny's doctors in Minneapolis, however, have advised that the search should continue, at least for a few years, and this has been the path taken, primarily with regular ultrasounds and occasional CT scans of the pelvic region.) The negative aspect to not finding the actual cause of the illness is that Jenny will be a candidate for a relapse for years to come. However, because we now know the signs, we are reassured of never having to relive the nightmare of those two and half months.

The most significant event of the day, of course, was that Jenny was finally able to come home. It was her first time there since we had left for the emergency room shortly after 8 a.m. on April 5, 2013, 74 days earlier.

As we turned the corner onto our street, after returning from Mayo at just after 8 p.m., Jenny said, "That's John's truck!" in a very sweet and excited voice, as she could see it parked in front of the house. Both John and Michelle were in the driveway with our two dogs and we had a nice "welcome home." Michelle had created some "sidewalk chalk art" to greet Jenny.

All things considered, the time that had passed and everything that had happened in order to get to this point, Jenny's arrival home was pretty much without fanfare. Other than a few hugs and smiles, it was a very quiet affair as all of us were already tired from a long day, not to mention a long two and half months.

The first thing we did was to show Jenny "her new room," which was actually the same bedroom she had occupied while she was growing up, but had been transformed back into a bedroom. Ironically perhaps, or perhaps not, Jenny took one more long walk before settling down for bed that night. Jenny, John, Michelle, Barb, and I, with the dogs Maya and Rossi pulling us along on their leashes, all took a walk through the neighborhood.

It had been a long and exhausting journey so far. Now the process would begin to bring Jenny all the way back to "a normal life." In the same way that Jenny would ask the doctors at Methodist hospital when she could go home every single time she saw them, Jenny only had one question for the doctors at Mayo. "When can I go back to work?" Jenny was not content, and it was time for the next step. That process would begin the very next day.

Because of Jenny's illness, I became possibly one of the only fathers in the world who actually wanted his 26-year-old daughter to move home. I finally had my wish. As I prepared for sleep that night, it was the first time in as long as I could remember that I had both of my daughters under the same roof with me and knew that they were staying for longer than just a weekend. For the first time in months, I felt good as I pulled back the sheets and climbed into bed.

CHAPTER 70

Jenny's First Day Home!

Jenny's first night home sleeping in a regular bed was interesting. She was clearly nervous. Perhaps the lack of routine and greater options than she was accustomed to in the hospital was a bit overwhelming, and we discovered Jenny needed very specific instructions as she prepared to settle in for the night.

After going to bed just after 10 p.m., Jenny must have been comfortable being home again because she slept until 10:00 the next morning. She had slept more hours in a row, or at least stayed in bed, longer than she had since March 27th when the whole journey began.

Jenny and Michelle's summer vacation together began as did Jenny's "outpatient" rehabilitation therapy. It was time to work on getting Jenny back to "a normal life." Her professional therapy sessions were scheduled to begin at the end of the week and we planned to provide as much or more "therapy" at home in an attempt to accelerate her recovery. Michelle had made it her mission to be Jenny's personal live-in therapist for the summer.

Jenny had provided us with two primary benchmarks that were her definition of a normal life: driving a car and returning to work at Barnes and Noble, not necessarily in that order. However, meeting those goals was a long way off yet. How far off, we had no way of knowing at that time.

Unfortunately, Jenny continued to need nearly constant supervision because her short-term memory was almost nonexistent. Redeveloping that critical component of her brain would require time and patience, accomplished in part by putting Jenny in situations in which she had to use her memory.

Jenny was the last one awake that first morning. Michelle had been up, ready to begin the day hours earlier, and waited for Jenny in the family room. Michelle had explained to Jenny the night before that she had made plans for their day, so Jenny sought out Michelle immediately after getting out of bed to find out what they were going to do. Michelle produced a very long but exciting list of things she had planned…chores that needed to be done around the house and yard that had been ignored for nearly three months.

Thus, Jenny's first full day home was spent outside doing yard work and, as Michelle put it, having a "normal" day. Conversation during their work included Jenny naming a number of things she wanted to do with her sister that summer that ran the gamut from playing Monopoly to going to the zoo. Jenny added a requirement to their list: "I want to do all of these before I go back to work."

In addition to the depression, the voices and noises in her head, the inability to hear the voices of singers and broadcasters that were not visible to her, and her sensitivity to loud noises, a new issue emerged that Jenny would have to contend with for the coming months: her emotions were "over the top." She would burst into tears at random and when asked what was wrong or why she was crying, most of the time she didn't know. It just happened. The speech therapist explained that the part of her brain that controls emotions needed to heal. As a result, Jenny would cry any time she was feeling stressed or frustrated.

The first example of her overemotional state came that day as Michelle and Jenny played Skip-Bo. Any time the game would take a negative turn for Jenny and Michelle would get the smallest advantage, Jenny would start to cry. Normally Jenny would enjoy the competitive aspect of any game and buckle down to gain back the advantage. In as much as Jenny worked hard at her therapy, setbacks of this nature seemed to stifle her. It took several weeks for the emotion issue to resolve itself.

Jenny also had a hard time "multitasking." Conversations with more than one person were difficult, if not impossible, as she could only focus on one thing at a time. Jenny also struggled with a sequential thought process. One of her first evenings at home, she wanted to play a game of Phase 10. Barb and I agreed, but also informed her that Mom needed to get some laundry out of the washer and I had to check my emails before we could play. A few minutes later, we found her standing in the family room crying in confusion that we had agreed to play but had then left the room.

It was impossible for someone to get Jenny's attention verbally if they were not in her line of sight. In other words, if Jenny was focused on something with her back to us, such as washing dishes in the sink, we had to tap her shoulder or arm to get her attention.

Other issues illustrated that Jenny was unable to process information, such as when she was helping me with something in the garage, and it required her to have a tool repeatedly rub across her hands. Soon her finger was bleeding because a blister had formed and then popped. She was so focused on what she was doing that she didn't even notice the pain until I pointed out the blood.

Additionally, speech continued to be a challenge. She could only speak one or two syllable words clearly, and she spoke so softly for the first month or so that at times it was necessary to put an ear right up to her mouth to hear her. She had the most success making very short, simple statements. When she attempted long sentences, especially if she got excited and tried to talk fast, it came out as mumbling or the words were slurred together and impossible to understand. Michelle was the most patient with Jenny and worked with her constantly to improve this. Even if she were able to decipher what Jenny had said the first time, Michelle had her repeat it until she said the words as close to perfect as Jenny was capable. Having learned by observing Jenny's speech therapy sessions, Michelle asked Jenny to read everything she could find aloud. When they played Monopoly, Michelle had Jenny name every property they landed on and had her repeat it until she said it correctly.

With all these issues to deal with, Jenny and Michelle's summer of therapy began with the short-term goal of Jenny being able to function independently and the long-term goal of her going back to work driving her own car. We all understood that this would happen in small steps and the entire process would take months. Mayo had predicted nine to twelve months before Jenny could even "talk about the possibility" of going back to work, but privately we refused to accept that prediction, in part because we knew that Jenny had the greatest advantage possible with her full-time, motivated "sister therapist" with her every waking moment of every day. Additionally, Michelle would be moving back to Wabasso in just over a month and we all needed to return to our own "normal" lives, so we worked toward improvement with absolutely everything we did involving Jenny.

There were good signs right from the beginning that Jenny was coming back and taking baby steps toward a "normal" life. At exactly 9 p.m. on that first full day home, Jenny headed downstairs without any prompting from anyone and said, "I need to take my pills." Barb, Michelle, John, and I stared at each other in awe because this demonstrated she was aware of the time and remembered that she needed to take pills on a very strict schedule. We let her go down to the bathroom alone wondering if she would select the correct pill bin in the medication sorter that Barb had used. John followed her shortly after and confirmed that she had emptied the correct bin. Ironically, as much as Jenny struggled with many things, she never seemed to have any issues with doing something that was truly critical or dealt directly with her goals of returning to "a normal life."

Perhaps the biggest frustration Jenny experienced during her rehab was that for the most part she considered herself perfectly fine. While she had lost the memory of two months of her life, she did not comprehend that she wasn't remembering things and that she was failing at even the simplest of tasks. Many conversations would take place over the coming weeks explaining why she could not just get back into her car and go to work that day.

On Friday of her first week home, Jenny started professional therapy. She had a combination of speech and occupational therapy five days a week. Jenny had tested out of physical therapy very quickly after it started at Bethesda, which was a testament to how strong she stayed despite being sick for so long. The best news was that her therapy took place at Methodist with the same therapists that had worked with Jenny right after the diagnosis was received before she left for Bethesda. Her schedule required that Jenny be driven to the hospital every day. Perhaps the largest blessing was having Michelle home for the remaining portion of the summer allowing Barb, John and me to get back to work without further interruption to our work schedules and not having to worry about who was taking Jenny where and when. We all understood that we were blessed with the timing of the situation.

In the same manner that she did at Bethesda, Jenny went to each session ready to work hard. She was impatient in the waiting room and quickly began performing tasks even before the therapist had the timers set and said "go." Jenny was showing the same fierce determination that we had seen in almost everything she had done the previous two months, and it did not waver.

However, Jenny also needed routine. She needed to wake up at a specific time and have certain "chores" that needed to be done. This helped establish "normal" but also aided in combating the depression she was experiencing, but it started out rough and slow. Jenny was still so tired due in part to the lack of sleep during her illness, but also because of her depression, that we tended to let her sleep in almost every day. However, once the therapists at Methodist discouraged it, we broke that habit very quickly.

For the first two weeks, much of Jenny's life at home may have been as boring for her as when she was in the hospital. There was a lot of time spent in the car for the daily trips to therapy (as well as the two trips to Mayo) and because of the suddenness of her hospital discharge, we hadn't had time to get a complete plan in place for her home therapy.

Having Michelle at our house as a full-time therapist was a benefit for all of us, but Jenny didn't see it that way. Barb and I saying, "Jenny is home" did not sit well with her because she considered her apartment with John her home. Jenny also believed she was more than well enough to be alone, so being at our home instead of hers made her feel like she had not yet accomplished her goal of "going home." This viewpoint made it especially exciting for her when I dropped her off at her apartment the Friday after her discharge from Bethesda. She was going to spend the entire weekend with John, sleeping either at the apartment or at his parent's home.

John took Jenny fishing that weekend, possibly the first truly exciting activity Jenny had engaged in since her release from the hospital. It was something they both enjoyed and of course hadn't had a chance to do yet that summer. John took care of the tackle and bait for Jenny, but she did enjoy a successful trip onto the lake. It was the first of many of a wide variety of excursions Jenny would have in the next two months.

Despite Jenny's frustrations, we knew she was blessed in terms of having so many opportunities to work hard at her recovery while staying active and having fun in the process. Michelle was able to take Jenny just about anywhere to do anything during the week, and between John, his family, and Barb's family, Jenny had the opportunity for the best summer ever.

CHAPTER 71

Going Public!

Jenny had made major strides in all areas of her life since bottoming-out in early May. During the two months that followed, it was clear that most of the improvements she made were accomplished through the process of experiencing them. For example, although Jenny struggled with any type of math when she first began therapy in spite of being a math major in college, once she was presented with a few complex problems on paper, and began working through them, she very quickly was able to solve a wide variety of math problems. There was no need to practice all types of math, as she was able to apply all the skills she had before she got ill.

This requirement for the experience and recognition process was evident not only in her mental and physical advances, but also in her emotional control. Once she actually did something, the skill would return quickly, but each skill first needed to be reintroduced and used in order to be applied.

We had gradually introduced some public outings other than going to therapy, such as going to church and Barb's work; however, Jenny had yet to actually be in a situation in which she needed to interact with a number of people who were not aware of her limitations, particularly her difficulty with speaking and controlling her emotions. By early July, Jenny was still unable to focus effectively on more than one thing at a time, so going into uncontrolled situations was somewhat risky. However, she needed to experience them and work through the results.

Michelle had spent the previous two weeks working with Jenny literally every waking hour at bringing back some of her basic skills, such as having her cook dinner. John had also presented Jenny with a few "safe" situations that slowly exposed her to various stimuli that were not necessarily "controlled," but provided a level of comfort, such as large gathering of friends in an active social environment.

On Wednesday, July 3rd, Michelle made what I believed to be the brave decision to take Jenny to the zoo after her morning therapy session at the hospital. The trip started rough in that Michelle's car would not start after a short pit stop when they left the hospital, and because they were very close to my office, I went to rescue them. Since none of us had eaten yet, we decided to have lunch together.

Although this was not her first restaurant experience since being home, Jenny's initial attempt at "going public" was to order her own yogurt for dessert after lunch. She and I looked at the menu and I had her rehearse saying the words clearly and speaking loudly enough for the person behind the counter to hear her over the noon crowd. Jenny placed the order on her own, thereby accomplishing another step back to "a normal life." She even managed to deal with a couple questions the server had to ask about the toppings she wanted on the yogurt.

From there Jenny and Michelle went on to Como Zoo in St. Paul for the afternoon. Michelle reported that Jenny did very well the entire time. Perhaps the most interesting aspect of the trip and, in a way, the most fun, was that it seemed as if Jenny was seeing the animals for the first time in her life. It was very hot that day and most of the animals were inactive, yet Jenny examined each display for quite a while, watching the monkeys for more than 30 minutes; and Michelle allowed Jenny to take as much time as she needed at each new display.

One of Como Zoo's featured attractions is a seal named Sparky. Sparky makes an appearance three or four times a day and does a series of tricks for the crowds gathered around his pool. He is the only seal that "performs" while other seals are swimming in the pool. In a sign that Jenny did not fully comprehend everything that she saw that day, she said that she saw three "Sparkys," and tried to describe to me where each one was located in the pool at different times during the performance. However, most important to me was that she had been attempting to focus on more than one thing happening at the same time and was even able to recount some of it for me.

Jenny in the Butterfly Garden at Como Zoo

On Thursday of that same week, Jenny insisted that we go to a movie in the morning before she and I went to our first Twins game of the season that afternoon. Jenny was still having a hard time following a conversation with a single person, so the movie would be another opportunity to see how she responded to multiple things going on at one time. However, she had been improving, and we were aware that the only way she could get better at anything was to do it. We were not sure how she would keep up with the dialogue of a movie, but there was no better way to learn so Barb, Michelle, Jenny, and I went to a movie.

We caught an early showing of *Despicable Me 2*. It was a new movie at the time so the theater was very full and loud – it's possible that every 5-year-old within a 20-mile radius attended. Jenny didn't seem to notice the crowd and never took her eyes off the screen once the movie started. We're not sure how much she followed the show because she never laughed, but she also never expressed concern about being confused either. Her "review" after the movie was, "It was kind of slow, but it was pretty good."

After the movie, Jenny and I headed for Target Field. I thought the Twins game would be great because Jenny is a huge fan, and as far as we were concerned, there was no better slice of "normal" for either of us. However, I was nervous about this event, probably as nervous as I had been about anything since her discharge. Jenny did not like crowds even when she was healthy and she had seemed frightened the few times she had been exposed to them since her illness. Additionally, she tended to react very poorly to loud noises and too many distractions at once. We had the advantage, however, of being able to leave at any time if necessary.

Jenny is a die-hard Twins fan. In fact, her knowledge of the team is almost scary. For example, one day in a previous season Jenny and I entered the room together when Barb had the Twins game on the TV and I asked her who was at bat. Barb said she wasn't sure, but Jenny immediately identified the batter. What was so remarkable was that on the TV screen at the time we entered the room was a close-up of the opposing catcher behind the plate as the announcers were discussing something about him. All that could be seen of the Twins batter was his legs from the knees down. I had doubted Jenny's answer of who the batter was, but when it was confirmed that she was correct, I asked how she knew and she said, "He's the only Twin that wears his socks like that."

As we approached the ballpark, I had many questions swirling around in my head. As always, I was most anxious for signs of how "aware" Jenny was and how her brain was functioning, and I knew this experience would present many clues about this.

I didn't have to wait long for the first bit of evidence to present itself. I parked the car in a spot from which the stadium was clearly visible, and we could even see a small portion of the scoreboard. We were behind schedule and I knew we were late for the game, but I had no idea how much we had missed. We got out of the car and had only taken a few steps toward the stadium when Jenny said, "We missed the start of the game." It took me longer to figure out how she knew that than it did for her to figure it out; the visible portion of the scoreboard displayed who the batter was and where they were in the lineup, and the second batter was up. This was a good sign.

We found our seats, but the game was off to a very rough start – for the Twins and for Jenny. The music that Jenny heard in her head at times was currently the most frustrating issue she had to deal with, mainly because it confused and distracted her, and many times it was so loud it was all she could hear. This became an issue as soon as we sat down and she cried for a few minutes. We had discovered that Tylenol helped, so I gave her some. By the fourth inning, she had started to feel better. Initially, Jenny knew she could not hear the batter introductions as they came to bat, but she started to smile as she heard more and more of the sounds that occur throughout a game and it was a pleasure to see her enjoy herself.

There was one very sobering moment late in the game when Jenny asked me to tell her who wore each of the symbolic "retired" jerseys displayed on a wall of the stadium. The question shocked me because I knew Jenny had known them all before her illness. We went down the list forward and backward many times until she was satisfied that she understood.

Jenny sat and watched the game intently. At times, I would ask her things about the game (the score, the count, who was batting, the inning, etc) and she always knew the answer. At one point Jenny decided she wanted ice cream and a pretzel, which was kind of a tradition for us, and said she wanted to go get them "after this half-inning is over." I was surprised when the third out was registered and I turned to her and said, "Let's go" and she clearly had no idea that there were three outs.

Although I am sure she enjoyed the game overall, I do wonder how much she knew about what was happening minute-to-minute. At one point she did say, "Dad, we're getting crushed," so I know she was aware enough of her surroundings to look at the scoreboard.

There was one final event for us at the game that would have been inconsequential under any other circumstance, but now it showed that Jenny was making at least some progress in being able to grasp more than one thing going on around her.

At one point Jenny started crying. I asked her what was wrong and she said, "The lady behind me is irritating and I wish she would be quiet." Luckily her voice wasn't much more than a whisper. I had to laugh because she was right. I was wishing the same thing.

On the other hand, in a sign that our life was still far from normal, I had to watch Jenny go to the restroom by herself at the end of the game, standing in a line that was 30 people deep outside the door. I saw Jenny having a rather extended conversation with a woman in front of her, and I could not imagine what they could possibly be talking about or how the woman could hear or understand Jenny. From 30 yards away, I felt the version of helplessness fathers feel when our little girls begin to spread their wings as four-year-olds and I wanted to go and stand in line with her.

My discomfort must have been obvious because the usher standing next to where I was said to me, "You alright, you look nervous." I said I was just watching my daughter. "Oh, that little girl in line at the bathroom? Isn't that her Mom with her?"

"Yeah, I'm watching the 26-year-old standing behind her." Awkward! I could tell he wanted to ask, so I gave him the 15-second version of what was going on. We talked for the 10 minutes it took Jenny to get through the line. Although he justifiably laughed at me, he was very sympathetic and even shared a personal story that reminded me that someone always has it worse. It's good to get a check on our perspective from time to time.

It was a GREAT day, a day I will cherish for the rest of my life. Going to a Twins game is my favorite thing to do with Jenny, and I felt like I had my kid back that day, at least an important part of her.

There was, however, one thing I missed. While she did sway back and forth during "Take Me Out to the Ball Game," which is something she always insists we do and it made me smile, she forgot she also always insists that we do it arm-in-arm. That was okay and she was smiling as she sang and did the "One...Two…Three outs…" with her hand waving above her head, but it was a good thing I had my sunglasses on so that she could not see the tears in my eyes. I am not sure if they were sad tears since she forgot to include me in the "tradition" of swaying arm-in-arm, or tears of joy in that at least we had come this far and were enjoying a Twins game together. Ultimately, it doesn't matter; both were true, I guess.

CHAPTER 72

The Follow-up Doctor Visit

There are a number of stories that could be told that demonstrate how truly special the people are at Methodist Hospital and how special Jenny was to all of them. In fact, some of them have already been mentioned in the pages of this book. My favorite stories are the ones in which the doctors and nurses were able to interact with Jenny during her recovery and enjoy the results of their hard work and commitment.

In mid-July, Jenny went in for a follow-up appointment with Dr. Tran, one of the team of Neurologists who helped Jenny, and who became the lead Neurologist once Jenny received the diagnosis. It was always great to see the caregivers in the more relaxed atmosphere of follow-up care as opposed to the intensity of the days when Jenny was ill. This was the first time Dr. Tran had seen Jenny since she left Methodist to go to Bethesda for rehab. It is dangerous for me to presume anything that Dr. Tran was thinking at any time during Jenny's care, but I am confident in saying that she was excited to see Jenny for the appointment that day. The smile on her face and the conversation she had with Jenny seemed indicative of someone who genuinely wanted to know the details of how Jenny was doing in her own words, rather than just hearing from her parents.

With every success story Jenny told her, Dr. Tran cheered as if Jenny was one of her own children. It was so fun to see. At times, the stories and details Jenny shared as she answered Dr. Tran's questions would get off track, and while I believe Dr. Tran wasn't necessarily interested in some of the details, it appeared she enjoyed hearing Jenny tell the stories because she had witnessed the weeks when Jenny could not communicate at all.

Every Neurologist that saw Jenny, regardless of what hospital or stage of her care, performed a standard series of tests to check on the status of various aspects of her condition, and this follow-up visit was no exception. It had both verbal and written aspects and was designed to demonstrate Jenny's basic brain function. The verbal questions were things like "describe an island" (if you're caught off guard by the question, it takes a moment to do that; now imagine having a brain injury and doing it), or a list of three unrelated words (tiger, car, Halloween) that she was asked to repeat three or four minutes later, after being distracted by other tasks. Dr. Tran seemed to get happier and happier with each stage Jenny successfully completed. Jenny had been asked to use a pencil to copy the drawing of a three-dimensional box onto a piece of paper almost every time she had taken these tests, but this was the first time that she adequately performed this portion of the test. When Jenny was done, Dr. Tran looked at the picture for a moment and appeared to be very pleased. Then she set the paper to the side.

What happened next will forever be another one of my most special memories that I have of this journey.

The appointment was nearly finished and we were saying our goodbyes when Dr. Tran asked if we had seen any of the other doctors today. When we replied that we had not, she immediately started to round up anyone she could find to reintroduce them to "the real Jenny" that they had cared for during the past two months. The surprise and joy on everyone's faces was so fun to see. These people had only seen Jenny when she was at her very worst and had not seen her since she had begun her recovery and was discharged from Methodist.

During the long search for a diagnosis, one doctor in particular, Dr. Worley, saw Jenny through the deepest and worst part of her "deterioration." During that time, it appeared that he was being tortured as much as we were by having to watch Jenny go through this while he could do nothing to help her. During Dr. Tran's exploration of the hallways to find people who knew Jenny and would want to meet her, she discovered that Dr. Worley was in an exam room with a patient. She asked her nurse to go down the hall to ask him to step out for a moment. I do not claim to know Dr. Worley well, but I am comfortable in saying that he does not like interruptions. The nurse prodded Dr. Worley out of the exam room he was in, saying, "Really, you want to see this." Dr. Tran disappeared from our view as she went down the hallway toward the room in which the nurse was talking to Dr. Worley, and Barb, Jenny and I heard her say, "Close your eyes. No really, close your eyes – I have a surprise for you."

The next thing I saw will be etched in my mind forever…

Coming into view through the door was one Neurologist guiding another who had his eyes closed tight. Once Dr. Worley was squarely in the doorway, Dr. Tran gripped his shoulders and turned him toward Jenny, so they were standing almost toe to toe, then said, "Okay, open your eyes!" Initially Dr. Worley looked at Jenny and it appeared that nothing registered. Jenny's appearance had changed dramatically since the time Dr. Worley cared for her. In front of him was a wide-eyed and smiling Jenny as opposed to the drooping, non-smiling face he was used to. Dr. Worley glanced towards me for a moment, showed some slight recognition, and then looked back at Jenny. His eyes nearly popped out of his head! "OH MY GOD! Hello!" He didn't hug her even though it seemed he wanted to, but it was obvious that he was awed at seeing Jenny and excited to hear what she had to say. They talked for a while and Jenny handled it very well, I thought, considering that she had no idea who he was. She just laughed in her new quiet, reserved way that was her style early in her recovery.

These two doctors, who I could not respect more, were like two little kids on "show and tell" day. Dr. Tran handed Dr. Worley the written portion of the test Jenny had taken earlier. Dr. Worley looked at the 3-dimentional box and acted as if his five-year-old had just created a clay ashtray for him at summer camp. His eyes appeared to be welling up with tears just a bit. It really was an extremely special moment that captured the ferocity with which they had worked to save Jenny from the demons that had such a firm grip on her brain, and now were enjoying seeing the person they rescued.

Dr. Worley eventually left to go back to his patient and Dr. Tran went off to find someone else. While we were waiting in the exam room, another nurse entered. She worked in the office and had not cared for Jenny while she was a patient on the 6th floor of the hospital, but she said, "I am so glad to meet you, Jenny. I remember the day the diagnosis came in, and all the doctors around here were running up and down the halls cheering. I was wondering who 'Jenny' was."

I was stunned and a little overwhelmed that my daughter's diagnosis had been so important to the doctors and staff that even people who weren't caring for her knew who she was. I suppose that I shouldn't have been surprised though. Methodist's commitment and compassion started the day Jenny was first admitted, and continued all the way through the therapies she received for months afterward. I thank God for helping Jenny find her way into the care of those amazing people.

CHAPTER 73

A Progress Report

A month into Jenny's outpatient rehab she was doing very well. She was making terrific progress at the regular sessions of professional therapy at the hospital, which dealt mainly with the clinical aspects of her rehab. In the meantime, Michelle was continuing intense sessions of home therapy; albeit informal and unprofessional, they nevertheless were very important to Jenny's overall recovery in my eyes.

As much as each small experience accomplished on her own would help Jenny improve, they also allowed Barb and me to regain confidence that she would be safe and make good decisions. In the same way that we had to help her through many experiences and situations while she was growing up, we now had to help her through many of them a second time. We were still hesitant to leave Jenny alone for any length of time, but we were working on small ways to gradually introduce it for short periods. One afternoon I decided to leave Jenny alone for about half an hour. Upon my return, I was pleased to note that she had taken it upon herself to care for Michelle's turtles, which showed that she was able to recognize a need and address it appropriately.

Michelle began to stay in bed each morning and pretend she was still sleeping to give Jenny the opportunity to get up on her own. In this way, Jenny made some of her own decisions, while Michelle was still able to listen to what she was doing and react if something went wrong. It was a very simple and effective test to see if Jenny was able to function on her own or would wait for instruction. One of Jenny's first few days home from the hospital, she woke up went into Michelle's room, and simply stood there and watched Michelle (pretend to) sleep until she woke up on her own. However, soon Jenny was doing things like cleaning the kitchen, including emptying the dishwasher and taking out the garbage, and we were very excited at the initiative and thought process she was showing.

At the one-month juncture, Michelle took Jenny for her first bicycle ride since her illness. The ride went well, and Jenny made it home in one piece. She did drive off a curb and into the street while taking a corner too fast, but she did not fall down nor was she hit by a car. Jenny laughed the entire trip, even when she was out of control driving off the curb, and talked non-stop about the bike ride in the car during the drive to therapy that day. Obviously she felt some version of freedom and normalcy.

Jenny also made her first visit back to Barnes and Noble since she had become ill. Michelle, Jenny, and I went together, and we managed to get to the back of the store to the children's books section without anyone recognizing us. Jenny walked slowly through each aisle looking at everything, and she was able to point out which books and products were new. 15 minutes later, Jenny went into the main portion of the store and began to greet her coworkers. Everyone was very happy to see her, and Jenny shed a few tears of joy. She was glad that she had made the decision to "give it a try," and was particularly impressed to see that her mailbox was still there and full of mail. She was so happy that they had left everything of hers just as she had left it, and that small gesture did so much for Jenny's confidence, reminding her that she would indeed have a job to go back to when she was ready. Everyone at Barnes and Noble – from the store she worked at to the corporate office – never wavered in their support of Jenny. They are an extremely classy organization.

A measure of Jenny's progress was that her professional therapy was reduced to three days a week. She attended speech therapy each of those days, with occupational therapy on two of them.

Jenny continued to stay focused and worked hard every day. One day the previous week, I had attended an "evaluation meeting" where I received status reports directly from each therapist. This meeting presented the opportunity for two-way conversation; they explained what they were doing and I was asked to share what we were seeing as a result. About halfway through the meeting with the occupational therapist, Jenny suddenly began crying. We stopped and asked, "Jenny, what's wrong?" Her response made me laugh: "I want you guys to stop talking because I'm just sitting here and I want to get to work!"

Her outburst summed up Jenny's attitude through the entire rehab process, even before she was completely in control of her thoughts and actions. She worked very hard every chance she got, not only at the hospital, but on all of the homework she was given as well. She also utilized various "apps" on computers and tablets to continue to improve her brain function, and in fact continues to do that to this day.

When Jenny had been released from the hospital, Barb and I had set what we felt was a very realistic goal of Jenny going back to work, at least part-time, by Christmas, six months away. In September, as the doctor at Mayo was leaving the exam room after one of Jenny's follow-up appointments, Jenny asked, "When can I go back to work?" The doctor replied, "We'll talk about that during your next visit in six months." I believe he was being cautious so as not to give Jenny any false hope, but it broke Jenny's heart.

We also still had no idea when she would be aware enough to drive a car…or when I would have the nerve to allow her to do so. However, Jenny had already made tremendous progress. She was doing better than all the doctors predicted she would be at this point in her recovery. I knew the day would come when all the pieces would fall into place and I, once again, would have the nerve to give her the car keys just as if she was 16 all over again. My goal had always been for Jenny to drive herself to Barnes and Noble, park the car in the same spot she had that day in March, and finish the walk into the store to begin her first full eight-hour shift. That would be my true measure of "normal."

CHAPTER 74

Bathroom Anxiety

Jenny's illness had many unique "stages." There was the very early stage of trying to determine why she was acting so "odd," then trying to figure out the cause once it was clear she was sick, then we watched her deteriorate before we began what felt like the excruciatingly slow process of her recovery, though the doctors now insist that it was very fast. We witnessed Jenny go from a healthy adult woman to someone reminiscent of a newborn baby, and now we watched her restoration. While not nearly as painful as watching our daughter regress the way she had early in her illness, the process of Jenny returning to a mature adult was extremely stressful in its own way.

Barb and I were well into the "empty nest" stage of our lives, and we were enjoying it. Before Jenny got sick, both of our kids were well on their way to establishing their own productive lives; we had no interest in becoming "parents" again. We had even converted Jenny's bedroom into a craft room. Ironically, about two months before Jenny got sick I was talking with a friend who still has grade school age children and I commented that, "Although I know you never stop being a parent, I have reached the point that I don't worry about my kids in the same way anymore. They're in a position to handle almost anything thrown their way now."

Oops, I forgot to knock on wood.

Now, here we were and Barb and I had to raise a child again, but in fast forward. Most parents get to deal with the various issues of raising a child over a period of 18 to 20 years. Barb and I had to go through it all over again, only condensing it into six months. From deciding when and how long to leave Jenny alone to helping her deal with the frustration of new limits put on what she could and could not do, Barb and I were dealing with an adolescent all over again.

One of my biggest fears was allowing Jenny to drive a car again. The first glimpse of what this would be like came during an occupational therapy session in late July when Jenny had the opportunity to "drive" in a car simulator. Jenny had been telling us that she was sure she was ready to drive for about a month. On her first venture behind the wheel, she killed a deer, rear-ended a car, and hit a van, all in the first five minutes. The second session a couple of weeks later didn't go much better, but Jenny wasn't concerned and would maintain her innocence by always stating, "It wasn't my fault" as she relayed the story of each "accident." Clearly, she wasn't ready to hit the open roads of the western suburbs of Minneapolis yet. We knew that. I was just hoping Jenny would understand that as well and stop asking to drive the car. One day Barb and I even contemplated hiding the car keys because Jenny seemed so intent on driving.

However, just as a vast majority of parents do, we managed to navigate these difficult years…I mean…rapid succession of dilemmas over the four or five months of Jenny's re-maturation process. We went through "separation anxiety" as well as "new driver anxiety."

Unlike many parents, however, we also went through "bathroom anxiety," a relatively surprising phenomenon that I didn't see coming, but was actually one of the first phases I had to deal with as Jenny went through her recovery. It reminded me of my years as a young parent, but, more importantly, it awoke me to the fact that we really were in for an adventure as Jenny began to improve.

Barb, Michelle, Jenny, John, Brad, and I all attended a presentation at the Chanhassen Dinner Theater and Barb and Jenny decided that they would use the restroom after dinner before the show started. Our seats were almost exactly between the restrooms to the left and the ones to the right, and while Barb stood and was trying to decide which one she would go to, Jenny stood up and immediately turned and went toward the one from which she had just seen John emerge. Barb didn't realize Jenny had walked away, so Jenny was on her own. Barb stood there and scanned the crowd of people until I finally mentioned that she might want to follow Jenny. She turned that direction, but there were already 15 people between her and Jenny, and given the narrow aisles, there was no way Barb was going to catch her. Since there was no chance of getting Jenny's attention in such a situation, we were helpless to stop her; she was on her own, for better, or for worse.

I watched Jenny wander off and turned to John saying that Barb had yet to experience the horribly helpless feeling of watching her 26-year-old daughter go to the bathroom on her own. John laughed and said something to the effect of, "She hasn't experienced the anxiety of watching Jenny go to the bathroom on her own in a public place like we have." It was true! Bathroom anxiety! I'd had to watch Jenny go by herself at a Twins game a few weeks earlier, while John had had to watch Jenny go in a crowd three times larger and more "influenced" at the Kenny Chesney concert he had taken Jenny to about a week ago. We were experiencing things because of this illness that I had never even contemplated. I've learned more about the brain than I ever cared to know, and now I am an expert on bathroom anxiety.

CHAPTER 75

But, we had some fun too!

As brutal as this entire experience was, we did try to find reasons to laugh as much as possible. During Jenny's recovery, some of her toughest work was in the area of regaining her speaking skills, one of the first motor skills she lost and the last to return. There was a time in early August when although Jenny could communicate fairly well, she struggled with words of three syllables or more. Possibly the funniest things we experienced during Jenny's illness were when she attempted to pronounce complicated words, though it really had to be heard to understand how funny and entertaining it was.

Many doctors from different disciplines had cared for Jenny while she was in the hospital. Whenever she went to one of them for the first time for a follow-up visit after her release, she had to fill out all the usual forms as if she was a new patient. During the time when Jenny was struggling to pronounce multisyllabic words, she had a first-time appointment with one of her doctors. The three of us arrived at the office, checked in, and after being given the proper forms, took our seats in the waiting area to fill them out. After looking over the questionnaire, Barb decided it would be a good idea for Jenny to answer the questions.

As part of her in-home therapy, Barb and Michelle had developed the habit of making Jenny read everything and anything she could aloud as a way for her to continue to work on her speaking skills. We had arrived very early, so Barb gave the questionnaire to Jenny and asked her to read the questions to us, which wasn't only about making every waking minute a part of her rehab, but also to help her answer the questions as well. Almost every question had a "complicated" word of one kind or another and many times three or four of them in the same sentence.

We were seated in a waiting room that actually served more than a dozen doctors, so it was extremely full with quite a few people. I am not sure what all of them thought of the three people in the corner laughing hysterically for the 45 minutes it took us to fill out the six pages of "personal information." Jenny would try to say a word and while she knew which ones were difficult for her, she couldn't always hear herself say them. At times, she would say a word and stop to ask, "Is that right?" She could tell by the way Barb and I laughed when it wasn't. When Jenny tried to say the word "alcohol," Barb said, "You sound like you've already had too much this morning." At times like this, Jenny laughed right along with us, especially when she could hear what she said and knew it wasn't right.

Laughter always made the situation easier for all of us.

Even with events that didn't go so well, we usually found a way to see the bright side of the situation. Such was the case in mid-August when Michelle and Jenny went for one of their nearly daily bike rides. This story is best told from Michelle's perspective, via a CaringBridge entry she made to share the experience with everyone:

...but, after a few mishaps we ended up just biking to Lake Rebecca (a nature preserve and park near Rockford). Jenny and I have been doing that most of the summer, but we usually just go to the playground and back. Today we decided to go a little further. After I showed her the map of the main route around the lake, Jenny decided that would be too far, so I pointed to a path that was unpaved, but it cut the ride by more than half. She wanted to do it. I warned her about the rough ride, but she looked at me and said, "I can do it!"

Okay, so we are biking and make it to the "off road" part of the trip. The cool thing was that most of this part was downhill. The part that was uphill had way too many roots and we had to walk our bikes up. We also walked one other time when Jenny wasn't going fast enough and her bike just stopped and I ran into her wheel. She kept reminding me over and over it wasn't that she was tired, she just didn't have enough speed to keep going. (I was fine with the small break.) But, this path had grooves and ruts all over the place and our tires would get stuck in them a few times. It was also really bumpy and Jenny is in need of a new bike, so when she was behind me all I would hear were clunks and clanks of her bike. I never knew if it was her falling over or just her bike. So that's when I decided to have her go in front of me. BUT! The problem with her in front of me is I try to focus more on what she is about to drive over than what I am. That wasn't easy. Jenny started going really fast down hills and I was yelling at her to use her brakes because I was so nervous she wasn't going to make a turn or hit a bump and fall. I literally was laughing out loud for 3 minutes watching her just take off down these hills, while trying to tell her to slow down and hearing her sound effects. It was so funny. Anyway, amongst all of this I failed to see a rut that my tire fell in. I was going pretty fast and I knew it was going to be hard to get out of. I could see it was going to end badly for me. I was going down. It all happened in slow motion. I swear as I was falling I tried to yell to Jenny that I was falling! Then down I went. If you go on that path you will see the layout of my body in all the tall weeds I fell in. I just laid there and had to laugh, right after I tried to yell at Jenny one more time. Of course, she didn't hear me, which is probably a good thing because she would have tried to turn around to look while still riding and

318

that would have ended in a disaster. Then in my head I wondered how long it will take her to figure out I was not behind her. I pulled myself back together and got my bike back in order (who knew your handle bars could turn so many times). I made my way down the rest of the hill waiting to see Jenny. I went about 30 seconds, which seemed like forever without seeing her. Then finally, as I was coming around a corner, there was Jenny RUNNING back to find me. I was laughing so hard, she looked so worried. She made her jokes at me that if anyone would fall off their bike on this trip it was supposed to be her. I was telling her I was focusing too much on her and not myself. She reminded me she was fine and she could do it. We had a few good laughs talking about it on the way home. I will never get the image out of my head seeing Jenny run around that corner. I'm not going to live this one down, especially from Jenny. But, I needed to share this story because even though I'm looking like the fool, it was one of the best moments of the summer so far because we laughed about it all the way home.

There is also the story of what took place in our backyard one day, a story best told by the CaringBridge entry Barb made:

We were going over to look at the plants that Jenny received while in the hospital and Brian planted in the backyard flowerbeds to keep for her until she can take them back. Jenny noticed a toad hopping among the flowers and decided she wanted to pick up the toad. But, she got distracted by another movement in the flowers and went to grab it. It wasn't another toad, it was a SNAKE! She grabbed it by its tail, held it up, turned to me and asked, "Now what do I do with it?" I told her she should go to the edge of the yard and throw it as far as she could. Meanwhile, Michelle heard all the commotion from inside and came out to see what happened. Jenny's face was priceless. She didn't listen to me and just stood there holding the snake asking what she should do with it. She eventually said, "Ask Michelle what I should do with it." Sure enough we ask her and she said the same thing I did. Of course, then Jenny heads over to the edge of the yard. Michelle told her to go up high behind the neighbor's shed, and she threw it as far as she could. When she came back, Michelle asked her why she picked it up and she said, "I saw a toad and wanted to pick it up." I don't think that will ever make sense.

Jenny, holding the snake

CHAPTER 76

Letting Go

Everything took a major turn in mid-August when Michelle had to move back to Wabasso in preparation for going back to work as a teacher. Her move actually translated to some good news for Jenny. She had been pleading to move back to the apartment with John, which she considered "home," and Jenny's speech therapist had been encouraging us to allow Jenny more alone time than we had been. The apartment was only a four and a half mile bike ride from Methodist Hospital where Jenny's therapy took place, so Michelle moving away proved to be a good thing in many ways.

While Barb and I were not as uncomfortable with Jenny moving back to the apartment as everyone seemed to believe we were, we were anxious during this phase and I won't apologize for any decisions we made during that summer. Looking back, I feel Barb and I did quite well, all things considered. While we appreciated the support, advice, and encouragement we received from many people during that time, none of them, not one, saw Jenny every single step of the way on a day-to-day basis the way Barb and I had. We had been through hell with our daughter. Between the last few days of March through the end of August, we had watched our daughter transform. In some ways, the trip back was as difficult as the deterioration. True, I'd never go back, but while Jenny was sick, we had the aid of the medical professionals at the hospital. Once Jenny was in recovery, we felt as if we were on our own in uncharted waters. In many ways, we were too old and too unprepared for the transitions we went through in guiding Jenny back toward what we always referred to as "a normal life." The truth was nothing would be ever "normal" again.

But, I digress.

Jenny's summer of therapy and recovery had gone well, and while many people played a role, it was in large part due to the blessing of Michelle staying with Jenny for the summer and her selfless dedication to preparing Jenny for the moment when she would, indeed, be on her own. There were, however, huge hurdles to cross.

The most immediate issue was how to get Jenny to and from her therapy sessions. Michelle had been driving her to and from them all summer and since Jenny had also been riding bike all summer and Jenny and John's apartment was in close proximity to the hospital, it made sense for her to get her wish to move back to the apartment and begin to ride her bike to therapy.

I once again had to "let go" and reenter the "empty nest" stage. I don't remember it being as scary the first time around.

Michelle had ridden the bike route between the apartment and the hospital with Jenny on two previous occasions. We intended for it to happen far more often, but various circumstances made that impossible. I am a control freak and there was a very real need to have Jenny make a couple of more trips with someone present just to be sure she was safe, so I decided to go with her at least once. The four and half mile trip each way follows a paved biking path most of the way, but there are two major roads to cross and many minor ones. Michelle had assured me that all went well during their trips and that she was very confident Jenny could handle it on her own. However, I had to see it for myself. It is also very worth noting that Jenny's own confidence level skyrocketed after that first bike trip.

I joined Jenny at the apartment the first day that she needed to get to therapy "on her own." I had barely engaged in exercise of any kind since Jenny had gotten sick and I had gained quite a bit of weight in the meantime. As I was leaving the office that morning to meet Jenny at the apartment to begin our trek, I mentioned to my business partner that I would dial 9-1-1 on my cell phone so chances were good that I could hit "send" before I hit the ground as I went unconscious from lack of oxygen.

While Jenny did challenge me on the ride, I was very pleased that I was able to see her do it firsthand. I rode behind her and never gave her a single cue. She was very safe and aware of what was around her, as best I could tell, and she followed all the rules we set for our 6-year olds when they first learned how to ride bike except to "walk the bike across streets," which I always thought was silly anyway. Jenny did not cross a street unless she saw the "walk" signal at intersections with traffic control lights, so I felt a lot better.

Believe it or not, I was actually pleased to see an extremely dangerous close call that could potentially have caused serious injury towards the end of the ride, which was, honestly, 100% the other bike rider's fault for going way too fast around a blind corner. I am very pleased to say that Jenny immediately recognized what was happening and made an excellent move that was the only reason a serious collision was avoided. I was maybe 20 to 30 feet behind her at the time and the man still hadn't gotten his bike back under control when I passed him. It felt good to have seen the whole ride, including that incident.

While I struggled to keep up at times, I managed to stay close enough for her to see me every time she looked back. I have to say that I was relieved when the hospital came into sight and we locked the bikes to the rack. I drank a bottle of water and strolled to the bathroom, pretending all was fine. I went to the bathroom so I could change my shirt, and lean against the wall to prevent collapse while I caught my breath. I met Jenny back in the waiting room for therapy and was feeling pretty good about myself until Jenny said, "Sorry that I was biking so slowly today. I think I'm tired from the tubing and skiing yesterday," effectively bringing my ego back to earth.

So Jenny was, in fact, ready to begin riding to therapy on her own. However, I wasn't ready to let her. On August 29th, I allowed Jenny to make the trip by herself…sort of.

Jenny was very happy and proud. I actually felt pretty good about it myself, but I was also very aware of the parking lot of the coffee shop that sat right next to the bike path Jenny would be on. More importantly, that parking lot was also right next to the busiest intersection Jenny would have to cross on her route. Yeah…so, that morning found me sitting in my car in the parking lot so I could watch Jenny without her knowing as she passed less than 30 feet in front of me. I was on the phone with Barb giving her a play-by-play. I'm horrible, I know. I can report that Jenny looked comfortable, happy, proud, and confident as she rode by. I felt better too.

CHAPTER 77

Going Back to Work

Once Jenny was clearly on the road to recovery, the biggest hurdle to get over was getting her back to work. When she was coherent and could actually communicate, Jenny switched from asking, "When can I go home" to "When can I go back to work." It was her measure of a normal life.

The initial plan, based on a process that most people who experience a devastating illness or injury follow, was that Jenny would participate in a "vocational transition job" to begin the process of going back to work. The blessing for Jenny, and where she was extremely fortunate, was that she was improving at an extremely rapid pace relative to most patients dealing with a severe brain injury. In fact, her rapid improvement is how she was able to qualify to get into the program.

Ironically, all of the programs that Jenny qualified for as part of these transitional jobs took longer to process the paperwork than we believed Jenny would have actually been in the program (which proved to be true). I went to meet with an admittance counselor at one facility, and Jenny and I attended an informational meeting at another. In both instances, the estimated dates for her admittance into the program were beyond our goal date for Jenny to actually be back working at Barnes and Noble. It was also clear that the programs had more demand than possible job openings, so if Jenny started the process, she would be taking away from someone who needed it more. We very quickly made the decision to go another route.

Throughout Jenny's illness, many people at Barnes and Noble stayed in almost constant contact with us. Most of Jenny's non-family visitors at the hospital were coworkers, and one of them came to sit next to Jenny's bed to read books to her when it wasn't even clear if she could comprehend. When Jenny's disability benefits were about to expire, an individual from the corporate office in New York called me to go over the entire situation to be sure they were clear on Jenny's condition, but more importantly, that I understood what options Jenny had available to her. Most relevantly, Jenny's supervisor, Jennifer Klein, contacted me no less than once a week to get direct updates on how Jenny was doing. She always kept the door open for Jenny coming back to work as soon as she was ready and was always kicking around ideas for how they could accommodate Jenny's specific needs.

This culminated in a meeting one afternoon in the café inside the store with all three of us, and the assistant manager, Stephanie, who had called me on the day Jenny had her first seizure outside the store on March 27th. That meeting laid out a very specific plan about when Jenny would be allowed to come back to work at a very slow pace, starting with just two hours a day two days a week, before the store was open in the morning. Her hours would be expanded to four hours a day and gradually increase to three or four days a week. Jenny's hours would eventually overlap into times that the store was open for business, and she would slowly be transitioned back into having contact with customers. The safety and professionalism of the store was always the primary concern for all involved, but they remained extremely flexible and open to suggestions and ideas to find a formula that could work for all of us. I can't express how excited and impressed I was as I listened to the detailed plan Jennifer had to slowly work Jenny back into the fold at Barnes and Noble. She clearly had given this a lot of thought and was willing to go out on a limb for Jenny.

This all resulted in an interesting conflict with the speech therapist with whom Jenny was working. Barnes and Noble required the doctor to sign off on Jenny coming back to work, and in turn, the doctor was looking to the therapist to give her approval, which she was not prepared to do. I could not understand why she was holding Jenny back, but I did my best to allow Jenny to deal with the situation. After about two weeks of waiting for her approval, however, I decided to go see her myself and discuss it face to face.

The therapist stated that she would not sign off on Jenny going back to work because she was not ready to go into a retail environment for an eight-hour period. The general practice of therapists is to wait as long as necessary to be sure that a patient had the skills necessary to ensure they avoided being put into a situation where they may end up being fired by their employer. The speech therapist believed that she was actually protecting Jenny, not holding her back. There was an irony to all of this as this was the same therapist that felt I was not allowing Jenny enough time alone earlier in her recovery. When I explained what arrangements we had made with Barnes and Noble, she was very surprised, said it was rare, and made sure I knew how lucky Jenny was. I did know. Barnes and Noble had always been a class act and a huge reason Jenny recovered as quickly as she did. By keeping the door open for Jenny to come back, they gave her a goal to work toward, and goals are wonderful things.

I also explained to the therapist that the bigger issue concerning why she needed to go back to work regarded Jenny's emotional well-being. Jenny already had been dealing with depression, and part of that was due to a lack of significant activity during the day. Michelle had kept her busy during the summer, but Jenny still could not drive, so now she was pretty much stuck alone at the apartment. Initially being home all day was fine and Jenny continued to use her computer apps to do additional brain therapy, but eventually that time became a detriment rather than a benefit. The fact was that Jenny needed to go back to work for many reasons.

The therapist understood the situation and saw that Jenny would be in good hands at Barnes and Noble. She realized Jenny would be able to move forward slowly, without the risk of losing her job and signed off on Jenny's work release immediately.

Thus on Tuesday, October 22nd Jenny went back to work at Barnes and Noble on a part-time basis and by December she was working full-time. In terms of the predictions made by the doctors, this was a remarkable recovery. All of us were lucky and blessed. Barnes and Noble had gone "above and beyond" what any of us had any right to expect from the company and the people there, and we will forever be grateful. It was an important step in the process of Jenny returning to a normal life. Jenny really is extremely lucky. The class, character, and care that everyone at Barnes and Noble has shown Jenny has been tremendous.

It was also at this time that Jenny applied for, and was chosen, as the Adult Recreational Volleyball Coordinator for Rockford Community Education. She started this "job" the Sunday before she started at Barnes and Noble. Jenny's supervisor for that position was Christa Larson, the same person who had done so much in putting together the benefit for Jenny in June of 2013. Christa has been instrumental in Jenny's life in many ways for a number of years. She had worked with Jenny when she was the Coordinator for the Youth Recreational Soccer League in Rockford a few years before, so in a way Jenny was coming back home there too. Christa and Scott helped our family in countless ways throughout Jenny's illness, and Christa followed that up by showing confidence in Jenny and giving her a chance to show how far she had come.

Thank God for the loyalty of friends. We truly have been blessed to have such wonderful people doing all they can to help Jenny with her recovery.

CHAPTER 78

Driving

Only days later, the process began for Jenny to get back behind the wheel of an automobile. It was toward the end of a follow-up appointment with Dr. Tran that Jenny was asked the usual, "Do you have any questions?" Jenny responded with a very definitive, "Can I get a referral to get into the Driving Simulator so I can maybe start driving again?" Driving is one of the ultimate signs of a normal life and I'm not sure if that has ever been truer than it was for Jenny. She wanted the freedom to come and go as she pleased and be able to get herself back and forth, anywhere, but in particular to and from Barnes and Noble.

Jenny's therapy sessions had reached a point that she needed a doctor's prescription for insurance to pay for the session needed to get into the simulator, which was actually the first step in a legal process for Jenny to get a valid driver's license again. Thanks, at least in part, to the results of a neuropsych exam done at the Mayo Clinic a few weeks earlier, along with what Dr. Tran had witnessed, Jenny got the referral. She was on her way, literally and figuratively!

Still, if I wasn't ready to let Jenny ride a bike on a bike path by herself, how was I going to let her drive a car? There was no way around it, I felt as if I had a 16-year-old all over again…and I was too old for that kind of stress. The truth was that I knew the day was coming and had no idea how I was going to deal with it.

Barb and I have always felt lucky to have landed in Rockford, Minnesota back in 1988 when Jenny was just a year old and Michelle wasn't even in the plans yet. We truly found a terrific community to live in and raise our kids. Part of that community is people like Becky Miller, Michelle's fourth grade teacher and a family friend ever since.

Most relevant at this time, Becky had been the Driver's Education Instructor in Rockford for a number of years. For whatever reason, this never crossed my mind while I freaked out over the issue of how to make sure Jenny would be safe once she got behind the wheel of a car. Jenny needed to experience things to get skills back, but a simulator was just that, a simulator, and she would only get an hour or two with that. How would we take the next step?

Thank God for sending us Becky Miller! Without being asked, Becky approached Barb and I about redoing some "driver's education" with Jenny. An amazing weight was off my shoulders. Becky and I had a few conversations so that she had a complete understanding of Jenny's condition, or more relevantly, my concerns about what problems Jenny would have while driving. I have to give Becky credit; she is such a wonderful person. Not once did she roll her eyes at me or tell me to stop being a Dad and just shut up. She assured me everything would be fine, and of course, it was. With the aid of an extra brake pedal on the passenger side of the car, Becky took Jenny out two or three times and put her into as many different difficult situations as she could find, including repeatedly entering and exiting rush hour traffic on the I-494 loop. Brave!

On November 3rd, Jenny drove out of the garage for the 1.2-mile trip to the high school on her way to her Volleyball Coordinator job. I was as nervous as when I gave her the keys the day she got her driver's license. In fact, I stood in the garage and operated the garage door for her – not that I was hovering. I said, "Send me a text when you get there," and that text couldn't arrive fast enough. I found out later that another former teacher and volleyball coach of Jenny's saw her pull into the school parking lot and greeted her with a huge hug. Jenny was back!

Now more than a year later, Jenny has driven without incident. Truly, she was ready.

On the other hand, Jenny still needs to text me when she "gets there." However, that's no big deal, so does Michelle. That will never go away.

EPILOGUE

On December 10, 2013, Jenny climbed into her car and drove from our home to Barnes and Noble. She parked in the same parking lot she had on March 27th, but this time she made it into the store and completed an eight-hour shift. It had been almost nine months since the journey began, and although her recovery was not yet complete, that day was momentous to me. It was the marker I had set in my own mind for knowing Jenny was back, and when I could have reasonable hopes of her leading a fully normal life. It occurred months sooner than any doctor predicted.

As it turned out, after further discussion with many of the people that surrounded Jenny on a daily basis back then, Jenny had begun showing symptoms of the illness about three weeks before the first seizure occurred. A primary example was she had been expressing interest in a higher position within Barnes and Noble that was due to open up soon. When it finally did, just days before her seizure, she had to be coaxed by a friend into even saying she wanted the job, and then she showed no confidence in her conversation with the manager, which was very unlike her.

There were other small things, but only in hindsight, knowing what we know now, do we view them as the beginnings of the "odd behavior." At the time, they were written off as fatigue or stress, and actually things we all do from time to time.

So we are all moving forward.

Obviously the most common question we get these days is, "How is Jenny doing?" It is amazing how difficult it still is to answer that question. For sure, when everything is considered, "Jenny is doing well," which is the easy answer to respond with and it is really how we look at it right now. As I often say to people, "Considering that at one time Jenny couldn't talk, eat, or walk and was wearing a diaper, she is doing great!" Jenny has regained all of her motor skills and other than the fact that she is still underweight, by all physical appearances she has recovered. In fact, without being aware of exactly what to look for, no physical sign of Jenny's illness remains.

This does not, however, address Jenny's memory, full brain function, and most importantly, the emotional toll the illness took on her. In terms of memory and brain function, I would challenge anyone that didn't know Jenny had been ill to notice anything; but the truth is that she is not as sharp as she was before she got sick. Jenny herself points to the fact that she still talks to people without making eye contact, and makes random comments without thinking.

Emotional health is a completely different issue. Jenny is working at getting closer to the way that she was before she got sick. She realizes that it is not realistic and at times her anger comes to the surface. Jenny is well aware that she lost many things because of the illness and she may never get all of them back. That is fine, that is life. Everyone has setbacks. Jenny just has a hard time, occasionally, with the frustration of dealing with the fact that she did nothing to bring this on herself.

So "good" is relative. We know how far she has come, but she still has a ways to go. We consider ourselves lucky because she blew away all the doctors' predictions regarding how far and how fast she would come back. It could have turned out so much worse.

Still, although we consider ourselves lucky, what cannot be ignored is that there was a huge price paid by everyone involved. Earlier in this book I discussed the price that people paid because of Jenny's illness, and as I said, no one paid a bigger price than Jenny. No one goes through the journey we shared together and comes out the other end the same as when they went in. Everyone in our family was strongly affected by what happened, but no one changed more than Jenny.

In terms of Jenny's long-term prognosis, I focus on something nurse Andi shared with me about her husband who suffered a brain injury; years later, she still sees improvement. So even though Jenny is "doing well," we know better days are ahead.

While the search continues, since no cancer of any kind has been found, we do live with the fear of a relapse, and in fact, she possibly had one in May 2014. The good news is that it was nothing like it was in 2013 in that we knew exactly what to look for and the doctors and insurance company allowed us to completely overreact to it and get treatment right away…just in case. The flip side to this is that when Jenny forgets something, anything, all of us ask questions. We often need to remind ourselves that all of us have brain farts from time to time.

Jenny is back working part-time at Barnes and Noble, but only because she is pursuing her passion of coaching high school volleyball again and is currently the JV coach at a large high school relatively close to Rockford. Overall, she is beginning to find happiness again, one small piece at a time.

The second most common question we get, from people that have not heard the whole story, is "How did Jenny get this illness?" Since the whole process is so very complicated and it has not been directly stated anywhere else in this book, I will state it here: It was an absolute fluke, the luck of the draw and completely random that Jenny was inflicted with NMDA. She did not contract it, she was never contagious, she did nothing to bring it on herself and there was nothing she could have done to avoid it. A phrase I coined fairly recently is that "she won the medical lottery."

There was a day in the early fall of 2013, a few months after Jenny had been discharged from the hospital and came back home that I saw a quote that said, "Life is what happens despite the fact that you have made other plans." I immediately thought of everything that had happened to

Jenny the previous spring and summer. Later that same day as I was cleaning my office for the first time since all of that had begun about six months earlier, I found my "to do list" from March 27, 2013 – the day I got the call that informed me that Jenny had been found unconscious in a snow bank. I had made the list that morning before leaving the house. Finding it reminded me of how busy I had believed that I was that day, of how important everything on that list seemed to be, and how I had wondered how I was going to get everything done that day, because, of course, it was vital that everything on that list got done.

As I reviewed the list, it was very clear to me who each item regarded and why it was so vital, yet, not one thing on that list was *ever* completed. Surprisingly, *life* went on anyway, regardless of the plans I had made.

I have heard of many people who had life-changing experiences and how it changed them and sent them in a new direction. Some say that they ultimately were glad some tragedy befell them because they found a new and wonderful path in life that they otherwise would not have discovered. You won't hear that from me.

This experience took a lot out of me, physically, emotionally and psychologically. I, like Jenny, am not yet back to the person I was beforehand and I have come to believe that I never will be. Not all of the changes that took place are bad, but the pain was not worth the very few areas where I improved. I can't say that I am so much wiser or a better person in any way or that the lessons learned were so valuable that I would never go back. Ultimately, there was no "silver lining" in all of this.

Michelle created t-shirts and wristbands for Jenny's benefit in June. The front of the t-shirt read, "Faith, Trust and Pixie Dust." I couldn't imagine anything more appropriate for describing how we were coping with the situation. All of us put our faith in God to one degree or another and the trust that we had to put in the doctors and other medical professionals was obvious. Yet, it did seem like it took some good old-fashioned Pixie Dust for Jenny to pull through.

On the back of the t-shirts and the wristbands was the phrase, "You are stronger than you think." I remember thinking at the time, although I never said it out loud, "Really? I don't think so." Yet, despite everything that happened during Jenny's illness, the single lasting image I have in my mind, what I come back to the most when I think of all the events that took place, was when Jenny refused to sit down in the wheelchair by the elevator toward the end of that first walk outside the hospital in May. It was then I knew that Jenny had a determination engrained in her that I admired and wished that I had. I know that I don't have her strength.

One of the good things that came from this was that we met a large group of wonderful and amazing people at Methodist Hospital who we now care for and love. It was incredible to watch people who are passionate about what they do and to see that flourish in how hard they worked and how well they cared for my daughter and the other patients on the 6th floor. Still, I know that each of them will understand when I say that all of us would be okay if we had never met. They know, because they saw all of this firsthand. They saw the price Jenny paid, but the experience also caused them stress and pain as well, because they cared so much and worked so very hard.

Yet, here we are. We make the best of the cards we have been dealt. We pick up the pieces and figure out what direction we go. I cherish the new relationships built and the old ones that were strengthened because of what happened, but there is no part of me that is glad it happened. The price paid by everyone was too great.

So, ultimately, since I couldn't find any positive that came from the experience, I figured I might as well try to create some…you are holding the results of that effort in your hands right now.

The genesis of this book is actually rooted in my initial efforts to bring together as much information as possible to aid Jenny in gaining some understanding of what happened to her. The compilation of all the information used to rebuild the scattered memories that make up this book came from a variety of people and resources. The CaringBridge entries I posted along with the notes I took during meetings, the journals created by Michelle and Debbie, and the medical records of Jenny's care each provided different perspectives and covered a different angle of the experience for Jenny.

It wasn't long after I began pulling everything together that I realized it was a good idea to put this information into a format that could be used to tell the entire story to distant family members who could not be present during the journey as well as close friends that still have so many questions.

Through all of that, this book was conceived.

My hope is that this book can help Jenny develop an understanding of what happened to her, and give her guidance so she knows what questions she still wants to ask. Additionally, perhaps by other people reading this story, word can get out and this book can play at least a small role in raising awareness of the illness so other victims can be diagnosed quicker and the deterioration and damage stopped sooner. I do not know if this book will serve that purpose, but I will put it out there and hope the word spreads.

We decided to make the final entry to the CaringBridge site for Jenny on Thanksgiving Day 2013, appropriate because we had much to be thankful for. Jenny, Barb, Michelle, John, and I each added something to the entry and I still smile when I see what Michelle wrote. It was all so relevant. Each item on that list represents a story that can be found in this book and shows that we did manage to learn something through all of this.

Life Lessons I learned from my sister in the past eight months:

1. It's not okay to climb on the windowsills of hospital rooms.
2. You can never have too many stuffed animals.
3. Naming machines makes life better.
4. When you sit in a bed all day, you have the strength to push your sister and dad out of the way.
5. You always want an imaginary friend when you are younger, but they get annoying when they become your reality.
6. When you spend a month in a hospital, you and your family can go almost anywhere without permission.
7. Life is just like watching your sister ride a bike: regardless of what others are doing, you still need to be sure your own wheels stay on solid ground.
8. EEG's are really uncomfortable.
9. The game of UNO will never get old.
10. You can watch monkeys at the zoo for 30 minutes and it doesn't get boring.
11. If you are trying to lose weight, just be admitted to the hospital.
12. There are 4 letters is in the word "WILD" and 11 in "BLUE JACKETS."
13. My small hometown really rocks.
14. Meal Trains mean the world.
15. Sunshine really is God's Gift.
16. You can never overuse the words, "I love you."
17. I need my family more than I thought I did.
18. You ARE Stronger Than You Think!

JENNY'S EPILOGUE

My name is Jenny Nichols. I am in recovery and suffer from the illness known as Anti-NMDA Receptor Encephalitis, whatever that means. As complicated as the name and the illness is, I will never fully understand it. What I do know and understand is that on March 27, 2013 the course of my life was changed forever. To me it was just an ordinary day when I was going to my work and looking forward to what the day would bring. Little did I know that I was completely wrong. Over the next 84 days, I would become a person not even my family or closest friends would recognize. Although I only recall a handful of blurbs of what happened to me, I still suffer every day with the aftermath.

What I know about what happened to me and what I went through I have learned through many stories told to me, looking at pictures, and now from reading this book. I still struggle to believe it. I have the journals of my family who wrote down, in detail, what they witnessed of the demons attacking me. To this day, I can't recall the events I went through. What my dad called "demons" in my head took control of me and took away a part of my life I can't get back.

I slightly recall Father's Day in that I was allowed freedom to enjoy the day with my family. To me it was just another day where I got to enjoy a picnic, play cards, and throw a Frisbee. I had no idea why this day was so special to my family otherwise. I do remember having John sneak in a present for my sister. I was still sneaky like that despite my state. What is funny however is I don't recall leaving the hospital and my journey to Mayo Clinic. Throughout the months of June and July, I still just have glimpses of memory of certain events. I remember parts of my zoo trip, looking at the monkeys and watching the other animals. However, the story of the seals was new to me to read about. The Kenny Chesney concert was an experience of its own. I was still suffering effects of the illness, which made it difficult for me.

After being released from the hospital, I was still experiencing noises and voices in my head. During the concert was a prime example of music that was deafening to my ears. I could barely understand any of the artist's lyrics or hear their tunes due to the music I was actually hearing in my head that was so loud I was surprised it wasn't something other people could hear. On my way to therapy, my sister would drive me and we had the luxury of listening to an audio book to and from. It took all of my concentration to listen to the book due to other sounds I was hearing. At some points during all this I would have to ask the people around me if they heard things too because I couldn't tell where they were coming from, if they even existed. The voices in my head didn't completely disappear until May 2014.

I have to say that going to therapy was a great thing that I did. The people I worked with at the hospital made sure I was pushed and never settled for just okay. Specifically, my speech therapist was one that I am grateful for. I had the pleasure of working with her up until Christmas at which time we were told insurance would not pay for any more visits. My therapist and I became good friends and were able to share stories from outside therapy. I always looked forward to seeing her each day.

My sister was someone that kept me sane through all of the aftermath. I guess that is a funny term being that I seemed to go insane in the hospital. However, Moe was someone that pushed me like no one else and wanted to make sure I got better. She drove me every day, took me on bike rides, and played games with me. She could have easily made other plans and actually worked at a job instead. I love her so much and am so grateful for everything she did for me.

Today I still experience many things as a result of the antibodies attacking my brain the way they did. I fully believe I will never be the same person I was before this all occurred. Some of the things that have changed are for the good, some for the bad. My relationship with John has completely changed as our lives have gone in different directions, but he is still there when I have questions about all this. I am working part-time now which I think is for the best because I found it hard to work consistently for eight hours. My attention span cannot handle all that time, and I get tired from it. Speaking of tired, no matter how much I sleep during the night I still love naps and take them quite often. Everyone tries to explain that this is part of the healing process, but sometimes I get frustrated in thinking of how long this healing process should really take.

My concentration and memory are still lacking and only last for a while. If I don't write down what I need to do, chances are I will forget to do them, important or not. Although it is getting better each day, I still struggle in my everyday activities.

I really hope that one day I will truly return to "normal." I do not really know what this term means anymore, but I know I do not feel like myself as often as I should. I still suffer from depression, especially on days I don't have much to do. My friends and coaching keep me busy some days so I don't think about it. I hope one day that my memory comes back fully to the extent I can remember names the way I used to.

This story is by no means meant to develop sympathy from anyone that reads this. This story is meant to bring about awareness of this rare illness. I wish that no family goes through what mine did. Although we do not know the cause of what made the demons invade in the first place, I still believe that it is my fault my family and friends endured this. I want them to

336

be able to live their lives as well. I want everyone to know what this illness can do to the person as well as the loved ones around them.

My name is Jenny Nichols. I am a survivor of the evil that attacked my brain and body. I will continue to recover every day, but I will not let it take me over again. I will conquer it, and I am stronger than I could ever think I was.

Brian, Michelle, Jenny & Barb
September 21, 2013

ACKNOWLEDGMENTS

Many people made this book possible. Of course, Jenny – there were many long discussions before we got to this point. I am sorry that you had to be part of any of this. I am sorry that we had a book to write at all.

My wife Barb. This was a painful process for both of us. Thanks for tolerating it…and me.

Moe (Michelle), you have always been my biggest, most honest and favorite critic. Thank you.

My sister Debbie, I love you sis. Of everyone who had a hand in this book, no way it ever happened without you.

To my friend and business partner, Bonnie Stein. There are too many things to say "thank you" for over the past year and half. Maybe, someday soon, I can get all of this behind me.

To John, a very special thanks.

A special thank you goes out to Kathie DeLude and the Bunco Babes Book Club in Chicago. Kathie, with your assistance and encouragement, this book moved along much faster than it otherwise might have.

Dean Smith, what can I say. Your friendship and support of all of my wild projects and pipe dreams is beyond value to me. It really is great having my very own "tech guy." Yet, I still wish I had smarter friends.

Mike Tauber: Your brutal honesty is always what I need – I just wish your memory wasn't so good. Thanks for all of the sports debates that allow me to escape the real world from time to time, even though it is getting old that I am right and you are wrong….85% of the time. Hey, it's now in print – it must be true. Get out that phone of yours, you now will find this statement on the Internet.

Andi Hillestad: you have been a great friend and resource for me since this whole thing began.

There are so many people at Methodist that deserve a thanks, both for their help in confirming the accuracy of what few medical details are in this book, but more so for how much they all did for Jenny. Thanks. Pat Lund, I know I created a lot of work for you. Thank you. To Lesa Boettcher and EVERYONE on "6Neuro" – we love you all. There are so many nurses and aides on the 6th floor that carried us through the worst part of this journey. I am not going to name any one, at the risk of offending someone that I may miss. It was your passion and compassion that helped us through it. However, I am making one exception: Leah. You had a connection with Jenny like no other. You were the only non-family member that could reach Jenny. To doctors Freking, Beattie, Worley, and especially "Teresa" Tran (the first doctor I began to address by her first name, without even realizing it), as well as the countless people behind the scenes – especially the EEG techs: words cannot express how grateful all of us are. To Donna and everyone in therapy at Methodist. You are the ones Jenny remembers and thinks about when she recalls who helped her with recovery. Thank you for working so hard and caring so much.

Jennifer Klein and everyone at Barnes & Noble (especially AJ). All of you have stuck by Jenny's side through this entire journey. Having a place to come back to and a group of friends that supports her made Jenny feel safe and comfortable, and was as important as any medication Jenny has taken.

I also want to acknowledge and thank Bethesda Hospital for their cooperation, professionalism, and attitude in working with me on this book. It is important to remember "this is our story" and is not a reflection of everyone's experience there. Jenny's illness was unique; so was this situation.

There were many people that contributed to bringing this book to a level of acceptability far beyond what my capabilities were: Peter Nikolai, Mary Wiest, Kari Tauber, Susan Kollman, Jane Burandt, and Tony Dahlberg. Thanks to Julie Merila for tolerating my ever-changing demands, and last, but by no means least, Brad Wiest, for stepping up the way you did.

Oh yeah – I almost forgot: Kevin! Thanks for moving the pillow!

ABOUT THE AUTHOR

A lifelong resident of Minnesota, Brian Nichols has been married for 28 years and is the father of two daughters. He takes great pride in his community, and has raised his children to share his values regarding love of family and friends.

Brian is a partner in a business serving various manufacturing industries. He has a passion for soccer and indulges that by coaching high school and traveling soccer teams for over 25 years. In his spare time he enjoys playing with his Pit Bull, Maya, and irritating but lovable Beagle, Rossi. Brian is also an avid fan of all Minnesota professional sports teams.

Made in the USA
San Bernardino, CA
26 February 2016